AS
Geography

OCR

Michael Raw

Philip Allan Updates, an imprint of Hodder Education, an Hachette UK company, Market Place, Deddington, Oxfordshire OX15 0SE

Orders
Bookpoint Ltd, 130 Milton Park, Abingdon, Oxfordshire, OX14 4SB
tel: 01235 827827   fax: 01235 400401
e-mail: education@bookpoint.co.uk
Lines are open 9.00 a.m.–5.00 p.m., Monday to Saturday, with a 24-hour message answering service. You can also order through the Philip Allan Updates website: www.philipallan.co.uk

© Philip Allan Publishers 2008

ISBN 978-0-340-94795-1

First printed 2008
Impression number 7 6 5
Year 2013 2012

Ordnance Survey map extracts reproduced by permission of Ordnance Survey © Crown copyright. Licence No 100027418

This textbook has been written specifically to support students studying OCR AS Geography. The content has been neither approved nor endorsed by OCR and remains the sole responsibility of the author.

Front cover photograph © Daniel Kerek Photography/photographersdirect.com

All efforts have been made to trace copyright on items used.

Printed in Dubai

Hachette UK's policy is to use papers that are natural, renewable and recyclable products and made from wood grown in sustainable forests. The logging and manufacturing processes are expected to conform to the environmental regulations of the country of origin.

P02160

Contents

Introduction

This textbook has been written specifically to meet the needs of students following the OCR AS Geography course. It provides comprehensive coverage of the specification and makes extensive use of detailed, up-to-date and original case studies.

The book has several special features.

➤ Each of the eight topics that cover the two AS units has a separate chapter and a structure that follows the same order as the specification.

➤ Within each chapter, sub-topics are introduced by a list of key ideas that use the same wording as the specification. These key ideas provide the framework for studying the text and are the themes used for setting examination questions.

➤ Feature boxes, separated from the main text, highlight important themes and challenge students to investigate some topics in more detail.

➤ Numerous case studies drawn from MEDCs and LEDCs, and at a variety of scales, illustrate geographical patterns, processes, issues and people–environment relationships.

➤ Examination questions consistent with the style of questions set by OCR are provided at the end of each chapter.

While the main aim of the textbook is to deliver the content of the OCR specification, the crucial area of examination matters are dealt with in the accompanying online resources (www.hodderplus.co.uk/philipallan). These include a synopsis of the scheme of assessment and mark scheme criteria. They also contain a table listing the textbook case studies and show how some are interchangeable between topics (e.g. the Three Gorges Dam, the La Plata drainage basin, and the Alaskan oil industry). In addition there is advice to students on preparing for the AS examination and on answering OCR's structured questions and extended-writing questions. Finally, structured examination questions and extended-writing questions are provided for each of the eight specification topics. These are supported by detailed mark schemes, which include links to the content and case studies in the textbook.

Taken together, the textbook and online resources provide a complete resource that covers all aspects of the course, from content to assessment and examination preparation. For each sub-topic, students might use the resources by:

1 learning the key ideas that introduce each sub-topic
2 learning the themes, principles and processes that underpin each sub-topic
3 using the themes, principles and processes as organising frameworks for learning relevant case studies
4 studying the mark schemes in the online resources for the exemplar examination questions and writing timed answers (or plans)
5 writing timed answers (or plans) to the examination questions in the textbook

Acknowledgements

I owe a debt of gratitude to a number of people who have assisted in the preparation of this book: in particular, to Philip Cross for his encouragement, astuteness and professionalism; to Patrick Fox for his helpful advice and editorial skills; and to Andy Palmer for his critical overview of the writing. The invaluable inputs of Peter Stiff, and Tom and Frances Baldwin are also much appreciated. Finally, I must thank my wife Diana for her tolerance and good humour and for doing so much, despite her own professional commitments, to ease the stress of writing.

Michael Raw
Ilkley, West Yorkshire
March 2008

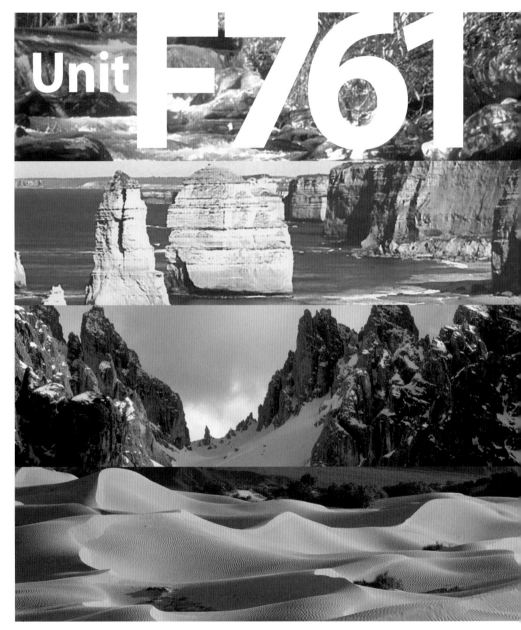

Unit F761

Managing Physical Environments

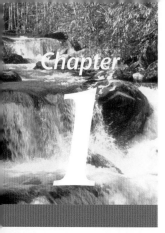

1

River environments

Fluvial processes

Key ideas
➤ Fluvial erosional processes are responsible for a range of landforms in river systems.
➤ Fluvial depositional processes are responsible for a range of landforms in river systems.
➤ The processes of weathering and mass movement contribute to the development of landforms in river systems.
➤ The character of landforms in river systems is also influenced by rock type, rock structure, slopes, climate and sea-level change.

Streams and rivers are natural bodies of water that flow in open channels. Today, in most natural environments, they are the dominant agents of landscape change.

Streams and rivers perform three important tasks:
➤ They erode the channels and valleys through which they flow.
➤ They transport sediments and solutes, which are the products of **erosion**, **weathering** and **slope processes**.
➤ Through erosion and **deposition** they create distinctive **landforms**.

Rivers as energy systems

Fluvial processes such as erosion and transport require energy. The amount of energy available depends on two factors: first, the vertical distance to sea level at any point in a river's course, known as potential energy; and second, the discharge (volume of flow per second). As rivers flow they convert potential energy to kinetic energy and perform work (Figure 1.1).

Rivers expend energy as it becomes available. Energy is primarily used in overcoming the frictional resistance to flow from water particles and channel boundaries (95%). Only then, if surplus energy is available, will erosion and sediment transport occur.

Changing energy inputs

Huge increases in energy occur during periods of high flow. This greatly increases a river's potential for erosion and sediment transport. On 6 July 2006, violent rainstorms occurred in the

Stream energy

Differences in elevation (head)

Discharge

Energy expenditure

Frictional resistance to flow from channel boundaries and water viscosity **1**

Transport of sediment load **2**

Erosion **3**

Figure 1.1 The fluvial energy system

Michael Raw

Photograph 1.1
*Bankfull conditions
and overtopping
banks*

headwaters of the River Calder in West Yorkshire. Thirty-five millimetres were recorded in less than an hour. The effect was dramatic. In the space of 15 minutes, discharge on the River Calder at Mytholmroyd increased from 0.2 to 37 cumecs while flow velocity quadrupled. Even though the peak discharge was sustained for less than half an hour, this was enough to increase the river's energy by a factor of 3000!

Streams and rivers achieve peak energy at **bankfull discharge** (Photograph 1.1). Bankfull is the maximum flow that can be contained by the channel. Any further increase in discharge results in the river overtopping its banks and flooding the adjacent valley floor. Bankfull discharge occurs infrequently (usually no more than once or twice a year) and is the principal control on channel shape and channel landforms. This is because at bankfull, streams and rivers are at their most efficient, moving the most water and sediment for the least amount of energy expended.

Box 1.1 Equilibrium and grade

Rivers operate to distribute energy evenly throughout their length. Within each section or reach, the river's channel adopts a form (e.g. gradient, cross-sectional area or cross-sectional shape), which allows just enough energy to transport its sediment **load**. A state of equilibrium exists when four variables — sediment discharge, particle size, stream flow and slope — are in balance. If the balance is disrupted, one or more of the other variables must change to restore equilibrium.

Rivers adjust automatically to changes in flow, sediment load, particle size and channel slope, which cause temporary disequilibrium. For example, a stream could respond to an increase in discharge by increasing channel erosion (**degradation**), which lowers the channel gradient and restores equilibrium. A reduction in energy could result in channel deposition (**aggradation**), steepening the channel slope and again restoring balance. Rivers are therefore self-adjusting systems: negative feedback mechanisms operate automatically to return the system to equilibrium.

Fluvial erosion

Fluvial erosion is the removal of rock and other mineral particles from the channel bed and banks by stream flow. Imagine a situation where flow velocity and discharge start to increase. Eventually a critical point is reached where the forces tending to move particles are just balanced by the resisting force of friction. This is the **critical erosion threshold** (see Box 1.2 on page 6). Any further increase in energy leads to erosion.

Sediments in stream channels also experience a lifting force that contributes to erosion. Flow velocities are higher over the tops of sediments than at their base, where they rest on the channel bed. Faster flows create lower pressure, and this sets up pressure differences that dislodge particles. Table 1.1 describes the four main processes of fluvial erosion.

Table 1.1 *Processes of fluvial erosion*

Process	Description
Abrasion	Abrasion is the grinding effect on the channel caused by sediments in transport. Cobbles, gravels and sand scour the channel, undermining banks and valley slopes. Where the channel is made of solid rock, gravels trapped by eddying flow drill potholes in the stream bed (see Photograph 1.5 on page 14). The sediments themselves are eroded by abrasion and by collision with other sediments. This process is known as **attrition**. It contributes to the downstream fining of river sediments (Figure 1.2).
Hydraulic action	Hydraulic action is the erosive effect of flowing water without the assistance of rock particles. Forces of shear stress and lift remove sediment from the stream bed and banks. Hydraulic action is particularly effective where channel banks consist of incoherent materials, such as sand and gravel.
Cavitation	Cavitation occurs when tiny bubbles of air implode in fissures and cracks in channel banks. The tiny shock waves that result weaken the banks and eventually lead to collapse.
Corrosion	Corrosion is the chemical action of stream water, which dissolves carbonate rocks such as chalk and limestone.

Figure 1.2 *Downstream changes in sediment roundness on the River Aire: Malham to Gargrave. This shows the downstream effects of attrition; the sharp decrease in roundness at 8 km is due to inputs of more angular sediment from a tributary stream (Otterburn Beck).*

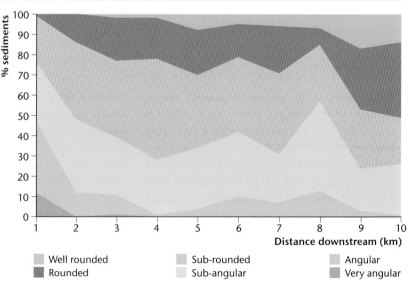

Fluvial transport

Solid and soluble particles eroded from the channel, together with materials input by mass movements and weathering from valley slopes, are transported downstream. Thus streams and rivers operate like giant conveyor belts, transporting materials from the upper to the lower parts of their catchments. All the material transported by a stream or river is known as the **load**. The load is divided into three fractions: bedload, suspended or wash load and **solution** load (Table 1.2).

Type of load	Sediment characteristics	Transport processes
Bedload	Coarse **calibre** particles such as boulders, cobbles and gravel	Intermittent sliding, rolling and hopping along the stream bed at high velocity — for larger particles, lift and eddying are important
Suspended or wash load	Fine-calibre particles of silt and clay, and medium-sized sand particles	Silts and clays are entrained at high flow velocities and transported long distances in suspension — sand-sized particles move at lower velocities, bouncing along the stream bed and lifted into the current
Solution load	Dissolved minerals from the weathering and erosion of carbonate rocks that crop out in the channel and in the catchment	Minerals in solution — transport occurs continuously and is independent of velocity and discharge

Table 1.2 *Types of sediment load and transport processes*

Streams transfer sediment by the processes of traction, suspension, **saltation** and solution.

Traction

Traction is the process that transports coarse bedload particles. They move at or close to bankfull discharge, when streams and rivers have maximum energy. Bedload particles move intermittently by sliding and rolling along the channel bed (Photograph 1.2). This intermittent movement is due to (a) unevenness in the channel bed and the obstruction caused by other particles, and (b) the nature of turbulent flow, with unpredictable pulses of high energy associated with eddies and vortices. Studies of bedload movement show that coarse particles are transported only short distances — on average less than four channel widths — during each high flow event.

Photograph 1.2 *Bedload particles: sandstone and shale cobbles and gravels, Keasden Beck, North Yorkshire*

Suspension

Only the tiniest particles — silt and clay — are transported in suspension. Although it takes high velocities to entrain clay and silt, once in suspension they are transported long distances. This is partly responsible for the downstream fining of sediments in rivers. Fine sediments are removed selectively from headwater regions, and are transported in suspension tens or even hundreds of kilometres downstream, where they are deposited in the lowlands.

Saltation

Saltation is the skipping motion of sand-sized particles. Individual sand grains bounce with the current along the stream bed in an arc-shaped trajectory (Figure 1.3). Once initiated, the process is cumulative: the impact of saltating grains sets in motion more and more particles.

Figure 1.3
Saltation of sand-sized particles

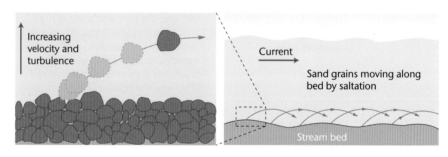

Solution

Streams and rivers draining catchments of chalk and limestone transport weathered minerals in solution. Unlike other transport processes, solution takes place continually, even at low flow. Because of this, and because solution is unseen, the solution load is often far more significant than it seems.

Fluvial deposition

Deposition occurs when a stream or river no longer has sufficient energy to transport its load (Box 1.2). Deposition may take place within the channel — a process called aggradation. Or, if a stream or river has flooded its valley, deposition (especially of suspended or wash load) will occur on the floodplain as **overbank deposits**.

Box 1.2 Hjulström diagram

The erosion, transport and deposition of sediments depend on flow velocity, flow type (i.e. laminar or turbulent) and sediment size. The Hjulström diagram (Figure 1.4) relates flow velocities to the erosion, transport and deposition of sediments of varying size (both are plotted on logarithmic scales). Generally, the higher the velocity the larger the sediments transported.

The upper curve in the Hjulström diagram shows that sand-sized particles have the lowest **critical erosion velocities** (0.2–0.3 m s^{-1}). In contrast, much higher velocities are needed to erode and transport the largest and the smallest sediments. The high critical erosion velocities needed to transport tiny clay and silt particles are unexpected. This phenomenon is explained by the cohesiveness of clays, which stick together because of electrical bonding.

The lower curve in the Hjulström diagram shows the velocities needed for sediments to either stop moving (e.g. bedload) or fall out of suspension. This curve supports our common-sense view that the smaller the sediment, the lower the velocity needed for deposition.

The difference between the upper and lower curves is also important. For example, the diagram tells us that only a slight fall in velocity below the critical erosion threshold causes large sediments to stop moving. Meanwhile, the large difference in the entrainment velocity and fall velocity for tiny particles shows that, once entrained, they will remain in suspension until flow rates are negligible.

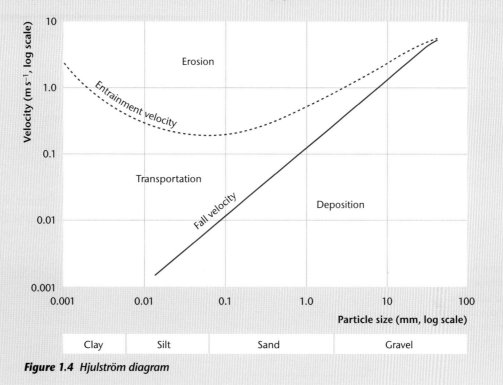

Figure 1.4 *Hjulström diagram*

Box 1.3 Estimating bankfull discharge

Bankfull discharge occurs when the volume of water in a stream or river channel just reaches to the top of the banks. At this stage the stream or river is most efficient (i.e. minimum energy lost to friction), moving the greatest quantity of water and sediment for the least amount of energy expended. Bankfull discharge is an important measure because it is the major influence on channel shape and channel landforms.

Bankfull channel cross-sectional area

Bankfull discharge is calculated by multiplying the channel bankfull cross-sectional area by its flow velocity at bankfull. Channel cross-section must be measured in the field. A site should be chosen on a length of stream with a straight **planform**; clearly defined banks of equal height; little bankside vegetation; and no obstructions in the channel such as boulders and bars. Bankfull width is measured with a tape, followed by depth measurement at equal intervals across the channel.

Bankfull velocity

Bankfull conditions occur infrequently and pose practical difficulties for measurement in the field. However, we know that bankfull velocity will be influenced by channel gradient, channel shape and the frictional resistance of sediment and vegetation to flow. These parameters are used in Manning's equation to estimate bankfull velocity:

bankfull velocity $(v) = (r^{0.66} \times s^{0.5})/n$

where:

r = hydraulic radius (see page 13)

s = slope of the water surface (tangent of the angle); the gradient of the adjacent valley floor is normally used as a substitute for the slope of the water surface

n = coefficient of roughness (estimated value, ranging from 0.025–0.035 for lowland streams to 0.04–0.07 for boulder-bed mountain streams, and 0.1–0.15 for flood-plain streams in dense woodland)

Fluvial features

Based on the work of streams and rivers as agents of sediment production and transport we divide drainage basins into three zones:

➤ the sediment supply zone
➤ the sediment transfer zone
➤ the sediment storage zone

Within each zone, a range of fluvial processes produces distinctive channel and valley landforms. Figure 1.5 shows the approximate boundaries of these three zones for the River Wyre's catchment in north Lancashire.

Figure 1.5 Wyre catchment divided into sediment supply, sediment transfer and sediment storage zones

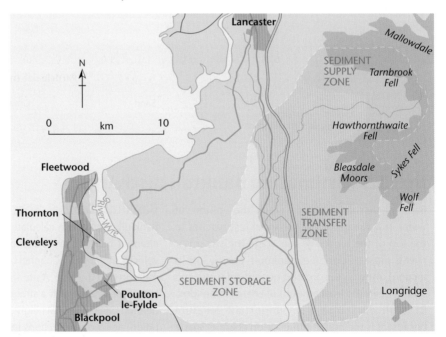

Processes and features in the sediment supply zone

In larger drainage basins, the sediment supply zone is usually an upland region. Inputs of sediment into stream channels from fluvial erosion, weathering and mass movements are quickly removed from this zone (Box 1.4, page 10). Sediment mainly comprises coarse rock particles, which are temporarily stored within stream channels as bedload and **alluvial bars**.

Although streams are short and drain small catchments (often no more than 2–3 km²), for short periods of time they have high energy levels. This is because:

➤ channel gradients are steep, so water moves swiftly
➤ runoff is rapid on steep upland slopes (especially if rocks are impermeable)
➤ a dense network of channels means that rainfall gets into streams quickly
➤ orographic uplift intensifies rainfall events
➤ cloudy upland climates and low temperatures reduce evaporation and help to saturate soils, which increases runoff
➤ snowmelt may inflate stream discharge during winter and spring

With steep channel gradients and high **peak flows**, many upland streams have surplus energy for sediment transport and erosion. They also have the 'tools' for erosion: coarse bedload particles abrade the channel and undercut channel and valley slopes.

Fluvial erosion

Fluvial erosion operates vertically, leading to deep incisions in upland surfaces (see Photographs 1.3 and 1.4) on page 11. There are three possible reasons for this. First, steep channel gradients reduce sinuous flow. Thus, upland streams on steep slopes have relatively straight channels. This limits erosion to a vertical plane. Second, peak discharge is relatively low compared with those of larger rivers in the lowlands. There the formation of meanders depends in part on a high volume of flow. Third, upland streams often flow in valleys confined by solid rock walls. In these circumstances, **lateral erosion** is minimal.

V-shaped valleys, interlocking spurs and waterfalls

V-shaped valleys are the most characteristic fluvial feature of the uplands. They provide clear evidence of the power of upland streams to erode vertically and incise their channels. However, if fluvial erosion was the only process operating, most upland valleys would be canyon-like. As it is, upland valleys are usually more open or V shaped. The explanation is that as streams cut down, weathering and **mass movement** wear back the valley sides. We call this process **backwasting** (Photographs 1.3 and 1.4).

Box 1.4 Weathering processes in the sediment supply zone

Weathering is the breakdown of rock *in situ*, at the Earth's surface or just below the surface, by physical, chemical and biological processes. In Britain's uplands, **freeze–thaw** is the main type of physical weathering. Rainwater penetrates joints and bedding planes in rocks exposed, for example, on valley slopes. When temperatures drop to zero and below, the water freezes, and its volume expands by approximately 9%. In confined spaces, the pressure exerted by this expansion is enough to shatter the toughest rocks. Frost-shattered rock particles litter the slopes of upland valleys and are a major source of the coarse sediment that feeds into streams and rivers (Photograph 1.3).

Chemical weathering is more complex and comprises several different processes such as **carbonation** (or solution), **hydrolysis** and **oxidation**. Carbonation is the solution of limestone by rainwater and soil water. Carbon dioxide dissolved in rain-water and soil water forms a weak carbonic acid that reacts with calcium carbonate to form calcium bicarbonate, which is soluble. Many sandstones are cemented with calcium-rich minerals. When attacked by carbonation, sandstones often disintegrate to form sand.

Granitic rocks are susceptible to weathering by hydrolysis, which involves a chemical reaction between rock minerals (e.g. feldspar) and water. The result is the formation of secondary minerals such as kaolin (china clay), and the breakdown of granite.

Oxidation is the absorption of oxygen either from the atmosphere or from water by rock minerals. Oxidised minerals increase in volume, weakening rocks and causing their breakdown.

In most instances, weathering weakens rocks, causing their disintegration. Then mass movements (e.g. mudslides) and runoff remove the debris from slopes. Much of it ends up in stream and river channels and is transported from the sediment supply zone, to the sediment transfer and sediment storage zones in the lowlands.

Case study Brandy Gill

Brandy Gill, near Mungrisdale in the northern Lake District, is a typical stream in the sediment supply zone flowing in a steep V-shaped valley (see Figure 1.6 and Photographs 1.3 and 1.4). Its valley slopes are currently being undercut by fluvial erosion and backwasted by weathering and mass movement. Since the end of the ice age, Brandy Gill has cut a deep, narrow valley into the landscape. Significant lateral erosion is impossible because of the rocky valley walls. Although the valley and stream channel are fairly straight, the view up-valley is interrupted by **interlocking spurs**. These features develop when incision occurs in a stream channel that follows a slightly sinuous path. Where more resistant bands of rock crop out in the channel, a series of small water-falls has formed (see Box 1.5).

Brandy Gill illustrates the coupling between the valley slope system and the stream system. The valley slopes are the main source of sediment. In places where the stream undercuts the base of slopes, slope instability and slumping occur (see pages 63–64). Higher on the valley slopes, freeze–thaw and rockfall supply coarse rock particles to the stream channel.

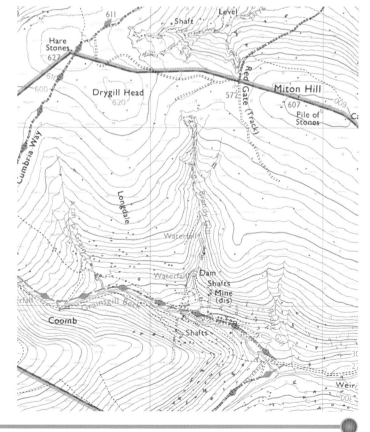

Photograph 1.3 *(Above) Brandy Gill flows in a narrow V-shaped valley with interlocking spurs*

Photograph 1.4 *(Right) Brandy Gill's V-shaped valley; note the rock particles, weathered from the valley slopes, feeding into the channel*

Channel characteristics

Brandy Gill's channel slope is typically steep. From its source on Carrock Fell to its confluence with Grainsgill Beck, Brandy Gill falls 250 metres in less than a kilometre. Channel sediments are mainly coarse; finer sediments are removed during periods of high flow and swept downstream into Grainsgill Beck, and ultimately into the River Caldew. In cross-section the channel is relatively shallow and wide with a high **width-to-depth ratio**, and a low **hydraulic radius** (see Box 1.3 on page 7). This, together with its coarse bedload, creates turbulent flow, which in turn helps to transport coarse sediment.

Figure 1.6 *Location of Brandy Gill, near Mungrisdale in the northern Lake District*

Box 1.5 The development of waterfalls

Abrupt changes in channel gradient lead to the development of waterfalls and rapids. Steep, almost vertical rock steps produce waterfalls, while less severe gradients are associated with rapids.

Most waterfalls and rapids form in one of these situations:

- A band of resistant rock crops out in a river's channel, e.g. the River Tees at High Force in County Durham.
- A fault line creates a sharp change in rock type along a river's course, e.g. Thornton Force near Ingleton.
- A river crosses a major structural boundary, e.g. Seljalandsfoss in southern Iceland has formed where the river plunges over the edge of the basalt plateau to the coastal plain.

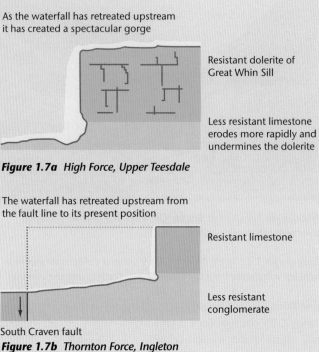

As the waterfall has retreated upstream it has created a spectacular gorge

Resistant dolerite of Great Whin Sill

Less resistant limestone erodes more rapidly and undermines the dolerite

Figure 1.7a High Force, Upper Teesdale

The waterfall has retreated upstream from the fault line to its present position

Resistant limestone

Less resistant conglomerate

South Craven fault

Figure 1.7b Thornton Force, Ingleton

Many upland streams have channels with a stair-like long profile known as **step-pool sequences**. Steep step sections alternate with longer pool sections with gentler gradients (Figure 1.8). Cobbles and boulders wedged across the channel form the steps, with finer sediments forming the pools.

Figure 1.8
Longitudinal profile of a step-pool sequence

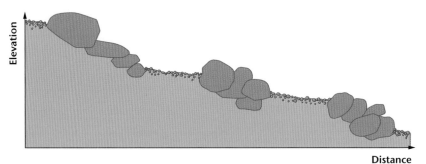

Elevation

Distance

Step-pool sequences are thought to be equilibrium features. They are an adjustment in a vertical dimension by upland streams confined to narrow, rocky valleys. Unlike low-gradient alluvial streams, upland streams cannot dissipate surplus energy by moving laterally (e.g. meandering). The formation of steps does two things: it increases channel length and thus reduces average gradient; and it creates turbulent flow, allowing surplus energy to be dissipated as heat.

Box 1.6 Measuring channel efficiency

The shape of a stream or river channel in cross-section affects its efficiency as a conveyor of water and sediment. The most efficient channel shape is the one that minimises the ratio between the cross-sectional area of the channel and the length of the cross-sectional channel boundary (wetted perimeter). This ratio is known as the **hydraulic radius** (r), and is widely used as a measure of channel efficiency. The higher the value of the hydraulic radius, the more efficient the channel (Figure 1.9).

$$\text{hydraulic radius, } r = \frac{\text{bankfull cross-sectional area (m}^2\text{)}}{\text{wetted perimeter (m)}}$$

Stream channels are least efficient in the sediment supply zone but increase in efficiency with distance downstream. Channels are most efficient at bankfull flow when least energy is lost to friction. This is the reason why flow velocities increase with discharge.

The **width-to-depth ratio** is an alternative, and simpler, measure of channel efficiency. This is obtained by dividing the bankfull channel width by the average bankfull depth. In contrast to the hydraulic radius, a low width-to-depth ratio describes an efficient channel (Figure 1.9).

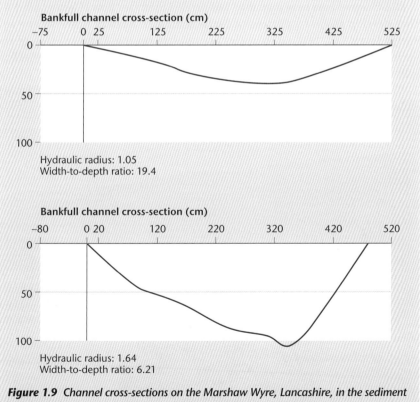

Bankfull channel cross-section (cm)

Hydraulic radius: 1.05
Width-to-depth ratio: 19.4

Bankfull channel cross-section (cm)

Hydraulic radius: 1.64
Width-to-depth ratio: 6.21

Figure 1.9 *Channel cross-sections on the Marshaw Wyre, Lancashire, in the sediment supply zone*

Many stream channels in the uplands comprise solid rock. Unlike streams with alluvial channels, they are unable to adjust to changes in discharge and sediment load. Solid rock channels are relatively smooth and provide little resistance to flow. Consequently, coarse bedload is often swept clear of these areas. Where flow is turbulent, gravel particles trapped by eddies and vortices drill potholes in the solid rock of the stream bed. Although localised, this erosion gradually lowers the stream bed, reducing the channel slope (Photograph 1.5).

Photograph 1.5
Potholes drilled in limestone; the pebbles that are responsible for abrasion can be seen in the potholes

Fluvial deposition

The absence of **floodplains** in the headwater zone confines sediment storage to alluvial bars within stream channels.

Mid-channel bars have their long axis parallel to stream flow (Photograph 1.6). They develop around a nucleus of coarse sediment. As peak flows decline and energy levels fall, bedload particles accumulate on the upstream side of the nucleus with finer particles deposited on the downstream side. Mid-channel bars split the stream into two channels and divert the flow against the banks (Figure 1.10). This accelerates bank erosion, and releases new sediment into the channel, which results in further bar development.

Photograph 1.6
Mid-channel bars comprising boulders and cobbles eroded from morainic deposits on the valley sides of Kingsdale Beck, North Yorkshire

Stage 1

Coarse sediment is deposited in mid-channel as flow competence declines

Stage 2

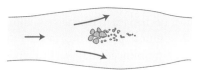

Obstacle to flow promotes further aggradation, and deflects flow against banks

Stage 3

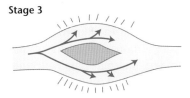

Bank erosion releases sediment; growth of mid-channel bar and shallowing of channel

Stage 4

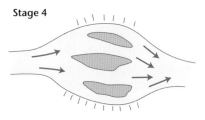

Bar stabilises with deposition of fine sediment and growth of vegetation

Figure 1.10
Formation of mid-channel bars

Alternate bars form on opposite sides of straight channels and like mid-channel bars are exposed at low flow. They owe their development to the meandering path of the main current (thalweg) within straight channels. Bars form from aggradation in low-energy areas of the channel.

Processes and landforms in the sediment transfer zone

Downstream from the sediment supply zone, rivers enter the sediment transfer zone. This is a lowland region with gentler gradients and more open valleys. Sediment production per square kilometre is less than in the supply zone, though inputs of sediment from the erosion of banks and valley slopes remain important. Overall there is a balance between sediment leaving the transfer zone and that being stored. Storage is often long term, in floodplains and terraces.

Despite gentler gradients and larger sediment loads, river energy increases downstream. This is due to:

➤ a more efficient channel shape (i.e. higher hydraulic radius) helping to increase flow velocity
➤ smaller bedload particles that offer less resistance to flow and increase velocity
➤ higher discharge because of the increased drainage basin area

These three factors create a smoother flow, rather than the more turbulent flow needed to transport coarse sediment in the uplands. Meanwhile the character of the sediment load also begins to change in the transfer zone. Due to attrition, sediments are finer, and the suspension load becomes more important than bedload.

Rivers in the transfer zone normally flow in alluvial channels and in valleys that are wider and less confined than in the uplands. As a result, they are able to adjust to changes in discharge, sediment load and velocity in a horizontal, as well as in a vertical, plane. Thus, lateral erosion, assisted by shallow gradients, becomes more pronounced than vertical erosion, and channels begin to migrate freely across valley floors.

Meanders

River channels become more sinuous in the sediment transfer zone. Single-thread, meandering channels extend across the entire width of the valley floor. Where they undercut the valley side they often form steep **river cliffs**.

Figure 1.11 describes the formation of meanders. We already know that even in straight channels, the flow is sinuous, causing deposition in low-velocity areas and the development of alternate bars. Once formed, alternate bars deflect the flow against the opposite bank, initiating erosion and channel curvature. Channel curvature (a) increases velocity in the curved sections and (b) directs flow against the outer bank, causing erosion. Meanwhile, faster flow around the outer bank

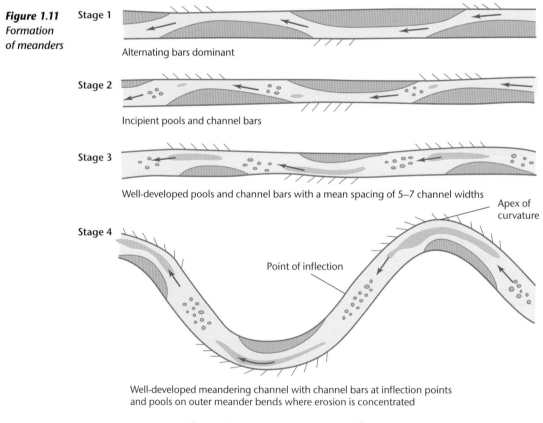

Figure 1.11 Formation of meanders

Stage 1

Alternating bars dominant

Stage 2

Incipient pools and channel bars

Stage 3

Well-developed pools and channel bars with a mean spacing of 5–7 channel widths

Stage 4

Apex of curvature

Point of inflection

Well-developed meandering channel with channel bars at inflection points and pools on outer meander bends where erosion is concentrated

Channel bar   Pool   Erosion

Source: Adapted from Knighton, D. (1998) *Fluvial Form and Processes*, Arnold

scours the river bed and creates a pool. Sediments eroded from the pool areas are then deposited a short distance downstream where they form channel bars.

Eventually, what started out as a straight channel is transformed into a meander, with pools located at the apex of curvature (Stage 4) and bars at the point of inflection.

Flow patterns in meanders

Flow patterns in meanders differ from those in straight channels. In addition to the main downstream flow, meanders have a secondary **helical** or spiral flow (Figure 1.12). As the river enters the meander, centrifugal force pushes the surface flow against the outer, **cut bank**. This gives a slight elevation in the water surface and creates a current, which flows close to the bed, towards the inner bank. This current transports sediment to the inner bank where it forms a **point bar**. Evidence of the current can be seen in the sorting of sediments on point bars: coarse material close to the inner bank with progressively finer sediments further up the point bar.

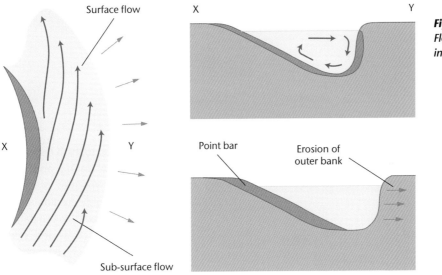

Figure 1.12
Flow patterns in meanders

Box 1.7 Meandering and braided channels

Meandering channels

Sinuous stream channels are also known as meandering channels. Strictly speaking, a meandering channel is one where the ratio of channel length to valley length exceeds 1.5. Meandering channels are usually single thread, develop in coherent bank materials such as silt and clay, and are formed by streams and rivers that have enough energy to effect the lateral erosion.

Why do rivers meander? One theory is that meanders are the outcome of excess energy in a river system. Rivers with excess energy, flowing through alluvial channels with gentle gradients, expend this energy on sediment transport and lateral erosion. Lateral erosion increases sinuosity, which lengthens the channel and therefore reduces its average gradient. In this way, surplus energy can be dissipated and equilibrium established.

Braided channels

Braided channels are multi-thread, with individual channels separated by bars or islands of sediment. Typical braided channels are shallow, wide and in-efficient, and have a high width-to-depth ratio. This type of channel generates turbulent flow, which is effective for transporting large volumes of coarse sediment. Unlike meandering channels, braided channels are unstable and shift position constantly.

Braiding is caused by rapid bank erosion and the overloading of the channel with coarse sediment. Braided rivers are usually powerful, with steep gradients and high (often seasonal) discharges. In southern Iceland, rivers such as the Markarfljót draining Myrdalsjökull icefield have braided channels (Photograph 1.7).

Photograph 1.7
Markarfljót River, Thórsmörk, Iceland

Michael Raw

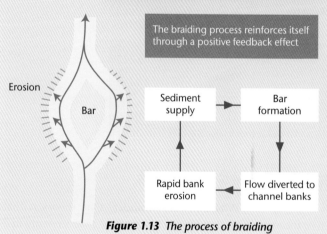

The braiding process reinforces itself through a positive feedback effect

Erosion

Bar

Sediment supply → Bar formation

Rapid bank erosion ← Flow diverted to channel banks

Figure 1.13 *The process of braiding*

Braiding is due to: high discharges of meltwater in spring and early summer; huge volumes of coarse glacial debris; highly erodible gravel banks, with little bankside vegetation; sparse vegetation cover and steep slopes, which deliver sediment to rivers by mass movement; and steep channel gradients (Figure 1.13).

Braided channels are the most energy efficient way for rivers to transport huge sediment loads that are too large and too coarse to be carried in a single channel.

Point bars

Point bars are semi-circular sand or gravel deposits located on the inner banks of meanders. They are depositional features, formed by the spiral or helical flow of water in meanders.

As meanders shift laterally across the valley floor, erosion on the outer cut bank is compensated by deposition on the inner bank. As we saw in the last section, sediments on the point bar are sorted — coarser sediments nearest the channel on the inner bank, finer sediments furthest away. Eventually point bar deposits are incorporated into the floodplain of the river. Figure 1.14 shows the sequence of deposition on the point bar of a meandering channel as the channel shifts position over time. The symbols T_1–T_3 are time intervals and show how the point bar deposits, sorted by size, gradually build up the alluvium of the floodplain.

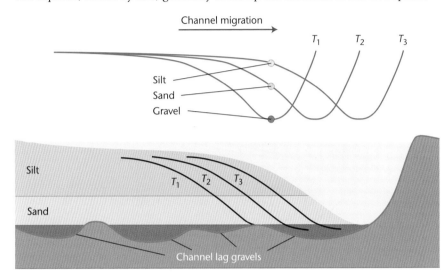

Figure 1.14
Formation of point bars and floodplain development

Floodplains

In the sediment transfer zone, valleys widen out. Now the river channel occupies only a small fraction of the valley floor, which is wide, flat and filled with alluvium. This is the active floodplain: the area across which the river floods when it overtops its banks (Photograph 1.8).

Photograph 1.8
Floodplain with point bar and river cliff on the Marshaw Wyre

Floodplains are formed both by erosion and deposition in meandering rivers (Figure 1.15). In meandering channels, erosion occurs along the outer cut bank, and is most concentrated just downstream of the apex of curvature. This lateral erosion, over many years, causes meanders to migrate slowly downstream and across the valley. Valleys are widened where the meanders contact the valley sides. Erosion undermines the slopes, causing them to slump and collapse. The scars of former slumps are often visible at regular intervals along the valley sides (Photograph 1.9).

Figure 1.15
Formation of
floodplains

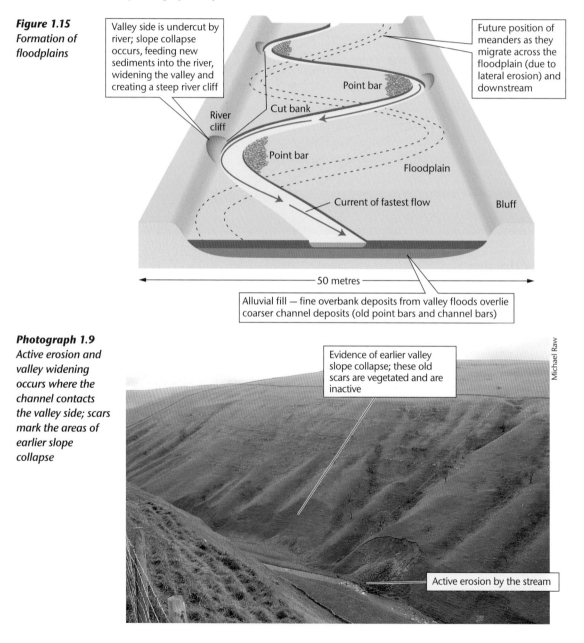

Valley side is undercut by river; slope collapse occurs, feeding new sediments into the river, widening the valley and creating a steep river cliff

Future position of meanders as they migrate across the floodplain (due to lateral erosion) and downstream

Point bar

Cut bank

River cliff

Point bar

Floodplain

Current of fastest flow

Bluff

50 metres

Alluvial fill — fine overbank deposits from valley floods overlie coarser channel deposits (old point bars and channel bars)

Photograph 1.9
Active erosion and valley widening occurs where the channel contacts the valley side; scars mark the areas of earlier slope collapse

Evidence of earlier valley slope collapse; these old scars are vegetated and are inactive

Michael Raw

Active erosion by the stream

Alluvial fans

Alluvial fans are lobes of sediment deposited by streams as they suddenly emerge from an upland course into the lowlands. In the uplands, these streams, with steep gradients and high peak flows, often have large sediment loads (Figure 1.16).

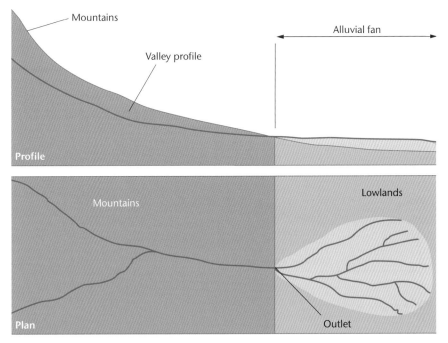

Figure 1.16
Alluvial fan
development
and form

As streams move into the lowlands, they experience a sudden loss of energy. No longer confined by steep rock walls, and with a marked reduction in gradient, stream channels become shallower and wider. The sudden loss of energy causes rapid deposition, with multiple channels separated by sediment bars. The resulting large-scale deposition leads ultimately to the formation of an alluvial fan.

Small alluvial fans are often found in the British Isles where upland streams enter large valleys such as glacial troughs. Alluvial fans are common in the Great Basin in the deserts of southwest USA. There, mountains alternate with down-faulted basins. Where streams leave the mountains they build extensive debris cones or alluvial fans (Photograph 1.10). So extensive are these fans that they often merge along the mountain fronts to form vast aprons of alluvium known as **bajadas**.

Photograph 1.10
An alluvial fan
at the base of
encircling
mountains in
Death Valley,
California; the area
in the foreground is
blown sand

Pools and riffles

Pools and riffles are common channel bedforms found in streams in the sediment transfer zone (Figure 1.17). They consist of alternating sequences of 'shallows', made up of gravel bars, and 'deeps' lined with finer sediments.

Pool and riffle formation is not fully understood. However, we know that they develop during high flow conditions when sediments scoured from the pools are deposited downstream on the riffles. Streams expend energy eroding sediment from the pools, and in the turbulent flow across the riffles. In this way, pools and riffles allow streams to dissipate surplus energy.

A feature of pools and riffles is their regular spacing — on average five to seven times channel width. This spacing is similar to the ratio between channel wavelength and channel width in sinuous channels, and suggests that pool and riffle sequences play some part in meander formation.

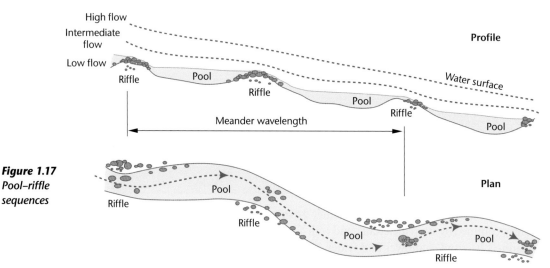

Figure 1.17
Pool–riffle sequences

River terraces

We have seen that fluvial erosion in the sediment transfer zone is mainly lateral. Lateral erosion causes stream channels to migrate downstream and across floodplains. At the same time, some degree of vertical erosion occurs. One effect of this vertical erosion is the formation of a new floodplain surface inside the old one. Remnants of the old floodplain survive as terraces along the valley side.

There are two types of river terrace: unpaired and paired. Where terraces are at different levels, they are unpaired (Figure 1.18). Unpaired terraces are common features in river valleys in the sediment transfer and sediment storage zones. They result from the gradual incision of the channel into the valley floor. This is shown in Figure 1.18. As the channel migrates across the floodplain from T1 to T2 it also lowers the valley floor. This process continues as the channel migrates to T3 and so on. The outcome is a series of terraces at different heights on opposite sides of the floodplain.

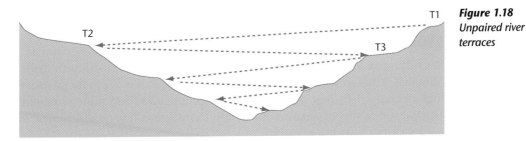

Figure 1.18
Unpaired river terraces

In contrast to unpaired terraces, paired terraces are at the same height on opposite sides of the valley (Figure 1.19). Each matching pair is the remains of the same floodplain surface, most of which has been removed by erosion. Whereas unpaired terraces develop where incision is a gradual process, paired terraces suggest a much more rapid downcutting (Photograph 1.11). This could be due to an abrupt increase in discharge caused by climate change (e.g. deglaciation), tectonic uplift, **isostatic recovery**, or a sudden fall in base level (e.g. lowering of sea level).

Figure 1.19
Paired river terraces

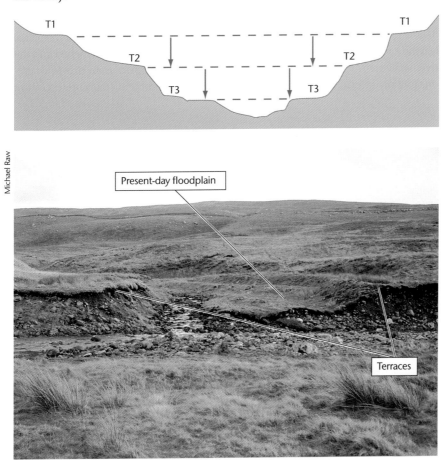

Michael Raw

Present-day floodplain

Terraces

Photograph 1.11
Paired river terraces at the confluence of Fall Gaze Beck and Kingsdale Beck; the terraces are associated with a fall in base level with the draining of a temporary glacial lake in the main valley

23

Processes and landforms in the sediment storage zone

Rivers flowing across lowlands close to sea level transport large sediment loads. Although slopes are gentle, energy levels remain high. This is due to three factors: high discharge; efficient channels in cross-section; and fine calibre sediment. The last two factors ensure that energy lost to friction is low. Most sediment is transported in suspension.

Meanders become more sinuous in the sediment storage zone, with numerous cut-offs or **oxbows**. In addition, the meander belt no longer extends from one side of the floodplain to the other. As a result, active valley widening no longer occurs. The absence of any coupling between the valley slopes and the river channel limits the input of fresh sediment in this zone. Instead, sediments that are not transported into the coastal zone enter long-term storage in floodplains, river terraces, deltas and estuaries.

Oxbows and cut-offs

In the sediment storage zone, meanders increase in amplitude and wavelength. As the meanders become more sinuous, lateral erosion causes the channels to converge leaving a narrow neck of land (Figure 1.20). Eventually the neck is breached and the river straightens its course. The abandoned meander is known as an oxbow or cut-off. Initially it forms a lake, but this is soon filled by sediment (rates of deposition

Figure 1.20
Formation of oxbows

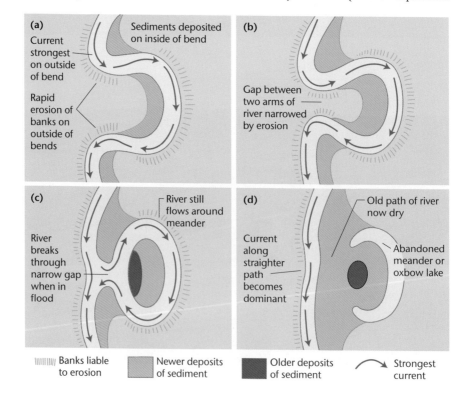

in oxbows may reach 5–15 mm a year). The scars of abandoned meanders litter floodplains and are clearly visible from the air. On the ground they are identified by shallow depressions or swales.

Levées

As floodwaters spill out of the river's channel onto the floodplain, the sudden reduction in flow velocity results in deposition of the suspended load. Close to the channel, larger, silt-sized particles are deposited. Here rates of deposition are highest, reaching 3–5 mm a year. Smaller clay-sized particles are deposited further from the channel where accretion is much slower — around 0.25 mm a year. Because deposition is greatest adjacent to river channels, natural embankments known as **levées** form there.

Photograph 1.12 *Meanders and oxbow lake on the Blackfoot River, Montana, USA*

Deltas

Deltas are large areas of sediment found at the mouths of many of the world's largest rivers. Deltaic sediments are deposited by rivers and by tidal currents.

Factors influencing the formation of deltas

Deltas form where rivers and tidal currents deposit sediments faster than waves and tides can remove them. Several conditions favour delta formation:

➤ Rivers carrying very large sediment loads, such as the Hwang Ho in China (80 g l^{-1}), and draining large basins.

➤ A broad continental shelf margin at the river mouth to provide a platform for sediment accumulation. For example, deltas occur on the Atlantic coast of South America where there is a wide shelf, but are largely absent from the Pacific coast where the continent falls steeply to the ocean.

➤ Low energy-receiving basins (i.e. seas and lakes). Environments with low-energy waves have limited capacity to erode sediments deposited in the coastal zone.

➤ Receiving basins with little or no tidal range, such as the Mediterranean. In these circumstances, the absence of tidal scour allows sediments to accumulate.

Delta morphology

Deltas consist of three separate landscape units (Figure 1.21). The **upper delta plain** is furthest inland and made entirely of river-deposited sediment. This area is above the reach of the highest tides. In contrast, the **lower delta plain** is submerged at regular intervals by high tides as well as river floods. Both river and marine sediments accumulate in basins between the **distributary** channels. These areas, isolated by levées, first form mudflats, and, later, salt marshes or mangroves. Gradually the basins fill with sediment until they are elevated above the high tide level. The third element — the **submerged delta plain** — lies below the mean low water level. Here the delta is advancing seawards.

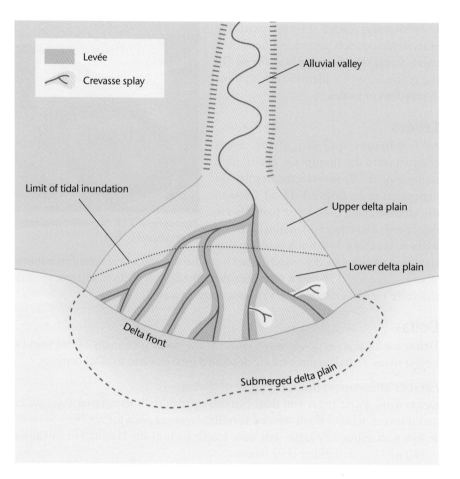

Figure 1.21
Delta structure

Distributary channels

Deltas are criss-crossed by a branching network of distributary channels. Overloaded with sediment, aggradation forms alluvial bars, causing channels to bifurcate (divide into two). Bifurcation reduces the energy in each new stream, leading to channel deposition and more bifurcation.

Natural embankments or levées line the distributary channels. They allow the delta to extend seawards. In conditions of high flow, levées may be breached. Rapid deposition may leave extensive lobes of sediment in the basins between the levées. These deposits, similar to alluvial fans in the sediment transfer zone, are called **crevasse splays**.

Types of delta

The main types of delta are: river dominant, tide dominant and wave dominant. Each type has a distinctive **planform**, determined by the relative importance of fluvial, tidal and wave processes (Figure 1.22).

River-dominant deltas have either an elongated or a bird's foot shape. The Mississippi is the classic example of this type of delta (Figure 1.23). Its

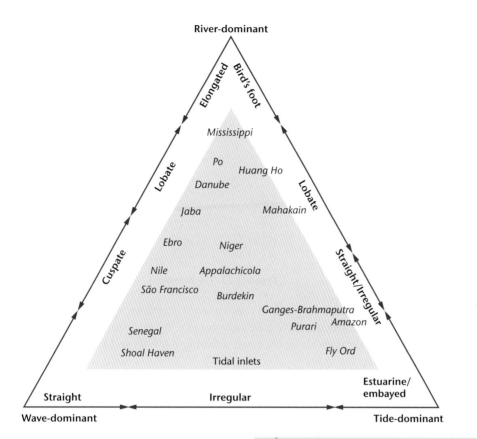

Figure 1.22 *Types of delta*

shape is due to distributaries, lined by levées, building out from the coast in a branching pattern. Two factors influence this process. First the Mississippi's very large sediment load; and second, the fact that the delta is built on a subsiding basin. Other factors that contribute to the delta's formation are the small tidal range and low wave energy in the Gulf of Mexico.

Tide-dominant deltas include the Ganges–Brahmaputra delta in south Asia (Figure 1.24), and the Amazon delta in South America. They consist of several major tidal inlets which run perpendicular to the coast. A high tidal range and strong tidal scour shapes the outline of these deltas.

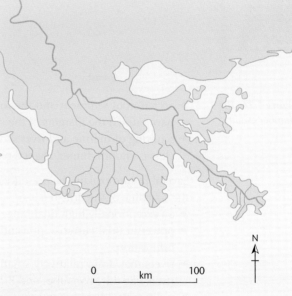

Figure 1.23 *The Mississippi delta*

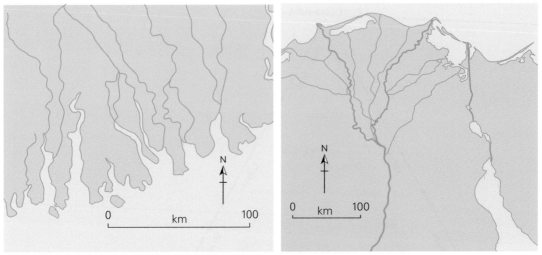

Figure 1.24 *The Ganges–Brahmaputra delta*

Figure 1.25 *The Nile delta*

In contrast, wave dominated deltas have smooth coastlines, with well-developed beaches and dune systems. They have been formed by strong **longshore currents** which sweep sediments along the coast, forming bay bars and shallow lagoons (Figure 1.25).

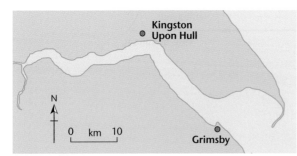

Figure 1.26 *The Humber estuary*

Estuaries

Estuaries are the funnel-shaped, tidal mouths of rivers (Figure 1.26). Most estuaries in the British Isles are river valleys, drowned by post-glacial rises in sea level. During the past 6000 years, sea level has stabilised and tidal action has modified the outline of estuaries to their present shape. Specifically, tidal action has led to:

➤ accretion of sediment and the formation of mudflats and saltmarshes, which have infilled the margins of the estuary
➤ scouring of marine and river sediments from the main channel, forming the classic smooth, funnel-shaped plan

Several factors explain the presence of estuaries and the absence of deltas around the coastline of the British Isles:

➤ an exceptionally high tidal range (up to 10 m) with strong tidal scour
➤ powerful tidal currents, preventing the growth of channel bars and channel bifurcation
➤ rivers that drain relatively small catchments and have, by comparison with rivers like the Mississippi and Brahmaputra, modest sediment loads
➤ well-vegetated catchments that produce low sediment yields

Key ideas

➤ River basins are multipurpose resources.

➤ River landscapes provide opportunities for a range of human activities, including industrial development, transportation, residential development, water supply, recreation and leisure, and conservation.

➤ Conflict can arise between different land uses in river basins.

Case study | **The La Plata drainage basin**

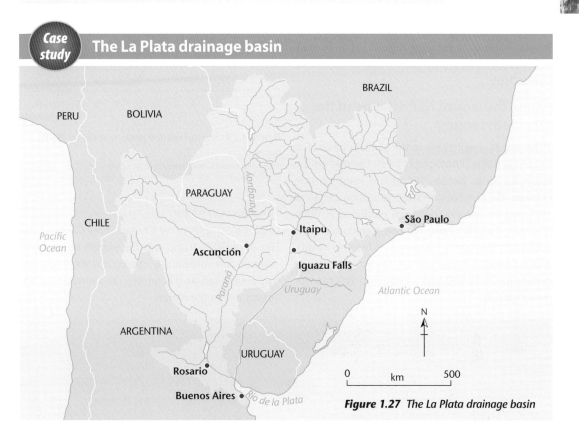

Figure 1.27 *The La Plata drainage basin*

The La Plata drainage basin is the fifth largest in the world, occupying an area more than five times the size of Spain. It consists of four main sub-basins: the Paraná, Paraguay and Uruguay basins, and the La Plata sub-basin itself (Figure 1.27). The Paraná is the most important river in the La Plata basin, and after the Amazon, South America's largest. From its headwaters in Brazil, to its mouth in the Rio de la Plata, the Paraná is nearly 4000 km long. The river discharges into the South Atlantic through an elongated delta, much of which is intensively cultivated.

The Paraná and its tributaries form an international river basin, which includes all of Paraguay, most of Uruguay, southern Brazil, northern Argentina, and eastern Bolivia. Peak flow occurs in February and March (17 100 cumecs) and is caused by intense summer convectional rainfall in the La Plata basin (Figure 1.28). Flow reaches a minimum in August and September (14 300 cumecs). The natural flow regime has been modified by several large dam projects. They have reduced seasonal variations in discharge, with lower flows in summer and higher flows in winter.

Over 100 million people live in the La Plata drainage basin. Most are urban dwellers, living in the region's 50 or so cities, including the megacities of São Paulo and Buenos Aires. Seventy per cent of the total GDP of Argentina, Brazil, Paraguay, Uruguay and Bolivia is generated within the La Plata drainage basin, underlining its huge economic importance. The river system also provides: a vital transport artery for Argentina, Brazil and landlocked Paraguay and Bolivia; water supplies for the region's urban populations; resources for tourism; and cheap hydro-electric power (HEP).

Itaipu: the largest HEP scheme of the twentieth century

There are 75 major dams in the La Plata basin. The biggest is Itaipu (Photograph 1.13). Located on the Brazil–Paraguay border, Itaipu is a joint venture between the two countries. Construction began in 1975 and the first electricity was produced in 1983. However, the project was not completed until eight years later. The dam is 196 m high, 7.76 km in length, and has created a reservoir 170 km long. Electricity generation is 12 600 MW — equal to ten nuclear power stations.

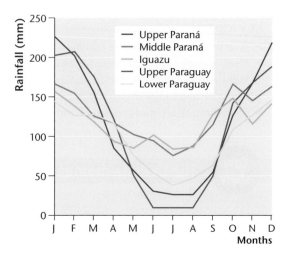

Figure 1.29 *Annual rainfall pattern in the La Plata basin*
Source: Camilloni I. and Barros, V. (2000) *Journal of Hydrometeorology*, Vol. 5, October, pp. 412–430.

The impact of Itaipu

Until the completion of China's Three Gorges Dam (see page 302), Itaipu was the world's biggest HEP scheme. Not surprisingly, given its scale, Itaipu has had a wide-ranging economic and environmental impact within the region.

Photograph 1.13 *Itaipu hydroelectric dam*

HEP project	Country	Ecological impact index (ha flooded per MW of electricity)	Displacement index (number displaced per MW of electricity)
Three Gorges	China	8.5	123
Itaipu	**Brazil–Paraguay**	**11.0**	**3.3**
Kariba	Zambia–Zimbabwe	370	38
Aswan	Egypt	190	57

Table 1.3
Comparison of the impact of Itaipu with that of other major HEP projects

Economic impact

Itaipu has brought both economic benefits and costs to the region. Because Paraguay is a much smaller country than Brazil, the relative importance of Itaipu to Paraguay is much greater. Itaipu's electricity provides 25–35% of Paraguay's income. Electricity production is divided equally between Paraguay and Brazil, but with a population of just 6.5 million, and GDP per capita of $4600, Paraguay uses only 3% of its share. The rest is sold to its giant neighbour, Brazil. With its rapidly growing economy and population of nearly 200 million, cheap electricity from Itaipu has been essential to Brazil's drive for economic development. Itaipu meets approximately one quarter of the country's electricity demand.

However, Itaipu's economic impact has not been entirely positive. The dam has severely disrupted navigation on the Paraná. It is impossible to navigate around the dam and small boats can no longer get to destinations in Argentina from Brazil.

Environmental impact

The reservoir impounded by the Itaipu dam flooded an area of 1350 km². Flooding meant the loss of 700 km² of forest and the extinction of several plant species, including a rare orchid. At an early stage, attempts were made to minimise the environmental impact of flooding. Over 27 000 animals, including 7500 mammals, were rescued from the rising waters and relocated in biological reserves. Forest reserves were created for transplanted trees, and areas already degraded before the dam was constructed were reafforested. Overall, 105 000 ha affected by Itaipu are protected as forest reserves, biological reserves and refuges.

Other environmental effects include:
- a lowering of water temperature in the Paraná downstream of the dam and its damaging effects on aquatic life
- interruptions of fish migrations on the river caused by the dam
- modifications to local climate caused by the reservoir, including increases in humidity and fog
- the growth of water weeds on the reservoir, clogging navigation channels
- concern that the threat of water-related diseases such as malaria and schistosomiasis could increase

Social impact

Forty-two thousand people were displaced in the flooded area behind the dam and resettled. Most native Indians and Mestisos were relocated to reservations. However, the scale of resettlement was far less than for other major dam building projects.

Transport on the Paraná–Paraguay waterway

The Paraná–Paraguay river system is an important inland waterway (Figure 1.29). It is navigable for much of its length and links large inland cities such as Asunción in Paraguay, and Rosario and Sante Fé in Argentina, with the Atlantic. The system also includes major international ports such as Buenos Aires and Montevideo in the Rio de la Plata, and smaller inland ports along the Paraná and Paraguay rivers in Argentina, Paraguay, Bolivia and Brazil. Cáceres in Brazil at the head of navigation is 3442 km upstream from Buenos Aires!

Although nearly 600 km upstream, Santa Fé can handle ocean-going vessels. It is a vital hub,

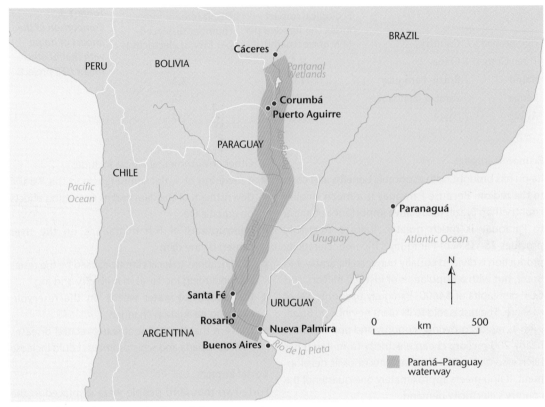

Figure 1.29 *Navigation on the Paraná–Paraguay waterway*

articulating trade with a large part of northeast Argentina. Its rich agricultural hinterland in the Pampas (Photograph 1.14) produces exports of grain, soya, cotton, citrus, livestock products and minerals. Further upstream, the waterway accommodates shallow draft vessels and barges only. Nonetheless, its economic importance to landlocked Paraguay and Bolivia is enormous. Puerto Aguirre, in eastern Bolivia, gives the country direct access to the Atlantic and sea-borne international trade. Since its completion in 1988, the port has reduced transport costs for Bolivian agricultural exports by 75%. It has also stimulated economic development in eastern Bolivia based on the growth of export crops such as grain and soya.

Improvements to the Paraná will increase the economic potential of central Argentina. Grain from the fertile Pampas — the 'breadbasket' of

Photograph 1.14 *Cattle being herded in the Pampas of Argentina; livestock products are among the exports from this rich agricultural area that use the Río Paraná.*

Michael Raw

Photograph 1.15 *Rosario and the Paraná river*

South America — is processed and exported from port terminals around Rosario. Currently a $100-million investment project is underway to widen the Paraná. This project has attracted $475 million of investments by foreign companies in export installations. These riverside locations will eventually make the area the largest grain milling centre in the world.

However, the relatively shallow depth of the Paraná (9.7 m) near Rosario is an obstacle to further development (Photograph 1.15). Shallow water means that Argentine exporters cannot fully load vessels. As a result, ships leave one-third empty and stop at the Brazilian grain port of Paranaguá on the Atlantic coast to get a full load. This increases shipping costs. Meanwhile, delays caused by congestion in Paranagua add further to costs. Once the Argentine grain terminals have been deepened, bigger ships will be able to load up on the Rio Paraná and will no longer have to call in at Paranagua for more cargo.

Tourism and Iguazu Falls

The magnificent Iguazu Falls (Photograph 1.16), rivalled only by the Victoria Falls in Africa, is one of South America's major tourist attractions. The Falls are 80 m high and 2.7 km in diameter. Straddling the Brazil–Argentina border, they have formed where the Rio Iguazu cascades across the edge of the Paraná basalt lava plateau. Over thousands of years the Falls have retreated from the confluence of the Paraná and Iguazu to their present position, 30 km upstream.

Iguazu has been designated by the United Nations as a World Heritage Site. The Falls are set within the context of a large conservation area. National parks have been established on both the Argentine and Brazilian sides of the Rio Iguazu. Alongside Argentina's Iguazu National Park there is also a national reserve. These conservation areas protect important tracts of sub-tropical rainforest and are home to over 2000

Image State/Alamy

Photograph 1.16 *The Iguazu Falls, Argentina*

plant species, and some of South America's most spectacular animals including tapirs, jaguars, giant ant-eaters and caymans.

Iguazu attracts over 1 500 000 visitors a year, two-thirds of them to the Brazilian side of the Falls. Most visitors arrive by air, at airports close to the river in Argentina and Brazil. A dozen or so hotels accommodate visitors at the Falls, most of them of four- and five-star status. Although Iguazu Falls is a mass tourism venue, because visitor numbers are relatively moderate, the current scale of development is sustainable.

Case study   The Colorado River

With a drainage basin covering 630 000 km², the Colorado is the third largest river in North America, after the Mississippi and the Columbia. Its source is the snowfields of the Rocky Mountains in Colorado and Wyoming; its mouth is the Gulf of California in Mexico, 2300 km to the southwest (see Figure 1.30). Apart from the Rocky Mountains, most of the Colorado drainage basin is desert. The climate at Moab on the Colorado Plateau is typical (see Figure 4.6 on page 164): mean annual rainfall is low and evapo-

transpiration in summer, when temperatures routinely rise above 40°C, is high (Table 1.4).

On the Colorado Plateau, the combination of erosion by the Colorado River, tectonic uplift and desert climate have produced some of the world's most spectacular landforms. They include the Grand Canyon (Photograph 1.17), Glen Canyon's Horseshoe Bend (Photograph 1.18) and the entrenched meanders or goosenecks on the San Juan River (Photograph 1.19).

Table 1.4 *Climate statistics for Moab, Utah*

	J	F	M	A	M	J	J	A	S	O	N	D	Total
Mean monthly temp. (°C)	−1.1	3.6	8.9	13.8	19.0	24.1	27.6	26.5	21.1	14.2	6.9	0.7	–
Mean monthly rainfall (mm)	14	11	22	25	18	12	21	22	19	29	19	17	229
Mean monthly potential evapo-transpiration (mm)	27	45	87	130	182	219	235	202	144	90	45	27	1433

Photograph 1.17 The Grand Canyon and the Colorado River

Photograph 1.18 Spectacular river-eroded canyons such as Horseshoe Bend in Glen Canyon have been carved into the Colorado Plateau by the Colorado River and its tributaries

Photograph 1.19 Entrenched meanders on the Colorado Plateau: goosenecks on the San Juan River

Managing water resources in the Colorado basin

From its source in the Rocky Mountains, the Colorado River flows across the arid Colorado Plateau and Great Basin. There, water is scarce: significant amounts are only available from the Colorado River and its tributaries. This explains why the Colorado is the most dammed river in the USA. Indeed, in its lower course in Nevada, Arizona and California, the Colorado is little more than a series of reservoirs created by the Hoover, Davis, Parker and Imperial dams (Figure 1.30).

Figure 1.30
Colorado drainage basin and annual water allotments by state

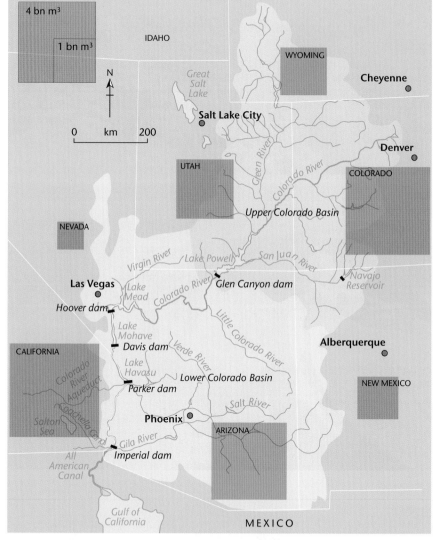

The Colorado River Compact

The 1922 Colorado River Compact (CRC) is a legal agreement between the seven US states in the Colorado drainage basin to share the water resources of the Colorado River and its tributaries. (Mexico was belatedly granted a water allocation in 1944.)

Between them, the eight interested parties divert the river's entire annual flow. Ninety per cent of the water is used for irrigation in agriculture; the rest supplies the needs of municipal authorities such as Los Angeles, San Diego, Phoenix, Denver, Salt Lake City and Las Vegas.

The CRC divides the Colorado's water equally between the Upper and Lower Basin states (Table 1.5). Hitherto, demand for water in the Upper Basin states has generally been less than their allocation. This has enabled California, with its large population and fast-growing economy, to exceed its legal share. However, rapid population growth and economic development in Arizona, Nevada and Colorado in the past 25 years has put a squeeze on California. It has also called into question the sustainability of current rates of water consumption in the southwest USA.

Four major dams control water resources in the Lower Basin: the Hoover, Davis, Parker and Imperial (Figure 1.30). Water is first diverted from Lake Mead to Las Vegas (Nevada) by aqueduct. However, Nevada receives only a tiny share of Colorado water. This, coupled with the explosive growth of Las Vegas in the past 30 years threatens the city with major water shortages in future. Nevada already uses its full allocation of water under the CRC and is urgently searching for new groundwater supplies in the Mojave Desert north of the city.

Fifty per cent of southern California's water comes from the Colorado River. A series of aqueducts downstream of the Hoover Dam provide water for irrigated agriculture in the Imperial Valley, and the Paulo Verde

Table 1.5 *Annual allocation of Colorado water by US states and Mexico*

	% allocation of Upper Basin water	Water allocations in billlions m^3
Upper Basin states		
Colorado	51.75	4.79
Wyoming	14.0	1.30
New Mexico	11.25	1.04
Utah	23.0	2.13
Lower Basin states		
California	58.7	5.43
Arizona	38.0	3.70
Nevada	4.0	0.37
Mexico	n/a	0.90

and Yuma irrigation areas. Water is also supplied to the metropolitan areas of Los Angeles and San Diego.

Like Nevada, Arizona's demand for water has increased massively in the past 30 years. Formerly a state with a water surplus, Arizona is now close to using its full allocation from the Colorado. Water abstracted at Lake Havasu is transferred by the Central Arizona Project (CAP) aqueduct over 500 km

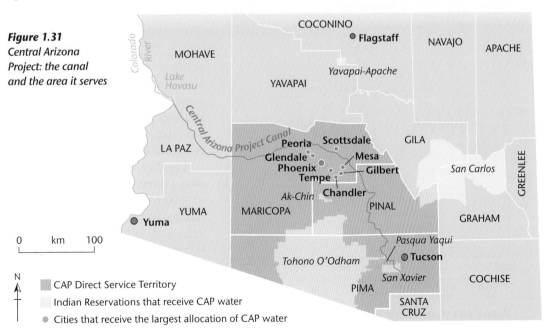

Figure 1.31
Central Arizona Project: the canal and the area it serves

CAP Direct Service Territory
Indian Reservations that receive CAP water
Cities that receive the largest allocation of CAP water

to the booming 'sun belt' cities of Phoenix, Scottsdale and Tucson (Figure 1.31).

What is left of the Colorado's flow when it finally reaches Mexico is diverted mainly to irrigation. There have been major issues concerning the quality of this water. Much of it is runoff from irrigated land in southern California, and has high levels of salinity that make it unfit for agriculture. Meanwhile, 90% of the Colorado delta has dried out, destroying what was one of the richest and most biodiverse wetlands in North America.

Glen Canyon dam

Glen Canyon was last major dam built on the Colorado. Completed in 1963, it was sited at the narrowest point in the canyon close to the Utah–Arizona border. Its location was so remote that a small town, Page, was built to accommodate the construction workers (Figure 1.32).

The primary purpose of the Glen Canyon dam was to improve water management in the Lower Basin. The dam created a huge reservoir — Lake Powell — over 300 km long and with a surface area

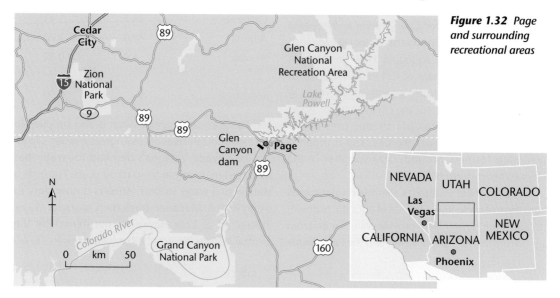

Figure 1.32 Page and surrounding recreational areas

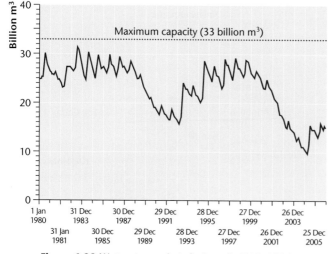

Figure 1.33 Water storage in Lake Powell, 1980–2006

of nearly 1650 km². A reservoir on this scale is a massive water bank: storing surplus water in times of flood and securing water supplies to the Lower Basin states and Mexico even in drought years (Figure 1.33).

Glen Canyon and Lake Powell have other purposes. The dam generates up to 1300 MW of hydro-electric power. Lake Powell supplies water to the 7500 inhabitants of Page, and to the nearby Navajo coal-fired power station. Meanwhile, Lake Powell has become a magnet for water-based recreation and leisure, such as sailing and fishing (Photograph 1.20).

Michael Raw

Photograph 1.20
Recreation and tourism on Lake Powell

Counting the cost: the environmental impact of Glen Canyon dam

Glen Canyon and Lake Powell have always been controversial. Securing water supplies for downstream users and generating over 1000 MW of hydro power have been achieved, but only at considerable environmental cost.

Glen Canyon's ecological impact has been greatest downstream of the dam. Controlling the flow of the Colorado has degraded the river ecosystem between Glen Canyon and Lake Mead. Before the construction of the dam the Colorado was wild and unpredictable. Violent floods scoured its channel every spring, and its waters were muddy and warm. Lake Powell changed all that. Because it acts as a sediment trap, the water leaving Lake Powell is clear; and because the lake is deep, the river water is cold — a constant 8° C. Floods are now a thing of the past: the entire annual floodwaters are stored in Lake Powell.

What are the ecological effects of these changes? Deprived of sediment and floodwaters, sandbanks that previously formed within the river channel have been eroded. Their absence has meant the loss of important habitats for fish, amphibians and birds. Meanwhile three native fish species, unable to tolerate cold, clear water, have become extinct — replaced by species such as trout, which thrive in these conditions. Today five other native fish species are endangered. Finally, the Glen Canyon dam is a barrier to fish migration on the river.

The annual floods on the Colorado had another beneficial effect: they cleared out bankside vegeta-tion. Without the floods, alien plant species such as tamarisk have been able to colonise the canyons. Tamarisks now dominate large tracts of the river bank, creating new habitats and ecosystems.

The upstream effects of Glen Canyon have been just as damaging. As the waters of Lake Powell rose they flooded some of finest canyonland scenery in the world. For example, the 'Cathedral in the Desert', an awe-inspiring canyon with sheer sandstone walls and waterfalls, disappeared beneath Lake Powell in 1966.

Draining Lake Powell

Since the late 1990s, a growing number of conservationist groups, led by the Sierra Club and the Glen Canyon Institute, have lobbied for the unthinkable: to drain Lake Powell. They want to restore the Colorado to its wild state, rehabilitate its unique ecosystems, and reclaim hundreds of square kilometres of desert canyons submerged by the lake's waters.

Needless to say, opposition to such a drastic scheme has been fierce — no more so than in Page, whose economy depends heavily on the recreation and tourism generated by the dam and Lake Powell. Over three million people a year visit the Glen Canyon recreational area — worth an estimated $400 million to the local economy (Photograph 1.20). Page draws its water supply from Lake Powell, as does the 2400 MW Navajo coal-fired power station nearby. Draining Lake Powell would also mean losing the 1300 MW of HEP generated by the Glen Canyon dam.

Yet there is no doubt that surface water storage in

this environment is wasteful. Around 10% of all the water that flows into Lake Powell is lost through evaporation and seepage.

The conservationists argue that Page, situated close to several of the USA's most popular national parks (see Figure 1.32), including the Grand Canyon, Bryce Canyon and Zion, would remain an important tourism centre even without Lake Powell. Water supplies for Page and the Navajo power plant could easily be abstracted from the Colorado River. More contentiously, they claim that Lake Powell has little value as a storage reservoir, and that its water could be stored either in underground aquifers or in Lake Mead.

The future

Dam building on the Colorado River goes back to the early twentieth century. At that time, the overwhelming view of society was that natural resources should be developed, that nature should be 'tamed', and that any environmental problems were of little consequence. The exploitation of the Colorado's water resources was crucial to the agricultural development and urbanisation of southern California, Arizona and Nevada.

Nearly a century later, societal values have shifted. Wilderness and its ecosystems are valued as a resource. The Colorado has suffered more than any other river, largely because it flows through a desert region where it is virtually the only source of water. But as we have seen, economic development in the Colorado basin has come at a cost. It has resulted in the destruction of the Colorado delta's ecosystem, the degrading of the river ecosystem between Glen Canyon and Lake Mead, including the Grand Canyon, and the flooding of huge areas of canyonlands in Utah.

It seems unlikely that environmentalists will succeed in their quest to drain Lake Powell. Yet, ironically, the issue could be resolved by nature itself. By 2005, a combination of drought and rising demand for water had reduced the volume of water in Lake Powell to its lowest level ever. By the end of 2007, Lake Powell was only 40% full. The effect on Glen Canyon has been remarkable. Vast areas of canyonlands, unseen for 40 years, have emerged from the lake. With no let-up in demand, and climate change likely to produce more frequent droughts, some experts believe that Lake Powell will never reach its full capacity again.

Key ideas
➤ Issues arise from the development of river basins.
➤ Some river basins are naturally vulnerable to flooding.
➤ The development of river basins can increase the risk of flooding.
➤ Flooding has social, economic and environmental impacts.

Flooding and the development of river basins

When river discharge exceeds bankfull channel capacity, flooding occurs across the adjacent floodplain. Flooding is part of a natural cycle and on wild rivers, unaffected by human activity, normally occurs once or twice a year. However, in densely populated countries like the UK, development has modified land use in most drainage basins, increasing runoff and potential flood risks.

Some rivers are more vulnerable to flooding than others. The natural factors that influence potential flood risks are summarised in Table 1.6. Rivers that pose significant flood risks typically have high peak flows and short **lag times** (Box 1.8 and Figure 1.34, p. 42); on longer timescales their flows are highly variable and erratic. The evidence of the hydrographs in Figure 1.35 (p. 42) suggests that the River Kent in Cumbria is more vulnerable to flooding than the River Avon in Wiltshire.

Factor	Effects on flooding
Geology	Porous rocks such as chalk and sandstone act as underground reservoirs, storing water and releasing it steadily through groundwater flow to rivers (e.g. River Avon). Drainage basins underlain by non-porous rocks such as shale and slate lack this storage capacity. As a result, runoff occurs rapidly and contributes to high peak flows and short lag times (e.g. River Kent).
Slopes	Steep slopes are typical of upland catchments. Rain falling on steep gradients will quickly run off into rivers. In these circumstances, response times are short and peak flows are high (e.g. River Kent).
Vegetation	In well-vegetated catchments (especially afforested catchments) interception is high. High rates of interception have two effects: they slow the movement of water to the ground and to rivers, and they increase evaporation. The net result is to extend lag times and reduce peak flows.
Drainage density	Drainage density is the average length of stream channel per km² in a drainage basin. The greater the density the shorter the distance water has to travel overland or within the soil to get to a stream or river. Thus high drainage density also tends to shorten lag times and increase peak flows.
Rainfall duration and intensity	The amount of rain that falls in a given time is a major determinant of flooding. High-intensity storms of short duration (often in the summer months) are responsible for 'flash' floods. Rivers with headwaters in hilly and mountainous areas are most vulnerable to flash floods because rainfall intensity is amplified by orographic uplift. Prolonged periods of rainfall, lasting several days or even weeks, produce slow floods (e.g. monsoon in south Asia). In these conditions, flooding is due to the sheer volume of rain and the saturation of the ground.
Precipitation type	Hilly or mountainous headwaters may support considerable snow cover in winter. The snowpack by the end of the winter may represent several months of precipitation. Rapid melting in the spring often gives rise to seasonal floods (e.g. Colorado River, USA; Isère River, France).

Table 1.6 Some natural features of river basins that influence flooding

Box 1.8 Storm hydrographs

Storm (or flood) hydrographs show the short-term response of a river to a specific rainfall event. Figure 1.34 is a typical storm hydrograph. Rainfall is shown as a bar chart at 15-minute intervals, and discharge as a line chart at similar time intervals. The highest discharge is known as the **peak flow**, and the difference between the time of highest rainfall and peak flow is the **lag time**. Rivers that respond rapidly to rainfall have high peak flows. They are said to be 'flashy' and are at high risk of flooding.

Figure 1.34 shows the storm hydrograph for the River Calder for 6 July 2006. This event caused widespread flooding in Hebden Bridge and

Mytholmroyd in the Upper Calder valley. The Calder catchment is vulnerable to flooding because of its impermeable geology, steep slopes and sparse woodland cover. In this instance, the heavy rain was intensified by the surrounding hills.

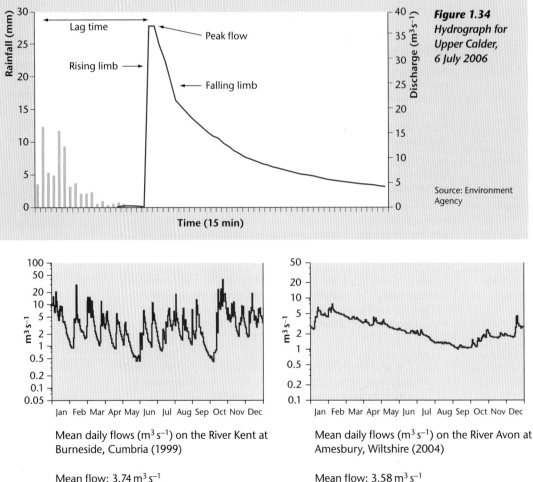

Figure 1.34
Hydrograph for Upper Calder, 6 July 2006

Source: Environment Agency

Mean daily flows (m³ s⁻¹) on the River Kent at Burneside, Cumbria (1999)

Mean flow: 3.74 m³ s⁻¹
Mean annual rainfall: 1732 mm
Geology: impermeable slate, flagstone, shale, boulder clay

Mean daily flows (m³ s⁻¹) on the River Avon at Amesbury, Wiltshire (2004)

Mean flow: 3.58 m³ s⁻¹
Mean annual rainfall: 745 mm
Geology: mainly chalk

Figure 1.35 *Annual hydrographs for the River Kent and River Avon*
Source: National Water Archive

How development can increase the risk of flooding

Human activities within drainage basins can significantly increase the risk of flooding. The main cause of increased flood risk is land use change that accelerates runoff or increases the ratio of runoff to precipitation. Deforestation and urbanisation are two examples of land use changes that are likely to heighten flood risks.

Other examples of human activity that increase flood risk include: the artificial land drainage of moorland (i.e. gripping) that speeds runoff; and flood defences such as levées, which protect immediate floodplain areas but contribute to higher discharges downstream.

Deforestation

Deforestation both increases and accelerates runoff. This is because there is less interception of rainfall by forest trees, less rainwater evaporation from leaf surfaces, and less moisture removed from the soil by transpiration. The impact of deforestation on river flow and potential flooding is shown in Figure 1.36.

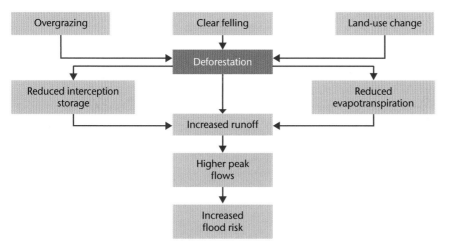

Figure 1.36
The effect of deforestation on rainfall–runoff relationships

Figure 1.37 illustrates the effect of deforestation on river flows. The Laval and Brusquet catchments in southeast France are adjacent to each other. They have the same climate, geology and relief. However, they differ in one important respect. The Laval catchment has been extensively deforested. Only 22% of the Laval's catchment is afforested, while the Brusquet retains 87% of its forest cover. As a result, peak flows on the Laval are four to five times higher than those on the Brusquet, and the flood risks proportionately greater.

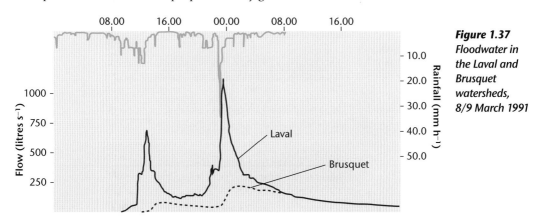

Figure 1.37
Floodwater in the Laval and Brusquet watersheds, 8/9 March 1991

Urbanisation

Urbanisation converts farmland, grassland, wetland and woodland to housing, offices, factories and roads. These urban land uses have a very different hydrology from natural surfaces such as vegetation and soil.

➤ Urban areas comprise more impermeable materials such as tarmac, concrete, tiles and bricks. These materials provide little storage capacity to buffer rapid runoff.

➤ Urban areas have artificial drainage systems — pitched roofs, gutters, sewers — to shed water quickly and efficiently. The effect on urbanised catchments is to shorten lag times and increase peak flows (Figure 1.38).

Figure 1.38
Hydrographs
for a catchment
before and after
urbanisation

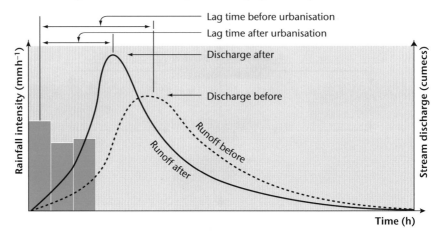

In addition to the transformation of land use, urbanisation is often accompanied by urban expansion onto floodplains (Figure 1.39). In their natural state, floodplains contain wetlands, which are important stores for floodwater. With urbanisation, these wetlands are drained and concreted over, reducing the catchment's storage capacity and increasing runoff and the potential for flooding.

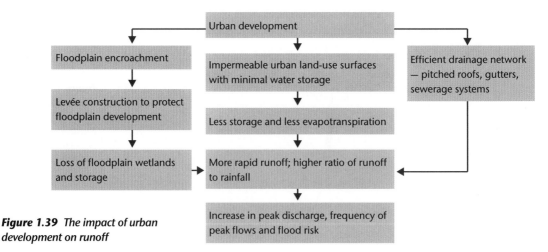

Figure 1.39 The impact of urban development on runoff

The impact of flooding

Case study **Prague floods: August 2002**

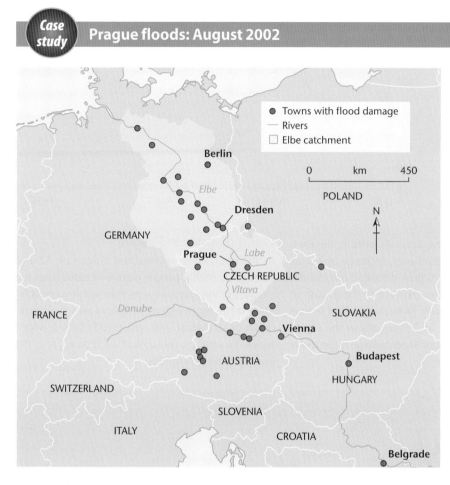

Figure 1.40
Flooding in central Europe and in the Elbe drainage basin, August 2002

Source: Risk Management Solutions

Many parts of central Europe, including the Czech Republic, Germany and Austria, experienced severe floods in August 2002 (Figure 1.40). The floods in Prague, capital of the Czech Republic, were unprecedented, with an estimated return period of 500 years. Flood damage in the Czech Republic alone amounted to €3 billion, with one third of the damage in Prague itself. The death toll in the Czech Republic from the floods was 110 lives.

The flood event

The Prague floods followed several days of torrential rain. There were two periods of particularly intense rainfall. The first, 6–7 August, was heaviest. Between 125 mm and 255 mm of rain fell in 2 days in the southwest region of the Czech Republic and in northeast Austria. However, reservoirs in the Vltava catchment upstream from Prague held back most of the floodwater. Then a second downpour occurred, on 11–13 August, as a slow-moving depression deposited 320 mm of rain in the Erzgebirger Mountains on the Czech–German border, and in southern Bohemia (Figure 1.41).

This exceptional rainfall event, following so soon after the 6–7 August rains, triggered a flood wave in the Vltava basin, and this time the floodwaters could

Figure 1.41
Hydrographs for Prague and Dresden, 7–22 August 2002

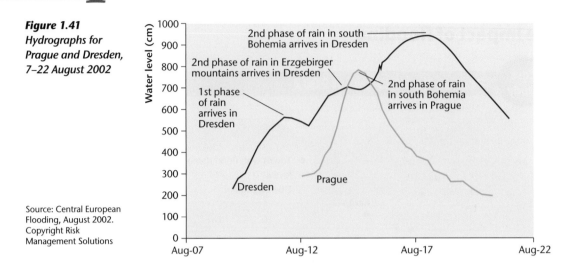

2nd phase of rain in south
Bohemia arrives in Dresden

2nd phase of rain in Erzgebirger
mountains arrives in Dresden

1st phase
of rain
arrives in
Dresden

2nd phase of rain
in south Bohemia
arrives in Prague

Dresden

Prague

Source: Central European
Flooding, August 2002.
Copyright Risk
Management Solutions

not be contained by the dams. As a result, the River Vltava recorded its highest-ever discharge at Prague — 5300 cumecs on 14 August. It took 12 days for the flood wave to travel downstream to the mouth of the River Elbe in Germany. En route it caused serious flooding in Germany, and especially in the city of Dresden. The total cost of flood damage in Germany was €12 billion.

Flood disaster in Prague

As the flood wave approached Prague on 12 and 13 August, 50 000 people were evacuated from the city. Half of the evacuees were elderly and vulnerable. Among the most urgent problems was the breakdown of sanitation and refuse collection services, which threatened the spread of disease, and the loss of power to hospitals.

isifa ImageService s.r.o./Alamy

Photograph 1.21 *The 2002 flooding in Prague was the worst for over a century*

All bridges across the Vltava were closed to traffic and temporary flood barriers were erected to save the city's historic core. Even so, flooding was the worst for over a century (Photograph 1.21). Many historic buildings in the Old Town, dating from the seventeenth and eighteenth centuries, were flooded to a depth of 4 m. The National Theatre, the city zoo and the National Library, which housed important archives and historical collections, were damaged. The floods overwhelmed Prague's Metro, the city's rapid transit system. Thirteen underground stations were flooded. It took six months and €230 million to repair the damage.

In the Karlin district, a residential quarter downstream from the centre, 1100 buildings were flooded and 25 000 people evacuated. Three blocks of flats collapsed and 40 buildings were considered too dangerous to reoccupy. In the immediate aftermath of the flood, the worst affected districts had no gas or electricity and were uninhabitable. Twelve weeks later, only one-third of the evacuees had been able to return to their homes.

Conclusion

The 2002 floods followed similar flood disasters in central Europe in 1993, 1995 and 1997 and suggest that both the frequency and costs of flooding have increased.

A number of factors are blamed for this, including: river straightening; uncontrolled floodplain development; underinvestment in flood defences; a lack of flood insurance (only half of those affected in the Czech Republic had cover against flood hazards); and climate change.

Key ideas

➤ Managing river basins often involves balancing socio-economic and environmental needs.
➤ Managing river basins often requires detailed planning to resolve land-use conflicts, development and flood risk issues.

Managing river landscapes

The use of drainage basins and water resources often gives rise to conflict. For example: discharges of sewage effluent may pollute public water supplies; farmers, applying nitrates to crops, may damage aquatic ecosystems; the building of dams and weirs may hinder recreational activities and fish migrations; and urban development may increase flood risks.

River Basin Management Plans (RBMPs) are a recent EU initiative. They emphasise a new integrated (or holistic) approach to drainage basin management, recognising that drainage basins are complex, interrelated systems, which function as whole. RBMPs aim to:
➤ protect and enhance the status of aquatic ecosystems
➤ promote sustainable water use
➤ supply sustainable, good-quality surface and groundwater
➤ reduce, and eventually eliminate, polluting discharges and emissions
➤ mitigate the effects of floods and droughts
➤ delimit conservation areas designed to protect habitats and species

The first RBMP in England is for the River Ribble drainage basin in northwest England.

Physical background

The Ribble has its source in the central Pennines and flows in a southwesterly direction to its estuary on the Irish Sea coast. It drains a total area of around 2100 km^2 (Figure 1.42). Its major tributaries are the Calder, the Hodder, the Darwen and the Douglas. The physical geography of the catchment is extremely varied. In the upper basin the hills of the Yorkshire Dales, the Forest of Bowland and the Pendle Anticline rise to nearly 700 m. The lower basin includes the Fylde plain and the lowlands south of the Ribble estuary between Preston and Southport. Carboniferous limestone, millstone grit and coal measures rocks dominate the geology of the upper basin. In the lower basin younger sandstones and marls are covered by boulder clay. Fen peat occurs on the south side of the Ribble estuary. Much of this area was drained and reclaimed for farming in the late eighteenth century.

Because of its westerly situation and hilly catchment, average rainfall is high. In the hills the orographic effect pushes mean annual rainfall totals above 2000 mm. Nowhere does rainfall average less than 900 mm a year.

Flows on the River Ribble at Salmesbury (10 km upstream from Preston) average 33 cumecs a year.

But discharge is highly variable: the highest recorded mean daily flow is 675 cumecs; the lowest just 1.8 cumecs. In general, the Ribble and its tributaries are free-flowing. Apart from Stocks Reservoir on the River Hodder and the Rivington reservoir complex in the Douglas catchment, there are no large surface reservoirs.

Land use and biodiversity

Ninety per cent of the Ribble catchment is rural, most of it moorland and pasture. Livestock farming and other rural uses dominate the northern half of the

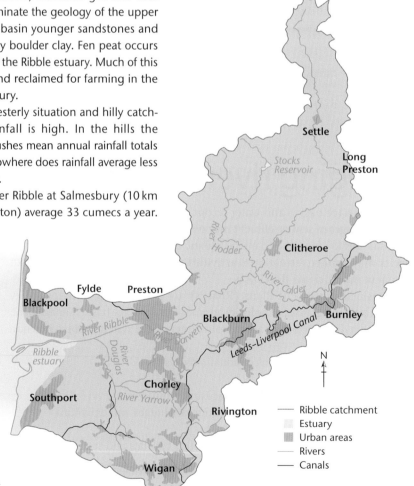

Figure 1.42
The Ribble catchment

catchment. Dairy farming is important in the Fylde and intensive horticulture on grade 1 land is found south of the estuary. The western and southern parts of the catchment have large urban populations, mainly concentrated in three areas: Preston in the Ribble Valley; Blackburn, Burnley and several small industrial towns in the Calder–Darwen catchments; and Wigan and Chorley in the Douglas basin.

In the sparsely populated upper basin, water resources are relatively unpolluted. As a result, the

Activity	Detail	Conflict
Recreation, leisure and tourism	The Ribble drainage basin includes parts of two national conservation areas: the Yorkshire Dales National Park and the Forest of Bowland Area of Outstanding Natural Beauty. Riverside locations and footpaths are visitor attractions in these areas. The upper reaches of the Ribble, and the Hodder, are important game fisheries. Coarse fishing is popular throughout the Ribble basin; even the more polluted rivers such as the Calder support healthy fish stocks.	Recreational activities such as angling and canoeing require pollution-free rivers for aesthetic, health and ecological reasons. There is conflict with activities that lower water quality (e.g. sewage treatment, industrial effluent), divert water from rivers (for public supply and irrigation), create artificial barriers (e.g. weirs) and reduce **biodiversity**.
Industry	Some water is abstracted for industrial use (e.g. manufacture of paper) but the main industrial use of rivers is the disposal of liquid effluent. Sewage treatment works (STWs) are a major source of effluent. STWs and some industries input small quantities of toxic waste, such as zinc, copper and mercury.	Construction of weirs stops migration of fish and may prevent salmon and trout from extending their range. Pollutants may get into the food web. Pollution may reduce oxygen levels and biodiversity. Pollution lowers the aesthetic quality of rivers and their value for recreation.
Water supply	The catchment provides some water for public supply, e.g. Stocks Reservoir.	May affect river flow in times of drought. This may have an impact on aquatic ecosystems and limit the use of rivers for leisure activities.
Agriculture	Water is abstracted for agriculture, especially in the lower basin where intensive farming occurs.	Runoff from farmland may input nitrates and phosphates into streams and rivers causing eutrophication. Spillages of silage liquor and farm slurry may kill aquatic life.
Ecology	The Ribble basin's stream and river network supports a range of wetland/aquatic habitats and considerable biodiversity, which includes invertebrates, fish, birds and mammals.	To maximise biodiversity and conserve habitats, wildlife conflicts with economic activities that reduce oxygen levels, increase pollution loads and create physical obstacles which hinder the free movement of aquatic life.

Table 1.7 Water resources and land use conflicts in the Ribble drainage basin

biological status of the Ribble and Hodder, and their tributaries, is high. Well-oxygenated water supports healthy populations of invertebrates such as freshwater shrimps, beetles and insect larvae. Salmonids (including Atlantic salmon and sea trout), whiteclawed crayfish, water voles and even otters thrive in the upper basin — a sure indication of high water quality.

Flood control management

There are historical records for 40 major flood events on the Ribble and its tributaries. The worst flood was in 1866, and the most recent ones were in 1995, 2000 and 2002. Most floods have occurred in autumn and winter, associated with prolonged frontal rainfall. However, August is the month with the largest number of floods. These summer floods are caused by heavy convectional storms. Tidal flooding is also a significant hazard in the lower reaches of the Ribble, downstream from Preston.

In total, 34 000 people live in areas with an annual flood risk of 0.1%. Some of these areas are protected by flood embankments built and maintained by the Environment Agency and local authorities (Photograph 1.22). Temporary storage of floodwaters

is possible in the upper basin on the wide floodplain between Settle and Long Preston (see Figure 1.42 on page 48). This washland area significantly reduces the flood risk downstream. Elsewhere, floodplain storage is limited either by the narrowness of the Ribble's floodplain, or by channel incision that has disconnected the river from its floodplain.

Much of the housing, commercial and industrial properties and infrastructure most at risk from flooding has been there for many years. Today, planners strictly control all new building developments on the floodplain (Box 1.9). The aim is to restrict development and not increase the area at risk from flooding.

Preston Riverside: balancing socio-economic and environmental needs

Just before the River Ribble reaches its estuary, it flows through the city of Preston. However, the city and the river have always been geographically separate. The city centre occupies a plateau 30 m above the river. Urban growth has taken place to the north, away from the river. In fact, most visitors to Preston are unaware of the river; and most residents rarely visit the river and its environs.

Photograph 1.22
The River Ribble at Walton-le-Dale, near Preston; housing areas at risk of flooding on the left are protected by levées

Michael Raw

Box 1.9 Controlling development on floodplains

Eight per cent of the land in England (around 10 000 ha) is at risk from river and coastal flooding. Within the flood risk area there are 1.7 million homes, 300 000 commercial properties and 12% of the nation's farmland. Historically, floodplains have always attracted development. Many of England's oldest towns and cities, such as York, Chester, Shrewsbury and Tewkesbury, occupy sites that are regularly flooded. Floodplains are attractive because they offer flat and fertile land, are easily developed, and provide locations for river crossings and transport routes.

However, development on floodplains is exposed to significant flood risks, which endanger lives, property and the environment. Floodplain development also creates additional discharges of water into rivers and reduces temporary storage areas for floodwater. For these reasons, planners in the UK guide new development away from floodplains. Where new development is permitted, developers must evaluate flood risks

and take measures to mitigate them. This can include building flood defences and maintaining them.

Although the frequency of floods appears to be increasing (due to climate change and land use changes in drainage basins) and the impact of flooding is far greater than any other natural hazard, pressures to develop floodplains are stronger than ever. In the southeast region of England, rapid population growth (and future growth), coupled with social changes such as increases in life expectancy and single-parent households, have led to acute housing shortages. With restrictions on development in the green belt, and brownfield sites able to meet only part of the demand, the government proposes to build thousands of new houses on floodplain land bordering the Thames estuary, east of London, by 2020. The proposals, which conflict with government policy on floodplain development, are highly controversial.

Developing the riverside

Since the early 1980s, river and other waterfront sites in many UK cities have proved attractive locations for housing and offices. London's Docklands is the outstanding example, but many smaller cities such as Bristol, Cardiff and Leeds have successfully re-developed waterfront sites.

So far, most waterfront development has been concentrated on regenerating run-down docklands and decaying industrial areas. The Ribble at Preston is different: the proposed site has a rural character (Photograph 1.23), made up of mainly farmland and parkland on the floodplain. The river itself is wide, shallow and tidal. This, however, creates a problem because in its present state it is unsuitable for most water-based recreational activities.

The riverside plan: opportunities

Preston and South Ribble councils want to develop the riverside at Preston. They see the river as a resource — hitherto underutilised — that has the

potential to create a new focus for development. They contrast the Ribble at Preston, which flows virtually unnoticed around the city, with the attractive waterfronts of the River Ouse at York, and the River Dee at Chester.

Key to the proposal is the construction of a barrage across the River Ribble (Figure 1.43). The barrage would permanently raise water levels, replacing the tidal river with a freshwater lake. The lake would attract recreation and leisure amenities such as sailing, waterskiing, angling and rowing. Raised embankments would protect riverside developments from flooding and provide walkways. Four thousand new homes, together with shops and offices, would be built on the floodplain on the south side of the river. An urban park would occupy the centre of the new complex, connected to the existing Avenham and Miller parks on the opposite bank by a new pedestrian bridge. The project would promote the sustainable city concept, with new housing, office and shopping developments within

Michael Raw

Photograph 1.23
Proposed site of
Preston Riverside
development

walking distance of Preston's central business district (CBD) and train station. The emphasis would be on pedestrian movement rather than motor vehicles.

Local councils see the development as boosting Preston's image and its status as the third largest urban centre in the northwest region. It would also create jobs, attract visitors and tourists and, most

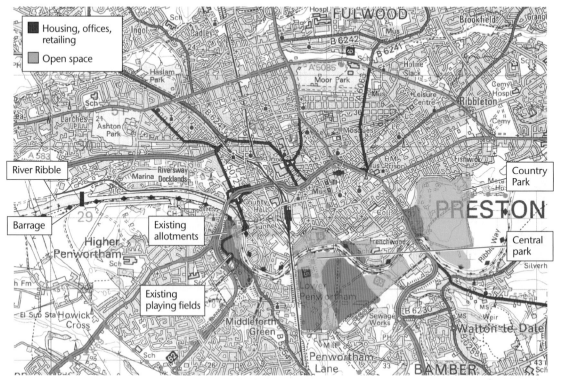

Figure 1.43 *The proposed Riverside development scheme, Preston*

importantly, it would at last integrate Preston with its river.

Problems

Many local people and conservation groups do not share the council's enthusiasm for the riverside scheme. There has been fierce opposition from the Save the Ribble Campaign, organised through its own website. Opponents of the scheme cite the following disadvantages:

■ loss of green belt land on the floodplain
■ loss of footpaths alongside the river, currently used for recreation
■ increased flood risks with building on the flood-plain, which is contrary to government guidelines (see Box 1.9)
■ loss of allotments and playing fields on the flood-plain
■ barrage would be an obstacle to migrating Atlantic salmon and sea trout

■ loss of the tidal river's unique habitat and wildlife, with its daily variations in salinity and exposed mudflats at low tide

The barrage could also have damaging ecological effects downstream. Sediment trapped behind the barrage will drastically reduce deposition in the estuary. Without this sediment, erosion of estuarine mudflats and saltmarshes would almost certainly take place.

Moreover, the Ribble estuary (Photograph 1.24) is internationally recognised for its biodiversity and the British government has legal obligations to protect it. Half of the estuary is a Ramsar site, a status reserved for internationally important wetlands.

The estuary is also protected by several nature reserves and Sites of Special Scientific Interest (SSSIs). Low tides expose mudflats and sandflats which in winter support 250 000 migrant birds, mainly waders and wildfowl.

Photograph 1.24
The Ribble estuary — a landscape of mudflats and saltmarshes

Examination-style questions

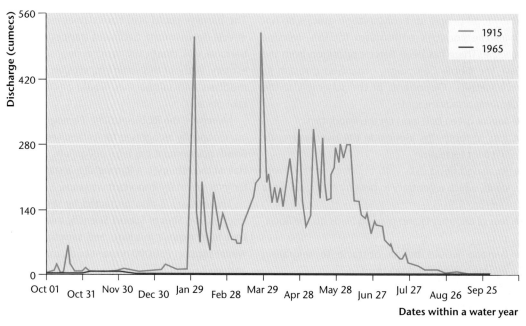

Figure 1 *Trinity River daily flows at Lewiston before and after dam construction*

Figure 1 shows the effects of dam construction on the Trinity River at Lewiston, northeast California.

The dam was completed in 1963.

1 (a) Describe the main features of flow on the Trinity River before and after the construction of the dam. (4 marks)

(b) Explain how dam construction might alter the fluvial processes operating in a river system. (6 marks)

(c) In what ways can rivers provide opportunities for a number of human activities? (6 marks)

(d) With reference to one or more examples, explain why some river basins are more vulnerable to flooding than others. (9 marks)

2 With reference to named examples, explain how river basins can be managed to reduce the risk of flooding. (25 marks)

Figure 2

3 (a) Describe the main fluvial features of the river channel and valley
        shown in Figure 2.   (4 marks)

  (b) Explain the processes responsible for the formation of the features
        identified in Figure 2.   (6 marks)

  (c) Show how development can make rivers increasingly vulnerable
        to flooding.   (6 marks)

  (d) With reference to one or more named examples, explain how
        different land uses can lead to conflict in river basins.   (9 marks)

4 With reference to named examples, explain how detailed planning
    and management of river basins is needed to balance economic and
    environmental needs.   (25 marks)

Chapter 2

Coastal environments

Coastal zones

Key ideas

➤ A range of physical processes, including erosion, deposition, transportation, weathering and mass movement (sub-aerial) give rise to distinctive coastal landforms.

➤ The processes responsible for coastal landforms vary from place to place.

➤ Rock type, rock structure, sea-level change and wave characteristics affect the development of coastal landforms.

➤ There are a range of coastal erosional and coastal depositional features and landforms.

The coast is the dynamic interface between land and sea. We subdivide the coast into three major zones: the **offshore zone**, the **nearshore zone** and the **backshore zone** (Figure 2.1). The offshore zone is an area of relatively deep water. Here, wave-induced sediment movement is limited, especially in water more than 20 m deep. In contrast the nearshore zone is vitally important to coastal geomorphology. As waves enter this zone they break and move towards the shore. Finally they travel up the beach as **swash**, and return to the sea as **backwash**. The extent of the area

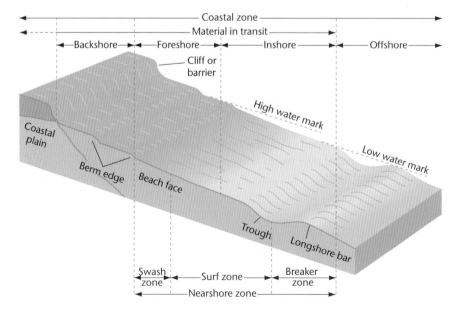

Figure 2.1
Coastal zones

Michael Raw

Surf zone

Swash zone

Photograph 2.1
The surf and swash zones on a beach in southern Iceland

affected by swash and backwash is determined by the tidal range and the gradient of the nearshore zone. The backshore zone lies beyond the reach of waves. It is often an area of sand dunes and old shingle ridges.

The coastal energy system

The coast is an example of an open system. It is powered by the energy of waves, tidal currents and the wind. These energy inputs then interact with the system's geological structure and sediments through processes of erosion, transport and deposition. The outcome is distinctive coastal landforms such as cliffs, beaches and dunes. The coastal system is 'open' in the sense that both energy and materials (e.g. sediment and seawater) can enter and leave the system (Box 2.1).

Box 2.1 Dynamic equilibrium and the coastal system

The coast is an energy system where there is a balance between inputs and outputs of energy. Ninety-five per cent of the energy input is from waves. This energy is used by:

- waves breaking in the surf zone
- friction between waves and the seabed in the nearshore zone
- erosion of sediments and solid rock
- sediment transport by waves and currents (in the swash zone and the nearshore zone)

Coastal landforms such as beaches achieve a steady state when their shape is in balance with the energy environment (energy is input and expended with no net movement of sediment). We call this **dynamic equilibrium**. Providing there is no change in energy inputs, the **profile** and the **plan** of the beach remain unchanged. Dynamic equilibrium is possible because beach sediments such as sand and shingle adjust rapidly (in just a few hours) to changing energy, inputs. Suppose, for example, that an abrupt increase in wave height and wave period occurs (the interval between waves in seconds). Because of the increase in energy, the beach must change. Sediments will be eroded and transported offshore. The effect on the **beach profile** will be dramatic. A wider, flatter beach will form that is able to absorb the extra wave energy. The beach now has a new steady state form which will persist for as long as energy inputs remain constant.

On solid rock coasts, short-term increases in wave energy (measured in hours) make little difference to landforms. Just as rivers cannot adjust their channels when flowing over solid rock (Chapter 1), so waves make little impression on solid rock coasts. Even if significant erosion occurs during a single storm, it will take thousands of years for the coast to achieve dynamic equilibrium. For this reason, many erosional features such as **shore platforms** and raised beaches cannot be understood by present-day processes. They are relict features formed by energy systems in the past.

Yet even on rocky coasts, equilibrium could in theory be achieved providing sea levels remained stable for long enough. Cliff erosion and recession would eventually form a shore platform wide enough to dissipate all wave energy before reaching the cliff line. Cliffs would then degrade through weathering and slope processes and achieve a new equilibrium form. However, given the enormous climatic shifts of the past 2 000 000

years, and the accompanying worldwide changes in sea level, equilibrium on such a timescale is highly unlikely.

So some landforms in the coastal system are in dynamic equilibrium, and others are not (and probably never will be). The system can adjust to short-time energy changes by shifting sediments (similar to a river flowing across floodplains and in alluvial channels) but little, if any, adjustment is possible on rocky and upland coasts. This means that in stormy conditions surplus energy will be expended pounding cliffs, gradually changing the shape of the coast in profile and plan. The evidence of change, which over thousands of years could lead to equilibrium, are the erosional features of cliff recession, such as **caves**, **arches** and **stacks**.

Wave energy

Waves are undulations of the water surface caused by winds blowing across the ocean. Energy is transferred from the wind to waves by friction. Water particles in waves have a circular motion in the open ocean. Only when waves enter the coastal zone, and start to slow down, does any significant forward movement of water take place. Thus when we observe waves we are not witnessing a mass movement of water, but a movement of energy flowing through the water.

Box 2.2 Wave energy

The amount of energy in a wave in deep water is approximated by the formula:

$$P = H^2T$$

Where P is the power in kilowatts per metre of wave front, H is height in metres and T is the time interval between wave crests in seconds (i.e. wave period).

The relationship between wave height and wave energy is non-linear. In this example (Table 2.1) the waves in the North Atlantic at 53.5° N are just over eight times bigger than those in the Straits of Dover at 51.1° N. However, the Atlantic waves have nearly 70 times as much energy!

Table 2.1 *Moored buoys: wave height and wave period, 7 February 2007*

Location	Wave height (m)	Wave period (sec)	kW per m
53.5° N 19.5° W	5	8	200
51.1° N 1.8° E	0.6	6	2.16

The height of waves depends on three things: **fetch**, wind speed and wind duration. Fetch is the open expanse of water over which the wind blows. Coastlines with a long fetch such as the Atlantic coast of Cornwall will generate bigger waves than coastlines with short fetches such as southeast England. The biggest waves are found where strong winds blow consistently from one direction. For example, waves in the Indian Ocean between 40° S and 60° S average 7 m in height. The effect of wind speed and wind duration on wave height is shown in Table 2.2.

Wind speed (km h⁻¹)	Wind duration (wave height)	Wind duration (wave height)
18.5	3 hours (0.4 m)	12 hours (0.6 m)
37	3 hours (0.9 m)	12 hours (1.9 m)
56	3 hours (1.8 m)	12 hours (3.4 m)
74	3 hours (2.7 m)	12 hours (5.3 m)

Table 2.2
Wind speed, wind duration and wave height

Waves in shallow water

Waves entering the nearshore zone undergo significant changes (Figure 2.2). As the water depth shallows to just half a wavelength, frictional resistance with the seabed starts to slow waves down. This has two effects. First the waves increase in height and develop sharper crests, and second the wavelength shortens. Despite these changes, the wave period remains the same. As waves move further onshore they become increasingly unstable. Eventually, at a depth of less than 1.3 times their height, they break as surf.

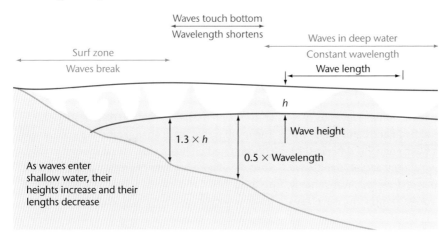

Figure 2.2
Transformation of waves as they enter shallow water

This process expends large amounts of wave energy. Most of the remaining energy is absorbed by sand and shingle, moved up and down and along the shoreline by the swash and backwash.

Wave refraction

Waves are also transformed in planform as they approach the coastline. Most waves travel obliquely towards the coast. As they enter the nearshore zone they are bent or refracted. Fully refracted waves break parallel to the shore.

Refraction is caused by variations in water depth in the nearshore zone (Box 2.3). Those sections of the wave crest that reach the shallower, nearshore zone first, are slowed by frictional drag. Meanwhile, sections of the wave crest that lie seaward, in deeper water, continue to travel at a constant speed. These processes cause wave fronts to bend and take on the planform of the coast. When waves are fully refracted, the swash and backwash follow the same path up and down the beach. With no net transfer of sediment along the beach, we describe these beaches as **swash-aligned**.

Box 2.3 Wave refraction and the unequal distribution of energy along the coast

Figure 2.3
The effect of refraction on energy inputs along an indented coast

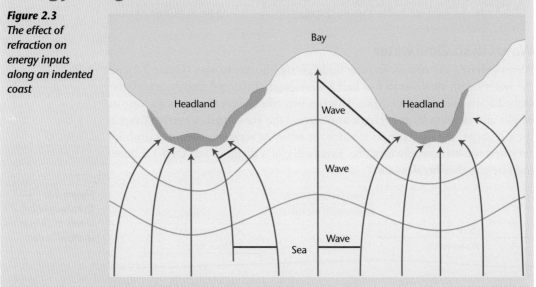

Figure 2.3 shows the refraction of waves as they approach a coastline of headlands and bays. The effect of refraction on wave energy is described by wave rays — lines drawn at right angles to the wave crests. Between each pair of wave rays, wave energy is constant. As the waves bend, the wave rays converge on the headlands and diverge in the bays. The result is that wave energy (and wave height) is concentrated on headlands, and dispersed in bays. Thus, headlands are sites of erosion and landforms such as cliffs and caves, whereas depositional features such as beaches dominate bays.

Wave-induced currents

Wave movements generate two types of current: shore-normal currents, which occur at right angles to the shore, and shore-parallel currents, which flow along the shore. The latter are better known as longshore currents.

Rip currents

Rip currents flow away from and at right angles to the shore. They form when there are marked differences in wave height in the nearshore zone (Figure 2.4). Water levels in areas of higher waves are greater than in adjacent areas of lower waves. The resulting head of water induces a convergent gravity flow of water towards the area of low waves. The two opposing longshore currents meet close to the shoreline and then flow seawards as a rip current.

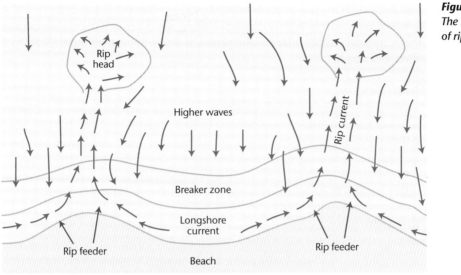

Figure 2.4
*The formation
of rip currents*

Longshore currents and longshore drift

Longshore currents develop when waves approach the shoreline obliquely. These currents flow parallel to the shore and transport large volumes of sand and shingle.

Longshore drift is the lateral movement of sand and shingle along beaches (Figure 2.5). Waves that are not fully refracted will approach the shore obliquely. When they break, the swash runs up the beach at the same oblique angle. The backwash, however, is pulled down the beach by gravity at right angles to the shore. This zig-zag pattern of swash and backwash transports sediments in the direction of the dominant waves. Longshore drift is responsible for **drift-aligned** beaches such as **spits**.

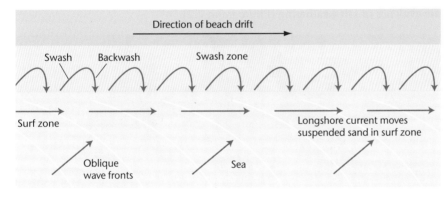

Figure 2.5
*Longshore current
and longshore drift*

Marine erosion

Waves are the most effective agents of erosion in coastal environments. Storm waves, which are high and fast moving, are the most destructive. They can erode solid rock cliffs as well as features made of loose sediments such as beaches. However, wave energy is only expended when waves break. Where cliffs plunge steeply into deep water little erosion occurs as waves bounce off the cliffs and are reflected seawards.

Quarrying

The impact of masses of water by wave shock and wave hammer can dislodge rocks and loose particles. This process is known as **quarrying** or hydraulic action. Well-jointed rocks and weak materials such as clay, sand and gravel, are most susceptible to quarrying. Quarrying also involves pressure release. Air trapped in rock joints is compressed by breaking waves, and water is also forced into cracks under pressure. These processes weaken rocks and cause their disintegration.

Abrasion

Breaking waves pick up rock particles, which are thrown against the shoreline. This scouring action wears down the rocks mechanically. Eventually it erodes a notch in the base of the cliffs, close to the mean high water mark. The effectiveness of abrasion depends on several factors: the availability of loose rock particles for erosion; the hardness of the rock particles compared with shoreline materials; the resistance of the rocks on the shoreline; and the depth of water adjacent to the shore.

Weathering

Weathering is the *in situ* breakdown of rocks exposed at the surface, or close to the surface, by chemical, mechanical and biological processes. All three weathering processes operate on cliffs and shore platforms.

Wetting and drying, due to waves, spray and tides, is responsible for **salt weathering**. Salt crystals forming in rock joints, crevices and pore spaces cause the mechanical destruction of rocks. Honeycomb rock surfaces in the spray zone are evidence of salt weathering (Photograph 2.2).

Photograph 2.2
Honeycomb rock surface, caused by salt weathering in the spray zone, Monterey, California

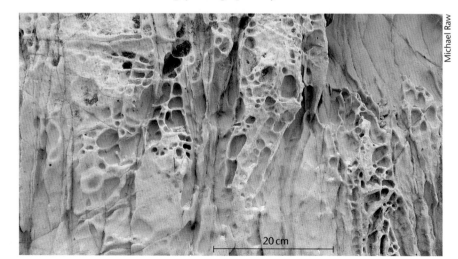

Michael Raw

20 cm

In coastal areas in middle and high latitudes, where temperatures fluctuate above and below freezing, cliffs and shore platforms are susceptible to **frost weathering**. Frost weathering can even have an effect in the relatively mild climate of the British Isles. In February 1996, Marsden Rock, a spectacular natural arch in northeast England, collapsed. At the time sea conditions were calm. But significantly, collapse followed several nights of frost.

Chemical weathering by solution is an important process on carbonate rocks. Rainwater and seawater containing carbon dioxide in solution react with calcium carbonate to dissolve rocks such as limestone and chalk (Photograph 2.3).

Rocks on the shoreline are also destroyed by organisms such as molluscs, sponges and sea urchins. Softer sedimentary rocks such as mudstones are attacked by rock-boring molluscs and acidic secretions from algae. The destruction of rocks by marine organisms is a form of biological weathering.

Photograph 2.3 *Solution weathering of limestone by salt spray, Mallorca*

Mass movements

Mass movements such as landslides, mudslides and rockfalls are common on cliffed coastlines. This is not surprising: cliffed coastlines are steep, and gravity is the main driver in mass movement. But other factors also favour mass movement. Coastal vegetation, which helps to bind slope materials, is often sparse; and the undermining of cliffs by wave action makes coastal slopes potentially unstable.

Rockfall

Rockfall is found on steep cliff faces. Detachment of rock particles and blocks occurs along joints (Photograph 2.4.). The trigger to rockfall in this example from the Mediterranean coast of Spain is undercutting of the cliff base by wave action. The cliffs are made of granite and the rock is well jointed.

Rotational slide

This is a type of slide which has a distinctive curved slide plane. It often occurs in weak materials such as clay, as has happened at Flamborough Head (Photograph 2.5, p. 64). The other factors contributing to slope failure are: steep slopes; wave erosion at the base of the cliff, undermining the basal support; and heavy rain, which loads the slope and weakens the clay.

Mudslide

After a rotational slide has occurred in clay or sandy materials, loose weathered debris absorbs water and accumulates, below the back scar. When sufficient material has accumulated, it

Photograph 2.4 *Rockfall on the Mediterranean coast of Spain*

Michael Raw

Michael Raw

Photograph 2.5 *Rotational slide at Flamborough Head*

Photograph 2.6 *Mudslide, Black Ven, Dorset*

slides downslope. Black Ven in Dorset (Photograph 2.6) is the largest active mudslide in Europe. There, permeable marls overlie impermeable Lias Clay. They absorb rainwater. Eventually high pore-water pressure builds up in the marl causing slope failure and rotational sliding. The saturated marl then slides slowly downslope towards the sea, where it forms two distinctive lobes.

Rocky coastal environments

Rocky coastal environments are dominated by erosional features such as cliffs, headlands and shore platforms. The shape of rocky coastlines, both in plan and profile, is strongly affected by geology. Specifically, this means their **lithology** and **structure**.

Box 2.4 Lithology and structure

Lithology describes the physical and chemical composition of rocks. Some rock types, such as clay, have weak lithologies, with little resistance to erosion, weathering and mass movements. Others, such as basalt, made of dense interlocking crystals, are highly resistant and are more likely to form prominent coastal features such as cliffs and headlands.

Structure concerns the properties of individual rock types such as jointing, bedding and faulting. It also includes the permeability of rocks. In porous rocks, such as chalk, tiny air spaces (pores) separate the mineral particles. These pores can absorb and store water — a property known as primary permeability. Carboniferous limestone is also permeable, but for a different reason. Water seeps into limestone because of its many joints, which are easily enlarged by solution.

Structure is an important influence on the plan-form of coasts at a regional scale (Figure 2.6). Rock outcrops that are uniform, or run parallel to the coast, tend to produce straight coastlines. These are known as **concordant** coasts. Where rocks crop out at right angles to the coast they create a **discordant** planform: the more resistant rocks form headlands; the less resistant form bays. The contrasting coastlines of east and south Dorset provide a classic example of the effect of structure on planform.

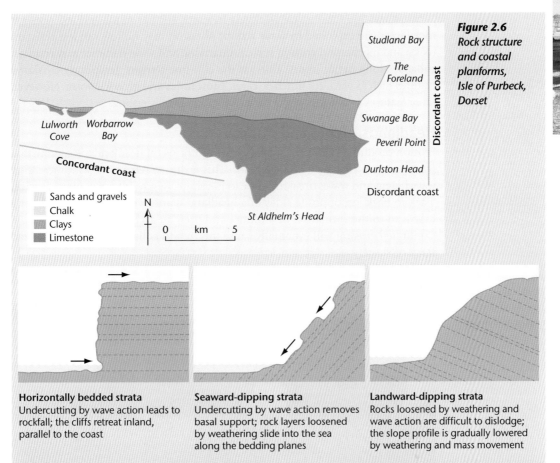

Figure 2.6
Rock structure and coastal planforms, Isle of Purbeck, Dorset

Horizontally bedded strata
Undercutting by wave action leads to rockfall; the cliffs retreat inland, parallel to the coast

Seaward-dipping strata
Undercutting by wave action removes basal support; rock layers loosened by weathering slide into the sea along the bedding planes

Landward-dipping strata
Rocks loosened by weathering and wave action are difficult to dislodge; the slope profile is gradually lowered by weathering and mass movement

Figure 2.7 *The effect of rock structure on cliff profiles*

Structure also includes the angle of dip of rocks and has a strong influence on cliff profiles (Figure 2.7). Both horizontally bedded and landward-dipping strata support cliffs with steep, vertical profiles. Where strata incline seawards cliff profiles tend to follow the angle of dip of the bedding planes.

The formation of cliffs and other erosional landforms

Cliffs

On upland coasts, the land often meets the sea abruptly in steep cliffs. Cliffs are not confined exclusively to coastal environments. They are, for example, common in glaciated uplands and even hot deserts. However, away from the coast, as cliffs weather and erode, most are gradually replaced by gentler debris slopes. On the coast this does not happen. Wave action scours the cliff base at high tide and removes any debris produced by rockfall and mass movement. Without any basal accumulation of debris, coastal cliffs retain their steep profiles as they retreat inland.

Structural and lithological weakness in strata, such as joints and less resistant rock layers, are exploited by wave action. Abrasion may hollow out less resistant rocks; and mechanical erosion such as quarrying and wave hammer may result in collapse along major joints. Thus, as the cliff-line retreats, temporary erosional features such as wave-cut **notches**, **caves**, **blow holes** and **geos** will form. However, these features only form where rocks are mechanically strong.

Headlands, arches and stacks

Erosion produces a different sequence of landforms on headlands. We know that wave energy is high around headlands. This is due to refraction, with increasing wave height and waves breaking close to the shore. As a result, caves often develop 'back-to-back' on opposite sides of a headland. Further erosion and weathering may lead to the formation of a tunnel and then an **arch** (see Photograph 2.7). Continued erosion will eventually cause the arch to collapse, leaving an isolated **stack** offshore.

Photograph 2.7
Dyrholaey headland and arch, southern Iceland

Michael Raw

Shore platforms

The ultimate erosional landform in rocky coastal environments is the **shore platform**. Shore platforms slope gently seawards at an angle of up to 3°. Their maximum width is around 1 km. A number of processes are involved in platform development. Wave action, through abrasion and quarrying, is clearly important. But so too are weathering processes such as salt crystallisation, hydration solution and biological action.

The profiles of shore platforms are linked to tidal range (Figure 2.8). During the tidal cycle, water levels are constant for longest during high tide and low tide (Table 2.3). As a result, erosion is greatest at these times. This explains the formation of a ramp at the high tide mark, and a cliff at the low tide mark.

Table 2.3 Tidal duration at Whitby during two tidal cycles: 14–15 February 2007

Tide height (metres)	Tidal level	Duration (hours)
4–5	High tide	9.25
3–3.99	Mid-tide	6.50
2–2.99	Low tide	8.75

Source: British Oceanographic Data Centre

Between the high and low tide marks, where erosion is less intense, the platform slopes more steeply. These three units are best developed on platforms that experience an average tidal range of less than 4m. On coastlines with a much greater tidal range, erosion is spread over a wider area of platform. This creates more uniform and more steeply sloping platforms (Figure 2.8).

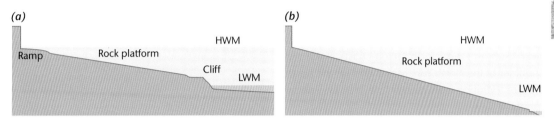

Figure 2.8 *Shore platforms: (a) average to low tidal range, (b) large tidal range*

The Yorkshire coastline from Saltburn to Flamborough

The Yorkshire coast from Saltburn to Flamborough Head is a hard, rocky upland coastline. Here geology is the main influence on landforms. Glaciation has also had a significant impact. Devensian till of variable thickness is a prominent feature of cliff profiles. Meanwhile, rivers draining the North York Moors often reach the coast in deeply incised valleys. These valleys were probably cut during glacial periods when sea level was 100–120 m lower than today and when most of the southern North Sea was dry land.

Geology and relief

Between Saltburn and Scarborough, the North York Moors dominate the coastline. This upland, which is 400 m above sea level, forms the highest cliffs in England. The rocks, of Jurassic age, are mainly sandstones, shales, ironstones and limestones (Figure 2.9). Differences in rock hardness are responsible for the varied coastal scenery, which includes impressive cliffs, headlands and bays.

Flamborough Head marks the southern limit of the upland coast of northeast England. There the

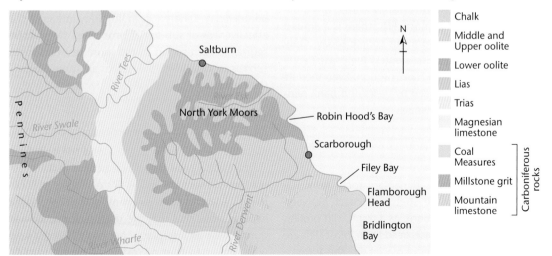

Figure 2.9 *Geology of the Yorkshire coast from Saltburn to Flamborough Head*

Yorkshire Wolds form a massive chalk headland. Flamborough has spectacular chalk cliffs capped with boulder clay, and a full range of erosional landforms.

Energy system

The stretch of coast from Saltburn to Flamborough is a high-energy environment. The dominant waves are from the north and northeast where the fetch is over 1500 km long. North-facing coasts along the shoulder of the North York Moors and on the north side of Flamborough receive the highest-energy inputs.

In some places, where weaker rocks such as shale and clay crop out, erosion rates can average 0.8 m per year. But overall, erosion rates are low — often less than 0.1 m per year. This is explained by the coast's hard geological structure.

Wave energy also transports sediment along the coast. Longshore drift, driven by powerful northerly waves, is from north to south. However, sediment movement is interrupted by major headlands and sand and shingle are often trapped in deep bays such as those at Runswick, Scalby and Ravenscar.

Sediment supply

Some sediment has come from the nearshore area, driven onshore as sea level rose at the end of the last glaciation. Sediment supply from cliff erosion (both hard rock and gravels released from till) is also important locally (Figure 2.10). However, given the resistant lithology of most cliffs, there is a limited supply of sediment from this source today. Only one large river — the Esk — enters the coastal zone between Saltburn and Flamborough. Even then its sediment load is reduced by weirs and bank reinforcements along its channel.

Landforms

Cliff profiles

Horizontally bedded sedimentary rocks form the cliffs along the entire stretch of coast between Flamborough and Saltburn. As a result, cliff profiles usually have a vertical face. In addition, most cliffs are overlain by a thick layer of glacial till. This forms a characteristic lower angle.

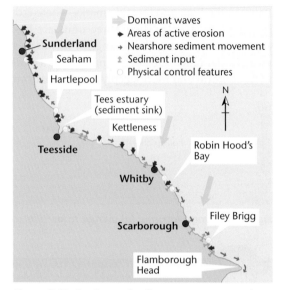

Figure 2.10 *Erosion and sediment movement on the northeast coast of England*

At Flamborough, the cliff wall is chalk (Photograph 2.8). Mechanically strong and horizontally bedded, chalk produces a vertical face 20–30 m high. Overlying the chalk a capping of glacial till is lowered by **sub-aerial processes** to an angle of around 40°.

Along the North York Moors coastline the cliffs are higher and have a step-like profile. This complex shape is explained by a more varied geology, with beds of sandstone, ironstone, limestone, shale and boulder clay. Differences in lithology influence the effectiveness of **sub-aerial processes**: steep slope segments correspond to the more resistant rocks such as sandstone; gentler slopes are more typically shale and clay.

Shore platforms

Powerful waves and relatively narrow beaches mean that marine erosion is active along the coastline. As the cliffs retreat they leave behind rocky shore platforms. There are impressive examples at Robin Hood's Bay and Staithes (Photograph 2.9). Some experts argue that they are relict features, formed during warmer interglacial periods when sea level was similar to that of today. At Flamborough, however, the cliffs are retreating at an average of

Photograph 2.8
Chalk and boulder clay cliffs at Flamborough Head

Boulder clay at a stable angle of 40°; susceptible to sub-aerial processes in wet weather, especially rotational slides and mudslides; run-off and gullying occur where plant cover is broken

Chalk — horizontally bedded; undercutting by waves causes collapse and parallel retreat and a near vertical cliff face; current rates of erosion average 0.3 m per year

Recent rockfall

Photograph 2.9
Cliffs and shore platform at Robin Hood's Bay; the cliffs comprise sandstones, ironstones and shales, capped with boulder clay

0.3 m per year. If this is typical, then Yorkshire's shore platforms could have formed within the past 6000 years.

Coastal planforms

Headlands and bays are common on the Yorkshire coast where there is considerable variation in rock type and where the geological structure is often discordant. Robin Hood's Bay is cut into weaker lias shales. The bay is anchored by the more resistant sandstones which form headlands at Ravenscar in the south and Ness Point to the north. Further south, Filey Bay has developed where the weak Kimmeridge clay reaches the coast. It is flanked by the more resistant corallian limestone and chalk. Flamborough Head is formed where the chalk Yorkshire Wolds meet the North Sea. Clay rocks that crop out to the north and south form deep bays, and make Flamborough the most prominent headland on England's east coast. At a smaller scale, structural weaknesses in the chalk

Michael Raw

Photograph 2.10 *Classic erosional landforms at Selwick's Bay, Flamborough: (a) cliff and shore platform, (b) cave and arch, (c) stack*

such as fault lines have been exploited by wave action and eroded into small bays or coves.

Erosional features around headlands

Landforms such as caves, arches and stacks, the result of wave erosion and cliff retreat, are well developed on headlands such as Kettleness and Flamborough (Photographs 2.10 (a)–(c)). There are two reasons for this. First, the rocks are mechanically strong and well jointed; second, refraction concentrates wave energy.

Cliffs and shore platforms

Horizontally bedded, mechanically strong chalk forms vertical cliffs. A boulder clay capping rests at a gentler angle on the cliffs tops. The shore platforms slopes at a constant angle of 3° (compare the angle of the platform with the horizontal tide level on the cliffs) (Photograph 2.10 (a)).

Caves and arches

Caves develop where mechanical wave action exploits lines of weakness. The master joint in the cliffs to the left in Photograph 2.10 (b) has been hollowed out to form a cave. Where a narrow ridge or 'fin' of rock projects seaward, cave development may lead to roof collapse and the formation of an arch.

Stacks

Following the formation of an arch, further erosion that results in arch collapse often leaves a stack — an isolated pinnacle of rock separated from the cliff line. Eventually, erosion reduces stacks to stumps (covered at high tide) and the base becomes part of the shore platform (Photograph 2.10 (c)).

Beaches

Along much of the coastline between Saltburn and Flamborough, beaches are not well developed. The most extensive beaches have formed in sheltered, low-energy bays, such as those at Runswick, Filey and Scarborough. Beach development is constrained by the following factors:

■ High wave energy backed by an upland coast creates conditions that remove sediments from beaches.
■ Gradients are relatively steep offshore.
■ Supply of sediment from cliff erosion and rivers is limited.

Although there is considerable longshore sediment movement, the coast has a notable absence of spits and other detached beach forms. There are a number of possible explanations:

■ There is an absence of shallow embayments or broad estuaries to act as sediment sinks for sand and shingle.
■ It is a predominantly straight coastline, with few abrupt changes in direction.
■ There is a relatively high tidal range of around 4 m.

Beach environments

Beaches are accumulations of sand and shingle deposited by waves in the inter-tidal zone.

Beach sediment: sources, stores and sinks

There are three principal sources of beach sediment: rivers, cliffs, dunes and the offshore zone. Of these, rivers are thought to be the most important. Cliff and dune erosion can also input large amounts of sediment and can be locally important. For example, cliff erosion on the Holderness coast of East Yorkshire inputs 2.4–4 million m² of mud, sand and shingle into the coastal system every year. This is by far the main source of sediment on this coastline.

Sediments are also transported onshore by waves and currents from sandbanks in the offshore zone. These sandbanks are important sediment sinks. A significant part of the beach sediment around Britain's coast was transported onshore as sea

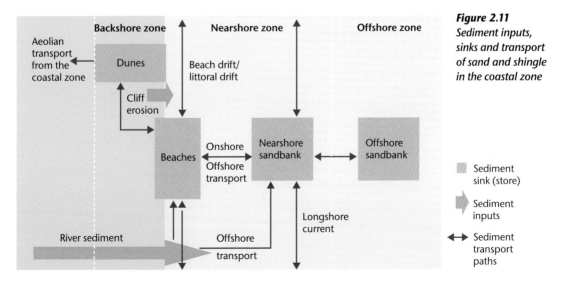

Figure 2.11
Sediment inputs, sinks and transport of sand and shingle in the coastal zone

levels rose after the last **glacial period** (20 000–6000 BP). Shingle from this source has helped to build impressive beaches in southern England, such as Chesil in Dorset, and Dungeness in Kent.

Sediment sinks are medium- to long-term stores of sediment. As well as sandbanks, they include beaches, dunes, mudflats, sandflats and saltmarshes (Figure 2.11). The term **sediment budget** refers to the net transfer of sediment between stores within the coastal zone.

Sediment cells

Coastal sediments are often confined to specific stretches of coastline known as **sediment cells** (Figure 2.12). Sediment cells are thought to be largely self-contained, with little movement of sand, shingle and mud into adjacent cells. They are defined by prominent physical features such as headlands, which are barriers to sediment transport. Each cell contains several sub-cells. Sediment cells have become the basic unit for coastal management in the UK.

Figure 2.12
Sediment cells in England and Wales

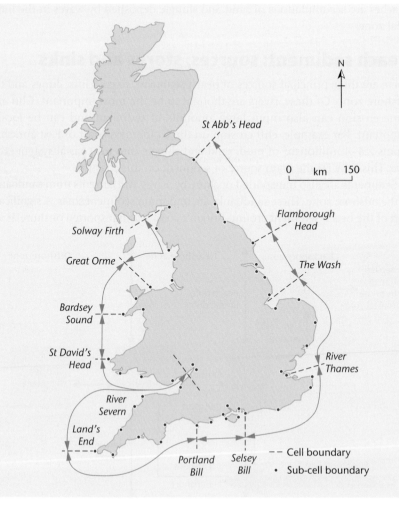

Beach profiles

The term beach profile refers to the cross-sectional shape of a beach from the high-water mark to the low-water mark. The main features of beaches are **berms**, **beach faces**, **ridges** and **runnels**, and **breakpoint bars**. These features are described in Table 2.4.

Berm	A flat-topped ridge at the back of a beach which marks the upper limit of the swash zone.
Beach face	The steepest, sloping part of a beach below the berm.
Ridges and runnels	Linear features on the foreshore that run parallel to the shoreline. Ridges are sandy bars; runnels are depressions between the ridges. Ridges and runnels form as the tide migrates across the swash zone.
Breakpoint bar	Ridges of sand and shingle that form parallel to the shore in the nearshore zone. They result from the offshore transport of sediment and are important sediment stores.

Table 2.4 *Main features of beach profiles*

Two factors explain the shapes of beach profiles: sediment type and wave energy.

Beach profiles and sediment type

Shingle beaches are steeper and narrower than sand beaches (Photograph 2.11). There is a simple explanation for this. Because shingle is coarser than sand it has a higher percolation rate. Swash running up a shingle beach quickly loses energy so that pebbles are only carried a short distance. However, percolation is rapid so there is little backwash to drag the sediments back down the beach. As a result, sediment moves in one direction only — up the beach — and piles up to form slopes of up to 12°. By comparison, sand beaches have lower percolation rates, a longer swash and a more powerful backwash. This produces a wider beach with lower slope angles (Figure 2.13).

Michael Raw

Photograph 2.11 *A steep, narrow beach of limestone shingle at Arnside, Cumbria*

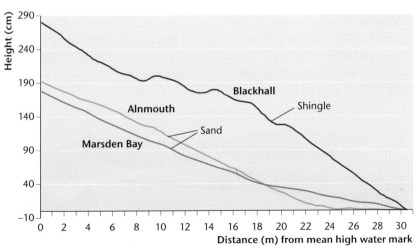

Figure 2.13 *Beach profiles and sediment types in northeast England*

Photograph 2.12
A wide sandy beach flattened by Pacific swell, Newport Bay, California

Sometimes beaches made of similar sediments have different profiles. This is due to differences in wave energy, the second factor that influences beach profiles. High waves, separated by long troughs, input huge amounts of energy to the nearshore zone. With long swash times and powerful backwashes they flatten sand beaches and transport sediment offshore, where it is stored in breakpoint bars. Wide, flat beaches are a response to the huge energy inputs from storm and swell waves (Photograph 2.12).

In contrast, low-energy waves are just a few centimetres high and have a short period. Their effect on beach profiles is altogether different. They induce a net transfer of sediment onshore, creating steep beaches, with a prominent beach face and berm.

In mid to high latitudes, beaches often have a seasonal profile. In winter, storms are more frequent, and many beaches develop wide, flat profiles. During the summer, beaches experience lower-energy waves, and consequently have steeper profiles.

Beach plans

Beaches in planform are either swash-aligned or drift-aligned.

Swash-aligned beaches

Swash-aligned beaches develop along coasts where wave crests approach parallel to the shore. In other words the dominant waves are fully refracted (see Box 2.3 on page 60). Thus swash and backwash, and beach sediments, follow the same path up and down the beach. Under these conditions there is no net lateral transport of sediment or longshore drift. Pocket beaches in bays and coves, which have a crescent-shaped plan, are swash-aligned (Photograph 2.13).

Photograph 2.13
Cove with swash-aligned pocket beach, Pineapple Beach, Antigua

Pocket beaches are attached to the coastline for their entire length. However, a number of other beach types, including **barrier beaches**, cuspate forelands, and **tombolos**, are often swash-aligned (Figures 2.14 b–d).

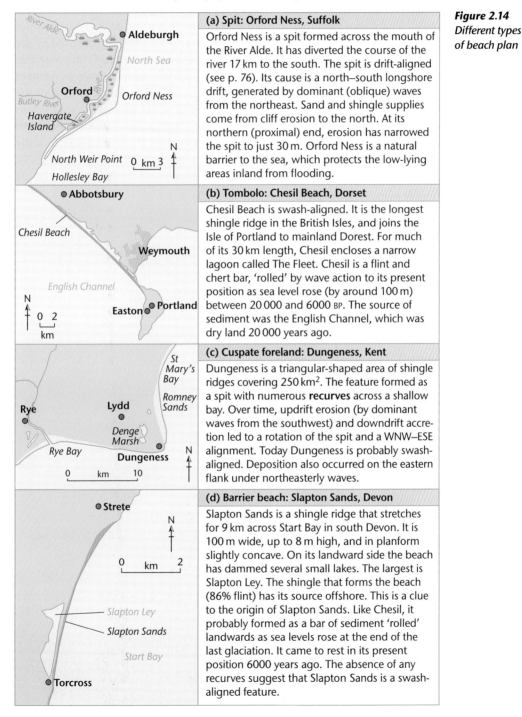

(a) Spit: Orford Ness, Suffolk

Orford Ness is a spit formed across the mouth of the River Alde. It has diverted the course of the river 17 km to the south. The spit is drift-aligned (see p. 76). Its cause is a north–south longshore drift, generated by dominant (oblique) waves from the northeast. Sand and shingle supplies come from cliff erosion to the north. At its northern (proximal) end, erosion has narrowed the spit to just 30 m. Orford Ness is a natural barrier to the sea, which protects the low-lying areas inland from flooding.

(b) Tombolo: Chesil Beach, Dorset

Chesil Beach is swash-aligned. It is the longest shingle ridge in the British Isles, and joins the Isle of Portland to mainland Dorset. For much of its 30 km length, Chesil encloses a narrow lagoon called The Fleet. Chesil is a flint and chert bar, 'rolled' by wave action to its present position as sea level rose (by around 100 m) between 20 000 and 6000 BP. The source of sediment was the English Channel, which was dry land 20 000 years ago.

(c) Cuspate foreland: Dungeness, Kent

Dungeness is a triangular-shaped area of shingle ridges covering 250 km². The feature formed as a spit with numerous **recurves** across a shallow bay. Over time, updrift erosion (by dominant waves from the southwest) and downdrift accretion led to a rotation of the spit and a WNW–ESE alignment. Today Dungeness is probably swash-aligned. Deposition also occurred on the eastern flank under northeasterly waves.

(d) Barrier beach: Slapton Sands, Devon

Slapton Sands is a shingle ridge that stretches for 9 km across Start Bay in south Devon. It is 100 m wide, up to 8 m high, and in planform slightly concave. On its landward side the beach has dammed several small lakes. The largest is Slapton Ley. The shingle that forms the beach (86% flint) has its source offshore. This is a clue to the origin of Slapton Sands. Like Chesil, it probably formed as a bar of sediment 'rolled' landwards as sea levels rose at the end of the last glaciation. It came to rest in its present position 6000 years ago. The absence of any recurves suggest that Slapton Sands is a swash-aligned feature.

Figure 2.14
Different types of beach plan

Drift-aligned beaches

Drift-aligned beaches are features of open, lowland coastlines. There the dominant waves are rarely fully refracted. This generates a longshore movement of sediment along the coast. In these circumstances, any abrupt change in the direction of the coastline or major river mouth often leads to the formation of detached beaches such as spits and tombolos (Figures 2.14 (a) and (b)). These beaches, fed by the longshore transport of sediment, grow outwards from the coast. Evidence of this growth is provided by hook-shaped sand and shingle ridges known as recurves (Photograph 2.29, p. 104). Each recurve represents stages in the growth of the beach. The recurve shape is due to the refraction of waves around the seaward (or distal) end of the feature.

Spits are the most distinctive drift-aligned beaches. Their distribution in the British Isles corresponds closely with coastlines of low tidal range (Figure 2.15). This suggests that spits only form where wave action is concentrated over a narrow vertical zone of the shore.

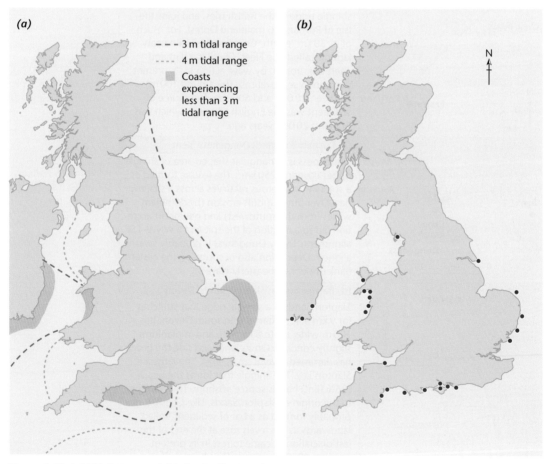

(a)

- – – – 3 m tidal range
- ⋯⋯⋯⋯ 4 m tidal range
- ▨ Coasts experiencing less than 3 m tidal range

(b)

N

Figure 2.15 *(a) Tidal range and (b) the distribution of spits in the British Isles*
Source: Pethick, J. (1984) *An Introduction to Coastal Geomorphology*, Arnold.

Sea level change

Huge fluctuations in sea level have occurred in the past 20 000 years. During this period, sea level rose by 100–120 m (Figure 2.16). Present-day sea level has been more or less stable for 6000 years — a relatively short time.

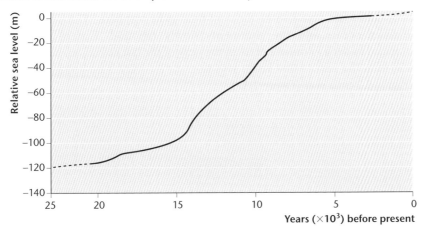

Figure 2.16 *Global sea level change in the past 25 000 years*

Sea level change profoundly alters the coastal system. Everything changes: the position of the coast, the vertical distance over which coastal processes operate, energy budgets, sediment budgets and coastal landforms. Some landforms such as raised beaches are abandoned altogether; others, such as **fjords**, develop for the first time.

Types of sea level change

Sea level changes can be worldwide or local, absolute or relative.

Eustatic change

A worldwide rise or fall in sea level is known as a **eustatic** change. This is an absolute change, caused by either an increase or decrease in the volume of water in the oceans. Eustatic changes are due to major shifts in the global climate that trigger glacial and interglacial periods. This is known as **glacio-eustacy**. During glacial periods, there is a net transfer of water from the oceans as snow and ice accumulate on the continents. The result is a worldwide fall in sea level of up to 120 m. Much of the seabed on the continental shelf is exposed as dry land and the coastline extends seawards. This sea level **regression** meant that during the last glacial period, large parts of the southern North Sea, the English Channel and Irish Sea were dry land.

During warmer periods or **interglacials**, these effects are reversed. Rising sea levels cause the coastline to retreat, and **transgression** occurs, flooding the continental shelves. Now the dominant process is the drowning and submergence of coastlines.

Isostatic and tectonic change

Local sea level changes involve a *relative* rise or fall of the land. The causes of these movements are either tectonic or isostatic. Rapid movements occur during earthquakes. For example, the great Alaska quake of 1964 raised parts of the coastline by 5 m.

During glacial periods, masses of ice load the continents, causing the crust to sink by hundreds of metres into the semi-fluid **asthenosphere**. With deglaciation unloading occurs and the continents slowly rebound. Eastern Scotland, submerged under a kilometre of ice at the peak of the last glaciation, has risen by 40–50 m in the past 12 000 years. This isostatic recovery is on-going, currently averaging 0.2 cm a year (Figure 2.17).

Figure 2.17
Isostatic change in Britain (cm year⁻¹)

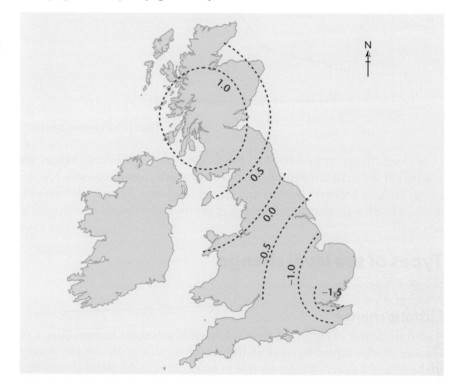

Rapid sedimentation

Coastlines can advance seawards where rivers deposit large amounts of sediment into shallow coastal waters. This building out of the coast is called **progradation**. It is particularly rapid in southern Iceland. Here, sediment-rich rivers draining **icefields** such as the Myrdalsjökull have formed extensive outwash plains or sandar (see Photograph 3.13 on page 126). In places, the coastline has advanced up to 40 km in the past 10 000 years. Spectacular advances occur during sudden outbursts of glacial meltwater known as jökulhlaups. The last one, in 1996, was caused by a subglacial volcanic eruption, which melted part of the Vatnajökull icefield. At its peak, the flood discharge reached 45 000 m³ s⁻¹.

Sea level change and coastal landforms

Rias and fjords

The eustatic rise in sea level between 20 000 and 6000 BP created submerged coastlines, flooding valleys to form **rias** and fjords.

Rias are drowned river valleys with elaborate branching networks. They form along upland coasts where fluvial erosion has incised deep valleys. Flooding penetrates far inland, submerging the main valley as well tributary valleys (Figure 2.18).

Drowned glacial troughs are known as fjords. Often they are sheer-sided and extremely deep. They shallow towards their mouths where a submerged sill or threshold restricts tidal flow (Photograph 2.14). Fjords are found in mid and high-latitude areas such as Norway and Alaska, where glaciated uplands reach the coast.

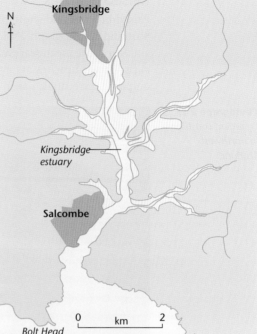

Figure 2.18 *A ria: the Kingsbridge estuary, south Devon*

Photograph 2.14 *Entrance to Milford Sound fjord, New Zealand*

Shingle beaches

During the low sea levels of the last glaciation, large amounts of coarse sediment were deposited by meltwater on the continental shelf. Then, as the climate warmed and sea level rose, much of this sediment was swept up into beaches. Shingle beaches such as Chesil in Dorset, Dungeness in Kent, and Slapton Sands in Devon are directly related to deglaciation and rising sea levels over the past 15 000 years.

Raised beaches

Raised beaches and shore platforms are common along the coast of northwest Scotland (Photograph 2.15). Several beaches can be recognised at 30 m, 15 m and 8 m above mean sea level. These ancient beaches are often backed by degraded cliffs. Raised beaches are evidence of isostatic rebound which in Scotland has outpaced the eustatic rise in sea level and continues today.

Photograph 2.15
Emergent coastline in northwest Scotland

Peter G. Knight

Fossil cliff-line

Raised beach

Recently abandoned cliff-line due to ongoing isostatic recovery

Mudflats and saltmarshes

Mudflats and saltmarshes are features of low-energy coastlines such as estuaries, saline lagoons and the landward side of spits and barrier islands. The UK has an estimated 588 000 ha of mudflat and 45 500 ha of saltmarsh. The main concentrations are in eastern and northwest England.

Mudflats are formed by deposition of silts and clays. Submerged for most of the tidal cycle, they are devoid of plants, but have a covering of algae (Photograph 2.16). In contrast, saltmarshes are vegetated and display a marked zonation. Halophytic (salt-tolerant) plants such as glasswort and cord grass colonise the higher mudflats to form the low marsh. High salinity levels, turbid (i.e. muddy) water and long periods of inundation mean that few species can survive in the lower marsh. Hence the low marsh is species poor. The upper marsh habitat is more favourable (Photograph 2.17). Salinity and the frequency and duration of submergence by the tide are much lower. As a result, biodiversity is higher. Typical species of the upper marsh include sea lavender, sea aster, sea blite and sea purslane (Figure 2.19).

Michael Raw

Photograph 2.16
Unvegetated mudflats around Morecambe Bay

Photograph 2.17
Saltmarsh at Flookburgh, Cumbria

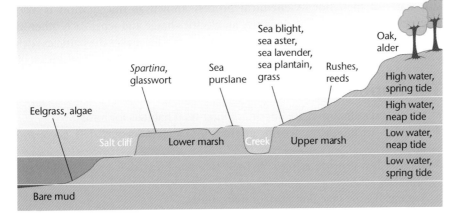

Figure 2.19 *Cross-section through a saltmarsh*

Sea blight, sea aster, sea lavender, sea plantain, grass

Oak, alder

Spartina, glasswort

Sea purslane

Rushes, reeds

Eelgrass, algae

High water, spring tide

High water, neap tide

Low water, neap tide

Low water, spring tide

Salt cliff   Lower marsh   Creek   Upper marsh

Bare mud

The morphology of saltmarshes

Saltmarshes have a shallow gradient, which slopes seawards. This is interrupted in two places. A low cliff, a metre or so high, often separates the unvegetated mudflats from the vegetated low marsh. A second, less steep, break of slope also occurs between the low marsh and the upper marsh (Figure 2.19).

The shape of the marsh in profile reflects rates of accumulation or accretion of sediment. This in turn is influenced by vegetation cover, and the frequency and duration of inundation. The abrupt transition from mudflat to low marsh is explained by the colonisation of the low marsh by vegetation, which traps sediment.

Although the upper marsh is inundated less often, deposition rates are nevertheless high. This is because deposition is most effective at high tide when slack water conditions last for 2 to 3 hours. Furthermore, the greater density of vegetation in the upper marsh encourages deposition.

Dense networks of steep-sided channels or creeks drain the marsh and bring water in on the flood tide. Between the creeks, shallow pools known as salt pans develop on the marsh surface. Where salt concentrations are particularly high, plants are largely absent.

The formation of saltmarshes

Saltmarshes form by the accumulation of silt and clay carried into low-energy environments, such as estuaries, by tidal currents and rivers. Under favourable conditions, deposition rates can reach 10 cm a year. Plants play a vital role in the development of saltmarshes, acting as baffles to the incoming tide, reducing current velocities and encouraging deposition. Gradually they raise the surface of the marsh and reduce the frequency and duration of tidal inundation. These changes create conditions that allow other species, less tolerant of salinity and inundation, to invade. This sequence of **invasion** and **succession**, and the development of high marshes from mudflats, has been observed at Scolt Head on the north Norfolk coast. There it took just 200 years.

The fall-out of silt and clay from suspension is not simply due to gravity and still water at high tide. A chemical process known as **flocculation** is also important. Tiny particles of clay carry an electric charge and repel each other in fresh water. However, in salt water attraction occurs. This makes the particles stick together forming flocs, which can settle out of suspension at higher velocities.

The importance of mudflats and saltmarshes

Mudflats and saltmarshes are important inter-tidal habitats for birds.
➤ Mudflats are productive feeding grounds for large flocks of waders, geese and ducks.
➤ Saltmarshes provide refuges at high tide for birds that feed on adjacent mudflats.
➤ Saltmarshes are breeding sites for many birds.

➤ Mudflats and saltmarshes are resting and refuelling stops for migrating birds.
➤ Mudflats and saltmarshes are important nurseries for many species of fish, molluscs and crustaceans.

As well as their ecological value, mudflats and saltmarshes are important natural defences against coastal erosion and flooding. They are extremely effective in dissipating wave energy.

Threats to saltmarshes

Saltmarshes are currently under threat in the UK. Every year, around 100 ha of marsh are lost to coastal erosion. The problem is worst in southeast England: Kent and Essex lost 20% of their saltmarsh area between 1973 and 1988.

There are several pressures on saltmarshes. Land reclamation in eastern England continued until the 1980s. In The Wash, between 1970 and 1980, 858 ha of saltmarsh were converted to farmland. Recently, some of this land has been deliberately flooded and allowed to revert to saltmarsh under managed realignment policies (see page 97). More will follow in the coming decades as rising sea levels make the defence of large stretches of our coastline unsustainable.

Coastal squeeze (see page 98) has also contributed to the erosion of mudflats and saltmarshes. Backed by seawalls and other hard defences, mudflats and saltmarshes cannot retreat inland as sea level rises. The result is erosion. Coastal defence works that stop erosion also add to the pressures. Erosion control reduces sediment input into the coastal system and upsets the sediment budget. With less sediment available for deposition, mudflats and saltmarshes start to contract. One other factor has contributed to the decline of mudflats and saltmarshes: cord grass, a pioneer species on saltmarshes, has suffered widespread die-back in recent years. Without this species to anchor the mud, erosion is rapid and unchecked.

Figure 2.20
Distribution of fixed (grey) dunes in the UK
Source: Joint Nature Conservation Committee

Coastal dune environments

There are approximately 500 km² of coastal dunes in England, Scotland and Wales, and 330 km² in Scotland. They are widely distributed (Figure 2.20). The most extensive dunes are associated with the following conditions:
➤ an abundant supply of sand in the inter-tidal zone
➤ a shallow offshore gradient exposing a wide foreshore at low tide
➤ prevailing onshore winds
➤ a lowland coast with a large backshore area for sand accumulation

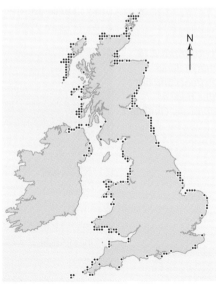

Dune-forming processes

Sand dunes are important sediment stores. Wind transports loose sand into dune systems. Meanwhile, sand is also removed by the wind (a process known as **deflation**) and by wave erosion.

Sand dunes owe their formation to two agents: wind and vegetation. The wind transports dry sand by **creep** and saltation. Creep is the movement of sand particles across the ground surface in a rolling and sliding action. Saltation, on the other hand, describes the entrainment of sand particles and their movement in a skipping motion. When each particle hits the surface it collides with other particles, setting them in motion. Eventually, when winds speeds fall below a critical level, sand is deposited.

However, the processes of sand transport and deposition alone cannot explain the formation of dunes. Another factor is needed: vegetation. Plants provide resistance to the wind, and by lowering velocities encourage sand deposition. Some plants such as marram grass can tolerate being buried by sand. Swamping merely stimulates growth. In this way, marram provides a permanent obstruction to wind flow, and creates an environment that favours deposition. It is this interaction between wind, transported sand and plants that allows coastal dunes to reach heights of 25–30 m.

The morphology and development of dune systems

Coastal dunes form ridges parallel to the coast (and perpendicular to the prevailing wind) separated by shallow depressions. The youngest dunes are located nearest to the shoreline (Photograph 2.18). These so-called yellow dunes are mobile, unstable and have variable plant cover. Further inland the dunes get older. These are the grey dunes: they are fixed and have a complete vegetation cover (Figure 2.21).

Photograph 2.18
Embryo dunes, foredunes and first dune ridge at Sandscale, Cumbria

Figure 2.21 Vegetation and plant succession on coastal dunes. Wind flow controls the shape and height of dunes. Erosion occurs on the exposed windward face with deposition on the sheltered leeward slopes. The dune ridges create turbulence and eddying downwind, which erodes the depressions and slacks. As wind speeds increase, dunes reach a height where the vegetation can no longer protect the dune surface from wind erosion.

Embryo dunes: sea couch grass Yellow dunes: freshwater is scarce Grey dunes: fully vegetated, biodiverse and fixed

A Embryo dunes just a few centimetres tall, form above the strandline. Salt-tolerant species such as sea couch grass and sea rocket, colonise this area, slowing wind speeds and encouraging further sand accretion.

B The yellow dunes are a harsh environment for plants — the reason why there is so little biodiversity. Fresh water is scarce due to the high porosity of sand and the absence of soil. Sand, blown by the wind abrades plants, while the instability of the dunes makes it difficult for plants to root. Marram dominates the first dune ridge; it is well adapted to the environment. Its long roots tap fresh water deep below the surface; growth is stimulated when it is buried by sand, and stomata on the inside of its rolled leaves reduce moisture loss.

C Once the supply of fresh sand diminishes, marram starts to die out. The grey dunes have much greater biodiversity and complete vegetation cover. Environmental conditions are more favourable to plant growth in the grey dunes because it is more sheltered; blown sand no longer creates problems. The dunes are fixed allowing plants to get a firm anchor, and shallow soils provide more moisture. Typical species of the grey dunes include sea buckthorn, hawkweed, burnet rose and wild pansies.

D The water table is at the surface depressions or slacks, and often produces shallow freshwater lakes and wetlands. This is a wholly different habitat from the dunes, and supports distinctive plant assemblages (e.g. creeping willow, reeds, flag iris, marsh orchids), as well as amphibians and reptiles.

Vegetation on a second dune ridge: sea spurge, moss, dandelion and marram.

Figure 2.22 *Cross-section through a dune system at Ainsdale on Merseyside*

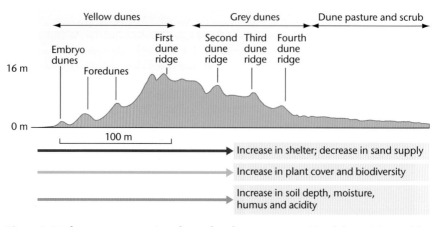

Figure 2.22 shows a cross-section through a dune system at Ainsdale on Merseyside. The sequence of dunes, from the upper beach inland, comprises embryo dunes, foredunes, first dune ridge, second dune ridge and so on. Dune morphology is controlled by the wind. Sand is transported from the windward faces of the dunes and is deposited on the sheltered leeward slopes. Meanwhile, the dunes interrupt airflow, causing turbulence and eddying between the dune ridges. This leads to erosion and the formation of depressions. Often erosion in the depressions brings fresh water to the surface. These waterlogged depressions, known as slacks, are important habitats for aquatic plants, reptiles and amphibians.

The migration of dunes inland slows as the older dunes are stabilised by vegetation. Where supplies of fresh sand are plentiful, dune systems will extend seawards. This process is called progradation and is likely to produce many parallel dune ridges. Where sand supplies are limited, beaches may be lowered, and dune systems will be eroded by wave action.

Human impact on sand dune environments

Sand dune systems in the UK are under pressure from a number of human-related activities. Their effect is twofold: to reduce the supply of sand for dune building, and to accelerate the loss of sand by wind erosion. Table 2.5 summarises the main impacts.

Table 2.5 *Pressures on dune systems in the UK*

Grazing of livestock	**Overgrazing** of the fixed dunes can damage the vegetation cover and cause erosion by wind. Overgrazing leads to the invasion of coarse grasses and scrub and the loss of typical dune plant communities.
Recreation	Recreation is a major land use on dunes. Excessive pedestrian use on popular routes between car parks and beaches destroys the vegetation cover by trampling and causes erosion (Photograph 2.19). The impact of four-wheel-drive vehicles and motorcycles is even more severe. Many dune systems support golf courses. Much of the original vegetation is modified by mowing, fertilising and re-seeding.
Sand stabilisation	Sand fencing and marram planting is found on more developed coastlines to prevent sand drifting towards tourism and urban developments. These measures help to tackle erosion problems but at the same time can reduce biodiversity, and cause sediment starvation downwind.

Beach management	The seaward development of dune systems leading to the formation of embryo dunes may be arrested on some popular coastlines by trampling. Beach cleaning, using mechanical methods, also destroys embryo dunes.
Forestry	Afforestation has had a major effect on some dune systems. Some sites have large conifer plantations. These prevent the development of dune vegetation communities and lower the water table.
Military	During the Second World War, dunes were extensively used for military training and as a source of sand for building military installations. The result was widespread wind erosion. A number of dune systems are still used for military training, especially in Scotland. However, military use can be beneficial because it excludes other potentially damaging activities and developments.

Michael Raw

Photograph 2.19
A blow-out in the Ainsdale dunes; blow-outs are areas of massive sand erosion, often caused by damage due to trampling of the dunes' protective vegetation cover

Key ideas

➤ Coastal areas are often valuable economic and environmental resources.

➤ Coastal areas provide opportunities for a number of human activities including industrial development, transportation, residential development, recreation and leisure, and conservation.

➤ Conflicts may result from the growth and development of different human activities on the coast.

Bangladesh, situated at the head of the Bay of Bengal, occupies the Ganges–Brahmaputra estuarine delta. The coastal zone is flat and low-lying and criss-crossed by hundreds of rivers, their tributaries and distributaries. It is a region of high population density: an estimated 36 million people occupy the coastal zone (Figure 2.23).

Bangladesh is a poor country. In 2006 it ranked 137th out of 177 countries on the UN's human development index, and its GDP per capita was just $1900. In the coastal zone, most people depend on agriculture, fishing, forestry and salt farming for their livelihoods. Everywhere, population pressure on limited farming and other natural resources is acute.

Resources and economic activities in the coastal zone

As in most rural areas of Bangladesh, farming is the main economic activity in the coastal zone. Fertile alluvial soils, together with fresh water from the rivers and high temperatures all year round, provide perfect conditions for farming. Rice is the main crop. It is cultivated in three seasons: *aus* (April–July), *aman* (August–November) and *boro* (January–April). Other *rabi* crops (grown in the dry season between December and March) include wheat, groundnuts, pulses and chillis.

Output per hectare is high. Even so, the vast majority of rural dwellers are poor. A number of factors are responsible. The sheer pressure of population ensures that farms are small. Although some farmers own the land they cultivate, others are sharecroppers and tenants. Often farms are so tiny that even owner farmers have to supplement their incomes with day labouring. Most day labourers belong to the large group of landless workers. At the top of the social hierarchy are the *jotedars*, a powerful landowning class who are often absentee landlords.

The coastal zone is a rich fishery which supports many rural households. In 2003, 445 000 t of marine fish were harvested. However, 86% of the fishery industry's output by value is from shrimp farming.

Figure 2.23 *Bangladesh: the coastal zone*

The coastal zone is the location of several types of industry such as jute, pulp and paper, textiles, fertiliser, rubber, plastic, pharmaceuticals and ship-breaking (Photograph 2.20). The main industrial concentrations are in the Khulna–Jessore corridor, around the Karnaphuly and Bukkhali River, and in

Photograph 2.20 *Shipbreaker yard at Chittagong, Bangladesh*

the Chittagong area (see Figure 2.23). Many industries use the coast as a convenient sink: a cheap way of getting rid of toxic effluent.

Mangrove forests

Mangroves are a salt-tolerant forest ecosystem found on low-lying coasts in the intertidal zone. Bangladesh has the largest area of mangrove forest in the world (Photograph 2.21). The most extensive area of mangroves, covering over 6000 km², is the Sundarbans in the southwest of the country.

Photograph 2.21 *Mangroves in the Sundarbans, Bangladesh*

The mangrove forest is an ecosystem of extraordinary biodiversity and is one of the most productive in the world (each hectare of mangrove generates between 1100 kg and 11 800 kg of harvestable fish a year). In 2001, the Sundarbans was designated an International Biosphere Reserve by UNESCO.

The mangroves have immense economic importance to Bangladesh and to people in the delta. They provide timber and fuelwood, and supply materials to industries such as paper making, matches, hardboard, boat building and furniture. In total, the mangrove forests and plantations support an estimated half a million people.

Environmental problems and conflicts in the coastal zone

We have seen that many economic activities exploit the resources of the coastal zone. Some of these activities are unsustainable and have degraded coastal ecosystems, while others conflict with each other as they compete for limited resources. Overall, there has been a significant decline in marine fisheries, mangroves and freshwater resources in the coastal zone in the past 25 years.

Specifically, the main problems are:
- pollution of coastal waters by industrial waste, sewage effluent and agrochemicals
- deforestation of mangroves
- saline intrusion into freshwater aquifers and soils
- uncontrolled growth of shrimp aquaculture

Coastal pollution

Pollution is a major issue in the coastal zone. Every year the Ganges, Brahmaputra and Meghna rivers pour billions of tonnes of sediment into the delta and the Bay of Bengal. Bound in these sediments are toxins from industrial effluent, farm chemicals, solid waste and sewage.

Today, pollution has become a serious environmental hazard: a threat not only to human health but to the marine ecosystems on which millions of people depend. Industries release a dangerous cocktail of heavy metals such as mercury, cadmium and lead into coastal waters. These pollutants, which persist in the marine environment, accumulate in marine organisms and enter the human food chain. Exposure to heavy metals can cause damage to vital organs such as the brain, heart, liver and kidneys.

Sewage from the 36 million people living in the coastal zone flows untreated into the Bay of Bengal. Khulna and Chittagong alone generate 900 t of human waste a day. Rapid population growth in the past 30 years has increased the scale of the problem. Pollution by sewage creates obvious human health risks. It also increases biological oxygen demand in coastal waters, creates eutrophic conditions, and damages fish stocks and other marine organisms.

There is one other important source of marine pollution in Bangladesh: agriculture. Bangladesh used 18 million tonnes of pesticides in 2003 — a sixfold increase in 20 years. One-quarter of all agrochemicals used by farmers runs off the land into rivers and coastal waters during the wet season. Persistent organic pollutants are the cause of most concern. These long-lasting toxic compounds used in pesticides

David Hosking/Alamy

do not easily break down in the environment and are known to be carcinogenic. Although the government has banned their use, farmers retain large stockpiles and their illegal use is likely to continue.

Deforestation

Not only are mangrove forests an important resource, supplying timber for building, charcoal, tannin and honey, they also provide a range of free services. For example, they protect coastal settlements against tropical cyclones and tidal surges; they reduce erosion and encourage accretion of silt and mud; and they are nurseries for fish and other marine organisms.

Yet, in spite of their value, the mangroves are under threat. Population pressure and poverty are responsible for the destruction of 20 km^2 a year of mangroves. Deforestation results from the use of mangroves as fuel and their clearance for shrimp farming, salt production, farming and human settlement.

Forest destruction increases the risk of tropical cyclones and storm surges to rural populations and to cities such as Khulna and Mongla in southwest Bangladesh. Current rates of forest destruction are unsustainable. Without management, the future for fisheries, timber production and wildlife is bleak in the coastal zone.

Salinity intrusion

The **salinisation** of water and soil are common problems in the coastal zone. Seventy per cent of agricultural land in the Khulna and Barisal divisions is affected by soil salinity. In the dry season, salinity penetrates far inland. The decrease in water flow during the dry season has contributed to surface water salinity in the southwest region. The main cause is the Farakka Dam on the River Ganges in India. As flow levels have fallen, salinity has advanced upstream. Meanwhile, reduced freshwater flow has led to salt water polluting underground aquifers. Shrimp farming has also added to the salinity problem. Salt water from the shrimp farms seeps into neighbouring farmland, making it useless for cultivation.

Shrimp farming

The shrimp-farming zone extends along the entire southeast fringe of the coastal belt, and has become a leading activity in Cox's Bazaar, Khulna, Bagerhat and Satkhira regions (Photograph 2.22). It accounts for 2.5% of the global shrimp production, generates

Images & Stories/Alamy

Photograph 2.22 *Shrimp farming in Shibsha River, Bangladesh*

$301 million of revenue annually, and is Bangladesh's second-largest export industry.

However, the economic success of the shrimp industry has been at considerable cost, both to local people and to the environment. Its development has led to massive deforestation and the conversion of newly accreted areas and mangroves to shrimp farms. For example, the mangroves of Chokoria Sundarban, covering 80 km², have been completely cleared for shrimp and salt farming. Despite its adverse environmental impact, the government has allowed the expansion of shrimp farming because of its importance to the Bangladesh economy.

Integrated Coastal Zone Management

Bangladesh's coastal zone is a complex system where physical, ecological, social and economic processes interact. In the past, coastal management has lacked integration. For example, separate government agencies have dealt with problems such as natural disasters, sea defences, salt water intrusion and the protection of ecosystems.

Since 1999 a more integrated management has been practised. This acknowledges that the problems of the coastal zone are closely interrelated and

that successful management is more likely with a 'joined-up' approach, which views the coast and its problems as a whole (Figure 2.24). In line with modern thinking, integrated management aims to be inclusive: to take account of the opinions of people that live in the coastal zone and whose livelihoods depend on its resources.

The Bangladeshi government's Integrated Coastal Zone Management (ICZM) strategy has received financial backing from the Netherlands, the UK and the World Bank. Its primary aims are to:

- achieve the sustainable use of resources
- preserve vital ecosystems
- balance the competing and often conflicting demands of different users
- reduce poverty and the risks and vulnerabilities to natural hazards associated with poverty

ICZM sets out a number of urgent priorities. These include:

- the protection of freshwater resources and countering the threat of salinisation
- improved protection from natural hazards (e.g. hard engineering structures such as flood embankments and cyclone shelters)

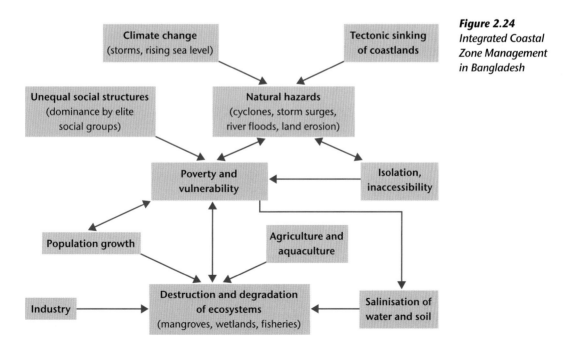

Figure 2.24
Integrated Coastal Zone Management in Bangladesh

- more controlled and organised use of newly accreted land — such as alluvial bars and islands — for development and settlement
- promotion of economic growth and the creation of small- and medium-sized businesses, many of which will be based on local skills and trades
- the sustainable management of resources, with particular emphasis on environmentally responsible shrimp farming, and marine and coastal fisheries
- environmental conservation, especially of the Sundarbans and other mangrove forests
- improving living conditions for the rural population, especially women
- developing the tourism potential of the coast, e.g. the Sundarbans

Key ideas

➤ There are a number of ways that coastal areas can be protected from natural processes, such as erosion and flooding.

➤ Approaches to coastal protection include hard engineering, soft engineering and managed retreat.

➤ Some coastlines need protection more than others.

➤ Different methods of coastal protection give rise to planning, management and environmental issues.

➤ Managing coastal areas involves balancing socio-economic and environmental needs.

➤ Planning and management are needed to resolve development issues and conflicts in coastal environments.

Case study Spain's concrete coast

Before the 1960s, the Costa del Sol was an isolated part of southern Europe, with an economy based on agriculture and fishing. Then came the package holiday boom, transforming the region into the Mediterranean's first mass tourism destination (Figure 2.25). Fifty years on, the environmental cost of the early, uncontrolled tourism development remains high. Hotels and apartments stretch for miles along the coast in a continuous ribbon (Photograph 2.23); buildings encroach to within 20 m of the shoreline; and pollution of beaches and coastal waters by sewage effluent is still widespread.

More recently, the Costa del Sol has experienced a second building boom: thousands of second-home

Figure 2.25
Costa del Sol and the populations of coastal settlements

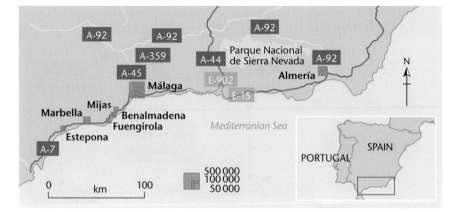

Duncan McNeill/Alamy

Photograph 2.23
High-rise
development on
the Costa del Sol

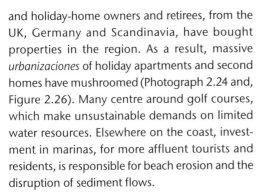

Mark Boulton/Alamy

Photograph 2.24
Urbanizaciones *of
holiday apartments
and second homes*

and holiday-home owners and retirees, from the UK, Germany and Scandinavia, have bought properties in the region. As a result, massive *urbanizaciones* of holiday apartments and second homes have mushroomed (Photograph 2.24 and, Figure 2.26). Many centre around golf courses, which make unsustainable demands on limited water resources. Elsewhere on the coast, investment in marinas, for more affluent tourists and residents, is responsible for beach erosion and the disruption of sediment flows.

Today, most of the Costa del Sol is fully developed. With land shortages and prices soaring,

Figure 2.26 *Population change: municipalities in Málaga province 1981–2002*

Michael Raw

Photograph 2.25 *Unspoilt coastline in Amería province*

development is increasingly shifting to the last remaining unspoilt stretches of coast to the east of Almería and west of Gibraltar (Photograph 2.25).

Urban growth

For the first 20 years of mass tourism in the Costa del Sol, development was subject to minimal planning regulations and controls. The priority was economic growth and raising levels of development in one of Europe's poorest regions. Thus development, driven by market forces, was uncoordinated and piecemeal. The outcome was high-rise hotels and apartment blocks that dominated the seafront townscape. Moreover, most buildings, cheap and shoddily constructed, only added to the poor quality of the urban environment. Lack of planning also meant little provision for promenades and access to beaches, while traffic management, parks and gardens and sewage treatment facilities were often ignored in the rush to development.

Modern planning policies aim to restrict urban development and remove some of the worst eyesores from the 1960s and 1970s. Even so, development has reached saturation point along many stretches of the Costa del Sol. Overdevelopment is most acute just west of Málaga. There coastal municipalities such as Torremolinos and Fuengirola have almost three-quarters of their shoreline fully urbanised, and extending for nearly a kilometre inland.

Nor has planning stopped thousands of illegal constructions in the coastal strip — 30 000 houses in Marbella alone — and there are reports of widespread corruption and bribery. Many developers, with the approval of planners and local politicians, have often ignored EU guidelines and local regulations. The problems of corruption and illegal development are illustrated by the El Algarrobico hotel scandal on the Costa Callida (Photograph 2.26). In 2003, the local authority gave permission for the hotel development on a 200 ha site on an unspoilt stretch of coast; this, despite the site's protected status and its location adjacent to the Cabo de Gata-Níjar natural park. The centrepiece of the development was a huge 20-storey hotel, which dominated the coast and extended down to the beach. Following protests from local pressure groups and Greenpeace, the Ministry of Environment in 2006 finally ruled that the half-finished hotel was illegal. Subsequently, the local authority purchased the site and the building was demolished.

Developments such as El Algarrobico have been fuelled by the huge foreign investment in second homes and holiday homes as well as a desire to move Spain's tourism industry upmarket. Sixty-five thousand foreigners own properties on the Costa del Sol: a number expected to increase to 200 000 by 2012. In addition, there was a 30% increase in the

Photograph 2.26 *Greenpeace's* **Rainbow Warrior** *ship, docked in front of the El Algarrobico hotel; environmental activists painted 'illegal' on the facade of the building*

number of new hotels built between 2000 and 2004. The building boom is far from over and is putting acute pressure on land, traffic circulation, water resources and the natural environment. Inevitably, urban development is extending beyond the core area of Málaga province and into the largely unspoilt coasts of Almería and Cadíz.

Golf tourism

Andalucia has 90 golf courses — the most in Spain — and has plans to increase this number to over 200 in the next few years. Half of the courses are on the Costa del Sol, in Málaga province. Golf courses are often a feature of upmarket urban developments comprising holiday homes and vacation villas. They also attract new hotels. It is argued that Spain's property boom fuels the demand for golf. Houses and apartments in *urbanizaciones* with access to golf on average cost 40% more. Also, the per capita spending of golf tourists is much higher than any other tourist group. No longer able to compete with cheaper 'sun and sand' holiday destinations such as Morocco and Croatia, development of golf tourism is in line with the government's aim to attract higher-spending visitors.

Environmentally, the key question is whether the golf boom is sustainable, especially in a drought-prone region where water is scarce. A typical golf course needs $700\,000\,\text{m}^3$ of water a year, enough to supply a town of 15 000 to 25 000 people. The combined demand from golf and upmarket residential zones puts huge pressure on the region's water resources.

Planners are trying to put a brake on golf course developments that are non-sustainable. Ecologists argue that planning for future golf courses should be decided at regional rather than provincial level, which is the current practice.

Figure 2.27
Environmental blackspots on the coast of Málaga province, 2006
Source: Greenpeace

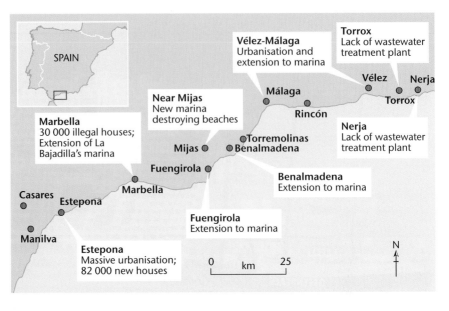

Marinas

Marinas for mooring pleasure boats have increased in popularity along the Costa del Sol (Figure 2.27). In 2006, several marinas extended their capacity. Marina developments involve the construction of harbours, piers and breakwaters, which have environmental implications. These fixed structures can disrupt sediment movement in the coastal zone, both longshore and offshore. Beach starvation and beach erosion often result. For example, the Puerto Banas marina just west of Marbella interrupted longshore drift across the mouth of the Rio Verde. To prevent beach erosion on the downdrift side of the marina, groynes were constructed to prevent the loss of beach sediments offshore. In addition, artificial beach replenishment has provided permanent beaches for the expensive properties in this area.

Government policy is not to replenish artificial beaches that lose sand due to coastal constructions such as groynes, piers and marinas. Artificial sand replacement is at best a temporary solution and in the long term is unsustainable. Furthermore, sand for beach replenishment is often mined offshore, destroying sea meadows and the marine animals that depend on them. Even so, the Ministry of Environment is still engaged in offshore sand extraction for beach replenishment, despite its adverse ecological effects.

Pollution of coastal water

Many new sewage treatment plants have been built and existing ones enlarged and repaired in the past 20 years. However, the work is slow and effluent discharged into the sea does not always comply with EU water quality standards. Thirteen per cent of Spain's wastewater is discharged untreated into the sea. By the end of 2005, all municipalities with more than 2000 people should have had secondary sewage treatment plants. Many failed to meet this target. Substantial coastal towns such as Algeciras, Benalmadena and Nerja still lack proper water treatment facilities. Untreated effluent is a direct threat to beaches and marine ecosystems.

Although bathing water quality in Andalucia is good, some sewage dumping at sea continues, despite being illegal. Too often in the past, urbanisation has occurred without appropriate sewage treatment facilities.

In 2006, the Ministry of Environment and the Andalucian Board agreed to invest €319 million to improve wastewater treatment.

Coastal management and planning

In England and Wales, shoreline management is the responsibility of coastal local authorities and the Environment Agency. Local authorities deal specifically with coastal erosion; the Environment Agency has responsibility for flood protection. Both problems are brought together in Shoreline Management Plans (SMPs) (Box 2.5).

Box 2.5 Shoreline Management Plans

In England and Wales, coastal management is coordinated through Shoreline Management Plans (SMPs). The basic unit of management is the sediment cell. Sediment cells are lengths of coastline that are self-contained in terms of inputs and movements of silt, sand and shingle. In other words, they are 'natural units', which cut across local authority boundaries. There are 11 sediment cells in England and Wales (see Figure 2.12 on page 72). Each is divided into 49 smaller units called sub-cells, which in turn are split into smaller management areas.

A feature of SMPs is a reduction in human intervention in the natural processes that operate on the coastal zone. This recognises that the coast is a self-adjusting system and that we should work with, rather than against, natural processes. Thus, a 'no active intervention' policy for most of the coastline allows natural change through erosion, sediment transport and deposition.

Managed retreat actually dismantles hard structures such as seawalls and flood embankments, allowing the coast to resume a more natural form.

Another 'soft engineering' response to coastal erosion is **beach nourishment**. Sand and shingle are imported to build up beaches and protect against erosion. Beaches, as we know, are highly effective absorbers of wave energy. However, beach nourishment can cause problems, especially if the sediments are mined offshore. Then gravel stores in offshore banks can be depleted, reducing the total volume of sediment in the coastal zone. Perversely, this could starve some beaches of sediment, narrowing them and accelerating erosion.

An integrated approach to shoreline management is essential. In the past, planning was piecemeal. Action taken by a single local authority often had adverse effects on adjacent stretches of coastline. For example, building seawalls, protecting cliffs from erosion or mining sand offshore could reduce sediment availability. This in turn could have serious consequences, such as the erosion of cliffs, beaches and saltmarshes.

Coastal problems
Global warming and climate change

Coastal management has to tackle the long-term problems caused by global warming and climate change. In a warmer world, sea levels are already rising. The most conservative estimate suggests a rise by nearly 1 m by the end of the century. A rise in sea level changes the area over which coastal processes operate. It also increases the flood hazard and threatens the erosion of beaches, dunes, mudflats and saltmarshes unless they can migrate inland. Furthermore, computer models predict increases in storminess: with more powerful waves hitting the coast more frequently, rates of erosion will accelerate. All of this has serious consequences for sea defences and their sustainability.

Sediment budgets

Today, coastal management and planning are based on natural units known as sediment cells (see Box 2.5). The key to successful management is an understanding of coastal processes, and in particular the supply, movement and storage of sediment within the coastal zone. Past human intervention has greatly modified the sediment budget of some coastlines. Supplies of sediment have been reduced by the construction of seawalls, cliff and sand dune stabilisation, the management of rivers and land reclamation in estuaries. Meanwhile, longshore sediment transport has been disrupted by hard-engineered structures such as groynes, piers and jetties (Figure 2.28). Finally, sand and shingle stored offshore has been depleted by dredging and mining for construction and beach nourishment.

Figure 2.28 Some hard engineering structures

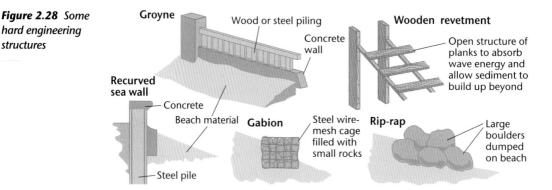

Coastal squeeze

Coastal squeeze is a widespread problem (Figure 2.29). It describes the erosion of beaches and saltmarshes and is caused by a combination of factors: hard coastal

Figure 2.29 Coastal squeeze

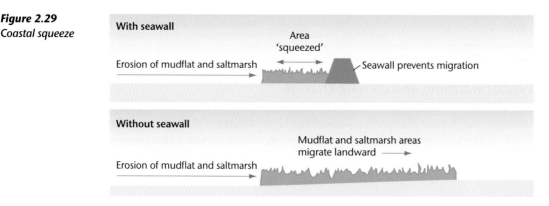

defences, rising sea levels and reduced supplies of sediment. Coastal squeeze occurs when beaches and saltmarshes are trapped between rising sea level and hard defences such as seawalls and flood embankments. On natural coastlines, beaches and saltmarshes would simply migrate inland. But hard defences make this impossible. The result is the erosion of these features, making the coast more vulnerable to flooding and wave attack.

Coastal management

Current practice is to reduce human intervention in the coastal sediment budget, allowing erosion to occur and sediments to move more freely into and out of store. It also means that the coastal system has more freedom to self-adjust in future (see Box 2.1, page 57).

Sediment depletion causes significant management problems — for example, beaches starved of sediment, either because of erosion control, obstacles to longshore movement or the mining of sand and shingle, provide little protection against erosion. Equally, erosion control and lower sediment loads of rivers entering the coastal zone reduce deposition on mudflats and saltmarshes, and exacerbate the problem of coastal squeeze.

Managed retreat and realignment

Managed retreat or managed realignment is a strategy option in SMPs. It involves setting back the shoreline and allowing the sea to flood areas that were previously protected by embankments and seawalls (Figure 2.30). The motives for managed retreat and realignment include:

➤ reducing the cost of maintaining non-sustainable or expensive sea defences
➤ allowing saltmarshes and mudflats that develop on abandoned farmland to create natural defences against flooding and erosion
➤ creating new wildlife habitats, i.e. inter-tidal mudflats and saltmarshes
➤ tackling the problem of coastal squeeze
➤ restoring valuable sediment sinks

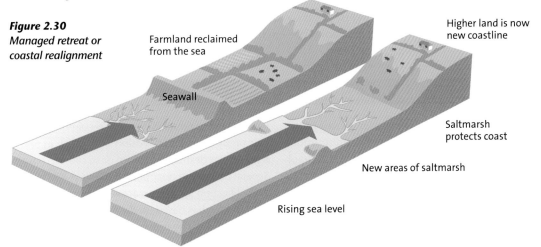

Figure 2.30
Managed retreat or coastal realignment

Farmland reclaimed from the sea

Seawall

Higher land is now new coastline

Saltmarsh protects coast

New areas of saltmarsh

Rising sea level

Case study: Managed retreat/realignment at Freiston Shore

In 1983, 66 hectares of saltmarsh at Freiston Shore, in Lincolnshire (Figure 2.31), was reclaimed from The Wash. The reclaimed land, protected by a flood embankment, was converted to arable farming. However, it was estimated that maintaining the sea defences over next 50 years would cost nearly £2.5 million. Such expenditure was difficult to justify, given the relatively low value of the land. Managed realignment offered a cheaper alternative. It would cost just under £2 million, be sustainable and have significant ecological benefits.

The outcome was a partnership between the RSPB, the Environment Agency and English Nature to complete a managed realignment project. The flood embankment was breached in three places in August 2002 creating 66 ha of saltmarsh and a 15 ha saline lagoon. The work was highly successful. The salt-marsh formed faster than expected: just 13 months after the breach, 60–70% of the realignment area had been colonised by 11 different species of saltmarsh plants. Eight species of fish were also recorded. As a result, birds such as dark-bellied brent geese, golden plover, lapwing, dunlin and oyster-

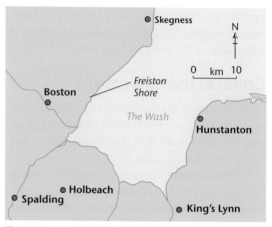

Figure 2.31 *Location of Freiston Shore*

catcher have all increased in numbers. Avocets have also started to breed on newly created lagoon islands for the first time.

Freiston Shore (now a RSPB nature reserve) has also had recreational benefits. It attracts 57 000 visitors a year, brings £150 000 into the local economy, and supports four full-time jobs in the local area.

Do nothing: no active intervention

This policy is applied to most stretches of coastline in England and Wales: coasts are unprotected, and natural processes operate without human interference. 'Do nothing' recognises that coasts are self-adjusting systems, and that it is neither economically feasible, nor environmentally desirable, to stop all erosion and flooding.

Case study: Happisburgh, Norfolk

Occasionally, a 'no active intervention' policy causes controversy. This has happened at Happisburgh, a village on the northeast Norfolk coast (Photograph 2.27). The coastline here, consisting of low cliffs made of sand and clay, is vulnerable to erosion. Revetments, built in 1958, protected the village. However, in 1990 a storm destroyed a 300 m section of the revetments. Under a policy of 'no active inter-

vention' the revetments were not repaired. The effect was predictable. Rapid erosion — as much as 5–8 m a year — has destroyed a dozen or so cliff-top homes. Several others will disappear in the next few years.

Justification for the 'no active intervention' policy for this stretch is based on the following arguments:

■ The value of the properties at risk is less than the cost of repairing the hard defences.

Photograph 2.27
The crumbling cliffs of Happisburgh; the current SMP's 'do nothing' policy means that the houses in the photograph will soon be lost to the North Sea

- Climate change and rising sea levels make hard defences non-sustainable in the long term.
- Stopping erosion at Happisburgh reduces sediment supplies to the coastal system and could create problems further along the coast.
- Erosion will realign the coast (already a small bay has been formed to the south of the village); eventually, erosion will slow until a new equilibrium and a stable coastline is established.

Understandably, there has been considerable opposition to this policy by local residents whose homes are at risk. In response to the situation, they formed a local pressure group — Coastal Concern Action Group — to lobby North Norfolk District Council and the government to either repair the sea defences or provide compensation. However, the government has no legal obligation to defend properties at risk or compensate home owners, businesses and farmers who lose land.

Case study   Coastal management between Saltburn and Flamborough

The Yorkshire coast between Flamborough Head and Saltburn forms part of sediment cell 1. This cell, one of 11 in England and Wales, extends from Flamborough to St Abb's Head in southern Scotland. The greater part of the Yorkshire coast (from Saltburn to Flamborough) occupies sub-cell 4.

There are no overriding management issues along the coast between Saltburn and Flamborough. The hard rock nature of the coast means that erosion is not a serious problem, while the coast's upland character and low population density minimises the risk of flooding (see *Case Study* on page 67).

Even so, coastal management is needed. The SMP includes strategies to manage coastal land uses. These include the built-up areas of towns and villages adjacent to the coastline, conservation areas such as the North York Moors National Park and the Yorkshire Heritage Coast, historically important buildings such as Whitby Abbey, archaeological sites, and Sites of Special Scientific Interest (SSSIs).

The SMP is based around three main strategy options: hold the line; no active intervention; and retreat/managed realignment. These options are applied to short stretches of uniform coastline known as management units (Figure 2.32).

Active intervention has to satisfy several criteria.

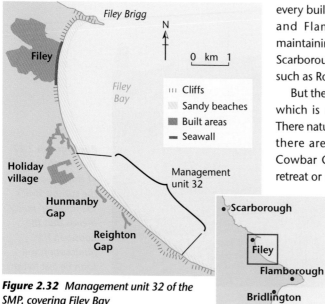

Figure 2.32 *Management unit 32 of the SMP, covering Filey Bay*

every built-up section of coastline between Saltburn and Flamborough. In practice, this involves maintaining hard defences in larger centres such as Scarborough, Whitby and Filey, and in smaller places such as Robin Hood's Bay, Runswick and Staithes.

But the preferred option for most of the coastline, which is not built up, is 'no active intervention'. There nature will be left to take its course. Meanwhile there are only small sections of coastline (e.g. Cowbar Cliffs near Staithes) where the managed retreat or realignment is in force.

Figure 2.32 shows management unit 32, just south of Filey. Natural erosion will be allowed to continue here under the policy of no active intervention. As a result, the entire stretch of coast will retreat significantly in the next 100 years, putting the villages of Hunmanby Gap and Reighton Gap at risk. At the moment, there are no plans to protect these places. However, the hard defences at Filey (i.e. its seawall) will be maintained. There the coastline will remain unchanged.

First, it must be sustainable and, second, the value of properties and infrastructure at risk from erosion or flooding must be weighed against the cost of engineering works. At the moment, the SMP protects

Christchurch Bay: a dynamic lowland coastline

Christchurch Bay in Hampshire (Figure 2.33), lies between Hengistbury Head and Hurst Spit. This is a dynamic coastline of active erosion, sediment transport and deposition. Being densely populated, it is also an area where coastal management is particularly sensitive.

Geology and relief

Most of Christchurch Bay is backed by low cliffs, 20–30 m high. The cliffs are made of weak tertiary rocks. Permeable sands and gravels overlie impermeable clay — a structure that makes the cliffs inherently unstable. Water seeps into the sands and gravels only as far as the clay. As water cannot escape easily, pressure builds up in the permeable rocks, making them vulnerable to failure by rotational slumping. Other mass movement processes, including mud-slides, mudflows and gulleying, are active on the unvegetated slumped masses (Figure 2.34).

Offshore, Christchurch Bay is shallow (averaging just 7 m in depth) and has a gentle gradient.

Wave energy, tides and currents

Although the average tidal range is just over 1 m (making it one of the smallest in the UK), tidal currents are strong and transport large volumes of sediment. The dominant waves are from the south-west, the direction of longest fetch. These waves are responsible for a net longshore transport of sediment in Christchurch Bay from west to east (Figure 2.35).

Cliff erosion and sediment inputs

A combination of soft rocks, narrow beaches and high wave energy are responsible for rates of erosion

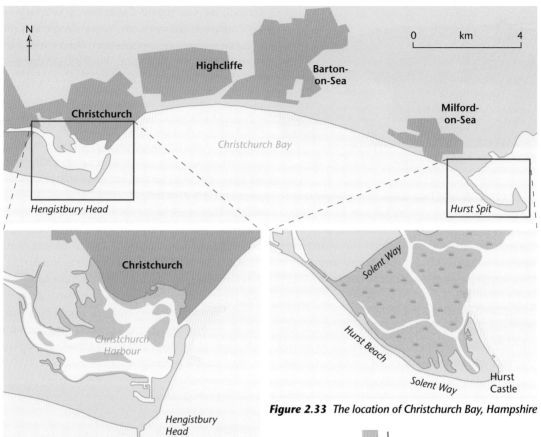

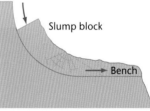

Figure 2.33 The location of Christchurch Bay, Hampshire

that are among the highest in the UK. At Highcliffe and Barton-on-Sea, erosion caused the cliffs to retreat by nearly 1 km between 1867 and 1959. Current rates of erosion at Barton are 1.9 m per year. While erosion creates obvious problems it has one major advantage. It inputs large amounts of sediment into Christchurch Bay, which builds beaches and gives protection against further erosion. The crumbling cliffs at Highcliffe and Barton provide an estimated 28 000–47 000 m^3 of sediment to the coastal zone every year (Photograph 2.28).

Figure 2.34 Geology and cliff failure at Barton-on-Sea, Christchurch Bay

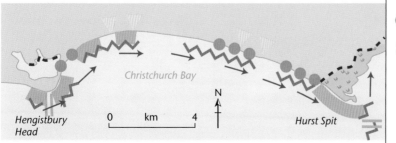

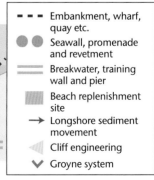

Figure 2.35 Coastal defence systems, Christchurch Bay

Kitchenham

Photograph 2.28 *Cliff erosion at Barton-on-Sea*

In contrast, the two main rivers flowing into Christchurch Bay — the Avon and the Stour — provide negligible inputs of sediment. Both drain chalk catchments and have naturally small sediment loads. In addition, what little sediment they carry is often trapped by weirs and sluices upstream.

Sediment stores and sinks

The Shingles and Dolphin banks are important offshore sediment stores. So too are the extensive mudflats and saltmarshes in the lee of Hurst Spit.

Overall, we can regard Christchurch as a largely self-contained sediment cell. Sand, shingle and silt circulate alongshore, onshore and offshore between stores such as beaches, spits, mudflats, saltmarshes and offshore banks.

Hurst Spit

Hurst Spit is a large barrier spit, 2 km long and multi-recurved (Photograph 2.29). It is located at a point where the coastline changes direction abruptly. Its distal section recurves sharply north-west and is 800 m long. Former recurves are also visible. They mark phases in the growth of the spit fed by longshore movement of sand and gravel from Christchurch Bay. The main source of sediment updrift is the eroding cliffs at Highcliffe and Barton. In recent years, coastal protection at these locations has severely reduced sediment inputs. Without artificial beach nourishment there would be a high risk of erosion and eventual breaching. Such an event would greatly increase the threat of flooding to coastal areas behind the spit.

© English Heritage

Photograph 2.29 *Aerial view of Hurst Spit*

The low-energy environment in the lee of Hurst Spit supports a large expanse of mudflats and salt-marshes. These expanded rapidly in the period 1880 to 1930 due to the invasion of hybrid cordgrass. Today the saltmarshes are being eroded, caused by the die-back of cordgrass.

Coastal management

Christchurch Bay is a heavily managed coastline. This is not surprising. After all, it has a large urban population, meaning that coastal defence is a high priority. Most of the coastline is protected from erosion by hard structures such as seawalls, groynes and revetments (Figure 2.35).

The rapidly eroding cliffs at Highcliffe and Barton threaten residential areas on the cliff tops. In response, seawalls have been constructed along the western side of Christchurch Bay and at Mudeford. Extensive groyne fields interrupt longshore drift, building up beaches and providing further protection. Revetments protect the base of cliffs. At Highcliffe and Barton, the cliffs have been regraded, strengthened with metal pilings, and drained (see Figures 2.33 and 2.35).

The visual impact of much of the Bay's coastal defences is unsightly. However, soft engineering such as beach nourishment is also currently in use. Gravel, mined offshore on Shingles Bank, is input to beaches at Mudeford Spit, Christchurch and Hurst Spit to compensate for the loss of beach sediment caused by cliff protection.

Shoreline Management Plan

The SMP for Christchurch Bay and Hurst Spit provides an integrated strategy for tackling the area's coastal issues. These issues include:

- cliff erosion at Barton and Highcliffe
- reduced longshore flows of sediment to Hurst Spit
- saltmarsh erosion in the lee of Hurst Spit

The first two issues are related. Erosion protection of the cliffs at Barton and Highcliffe has significantly reduced sediment inputs to the coastal system. Starved of sediment from longshore drift, Hurst Spit is eroding and breaching has become a serious threat.

The latest SMP adopts three management strategies for the coastline. In the west at Naish Farm, a managed retreat policy is in force, allowing the cliffs to erode naturally. The exposed cliffs are an SSSI and contain scientifically important fossils. Stopping erosion would result in their re-vegetation and greatly reduce their scientific value.

At Barton, Christchurch and Highcliffe, the policy is to 'hold the line'. This means maintaining existing sea defences, such as the 1.8 km of revetments and rock groynes at Barton, and the seawalls at Christchurch and Milford. Some of the cliffs have been regraded and drained (Figure 2.36). However, some areas are still at risk from erosion.

The third strategy is 'do nothing' and allow nature to take its course. This policy is used between Barton and Milford, and along the eastern end of Hurst Spit.

Cliff-top gravel drain removes water before it reaches the cliff face (cliff at Milford only)

Gullies are blocked with brushwood

Barrier of interlocking sheet piles

The water trapped behind the barrier is drained out at the base of the piles

Groynes to reduce longshore drift

Sand

Silty clay

Clay

Filter of coarse sand

Perforated drainage pipe

Cliff-foot protection by seawall or revetment

Figure 2.36
Cliff stabilisation measures at Barton

Examination-style questions

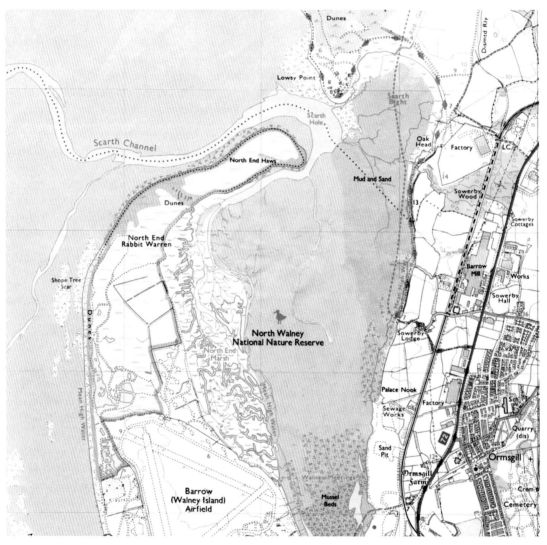

Figure 1

1 **(a)** Identify and describe the main coastal landforms shown in
Figure 1. (4 marks)

(b) Explain the formation of the coastal landforms identified in (a). (6 marks)

(c) Outline the evidence in Figure 1 that shows that coastal
environments have a variety of human uses. (6 marks)

(d) With reference to one or more examples, explain how stretches
of coastline can be protected from coastal erosion and flooding. (9 marks)

2 With reference to named examples, explain how detailed planning and management can resolve development issues and conflicts in coastal environments. (25 marks)

Michael Raw

Figure 2

3 (a) Describe the main features of the coastline in Figure 2. (4 marks)

 (b) Explain how erosion and sub-aerial processes are responsible for the formation of the features described in (a). (6 marks)

 (c) Explain why some stretches of coastline need protection against the effects of natural processes. (6 marks)

 (d) With reference to one or more named examples, explain how coastlines are valuable economic and environmental resources. (9 marks)

4 With reference to named examples, explain how managing coastal areas often involves balancing socio-economic and environmental needs. (25 marks)

Cold environments

Key ideas

➤ Cold environments are shaped by distinctive climatic and geomorphological processes.

➤ Climate and weathering have an important impact on the physical landscape.

➤ Ice and water shape the landscape to produce distinctive landforms.

Cold environments occur in two types of location: in high latitudes and in high mountains. In both locations, low temperatures dominate climate. The most extreme cold environments have a permanent cover of ice and snow. Virtually the whole of Antarctica and most of Greenland are smothered by ice sheets, in places up to 2–3 km thick. Over the Greenland ice sheet, temperatures average −33 °C in winter.

Antarctica is even colder. We can explain Antarctica's extreme cold by its high latitude: only the Antarctic peninsula lies north of the Antarctic Circle. In contrast, the southern tip of Greenland is the same latitude as northern Scotland. So why is it permanently covered by ice? The reason is **albedo**: snow and ice reflect most incoming solar radiation, keeping Greenland in its own deep freeze.

In this section we shall concentrate on the cold environments of high mountains, which support snowfields, icefields and glaciers; and the sub-arctic and tundra of the northern hemisphere. Table 3.1 defines the world's cold climates based on the Köppen's climate classification (Figure 3.1).

Table 3.1 Cold climates (Köppen classification)

Type	Description
Dfc	Cold boreal forest climates; coldest month <−3°C, warmest month >10°C
EF/ET	Ice and tundra; climate of perpetual frost on the Antarctic and Greenland ice sheets; tundra climate where the warmest month is 0°–10°C (i.e. too cold to support trees); highland; mountain climates, whose severity depends on latitude and altitude

Cold mountain environments

Temperatures in the lower atmosphere decrease with altitude at a rate of 6.5 °C per kilometre. This **lapse rate** of temperature greatly modifies mountain climates. Thus, a temperature of 25 °C in Nice becomes −1 °C at 4000 m in the nearby Alps.

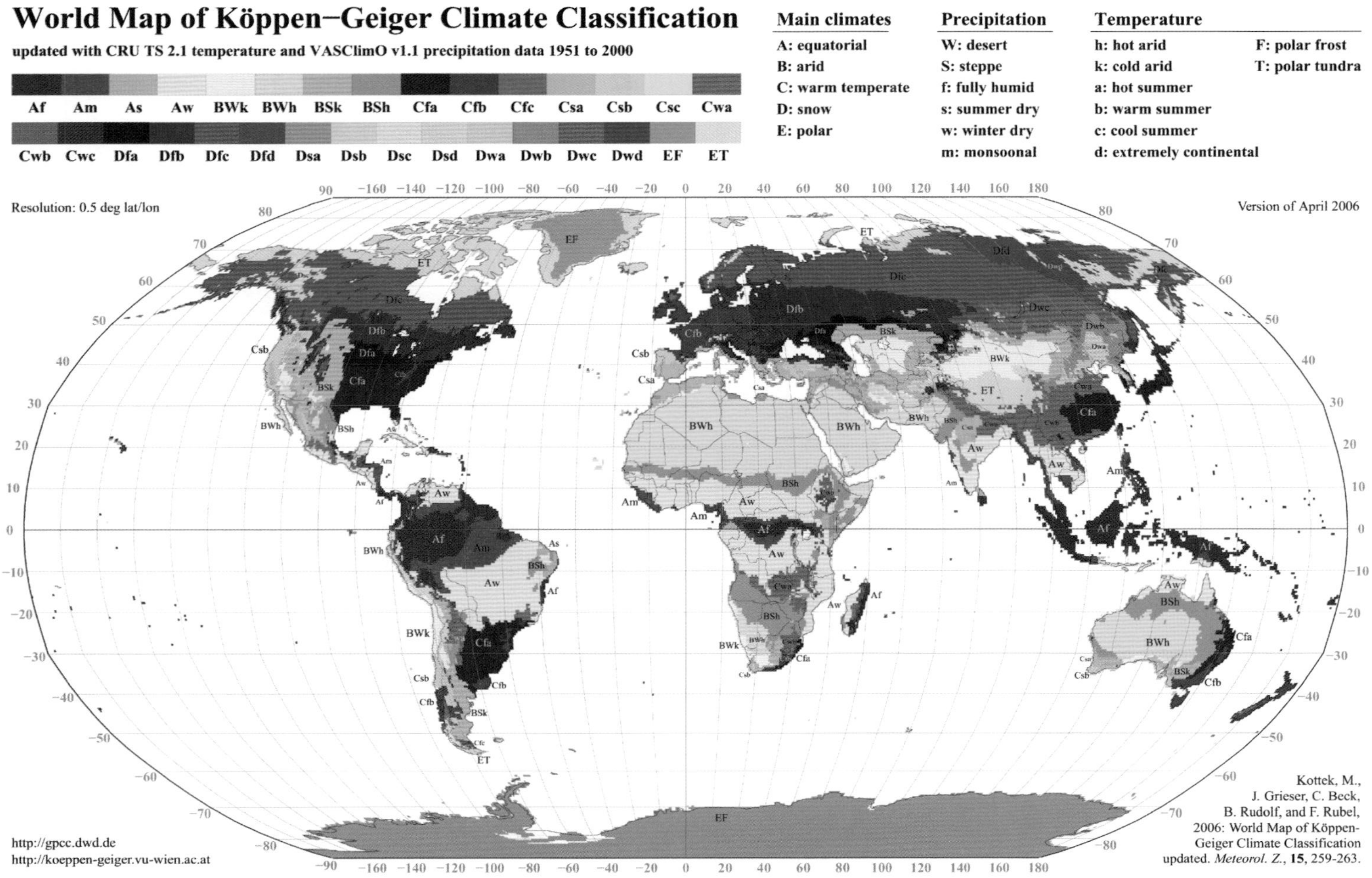

World Map of Köppen–Geiger Climate Classification

updated with CRU TS 2.1 temperature and VASClimO v1.1 precipitation data 1951 to 2000

Main climates	Precipitation	Temperature	
A: equatorial	W: desert	h: hot arid	F: polar frost
B: arid	S: steppe	k: cold arid	T: polar tundra
C: warm temperate	f: fully humid	a: hot summer	
D: snow	s: summer dry	b: warm summer	
E: polar	w: winter dry	c: cool summer	
	m: monsoonal	d: extremely continental	

Af Am As Aw BWk BWh BSh BSk Cfa Cfb Cfc Csa Csb Csc Cwa

Cwb Cwc Dfa Dfb Dfd Dfc Dsa Dsb Dsc Dsd Dwa Dwb Dwc Dwd EF ET

Resolution: 0.5 deg lat/lon

Version of April 2006

http://gpcc.dwd.de
http://koeppen-geiger.vu-wien.ac.at

Kottek, M.,
J. Grieser, C. Beck,
B. Rudolf, and F. Rubel,
2006: World Map of Köppen-
Geiger Climate Classification
updated. *Meteorol. Z,* **15,** 259–263.

Figure 3.1 *World climate map*

Little wonder that high mountain ranges in middle latitudes such as the Alps in Europe, and the Andes in Chile and Argentina, support permanent ice and snow (Figure 3.2).

Figure 3.2 The effect of latitude on the elevation of the snowline
Source: USGS

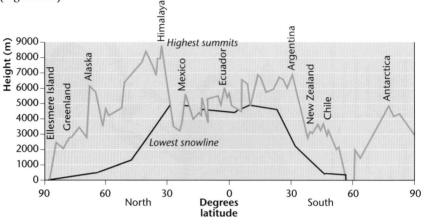

The snowline in the mountains — the level of permanent snow cover — varies with latitude. Higher temperatures in the tropics, caused by the greater intensity of solar radiation, increase the elevation of the snowline to around 5000 m at the Equator (Figure 3.2). By 75°N, the snowline has fallen to below 500 m. Precipitation also influences the snowline. Mountains in the same latitude often have variable snowlines because of differences in precipitation. Generally, the snowline is lower where precipitation is heavier.

Geomorphological processes in cold mountain environments

Frost weathering

Weathering is the *in situ* breakdown of rocks at or near the Earth's surface due to changes in temperature and moisture. In mountain and sub-arctic environments, freeze–thaw or frost weathering is important. Water, trapped in confined rock joints and crevices, expands by 9% of its volume on freezing. Pressures exerted by ice are sufficient to shatter even the hardest rocks (Photograph 3.1).

Several factors control the effectiveness of freeze–thaw weathering:
➤ the number of freeze–thaw cycles when diurnal temperatures fluctuate above or below freezing
➤ the availability of moisture
➤ the density of jointing in rocks exposed at or near the surface

Photograph 3.1 Limestone rock debris formed by freeze–thaw weathering

Freeze–thaw weathering occurs on exposed summit ridges in glaciated mountain environments, above the level of icefields and **valley glaciers**. In sub-arctic and tundra environments, freeze–thaw weathering is less effective because temperatures remain below freezing for 6 or 7 months, and precipitation is light.

Pressure release

Pressure release or **dilatation** is a type of physical weathering. During periods of continental glaciation, great thicknesses of ice load the continental crust, compressing rocks near the surface. However, when deglaciation occurs and pressure is reduced, the rocks expand parallel to the surface. Expansion creates parallel joints known as **pseudo-bedding planes**. These joints are lines of weakness, which are exploited by frost weathering and by glacial erosion should glacial conditions return.

Glaciation

Currently, 10% of the continental surface is covered permanently by snow and ice. Twenty thousand years ago this proportion was much higher. At this time, almost one-third of the land surface, including most of northern Europe and Canada, was buried by ice (Figure 3.3).

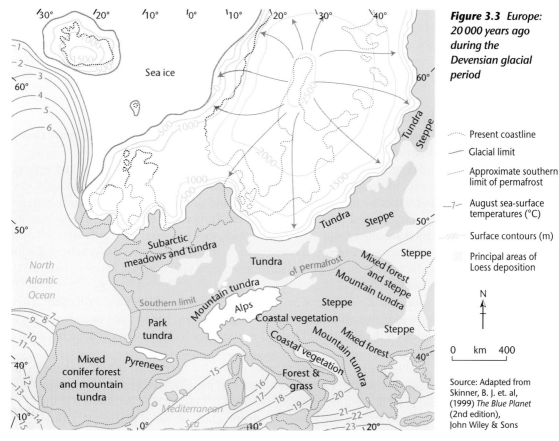

Figure 3.3 *Europe: 20 000 years ago during the Devensian glacial period*

Source: Adapted from Skinner, B. J. et. al, (1999) *The Blue Planet* (2nd edition), John Wiley & Sons

Box 3.1 Glacial and interglacial periods: the changing geography of cold environments

The area occupied by cold environments has fluctuated enormously over the past 2 million years (the Quaternary era). Twenty thousand years ago, the last ice age (the Devensian) reached its maximum in Europe and North America (Figure 3.3). Ice sheets up to 1 km thick covered Scotland, and most of northern England, the West Midlands, Wales and Ireland. As the climate warmed, the ice sheets retreated; valley glaciers occupied the mountains of northern Britain and Wales until c.13 000 BP. A brief cold snap between 12 500 and 11 500 BP — (the Loch Lomond Stadial) — saw the return of glaciers to the mountains. Since that time, the uplands of northern Britain have lain below the snowline.

During the Devensian glacial period, southern Britain remained ice-free. However, average annual temperatures were 5°C lower than today, and the ground was permanently frozen. With conditions too cold for forests, tundra vegetation, dominated by dwarf trees, evergreen shrubs, sedges, mosses and arctic alpines, was widespread.

Since the end of the last glaciation, the world's climate has warmed. Today we live in a warm interglacial period known as the Holocene. In the northern hemisphere, cold environments survive only in the mountains, northern Canada, Siberia and of course in Greenland, where the ice age never ended.

The causes of ice ages are astronomical. Cyclic changes in the shape of the Earth's orbit affect the amount of solar energy reaching the Earth. Changes in obliquity (the angle of tilt of the Earth's axis) influence the geographical distribution of solar energy, and the wobble of the Earth's axis (known as the precession of the equinoxes) alters the timing between perihelion (when the Earth is closest to the sun), aphelion (when the Earth is furthest from the sun) and the northern hemisphere's winter. These factors are responsible for forcing climate change that has given rise to the long succession of glacials and interglacials during the past 2 million years.

Types of glacier

Glaciers are large bodies of ice formed from compressed snow. They move slowly downslope under their own weight and gravity.

We recognise three main types of glacier according to their shape and size: ice sheets, icefields (or ice caps) and valley glaciers. Ice sheets are the largest glaciers. Today they are found only in Antarctica and Greenland, though during the last ice age they covered large parts of northern Europe and North America. Because ice sheets are often more than 2–3 km thick, they submerge the landscape. Today in Antarctica and Greenland only the highest mountain peaks project above the ice surface. These island peaks, surrounded by a sea of ice, are known as **nunataks** (Photograph 3.2).

Icefields are miniature ice sheets covering areas of less than 50 000 km². They form in plateau-like uplands. The largest icefield (or ice cap) outside the polar regions is the Vatnajökull located in southeast Iceland atop a 1500 m basalt lava plateau.

Valley glaciers are giant tongues of ice that flow down from the snowline in mountainous regions such as Alaska and the Alps (see Figure 3.4 on page 114). Some small mountain glaciers, confined to bowl-shaped depressions at the head of glacial valleys, are known as **cirque glaciers**. Valley glaciers that flow from

Michael Raw

icefields are called **outlet glaciers** (Photograph 3.3). Sometimes valley glaciers leaving the mountains spill out into lowland regions. There they merge, spreading out in lobes to form **piedmont glaciers**.

Photograph 3.2
Nunataks,
Greenland

Photograph 3.3
Solheim outlet
glacier, Iceland

Michael Raw

113

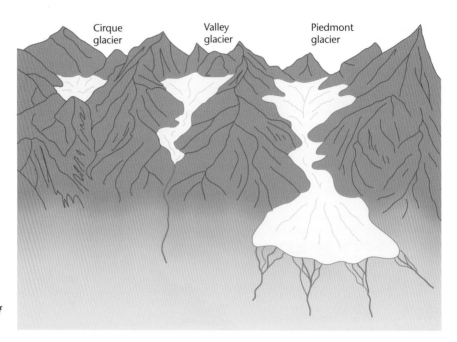

Cirque glacier   Valley glacier   Piedmont glacier

Figure 3.4 *Types of mountain glacier*

Formation of glacier ice

The story of glacier ice formation begins with snowfall. Snow is light, feathery and is mainly air. As snow accumulates, freeze–thaw and the weight of overlying snow convert it to loose ice granules, and eventually to opaque ice known as firn or neve. Further compression squeezes out the remaining air to form glacier ice (Figure 3.5). The whole process takes 40–50 years.

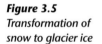

Figure 3.5 *Transformation of snow to glacier ice*

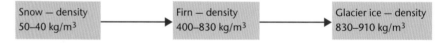

Snow — density 50–40 kg/m³   →   Firn — density 400–830 kg/m³   →   Glacier ice — density 830–910 kg/m³

Mass balance and glaciers

Mass balance is the difference between the amount of snow and ice accumulated on a glacier, and the amount lost to **ablation** (melting and sublimation). It is measured annually, and may be aggregated over tens of years.

Snow accumulates in the mountains where temperatures are low and precipitation is high. As glaciers move downslope, temperatures rise, and ablation increases. With ablation now exceeding accumulation, the mass of the glacier starts to shrink. The equilibrium line on the glacier marks the location where accumulation and ablation are equal (Figure 3.6).

Changes in mass balance or annual budget control the long-term behaviour of glaciers. A positive balance increases the total mass of ice, causing glaciers to advance. Conversely, a prolonged negative balance reduces the ice mass and results in glacier retreat. There is often a considerable time lag between changes in mass balance and glacier movement. Thus, a glacier may be advancing now due to heavy snowfall 20 or 30 years earlier.

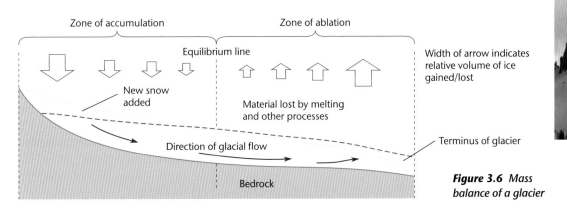

Figure 3.6 *Mass balance of a glacier*

Box 3.2 Global warming and glaciers

Glaciers are highly sensitive to climate change. Everywhere, glaciers are shrinking, providing unequivocal physical evidence of global warming and climate change. Nowhere have glaciers been more carefully monitored than in the Cascade Range in the US Pacific northwest. In the 22 years between 1984 and 2006, there were 16 years when glaciers had a cumulative negative mass balance. The impact was dramatic. Glaciers shrank in thickness by 12.4 m and lost 20–40% of their total volume (Figure 3.7). Similar trends have been observed in other mountain ranges such as the Himalaya, Andes, Alps and Rockies, and in Iceland.

Recent studies of the Greenland ice sheet suggest that it is melting three times faster than previously thought. It is losing some 215–260 km^3 of ice every year, and appears to be in negative mass balance. The main reason for this is an acceleration in rates of glacier flow. Rising temperatures produce meltwater at the surface, which then travels a kilometre or so to the base of the ice sheet. The meltwater causes the ice to slide faster, increasing the input of ice into the Arctic Ocean.

In Antarctica, the mass balance of the world's biggest ice sheet is also in significant decline. The most rapid decline is in west Antarctica. Large areas of ice shelf (ice sheets floating on the sea) have broken up in the past three decades. In 2002, the Larsen B ice shelf in the Antarctic peninsula collapsed. In just a few weeks, the ice shelf, which had been stable for 10 000 years, and occupied an area the size of Wiltshire, broke up, releasing 500 billion tonnes of water into the ocean.

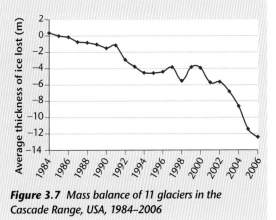

Figure 3.7 *Mass balance of 11 glaciers in the Cascade Range, USA, 1984–2006*

Glacier movement

Average flow rates in glaciers are around 100 m per year. However, some glaciers can move by as much as 20 m in a day! Flow rates depend on valley gradient and temperatures at the base of the ice.

There are two types of movement: **internal deformation** and **basal sliding**. Internal deformation is caused by the weight of the ice and gravity. Ice crystals in the glacier rearrange into parallel layers and slide past each other.

Basal sliding occurs when water is present under the glacier. Its presence is due to (a) intense pressure, which causes melting, and/or (b) meltwater seeping down from the surface through cracks in the ice. Meltwater lubricates the base of the glacier, reducing friction and allowing the ice to move freely. Pressure melting and refreezing is common at the base of the ice. Ice melts in high-pressure regions (e.g. as it moves across a rock outcrop) and freezes in low-pressure regions — a process known as **regelation**.

The surface layers of the glacier are known as the brittle zone. Fracturing and faulting of ice occurs in this zone and forms **crevasses**.

Box 3.3 Warm-based and cold-based glaciers

Glaciers can be classified by their temperature characteristics as well as by their shape and size. There are two types: warm-based and cold-based glaciers.

Glaciers in temperate regions like the Alps and the Rockies are warm-based. This means that temperatures at the base of the glacier are at pressure melting point. Heat from the Earth adds to melting. The resulting meltwater assists basal slipping and rapid movement. Warm-based glaciers are active agents of erosion and deposition.

In contrast, polar glaciers produce little meltwater: temperatures in the ice are often below pressure melting point. As a result, the most basal ice is frozen to the bedrock and glacier movement is largely by internal deformation. Thus, cold-based glaciers cause minimal erosion.

Continental and alpine glaciation

Continental glaciation is occurring in Antarctica and Greenland today. Ice sheets cover huge areas of the land surface, submerging the landscape under several kilometres of glacier ice. Similar conditions existed in northern Britain at the peak of the last glacial period, 20 000 years ago. The ice, nearly 1 km thick in the Scottish Highlands, smothered all but the highest mountain peaks.

Around 10% of continental ice sheets consist of gigantic, fast-moving rivers of ice called **ice streams**. They can move up to a metre a day and form where meltwater is present at the base of the ice. Flow velocities also depend on whether the stream rests on solid rock, or on soft deformable materials such as ice-deposited debris, known as **moraine**.

Sometimes glaciation is confined to mountain ranges and plateaux. Mountain glaciers, whose source may be in icefields or cirque hollows, flow downslope and occupy former river valleys. Glaciation on this smaller scale, confined to mountains and deep valleys, is known as alpine glaciation. Large, ice-free areas between valleys are exposed to weathering and mass movement processes. Continental and alpine glaciations give rise to their own distinctive erosional and depositional landforms.

Glacial erosion, transport and deposition
Erosion

Warm-based glaciers are fast-moving, effective agents of erosion. There are two important glacial erosional processes: **abrasion** and quarrying (or plucking). Box 3.4 gives details of their main characteristics.

Box 3.4 Glacial erosional processes

Abrasion

Glaciers transport huge amounts of coarse rock debris. This debris is derived from physical weathering and mass movements in areas exposed above the ice, and from erosion by glaciers themselves. As the glacier moves downslope, rock fragments embedded in the ice abrade the solid bedrock. Evidence of abrasion appears in the form of scratches or striations on rock surfaces over which the ice has flowed (Photograph 3.4).

Quarrying

Quarrying excavates far greater volumes of rock than abrasion. It depends on the presence of water, caused by pressure melting. For example, a small rock outcrop at the base of a glacier will cause frictional resistance to ice flow. Thus, its upstream side will experience high pressure, which results in some melting. Meltwater will run into joints and fissures in the rock. On the downstream side where pressure, is lower, freezing occurs. This means that as the glacier moves forward, rock will be quarried (or plucked) along joints in low-pressure areas. This process of melting and freezing is known as regelation. Evidence for quarrying is seen in rock outcrops called roches moutonnées (Photograph 3.5). The upstream side of this feature has been smoothed by abrasion; the downstream side is steep and uneven, showing the effect of quarrying.

Photograph 3.4 *Striations, Athabasca glacier, North America*

Photograph 3.5 *A roche moutonnée in Snowdonia*

Transport

Glaciers transport rock debris or moraine on the surface, within and at the base of the ice. Surface moraines are referred to as **supraglacial**; debris carried within the ice is **englacial**; and basal debris is **subglacial** (or **ground moraine**). The importance of surface moraine is obvious from the appearance of many valley glaciers. Below the equilibrium line, much of the surface ice is hidden under a thick mantle of debris derived from surrounding valley slopes (Photograph 3.6). Above the equilibrium line, surface moraine is quickly buried by new snowfalls and becomes englacial.

Photograph 3.6 *Nisqually glacier, Washington state, USA*

Deposition

Glaciers act as natural conveyor belts, transporting debris downslope, sometimes over hundreds of kilometres. However, rock debris cannot remain in transit indefinitely. Eventually, deposition occurs.

Direct (or ice contact) deposition occurs during deglaciation. Melting results in the random deposition of moraine *in situ*, known as ablation till. Moving ice can also deposit moraine, especially where frictional resistance to flow is high. This type of moraine, distinguished by rock particles whose long axes are parallel to the direction of ice flow, is known as **lodgement till**.

Glacial meltwater streams are also responsible for deposition. Unlike moraines, these so-called **glacio-fluvial** deposits have a layered or stratified structure. Glacio-fluvial sediments may be deposited beyond the ice front, in subglacial and englacial meltwater channels, and in **proglacial** and **marginal lakes**.

Alpine glaciation: erosional landforms

Most of the world's great mountain ranges — Himalaya, the Andes, the Alps and the Rockies — owe their spectacular landscapes to alpine glaciation (Photograph 3.7). The main features of this type of glaciation are cirque and valley glaciers, and erosional landforms such as U-shaped glacial troughs and **truncated spurs** (Figure 3.8 (a) and (b)).

Photograph 3.7 Alpine landscape in the Rocky Mountains, Colorado, with U-shaped valley, hanging valleys, truncated spurs and arêtes

Michael Raw

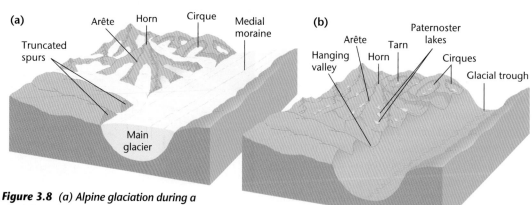

Figure 3.8 (a) Alpine glaciation during a glacial maximum and (b) the same region following deglaciation

Cirques

Cirques (or corries) are deep bowl-shaped depressions, enclosed on three sides by steep rock walls. Located at mountain heads, cirques are the source of valley glaciers in alpine regions (Photograph 3.8). The outlet to the cirque often has a raised lip of moraine or solid rock.

Smooth abraded slopes — the result of erosion by continental ice sheets during an earlier glacial maximum

More recent alpine glaciation responsible for steep slopes, overdeepened valleys, cirques and arêtes

Michael Raw

Photograph 3.8
Cirques on the eastern slopes of the Helvellyn range in the Lake District, Cumbria

Cirques develop where local relief and climate favour the accumulation of snow and ice. In the British Isles, aspect is critical. Slopes facing between north and east have a cold microclimate and are in deep shadow during the winter months. Even today, snow on these slopes is the last to melt. In addition, prevailing southwest winds cause drifting snow to pile up on these slopes. The importance of aspect can be seen in the northern highlands of Scotland. There, 71% of cirques have a north to east orientation.

The main cause of erosion in cirques is rotational flow. Cirque glaciers, under the force of gravity and lubricated by basal meltwater, slide downslope. At the back of the cirque and in the basin, this rotational flow quarries the bedrock. Meanwhile, basal ice, armed with rock debris, abrades the bedrock in the lower part of the basin and at the threshold (Figure 3.9). The steep headwall above the level of the glacier retreats by frost weathering. Rock particles, dislodged from the headwall, enter the glacier through the **bergschrund** crevasse, formed by the glacier's rotational downslope movement. These rock particles provide the tools for abrasion.

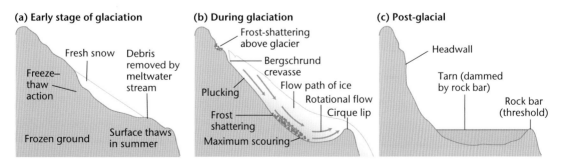

(a) Early stage of glaciation

Fresh snow

Debris removed by meltwater stream

Freeze–thaw action

Frozen ground

Surface thaws in summer

(b) During glaciation

Frost-shattering above glacier

Bergschrund crevasse

Flow path of ice

Plucking

Rotational flow

Frost shattering

Cirque lip

Maximum scouring

(c) Post-glacial

Headwall

Tarn (dammed by rock bar)

Rock bar (threshold)

Figure 3.9 *Cirques: processes and form*

Glacial valleys and related features

Glacial valleys are the basic landform of alpine regions. Their main characteristics are:

➤ a roughly parabolic or U-shaped cross-section
➤ an irregular, long profile
➤ a relatively straight planform

Whereas rivers occupy only a small fraction of the valleys in which they flow, valley glaciers are in direct contact with the entire valley floor and valley sides. In fact, glacial valleys are effectively the channels in which glaciers flow.

There are other differences between glaciers and rivers. Most obvious is the greater mass of glaciers. With volumes hundreds of times greater than rivers, glacial valleys are deeper and wider. And because glacial erosion is more extensive, valley shape is more uniform. So great is the erosional power of glaciers that valleys are overdeepened, leaving tributary valleys hanging high above the main valley.

Glacial valleys also differ from river valleys in long profile. Typical river valleys have smooth and linear profiles. In contrast, glacial valleys are irregular with frequent steps and rock basins. This irregularity is explained by the variable erosive power of glaciers. A common feature is the **trough end**: an abrupt termination to the head of a valley, below the main cirques. Trough ends are areas where tributary glaciers merge, increasing the glacier's erosive power. Overdeepened areas form rock basins, which on deglaciation may fill to create **ribbon lakes**. These basins often correspond to areas of intense quarrying and reflect differences in rock lithology, structure and glacier pressure.

The straight planform of glacial valleys is due to the bulldozing action of glaciers and the removal of spurs, which are blunted or truncated. Lateral erosion and weathering of adjacent glacial valleys and cirques often leads to convergence, reducing broad upland surfaces to knife-edged ridges called **arêtes**. High, three-sided peaks along the arêtes are known as **pyramidal peaks** or horns.

Roches moutonnées (Figure 3.10) are isolated hummocky rock outcrops which are common in glaciated valleys (see Photograph 3.5, p. 117). They have two contrasting slopes: a smooth, low-angled slope known as the stoss, which faces upstream and which has been abraded by glacial action; and a steeper and more rugged slope that faces downstream and owes its form to quarrying.

Figure 3.10
Formation of a
roche moutonnée

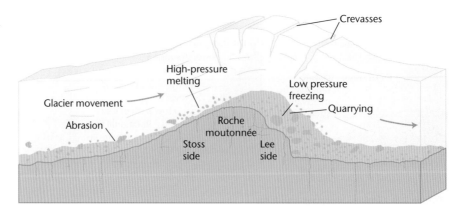

Continental glaciation: erosional landforms

Continental glaciation affects huge areas. During the last glacial period, the Laurentide ice sheet at its maximum covered the whole of Canada and the northern states of the USA. Continental sheets submerged all but the highest mountain ranges. This is the situation in Antarctica today. Elsewhere, regions of alpine glaciation, such as the Scottish Highlands and the Lake District, have at various times been overwhelmed by continental ice sheets. Some features, such as smooth abraded slopes, are evidence of the erosive power of ice sheets.

In many glaciated uplands, major cols have been breached by continental ice. The Lairig Ghru in the Cairngorms (Photograph 3.9) is a well-known example of glacial breaching. However, the main effect of ice sheets in glaciated uplands was to produce smooth, rounded slopes, which contrast with the steep, craggy slopes of more recent alpine glaciation (see Photograph 3.8 on page 119). In many cases, cold-based ice sheets, frozen to the bedrock, protected upland surfaces.

The most extensive effects of continental ice sheets are seen in ancient **shield areas** of Canada and Scandinavia. Thousands of lakes and valleys, carved out of weak or fractured rocks, stud these areas. Their orientation often follows the direction of ice flow for hundreds of kilometres. Roches moutonnées, with smooth abraded surfaces, are also widespread. Together with small lakes, they produce distinctive **knock-and-lochan** scenery. In northwest Scotland, the pre-Cambrian Lewisian gneiss has been eroded by ice sheets into classic knock-and-lochan landscapes (Photograph 3.10).

Photograph 3.9
The Lairig Ghru —
an example of
glacial breaching

Photograph 3.10
Knock-and-lochan
topography on
Lewisian gneiss,
Assynt, northwest
Scotland

Depositional landforms created by valley and outlet glaciers

Rock debris transported by valley and outlet glaciers comes from two sources:
➤ quarrying and abrasion at the base and margins of the glacier
➤ mass movements (e.g. rock avalanching) and frost weathering of rock particles from surrounding valley slopes

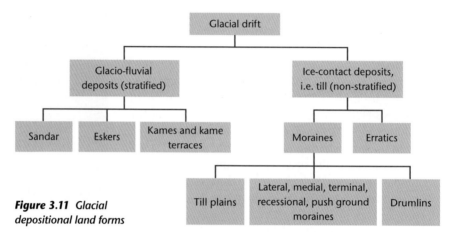

Figure 3.11 Glacial depositional land forms

Much of the moraine is transported to the snout of the glacier by the continual forward movement of the ice. Moraine is unsorted. In other words, it comprises a random mix of particles ranging in size from clay to large boulders. If the snout remains stationary for long periods, significant **terminal moraines** may develop, and extend across the valley. Glaciers retreating intermittently leave behind a series of smaller **recessional moraines** (Figure 3.11).

Push moraines form when glaciers recede and leave behind a terminal moraine. If the glacier then advances it pushes the moraine forward. As glaciers advance and retreat this process may be repeated many times. Moraines deposited by moving ice have a fabric of stones whose long axes are oriented in the direction of ice movement (e.g. lodgement till). Where moraines form from melting ice, the long axes of stones show no preferred orietation (e.g. ablation till).

Rock debris carried in a narrow belt along the edge of a glacier and derived from the adjacent valley slopes is known as **lateral moraine**. On deglaciation, lateral moraines accumulate along the valley side where they form irregular mounds, ridges and low hills. When two glaciers meet, two lateral moraines merge to form a central or **medial moraine** on the glacier surface. Ground moraine is glacial till deposited beneath a melting glacier (Figure 3.12).

Figure 3.12 Types of moraine

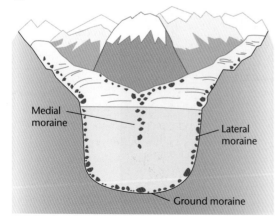

Medial moraine

Lateral moraine

Ground moraine

Michael Raw

Photograph 3.11
Granite erratic resting on limestone, Orton, Cumbria

Glaciers (especially ice sheets) often transport large boulders from their source regions and deposit them elsewhere, sometimes hundreds of kilometres away. These boulders, whose composition is different from the local (country) rock, are called **erratics**. Erratics are useful because they tell us about the direction of ice flows in the past. For example, granite erratics from Shap in Cumbria are found in northeast England and the East Riding of Yorkshire. They prove that ice streamed east and southeast across the Pennines during the last ice age (Photograph 3.11).

Ice sheets and depositional landforms

Ice sheets produce a variety of glacial and glacio-fluvial depositional landforms (Figure 3.13). These landforms are on a larger scale and occupy much more extensive areas than those associated with valley glaciers.

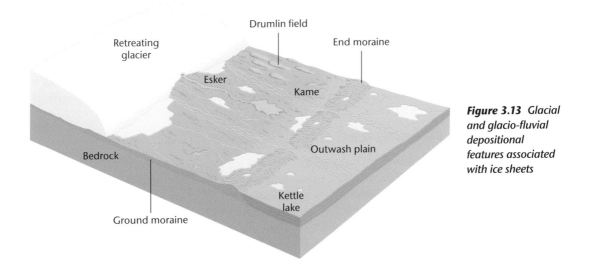

Figure 3.13 *Glacial and glacio-fluvial depositional features associated with ice sheets*

Alan Young

Photograph 3.12
Risebrigg Hill near Skipton is a drumlin, lying within a swarm of drumlins known as the Hills of Elslack

Low, rounded hills known as **drumlins**, are the most impressive landforms deposited by ice sheets (Photograph 3.12). In cross-section they resemble the bowl of an inverted spoon; in plan they are egg-shaped. The long axis is oriented in the direction of ice flow, with the blunter, steeper end or stoss facing upstream and the narrower **tail** downstream. Drumlin fields are widespread in northern England, with concentrations or 'swarms' in the Vale of Eden and around Kendal and Skipton.

The streamlined form of drumlins suggests moulding by fast-moving ice. To this extent they could be seen as erosional rather than depositional features. However, they consist of glacial deposits — mainly till — though some drumlins comprise stratified sediments originally laid down by meltwater. Drumlins are large-scale features, typically 50 m high and over half a kilometre long. Clearly landforms on this scale can only have been formed beneath continental ice sheets.

Gently undulating sheets of boulder clay laid down over vast areas by melting ice sheets form **till plains**. **Kettle holes**, filled with shallow lakes, stud the surface of many till plains. They formed during deglaciation. As stranded blocks of moraine-covered ice melted, subsidence created thousands of small depressions.

Box 3.5 Ice streams and drumlin formation

Scientists first recorded a drumlin forming beneath a glacier in 2007. The observed drumlin was 2 km below the surface of the Rutford ice stream, which drains part of the West Antarctica ice sheet. Ice streams are huge fast-moving 'rivers' of ice embedded within continental ice sheets. The Rutford ice stream is 150 km long, 25 km wide and 2–3 km thick. Ice movement is up to 1 m a day. This research (a) confirmed that drumlins are associated with fast-moving ice, and (b) found that they grow rapidly; in this example, ten times faster than expected.

Glacio-fluvial depositional landforms

Glacio-fluvial landforms are distinguishable from ice-contact features because they comprise sediment such as clay, sand and gravel that is layered or stratified. This is a clear signature that they were deposited by meltwater.

Meltwater is an important agent of sediment transport and deposition in warm-based glaciers and during phases of climate warming and deglaciation. It flows on the surface of glaciers (supraglacial), in tunnels within glaciers (englacial), at the base of the glaciers (subglacial) and beyond the ice front (proglacial).

Meltwater streams often have high energy and the capacity to transport large sediment loads. Typically their discharge is highest in late spring and summer when ablation reaches a maximum. Discharge also fluctuates daily, reaching a peak in mid-afternoon, and a minimum at night when temperatures often drop below freezing. Both alpine glaciers and continental ice sheets are responsible for a range of similar glacio-fluvial landforms.

Eskers

Eskers are long, sinuous ridges of sand and gravel, which can snake across the landscape for several kilometres. They vary in height from a few metres to several tens of metres. Formed from deposits laid down in ice-walled tunnels, either englacially or subglacially, they represent the bedloads of ancient meltwater streams. They are found close to the ice margins and formed during periods of retreat and stagnation.

Kames

Kames are conical, flat-topped hills which may reach 20–30 m in height. They are made from water-laid sands and gravels that were washed into holes, crevasses and depressions. In central Sweden, where they are called *ås*, kames provided attractive dry sites for village settlement. Kames develop in association with melting ice and often occur alongside kettles to form 'kame-and-kettle' topography (Figure 3.14).

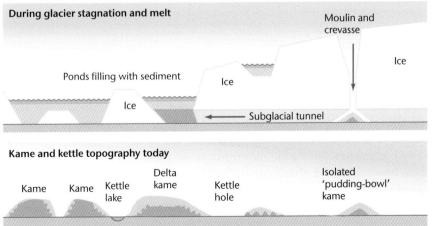

Figure 3.14
The formation of kame-and-kettle topography

Kame terraces

Kame terraces are flat-topped ridges located along the sides of glacial valleys. They form when a marginal lake, between a glacier and the valley side, is infilled with sediment from meltwater streams. Typically, the sediment comprises well-bedded and sorted sand and gravel.

Outwash plains (sandar)

Outwash plains or sandar (singular sandur) extend across areas of low relief beyond the margins of ice sheets and glaciers (Photograph 3.13). Fed by powerful braided streams, they consist of layers of sand and coarse gravel. The sandar in southern Iceland are actively prograding the coastline, extending it outwards into the North Atlantic. Today the distal end of the sandar are up to 20 km from the ice front. Iceland's dynamic sandar are due partly to volcanism and periodic jökulhlaups, when subglacial volcanoes erupt and cause catastrophic floods. The 1996 jökulhlaup delivered huge quantities of coarse sediment to the Skeið arársandur, raising its average elevation by 22 cm.

***Photograph 3.13**
Sandar, southern
Iceland*

Michael Raw

Case study   Glacio-fluvial erosional landforms

Glacial meltwater creates erosional as well as depositional landforms. **Overflow channels** are the most spectacular landforms carved by meltwater.

The North York Moors has several overflow channels thought to have been cut towards the end of the last glacial period. The largest is Newtondale (Photograph 3.14). Fifteen kilometres long and around 80 m deep, its peak flow was around 10 000 cumecs — not far short of the current maximum discharge of the River Rhine on the Dutch–German border.

How could a small area like the North York Moors sustain such a high discharge? The theory is that the North York Moors was surrounded by ice sheets in the last glacial period. As the climate warmed, meltwater flowing east down Eskdale and neighbouring valleys was blocked by ice. The result was a glacier-dammed lake. Its water level rose until it eventually spilled south over the lowest col (around 200 m above sea level) to glacial Lake Pickering (Figure 3.15). In the process, the huge volumes of meltwater cut the Newtondale overflow channel.

Photograph 3.14 *Newtondale: a glacial overflow channel incised into the North York Moors plateau*

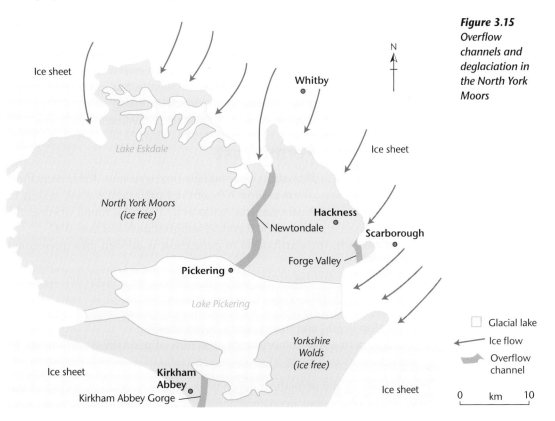

Figure 3.15
Overflow channels and deglaciation in the North York Moors

Glaciers also prevented the waters of Lake Pickering draining to the North Sea. As a result, it too overflowed at the lowest point in the surrounding hills, cutting the Kirkham Abbey Gorge (Figure 3.15). In this way, the drainage of the River Derwent was completely reversed. Instead of flowing east to the North Sea as it did in pre-glacial times, it now flowed southwest through the Kirkham Abbey Gorge to join the River Ouse near Selby.

Finally, the headwater tributaries of the modern River Derwent in the North York Moors were also diverted. With its route to the sea at Scarborough obstructed by North Sea ice, it formed a temporary lake around Hackness. This eventually drained south into Lake Pickering through the newly carved Forge Valley overflow channel.

Periglacial environments

Table 3.2 Climate at Godthaab, Greenland (64°N, 52°E)

Periglacial environments are high-latitude and/or high-altitude regions not covered by glaciers, where temperatures are so low that the ground is permanently frozen. In high latitudes, periglacial areas generally lie equatorwards of the polar ice caps. Periglacial environments also occur in lower latitudes in mountain ranges such as the Andes and the Rockies.

Month	Average temp. (°C)		Average ppt (mm)
	Min	Max	
Jan	−12	−7	36
Feb	−13	−7	43
Mar	−11	−4	41
April	−7	−1	31
May	−2	4	43
June	1	8	36
July	3	11	56
Aug	3	11	79
Sept	1	6	84
Oct	−3	2	64
Nov	−7	−2	48
Dec	−10	−5	38

Godthaab's temperatures (Table 3.2) are typical of much of the periglacial zone: a warmest month with a mean temperature below 10°C (the 10°C isotherm of the warmest month defines the treeline in the northern hemisphere); and a mean annual temperature of −1.7°C. But compared with the continental interior of Canada and Siberia, Godthaab's climate is far from extreme. Not only are its temperatures relatively moderate, but its coastal location boosts mean annual precipitation to nearly 600 mm — more than twice the amount in continental locations.

Permafrost

Permafrost is perennially frozen ground. Today permafrost covers around 20% of the Earth's land surface, mainly in Russia, Canada, Alaska and China. It is found wherever the mean annual ground temperature is less than 0°C.

Geographically, the distribution of permafrost is divided into three zones (Figure 3.16):

➤ Continuous permafrost occurs where the mean annual temperature at a depth of 10–15 m is below −5°C.
➤ Discontinuous permafrost occurs where temperatures are higher (−5 to −1.5°C at 10–15 m depth) and there is more surface thawing.
➤ Sporadic permafrost comprises small islands of permafrost surrounded by extensive unfrozen areas.

The thickness of the permafrost depends on climate, vegetation cover and soil types. In the continuous permafrost zone, it is commonly 300–600 m thick; in

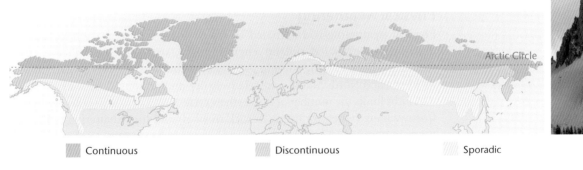

Arctic Circle

▨ Continuous   ▨ Discontinuous   ▨ Sporadic

Figure 3.16
The distribution of permafrost in the northern hemisphere

northern Siberia the permafrost reaches depths of 1500 m. As ground temperatures increase, the permafrost gradually thins. In the sporadic zone, the permafrost is usually less than 30 m deep.

Overlying the permafrost is a shallow surface layer (0.6–4 m deep) that thaws in summer. This is the **active layer**. It lies above the frost table, which marks the upper limit of permanently frozen ground. Areas within the permafrost that remain unfrozen are known as **taliks**.

Ground ice

Bodies of clear ice in permanently frozen ground are known as **ground ice**. Ground ice occurs in a number of forms. It may occupy pores between rock particles in the regolith or it may be sharply segregated into ice lenses and ice wedges below the surface. Ground ice occurs when (a) meltwater freezes at the surface (and is later buried) or in the ground, and (b) when water already held in sediments freezes. As ice crystals develop they attract surrounding liquid water which leads to the segregation of clear ice (Photograph 3.15).

W K Fletcher/SPL

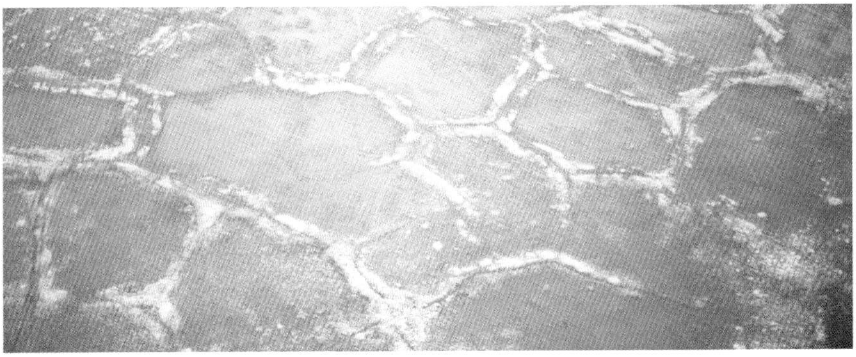

Photograph 3.15
Patterned ground, formed by frost cracking and segregated ice

Periglacial processes

The main geomorphological processes operating in periglacial environments are:
➤ physical weathering
➤ mass movement
➤ nivation
➤ river erosion, transport and deposition

None of these processes is unique to the periglacial zone.

Physical weathering

Physical weathering is dominated by freeze–thaw, a process we have already described in glaciated upland environments (see page 108). Freeze–thaw weathering has a variable effect in periglacial environments. Continental climates in Siberia and North America are relatively dry, and prolonged freezing over 7 or 8 months limits the number of freeze–thaw cycles. However, there is no doubt that frost wedging (when ice forms in rock crevices) and frost shattering (when ice forms in porous rock) are important in shaping the landscape.

Mass movement

Gelifluction is the slow flowing from higher to lower ground of masses of waste saturated with water. It occurs in summer on slopes where the saturated active layer rests above permafrost. In addition to the flow process, frost creep assists gelifluction (Figure 3.17). During freeze-thaw cycles, soil particles on freezing are raised at right angles to the sloping ground surface, but fall back more nearly vertical under the influence of gravity when the ice thaws. The result is a small downslope movement of soil particles with each cycle. Gelifluction is widespread in periglacial environments and operates on the gentlest of slopes. Solifluction is a similar flow of saturated regolith, but unlike gelifluction, solifluction occurs in the absence of permafrost.

Box 3.6 Gelifluction

There are three types of movement in solifluction (Figure 3.17):
- Potential frost creep (*PFC*) is the horizontal movement associated with the movement *P1* to *P2* caused by the freezing and heaving of the ground. Because heave takes place at right angles to the slope, the amount of *PFC* will increase in direct proportion to slope angle.
- Gelifluction (*G*) is the second major component of horizontal movement.
- Retrograde movement (*R*) is a negative or upslope movement acting in the opposite direction to gelifluction. Usually this movement does not exceed gelifluction.

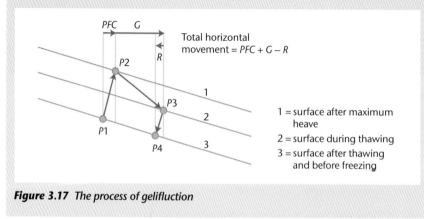

Figure 3.17 The process of gelifluction

Nivation

Nivation is an erosive process that operates under and around snow patches. It includes freeze–thaw, gelifluction and surface wash. Meltwater percolates into rocks beneath the snow patch and causes intense freeze–thaw weathering. The resulting rock debris is removed by gelifluction and surface wash. Nivation creates shallow hollows or basins on upland surfaces. Once formed, nivation hollows are self-generating, trapping snow, and prolonging the action of freeze–thaw, gelifluction and surface wash processes.

River action

Periglacial areas support dense networks of streams that are active during the short arctic summer. Several factors contribute to high peak flows: meltwater from snow and permafrost, sparse vegetation, which limits evapotranspiration and interception, and the impermeability of the frozen ground. In these conditions, streams have high energy levels, and significant erosion and transport potential. As a result, streams are usually braided (see pages 17–18) and flow in broad, flat-floored valleys.

Landforms of periglacial environments
Weathering and landforms

Some periglacial landforms result almost entirely from weathering processes. The principal ones are talus slopes, blockfields and tors.

Talus slopes

Talus slopes consist of coarse, angular rock debris that accumulates at the foot of vertical cliffs or free-faces (Photograph 3.16). The rock particles that form these debris slopes are known as scree.

Talus slopes are a distinctive feature of both modern and relict periglacial environments. Freeze–thaw weathering (see page 110) detaches rock particles from the exposed cliff, which form a new debris slope. This process is also common in glaciated uplands. However, in these areas most rock debris weathered from valley slopes is quickly removed by glaciers, so that talus slopes are poorly developed.

Many talus slopes show a degree of sorting, with particles increasing in size downslope. Two processes explain this. First, larger particles have greater momentum than smaller particles. Thus, when they fall from the cliff face, they tend to roll further. Second, smaller particles are more likely to get trapped in the voids between the scree. In practice, sorting is very variable. Where talus slopes are backed by high cliffs, even small particles have enough energy to reach the foot of the slope. Equally, where the debris slope has almost submerged the free-face, large particles have little momentum and are often left stranded at the top of the slope.

Photograph 3.16
Talus slopes, Dow Crag, Lake District

Between 10 000 and 20 000 years ago, rates of freeze–thaw weathering and talus accumulation in Britain were high. Today, freeze–thaw is less frequent. Indeed, most talus slopes are probably relict features — a legacy of a much colder climate.

Blockfields

On exposed ground with gentle slopes, and where rock joints are widely spaced, freeze–thaw weathering breaks up the surface into large, angular boulders. Without erosion or mass movement, these boulders remain *in situ* to form **blockfields** or **felsenmeer** (Photograph 3.17). Blockfields are common on plateau surfaces in Britain. Good examples are seen above 1000 m on the summits of the Glyders in North Wales, and Ben Macdui in the Cairngorms. These features probably formed during the last glacial period, at times when the plateau summits were free of ice, and glaciers were confined to adjacent valleys.

Michael Raw

Photograph 3.17
Blockfield comprising massive gritstone boulders

Tors

Tors are steep-sided, upstanding rock masses, often sited on isolated plateaux, ridges and on the top of valley slopes (Photograph 3.18). Usually formed from granite or gritstone, they have well-developed vertical and horizontal jointing. Boulders, weathered from the tors by frost action, often form extensive **clitter** slopes around the base of tors.

There are several theories explaining the origin of tors. Most involve periglacial processes.
➤ Granite (or a similar type of rock) is attacked below the surface by hydrolysis, a type of chemical weathering.
➤ Hydrolysis, concentrated where the joints are most dense, 'rots' the granite to produce saprolite (known locally on Dartmoor as 'growan').
➤ Periglacial processes such as gelifluction remove the rotted granite, leaving the more coherent rock standing as tors.
➤ Freeze–thaw dislodges boulders of granite which form clitter at the base of the tor.

Photograph 3.18
A granite tor in the Cairngorms

Mass movements and landforms

Gelifluction and solifluction movements give rise to a number of subtle, if unspectacular, landforms such as solifluction sheets, lobes and terraces.

Gelifluction/solifluction sheets

Extensive sheets of regolith, transported by gelifluction and solifluction, produce uniform expanses of smooth terrain, often at angles as low as 1–3°. The downslope edges of these sheets often have a lobate form backed by vegetation-covered risers just a few centimetres high (Photograph 3.19). Gelifluction and solifluction sheets are capable of transporting large boulders known as **ploughing blocks** (Photograph 3.20). They are rafted in the active layer with their undersides resting on or near the permafrost table.

Photograph 3.19 Solifluction sheet and lobes developed on impermeable shale (right-hand side of valley); the valley picks out a fault line and, to the left, on permeable limestone rocks, solifluction has been less effective

Photograph 3.20 A gritstone ploughing block — the boulder was 'rafted' to its present position by gelifluction during periglacial conditions that followed the last ice age

Gelifluction/solifluction terraces and lobes

Terraces are stepped, tread-like slopes. Vertical turf-covered risers range from 2–3 m to just a few centimetres in height. Each riser is separated by low-angled treads. Some terraces are marked by concentrations of stones and boulders at their downslope ends. The stones — known as **stone garlands** — are often tilted upwards and appear to be emerging from the terrace. **Stone-banked terraces** indicate that sub-surface rates of mass movement are greater than surface rates. **Turf-banked terraces** suggest the opposite (Photographs 3.21 and 3.22).

Lobes tend to follow well-defined linear paths and suggest that gelifluction flow is greater than frost creep. Locations immediately below snow patches favour the development of lobes.

Michael Raw

Photograph 3.21 *Stone-banked terrace*

Michael Raw

Photograph 3.22 *Turf-banked terrace*

Asymmetric valleys

In cross-section, many valleys in periglacial areas are asymmetric (Photograph 3.23). This could be due to either (a) one slope being steepened or (b) one slope undergoing decline. Either way, aspect (the direction in which a slope faces) has an important role.

One possible explanation of asymmetric valleys is outlined below:

➤ South-facing slopes receive more solar radiation than north-facing slopes.

➤ North-facing slopes remain shaded and frozen for large parts of the year; south-facing slopes experience more frequent daytime thawing and night-time freezing.

➤ Freeze–thaw weathering and solifluction are more active on warmer, south-facing slopes. These processes will lower slope angles.

➤ Lobes of soliflucted debris from south-facing slopes extend into the valley and divert meltwater streams against the north-facing valley slope. This leads to undercutting and slope steepening (Figure 3.18).

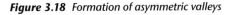

South ..... North

Original valley cross section

Sun's rays

Valley cross-section modified by frost action

(1) Reduced exposure to insolation
(2) Greater snow accumulation on north-facing slope

Ground permanently frozen
↓
No frost action or solifluction

Snow lingers providing continual source of meltwater ↓

Snow forms insulation against air temperature changes ↓

No frost action

(1) Increased exposure to insolation
(2) Less snow accumulation on south-facing slope

Ground thaws during day in summer
↓
Frost action and solifluction

Snow quickly thaws and slope dries out
↓
No solifluction

Ground not protected by insulating snow cover
↓
Frost action

Figure 3.18 *Formation of asymmetric valleys*

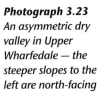

Michael Raw

Photograph 3.23
An asymmetric dry valley in Upper Wharfedale — the steeper slopes to the left are north-facing

Ground ice and landforms
Patterned ground

Intense freezing and thawing in periglacial climates sorts surface rock particles into a variety of geometric patterns (Figure 3.19). This so-called patterned ground includes polygons, circles, nets and stripes (Photograph 3.24).

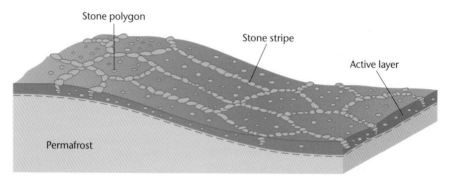

Figure 3.19 Types of patterned ground

Patterned ground results from frost cracking of the surface, the formation of ice wedges in these cracks, and frost heave. Frost cracking is caused by contraction of the ground at sub-zero temperatures. The fractures that form are often polygonal in plan. Frost heave is the vertical movement of the ground surface and rock particles in the active layer.

The following factors also influence patterned ground: thickness of the active layer, vegetation cover and slope angle. However, for patterned ground to develop in the first place there must be a range of particle sizes that can be sorted by frost action.

Photograph 3.24 Stone stripes on Skiddaw, Cumbria

Parallel stone stripes

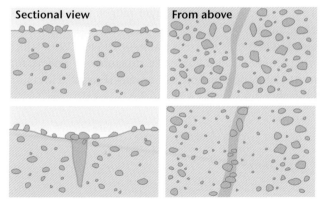

Sectional view	From above	

Cracking of ground occurs in vegetation-free, windswept areas without snow; intense frost activity occurs and sediment starts to fill cracks in the summer.

The snow-free ground between the sediment-filled cracks is affected by frost heave, which raises the surface. The removal of the finer material into the cracks has made the larger sediments unstable. These move by gravity towards the crack depressions, producing stone polygons.

Figure 3.20 The formation of stone polygons

In Iceland, the retreat of the Myrdalsjökull over the past 50 years has exposed new land surfaces in Maelifellssandur. Since the mid-1980s, stone polygons have developed on these surfaces. First the surface suffered frost cracking (up to 1–3 cm wide). The cracks, up to 20 cm deep and enclosing areas of 20 to 40 m^2, were quickly filled with gravel. Frost heave occurs within the polygons when fine, water-saturated particles freeze, raising the surface and causing larger particles to roll towards the infilled cracks (Figure 3.20).

On sloping surfaces, stone polygons are replaced by sorted stone stripes (Photograph 3.24). This type of patterned ground can be seen above 700 m in the Lake District, after short periods of intense freezing.

Pingos

Pingos are isolated dome-shaped hills that rise abruptly from alluvial plains in the permafrost zone (Photograph 3.25). They range in height from 2m to 50m and

Photograph 3.25 Aerial view of a pingo in tundra landscape, northwest Canada

Paolo Koch/SPL

may be up to 300 m in diameter. Some of the larger pingos have crater-like depressions around their summits.

Pingos owe their shape to enormous ice cores (talik — see page 129), which have pushed the overlying sediments into dome-like structures. To understand how pingos form, we need to know how the core ice becomes segregated into such large masses. There are two theories (Figures 3.21 and 3.22).

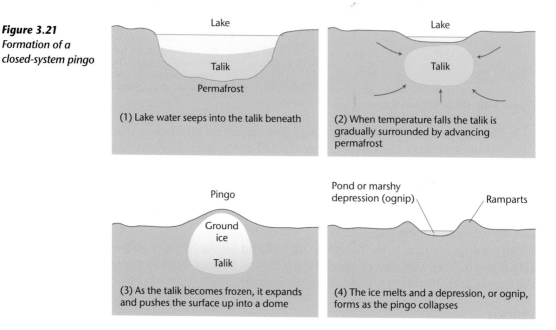

Figure 3.21
Formation of a closed-system pingo

Lake

Talik

Permafrost

(1) Lake water seeps into the talik beneath

Lake

Talik

(2) When temperature falls the talik is gradually surrounded by advancing permafrost

Pingo

Ground ice

Talik

(3) As the talik becomes frozen, it expands and pushes the surface up into a dome

Pond or marshy depression (ognip) Ramparts

(4) The ice melts and a depression, or ognip, forms as the pingo collapses

The 'closed system' theory suggests that pingos are preceded by shallow lakes. If a lake is infilled with sediment the underlying ground loses its insulation and allows the permafrost to advance on all sides. Water trapped in the lake sediments eventually freezes and the resulting expansion pushes the overlying sediments into a dome. Most of the pingos in the Mackenzie Delta in northern Canada fit this theory.

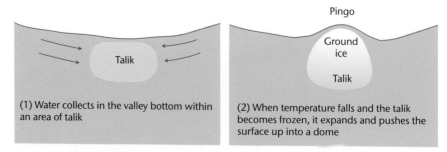

Figure 3.22
Formation of an open-system pingo

Talik

(1) Water collects in the valley bottom within an area of talik

Pingo

Ground ice

Talik

(2) When temperature falls and the talik becomes frozen, it expands and pushes the surface up into a dome

The 'open system' theory assumes that groundwater either in a talik or in the active layer, is trapped by freezing. Under pressure from the advance of the permafrost, water migrates until it forces its way to the surface, freezes and bulges the overlying sediments into a dome.

Thermokarst

Thermokarst is a type of landscape formed by the melting of ground ice, followed by surface subsidence. It results in the formation of pits, hollows and other depressions which are often filled with water (thermokarst lakes).

Thermokarst may develop over hundreds of square kilometres and is particularly common on the floodplains of Siberian rivers such as the Lena and Yenisey. It is found either where there are large amounts of ground ice or where unconsolidated sediments (e.g. sand, silt and alluvium) have a high ice content.

Climate change and global warming is likely to extend the area of thermokarst in future. Although most thermokarst forms naturally, at a local scale human activity can have a significant impact. For example, removal of the vegetation cover in the tundra alters the thermal balance at the surface, which may result in rapid melting of the permafrost.

Case study The cold environment of the Cairngorm plateau

The Cairngorm plateau in northeast Scotland supports a unique arctic–alpine ecosystem (Figure 3.23). It is the largest continuous tract of mountain above 1000 m in the British Isles. It is a high plateau, ringed by steep

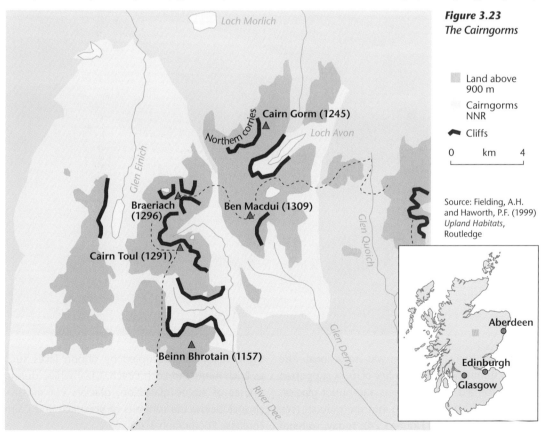

Figure 3.23
The Cairngorms

Land above 900 m

Cairngorms NNR

Cliffs

0   km   4

Source: Fielding, A.H. and Haworth, P.F. (1999) *Upland Habitats*, Routledge

Photograph 3.26
*Aerial view of the
Cairngorm plateau*

cliffs, and shows the effects of both continental, alpine glaciation (Photograph 3.26) and periglaciation.

Twenty thousand years ago, at the height of the last glacial period, a vast ice sheet covered Scotland, and froze to the bedrock of the plateau. It caused little erosion, protecting the older, rounded pre-glacial surfaces, and even leaving delicate tors intact (see Photograph 3.18 on page 133).

Photograph 3.27
*U-shaped valley in
the Cairngorms*

At other times, glaciation was more local. The plateau summit was variously free of ice or supported its own icefield. Valley glaciers and outlet glaciers carved deep glacial troughs into the plateau (see Photograph 3.27 and Figure 3.24). Today, some of these valleys are occupied by ribbon lakes such as Loch Avon and Loch Finich. Meanwhile, during phases of alpine glaciation, glaciers cut massive cirques below the summits of Braeriach and Cairn Toul (see Photograph 3.28).

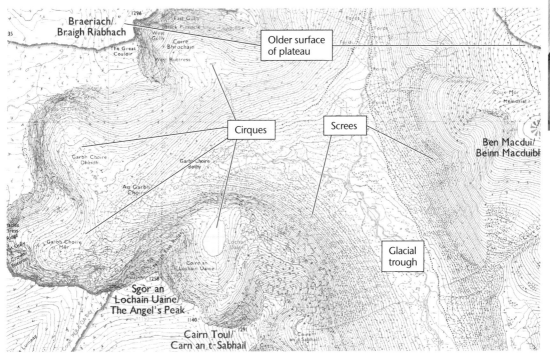

Figure 3.24 *Glacial landscape of the Cairngorm plateau*

Photograph 3.28
A cirque cut into the Cairngorm plateau

Then, 18 000 years ago, as Scotland began to emerge from the deep-freeze, periglacial conditions took hold. Periglacial processes such as freeze–thaw, frost heave and gelifluction created distinctive landforms such as blockfields, patterned ground, screes and ploughing blocks. Even now, on the high plateau, periglacial processes remain active in winter.

Tundra ecosystems

Key ideas

➤ Cold climates are extreme and lead to finely balanced ecosystems, which are easily damaged.

➤ Once damaged, cold environment ecosystems with their specialised flora and fauna, are slow to regenerate.

➤ Ecosystems in cold climates are vulnerable to climate change and human pressure, and are easily degraded.

There are two types of tundra ecosystem: arctic and alpine. Arctic tundra describes the level, wet country, north of the timberline in Eurasia and North America. Alpine tundra, on the other hand, occupies high mountain environments (Photograph 3.29). Both types support many similar plant and animal species.

Photograph 3.29
The treeline and the tundra plateau in the Rocky Mountain National Park, Colorado; the elevation of the tundra plateau is around 3500 m

Michael Raw

Arctic and alpine tundra are harsh environments for plant growth. Plants need to adapt to low temperatures, prolonged snow cover, strong winds, short growing seasons and thin, nutrient-deficient soils. However, there are important environmental differences between arctic and alpine tundra. In alpine environments, day length is less variable, solar radiation is more intense, slopes are steeper and aspect assumes greater significance.

Tundra ecosystems are dominated by low-growing, perennial plants. Apart from dwarf species of willow and birch, the tundra is treeless. Instead, ground-hugging species thrive, such as mosses, lichens and sedges; and woody shrubs such as heather, ling, bilberry, crowberry and mountain avens. Herbaceous flowering plants include species of saxifrage, moss campion, gentians and sorrel.

Arctic and alpine ecosystems have a number of common characteristics. These include:

➤ low biodiversity — few plants have adapted to such extreme environments.

➤ low productivity and low biomass — reflecting the low temperatures, lack of moisture, thin soils and short growing season
➤ low growth rates — these reflect the severe climatic conditions
➤ slow rates of organic decomposition and bacterial decay
➤ short **food webs** and food chain
➤ fragility — damaged vegetation is slow to recover

Specific problems for plant adaptation in the tundra (Table 3.3) include:
➤ short **thermal growing season**. Plant growth only begins when the average daily air temperatures reach 6°C. Thus, much of the tundra has a growing season lasting just one or two months. This forces plants to complete their life cycles (i.e. growth, flowering, fruiting and fruit dispersal) in a very short time. Net primary production is low. Averaged over the year it is around 0.01–0.66 $g\,m^{-2}\,day^{-1}$.
➤ limits to growth set by the **hydrological growing season**. Even if air temperatures are high enough for growth, water, frozen in the soil, may be unavailable.
➤ strong winds. There is little protection from the wind in the treeless tundra. Strong winds cause physical damage to plants and increase moisture loss through transpiration.

Table 3.3 *Plant adaptations to the tundra environment*

Environmental problem	Adaptations
Short thermal growing season	Most plants are perennial. The short growing season is unsuitable for most annuals. Perennials store food in tubers and rhizomes during the summer, which allows rapid growth in the spring in the following year.
	Some plants form flower buds a year in advance so as not to waste time in the growing season (e.g. alpine forget-me-not).
	Many plants are evergreen so have no need to grow new leaves before photosynthesis can take place.
Low temperatures	Many plants have dark leaves, which are more effective in absorbing insolation and raising their temperature.
	Many plants create their own microclimates by forming cushions, tussocks and rosettes (e.g. moss campion). Temperatures may be 5–10°C higher within these structures compared with outside. This may lengthen the growing season by 5–10%.
	The parabolic shape of some flowers helps to concentrate insolation on the developing reproductive parts. Other flowers track the sun on its path across the sky (e.g. mountain avens).
Strong winds	Low-growing (prostrate) habit of most plants offers minimal resistance to the wind (e.g. alpine willow).
	Growth in tussocks and cushions reduces wind speed by 99%.
	Many plants have waxy or leathery leaves, which helps to reduce moisture loss through transpiration.
Snow cover	Some plants can complete their life cycles in a few weeks after they emerge from the snow. Food stores in tubers and rhizomes mean that plants can survive buried in the snow for 2 or more years.

➤ poor drainage, especially in the permafrost zone. Although the active layer thaws in the summer, the sub-soil remains frozen and creates waterlogged conditions.

➤ poor soils. Well-drained soils are strongly **leached**, acidic and deficient in humus and mineral nutrients (especially nitrogen). There is minimal weathering of minerals in the soil to provide nutrients.

➤ slow recycling of nutrients. Low temperatures and waterlogged conditions inhibit bacterial activity and decomposition.

➤ slow rates of plant growth. This reflects limitations imposed by climate, drainage and soils.

➤ frost heave and solifluction. These disrupt plant growth.

Saxifrage is perennial and plants can live for many years

The plant grows on shallow soils, even on bare rock outcrops

The leaves are covered in dense hairs, which help the plant to retain heat

It grows in low dense clumps — this reduces wind resistance and helps the plant to warm up in spring

The plant can self pollinate — important if few pollinating insects are around in the early spring

Purple saxifrage is an arctic–alpine, distributed both in the arctic tundra and high mountains in lower altitudes

It is adapted to a short growing season — the plant flowers in the early spring (this photo was taken in northern England in March)

Michael Raw

Photograph 3.30
Purple saxifrage: an arctic–alpine species

Tundra food webs

With low primary production, arctic–alpine ecosystems support animal populations of low density. Apart from mosquitoes, insects are not present in large numbers, and the climate is too cold for amphibians and reptiles. Food chains are short and the lack of biodiversity, with just one or two species occupying each ecological niche, makes ecosystems fragile and susceptible to environmental change (Figure 3.25).

Even so, large populations of herbivores, such as the barren ground caribou in northern Canada, migrate to the arctic tundra during the short summer to calve and take advantage of the seasonal glut of food. They are followed by the ecosystem's top predator: the timber wolf. Smaller herbivores include rodents such as arctic hares, lemmings and voles. They are the principal prey species for arctic foxes, snowy owls and other raptors.

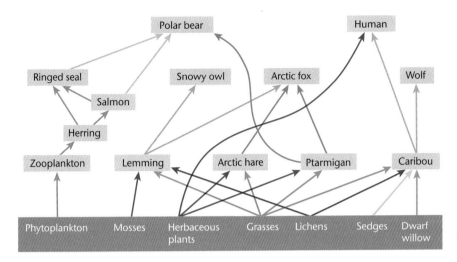

Figure 3.25 *Arctic tundra food web*

Some mammals in arctic–alpine environments in the autumn acquire white coloration as camouflage against the snow. Animals that adopt this habit include ptarmigan (a large grouse-like bird), stoats, arctic hares and arctic foxes.

A feature of arctic–alpine animal populations is their 'boom and bust' character. Cyclic changes in food availability lead to population explosions of small rodents during years of glut, and a corresponding rise in the number of predators. Years of scarcity, however, produce spectacular population crashes of both prey and predator species.

Animal adaptations to the seasonality of climate and low winter temperatures include migration. Many birds that breed in the arctic tundra, such as geese and waders, spend the winter in middle latitudes. Barren ground caribou migrate south to the boreal coniferous forest in winter. But other mammals such as musk oxen and arctic foxes, protected by thick fur, remain in the tundra throughout the winter.

Conflict in an arctic wilderness

Key ideas

➤ Cold environments provide opportunities and challenges for development.

➤ Opportunities include resource exploitation, and recreation and leisure.

➤ Challenges include environmental constraints and impacts, remoteness, high development costs and conflicts with indigenous people.

➤ Managing cold environments is often a balance between socio-economic needs and environmental needs.

➤ Careful management is needed to ensure that fragile, cold environments are not exploited for short-term gains, and that development is sustainable.

Ron Niebrugge/Alamy

Photograph 3.31 *Arctic tundra landscape of the North Slope, Alaska*

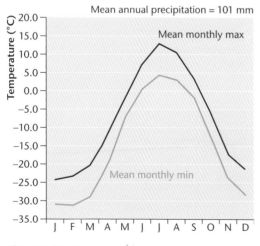

Mean annual precipitation = 101 mm

Mean monthly max

Mean monthly min

J F M A M J J A S O N D

Figure 3.26 *Mean monthly temperatures at Prudhoe Bay*

Physical environment

The coastal plain of northern Alaska, stretching from the Brooks Range to the Arctic Ocean, is known as the North Slope (see Figure 3.27 on page 149). This vast region, covering an area the size of the UK, lies in the zone of continuous permafrost. The permafrost impedes drainage and creates thousands of lakes and ponds that stud the North Slope. Most rivers originate in the Brooks Range and flow northwards across the plain to the Arctic Ocean. In this region of low relief, the most prominent landforms are river terraces, stone polygons and occasional pingos (Photograph 3.31).

The North Slope lies between latitudes 65° and 70° north. In these latitudes the climate is extreme. Winters are long, dry and cold and last from October to late May: summers are short, moist and cool (Figure 3.26). With only 125–375 mm of precipitation, the North Slope is essentially a cold desert. Day length varies from continuous darkness in mid-winter to continuous daylight in mid-summer.

The harsh climatic conditions, together with frost heave, poor drainage and the short growing season, limit primary production and plant biodiversity. There are just three main types of **plant associations**:

➤ wetlands, dominated by grasses, sedges, and rushes
➤ marsh grasses on the arctic coastal plain
➤ cotton sedge, lichens, mosses, heathers, dwarf birch and mats of mountain avens in the drier habitats

With few plant-eating insects, 20% of plant growth is consumed by mammals. **Nutrient cycles** operate on a very tight budget. About 80% of the annual plant tissue growth returns to the soil each year where it is decomposed by microorganisms and fungi.

Low biodiversity is equally a feature of animal populations (there are, for example, only five species of mammal that are **endemic** to the area). However, large migrations of birds and caribou herds swell animal populations during the short summer.

Food webs are short and highly interconnected. With food sources in limited supply, animals have not evolved the levels of specialisation found in tropical and temperate food webs. Animals such arctic foxes and wolves have varied and flexible diets which include fruit, insects and worms as well as mammals. Tertiary consumers, such as wolves and wolverines, depend on three basic primary consumers of vegetation: small rodents such as voles and lemmings; ground squirrels; and caribou. Being made up of so few species the North Slope ecosystem is both unstable and fragile, with populations of predators and prey undergoing dramatic shifts and cycles.

The total human population of the North Slope is only 7500. Most people belong either to the indigenous Inupiat and Gwich'in tribes, or are oil workers, employed by transnational oil corporations such as Exxon, Mobil and BP.

Case study **The oil industry and conflict in Alaska**

The challenge of economic development

Economic development in the Alaskan tundra is highly controversial. The problem is to find ways of ensuring that exploitation of the region's natural resources does no lasting damage to the environment. This goal is especially difficult because the tundra is a fragile ecosystem. For instance lichen, which grows at a rate of only 1–2 mm a year, may take 40 years to recover from grazing by a passing herd of caribou! Meanwhile, even small oil spills may persist in the environment for 30 years.

In spite of these concerns, since the late 1960s, large-scale development of the North Slope's oil and gas reserves has occurred. More than 4300 oil and gas exploration wells have been drilled, and Prudhoe Bay is North America's largest oilfield. A complex infrastructure of pipelines, pumping stations, roads and bridges supports the oil and gas industry.

Development in the tundra has posed significant challenges. Oil and gas companies have to cope with sub-zero temperatures for 8 months of the year, and averages of below −30°C in January and February. Exploration can only take place in winter when the ground is frozen. In summer, when the active layer thaws out, the ground becomes a morass, unable to support heavy machinery.

The key to sustainable development is to prevent the permafrost from melting. To this end, it is vital to keep the vegetation cover, which provides an insulating layer, intact. In addition, the permafrost must be protected from heat generated by buildings and pipelines. This is usually done in one of two ways: by elevating structures on piles driven deep into the permafrost; and by laying pads of gravel on the permafrost.

Despite precautions, the oil and gas industry have had an adverse effect on the ecosystem of the North Slope.

- The Trans-Alaskan Pipeline System (TAPS) has disrupted migration patterns of caribou herds.
- Oil spillages have degraded habitats. The worst and most recent incident was in February 2006.
- Seismic exploration disturbs animals both on the tundra and in nearshore waters in the Arctic Ocean.
- Gravel extraction from river beds has had damaging effects on fish populations and aquatic environments.
- Anthropogenic food sources around oil and gas installations have increased populations of predators such as arctic foxes, ravens and gulls, which prey on nesting birds.
- The disposal of solid wastes has caused problems because of (a) the difficulty of constructing sanitary landfill sites on permafrost, and (b) low temperatures that slow down rates of organic decomposition.

Oil exploration in the Arctic National Wildlife Refuge

The Arctic National Wildlife Refuge (ANWR) is a huge wilderness area covering nearly 80 000 km² of northern Alaska (Figure 3.27). It has protected status and is managed by the US Fish and Wildlife Service. Most of the Refuge is on federal land (i.e. owned by the US government).

Designated in 1980, the ANWR is an almost pristine ecosystem with remarkable biodiversity. Most spectacular are the 130 000 caribou that form the Porcupine herd. The refuge is home to: 45 mammal species, including wolves, wolverines, musk oxen, foxes, polar bears and grizzly bears; 135 species of migratory bird that breed or feed there; and 45 species of fish. The biological importance of the ANWR relates to its intense productivity during the short arctic summer. Many species arrive or awake from dormancy to take advantage of this richness, and leave or become dormant during the rest of the year.

The only two significant settlements in the ANWR are villages occupied by native people. In the north, the coastal village of Kaktovik is home to the Inuit Inupiaq tribe; in the south the native Indian Gwich'in are based in Arctic Village. Both groups continue to practise their traditional subsistence economies. The Inupiaq rely on marine ecosystems and hunting bowhead whales, seals and walrus. The Gwich'in ('people of the caribou') depend on the caribou herds, both economically and culturally (Photograph 3.32).

At the time of designation, Area 1002 was not given the same protection as the rest of the ANWR (Figure 3.27). This area, adjacent to the Prudhoe Bay, was thought to contain substantial reserves of oil (5–16 billion barrels) and gas. Exploration later confirmed this. In 2005, the US Senate gave approval for exploratory drilling for oil in Area 1002. This decision was the culmination of a long battle between the oil companies and conservationists going back 30 years.

Arco Images/Alamy

Photograph 3.32 *Caribou herds are important, both economically and culturally, to indigenous people*

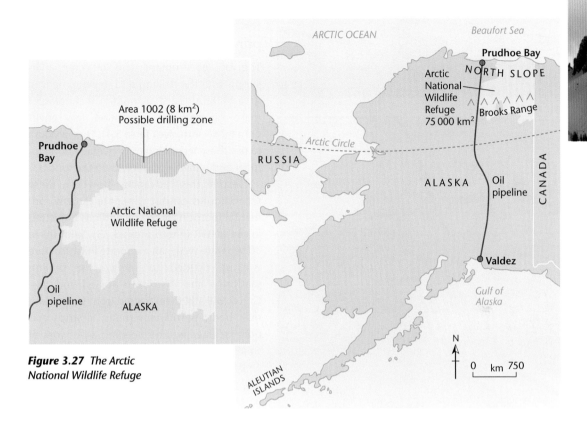

Figure 3.27 *The Arctic National Wildlife Refuge*

Although Area 1002 is less than one-tenth of the total area of the ANWR, it has a crucial role for the caribou herds and the regional ecosystem. The caribou spend the summer in this part of the coastal plain. This is their main calving ground, where they can graze, avoid mosquitoes and escape predators. Oil and gas exploration and development could seriously disrupt the behaviour of the caribou herds.

The exploitation of Area 1002's oil and gas reserves is a key part of the US government's energy policy. The government argues that drilling and development is essential to national interests because it would:

- give greater security of energy supplies, with less reliance on imports from politically unstable regions like the Middle East
- cut imports of oil and gas and therefore boost the country's balance of payments
- maximise use of existing oil and gas infrastructural features such as TAPS

- increase job opportunities in the North Slope region

Conservationists who oppose drilling argue that:

- the tundra ecosystem is more valuable than oil and gas and the ANWR should be off-limits to oil drilling and industrial development
- we have a moral obligation to save wild places like the ANWR for future generations
- the oil and gas from the ANWR would not provide a long-term solution to the US dependence on energy imports and would do little to strengthen energy security
- more investment should be made in alternative energy sources and energy conservation
- the migration and calving of caribou, and the migration of millions of birds, would be severely disrupted
- the subsistence way of life and culture of the Gwich'in Indians would be permanently harmed

Paul Andrew Lawrence/Alamy

Photograph 3.33 *Oil pipelines crossing the tundra at the Prudhoe Bay oilfields*

Reducing the environmental 'footprint' of oil and gas operations

The US government and oil companies supporting the drilling and development in Area 1002 argue that modern technologies make oil and gas extraction less environmentally intrusive (Table 3.4). They propose to use these technologies to manage development and minimise its impact on the tundra.

Despite their advances, however, these technologies cannot eliminate the environmental footprint of the oil and gas industries in the ANWR (Photograph 3.33). With up to 30 separate wells, an elaborate infrastructure will be needed to service the drilling platforms and distribute the oil and gas. Gravel will still be extracted from stream and river beds; permanent roads, airstrips and port facilities will be needed; a network of small pipelines and pumping stations must be provided; and oil spillages will still occur. Yes, compared with the Prudhoe Bay oil and gasfields, the environmental footprint in Area 1002 will be reduced, but it will still be considerable (Table 3.5).

Table 3.4 *New 'environmentally friendly' technologies for oil and gas extraction*

Seismic exploration	Geological sites likely to yield oil and gas can be identified using controlled explosions. This reduces drilling and the building of access roads etc.
Insulated ice pads	Roads and other infrastructural features can be built on new insulated ice pads, thus reducing the risk of melting the permafrost.
More powerful computers can pinpoint oil and gas-bearing geological structures	Fewer exploration wells are needed, which reduces the potential impact on the environment.
Drilling laterally beyond the drilling platform	New drilling techniques allow oil and gas deposits to be accessed several kilometres away from drilling rigs. Thus, less space is needed for drilling rigs. Modern rigs have reduced equipment volume and weight, produce less waste, and increase the proportion of hydrocarbons recovered from each well.

Table 3.5 *Viewpoints of proponents and opponents of drilling in the ANWR*

'It is our judgement...that we can have balanced and carefully regulated oil exploitation and development in the ANWR.'	Arctic Slope Regulation Corporation (Inuit organisation to safeguard drilling rights on their land)
'I am utterly opposed...we can only keep pointing out that this is an international herd of animals (i.e. Porcupine caribou). We have a long tradition of concern where animals cross borders.'	Canada's Minister for the Environment
'I believe we need to open up the ANWR and believe we can do it in an environmentally friendly way.'	George Bush, US President
'It will be at least 10 years before any oil from ANWR would reach the US. It will be developed by international oil companies...and it's possible that much of this oil would not even stay in the US.'	Bart Stupak, Congressman
'Opposition to drilling ANWR borders on being completely irrational. The oil companies would be drilling on a small isolated strip of land that is completely uninhabited...furthermore there is strong support in Alaska for drilling. Even the unions support drilling because it would create jobs.'	Article in *Conservative News and Views* (a right-wing subscription blog based in south California)
'Although the coastal plain is not a national park or formally declared wilderness, that's only a technicality. It's a critical part of the Refuge, which except for the plain has already been granted wilderness protection.'	*Los Angeles Times*
'ANWR can mirror projections of Prudhoe Bay. Dire predictions of environmental disaster advanced by the green lobby never came true.'	P.M. Weyrich, newspaper columnist
'Oil production is compatible with the protection of wildlife and habitat...North Slope caribou herds have remained healthy throughout previous oil development.'	Governor Murkowski (Governer of Alaska)
'The Gwich'in tribe have lived off the caribou for as long as they have existed...they have used caribou meat for food, skin for clothes, bones for tools and jewellery and antlers for spiritual ceremonies. In short, the tribe's entire livelihood would diminish.'	Kelly McNoldy, environmentalist
'We should not sacrifice one of the country's crown jewels for a few months' supply of oil. We can meet our energy needs without destroying our national treasures.'	Jason Pierce, environmentalist
'The 1002 area is the most biologically productive part of the Arctic Refuge for wildlife and is the centre of wildlife activity.'	Final Legislative Environmental Impact Statement (FLEIS)

Cold mountain environments: the Himalaya in Nepal

Cold mountain environments support unique and fragile ecosystems (Box 3.7). These ecosystems are increasingly under pressure, especially in many LEDCs. Conflicts arise between economic development and conservation. Misuse of resources by local people, and by economic activities such as hydro-electric power and tourism, are currently degrading mountain environments in many parts of the world. In this section, we illustrate these problems with a case study of Nepal, and the attempts at sustainable management in the Annapurna region of the Himalaya.

Box 3.7 Mountains as fragile ecosystems

Fragile ecosystems such as high mountains, tundra and deserts are particularly vulnerable to change caused either by environmental shifts or human activity. Any damage may be irreversible, or reversible only over long periods. There are several reasons why mountain ecosystems are fragile:

■ Mountain environments often form 'island' ecosystems, isolated from surrounding lowlands. Changing environmental conditions may result in the extinction of specialised (endemic) plant and animal species.

■ Mountains often support many varied and local ecosystems. This is because rapid changes in altitude compress habitats into short distances.

Although overall biodiversity is high, biodiversity within individual ecosystems is low.

■ Slow rates of soil formation and vegetative growth mean that ecosystems are slow to re-establish stability after change.

■ High degrees of **endemism** and lack of bio-diversity make these ecosystems vulnerable to the introduction of aggressive alien species.

■ Soils that are shallow and often on steep slopes are easily eroded if the vegetation cover is damaged.

■ Lack of biodiversity, with simple food webs, means that there are fewer negative feedback loops to buffer changes in external conditions.

The Himalaya

The Himalaya, formed by the collision of the Indian sub-continent with Eurasia, is the world's highest mountain range. Nepal, centrally located within the Himalayan chain, lies between latitudes 26° and 30°N; the east–west length of the country is about 800 km, and is roughly parallel to the Himalayan axis (Figure 3.28). The average north–south width is only 140 km. In terms of area, Nepal is comparable in size to England and Wales. Mountains occupy nearly 80% of Nepal and support just over half of the country's 28 million people.

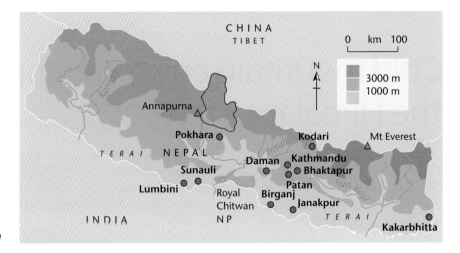

Figure 3.28 Nepal

The mountain zone in Nepal consists of two ranges:

➤ The High Mountains range from 2200 m to 4000 m. This is a region of metamorphic rocks and shallow soils. The climate is cool temperate and supports sub-alpine forest.

➤ The high Himalaya range from 4000 m to 8000 m, with eight of the world's highest peaks (including Sagarmatha or Mount Everest) as well as the world's deepest gorge (5791 m in the Kali Gandaki Valley). The climate is alpine and the snowline varies from 4000 m in the west to 5000 m in the east. The vegetation cover is alpine scrub.

High altitude and the heavy precipitation give the Himalaya the largest concentration of valley glaciers in the world. Nepal alone has around 3250 glaciers, which occupy 5325 km². Glaciation in the Himalaya has an alpine character: precipitous slopes and narrow ridges prevent the development of extensive icefields.

Ecological resources

Nepal's climate varies from subtropical monsoon in the lowlands of the Terai, to arctic tundra in the high Himalaya. These climatic contrasts, controlled by altitude, are largely responsible for the country's rich biodiversity (Photograph 3.34). Ninety-five different ecosystems have been identified in the hills and mountains. This mosaic of habitats means that an unusually large number of plants and animals are endemic, and found nowhere else in the world. However, the biodiversity within some ecosystems (e.g. alpine and sub-alpine habitats) is small.

Photograph 3.34
The Annapurna region, showing the diversity of habitats

Fragile ecosystems

High mountains with steep slopes dissected by deep valleys create delicate ecosystems, which are easily degraded (Box 3.7). Rapid erosion by meltwater rivers and glaciers undercuts hillslopes and causes frequent landslides. During the monsoon rains, topsoil is quickly removed from mountain slopes that have been deforested. Without forest cover, there is little to stop landslides, rock avalanches, mudslides and mudflows.

Economic resources

Healthy mountain ecosystems provide a wide range of resources and free 'services', not only to mountain communities, but also to people living in the lowlands. For those living in the Himalaya, the mountains provide water, soil, food, timber, fodder and grazing for livestock. Meanwhile, lowland populations in the Terai also rely on the mountains. They provide timber, glacial meltwater for irrigation and hydro-power, and generate income through tourism.

Today these resources are under increasing pressure (Figure 3.29). These pressures are both internal and external. The main internal pressure stems from rapid population growth (Figure 3.30) and widespread poverty. Externally, pressure comes from a huge growth in international tourism.

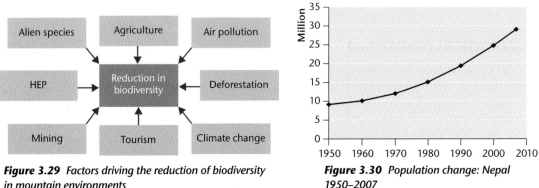

Figure 3.29 *Factors driving the reduction of biodiversity in mountain environments*

Figure 3.30 *Population change: Nepal 1950–2007*

Poverty and population growth

Nepal is an LEDC. In 2006 it ranked 138th out of 178 countries in the UN's human development index. Its estimated GDP per capita per year in 2003 was just $1400. Rapid population growth and chronic poverty, especially among mountain communities, place huge pressures on Nepal's natural environment and ecosystems and are the main drivers of environmental change.

Deforestation

Eighty-seven per cent of Nepal's mountain population depends on agriculture. Most of these people are subsistence farmers and 40% live below the poverty line. All of this places forest resources under intense pressure. Currently, forests are disappearing at a rate of 3% a year. **Overgrazing** by sheep, goats and cattle, fuelled by population growth, has speeded up deforestation. Deforestation is also due to clearance for cultivation and the ever-increasing demand for firewood, fodder and timber.

Tourism

Until recently, tourism in Nepal was unregulated. As a result, it has left a damaging 'footprint' on the mountain region.

➤ First, tourism has had a number of adverse social and economic effects. It has, for example, often alienated local people who have been swamped by the sheer number of visitors (in the main tourism season tourists in the Annapurna region outnumber residents by four to one). Tourism has also increased inequality between those engaged in tourism and those who are excluded, and has undermined traditional societal values.

➤ Second, the influx of around 25 000 trekkers a year, mostly in October and November, has imposed enormous pressure on mountain ecosystems. Although the use of fuelwood by trekking groups is forbidden, the rule is often ignored. For example, it is estimated that no more than 10% of visitors to the Sagarmatha National Park use other sources of fuel. Meanwhile, lodges on trekking routes burn an average of 75 kg of firewood a day during the peak season. In addition, pack animals overgraze areas close to trails.

➤ A third problem is human waste generated by tourists. It poses a threat to the environment, polluting streams and rivers. Much of the waste left by trekkers and mountaineers is non-biodegradable. The Everest region has been labelled 'the world's highest junkyard'. Waste includes food cans and wrappers, bottles, empty oxygen cylinders, spent batteries and ropes.

➤ Finally there is the problem of trail erosion. Many heavily used tourist trails are deeply gullied. Trekkers often avoid eroded trails, trampling adjacent vegetation and causing further damage. This contributes to loss of habitat and forces change in species composition (Photograph 3.35).

Jake Norton/Alamy

Photograph 3.35
Trekkers in the Everest region, which has been labelled 'the world's highest junkyard'

Conservation and sustainable management

Nepal has more than 13 000 km² of protected areas, including eight national parks. These areas are a magnet for trekkers, mountaineers and eco-tourists from all over the world.

The Annapurna Conservation Area Project

The Annapurna Conservation Area (ACA) covers 7629 km² and is one of the most spectacular regions in Nepal. Altitude rises from 800 m and culminates in Annapurna 1 — at 8091 m, the world's eighth highest peak. The ACA is Nepal's most popular trekking area, with 60 000 visitors a year. Visitors come to experience the region's spectacular mountains, waterfalls, gorges and wildlife. There are more than 1200 plant species, including: 40 orchids and nine species of rhododendron; 478 species of birds; and rare mammals such as snow leopards, blue sheep, bears and lynx.

The environment and natural resources of the ACA have been degraded over the past 40 years by overgrazing and intensive agriculture, which have resulted in deforestation and soil erosion. Although poverty and rapid population growth are most to blame, the huge increase in international tourism has also contributed significantly to environmental problems.

Management strategy

The ACA was given protected status in 1986 and a management plan (Annapurna Conservation Area Project) was launched to balance the basic needs of the local inhabitants, tourism development and nature conservation. The ACAP's approach is community-based. It recognises that protecting wildlife and maintaining biodiversity must (a) involve local people as stakeholders, and (b) deliver tangible economic benefits to them.

The ACAP's main source of income is a fee charged to foreign tourists ($7 per person) who visit the area. This money, together with donations from bodies such as the World Wide Fund for Nature (WWF) and the US government, supports 40 000 local people in the ACA. Thanks to the project, local people have been able to improve their standard of living, and at the same time protect the environment.

The ACAP supports reafforestation programmes, as well as water, soil and wildlife conservation. These programmes not only help the environment, but also, crucially, provide employment for local people. The projects generate a wide range of job opportunities. People work as forest guards, trekking guides and mountain rescue personnel. They also work in tree nurseries, tourism lodges, hotels and visitor centres; help to restore sites of historical and cultural interest; and take part in research projects investigating the region's biodiversity and wildlife. Income from tourism fees and donor organisations is used to build schools, maintain trails and improve sanitation facilities. Thus, conservation is linked to raising incomes and standards of living, and gives local people reasons to support the ACAP.

Conservation alone, however, will not protect the forests; hence the drive to reduce dependence on fuelwood by developing alternative energy sources such as small HEP generators and kerosene stoves. Finally, the problems of excessive population growth are being tackled by adult literacy schemes and family planning clinics.

Outcomes

Recent surveys have shown that the forest area is greater and the species diversity higher in the ACA than in neighbouring areas. The mean density of cut tree stumps is lower and this is explained by the decline in fuelwood as an energy source. Wild animal populations have also increased.

The behaviour of local people has changed. They have begun to alter their patterns of resource use and, thanks to environmental education, have increased conservation awareness. External agencies such as the ACAP have helped to improve the management of livestock, increased tree planting, and allowed secondary regeneration in areas previously cleared for farming.

Tourism has changed local people's attitudes towards nature and wildlife conservation. Many villagers (at least those who have benefited from tourism) now support wildlife conservation efforts. The ACAP demonstrates that conservation works when programmes engage local people as stakeholders. In a sense, tourism in the ACA has become a conservation tool, an important income and employment provider, and a catalyst for social change.

Examination-style questions

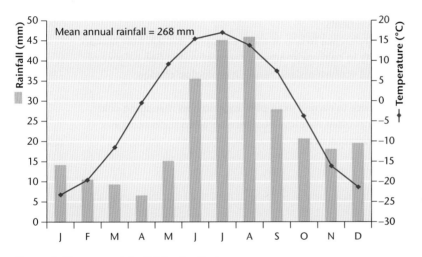

Figure 1 *Climate graph for Fairbanks, Alaska*

1 **(a)** Use Figure 1 to describe the main features of the climate at Fairbanks. (4 marks)

(b) Explain the weathering processes that operate in cold environments. (6 marks)

(c) Explain the formation of one named landform found in cold environments. (6 marks)

(d) With reference to one or more named examples, outline the opportunities for, and the problems caused by, resource exploitation. (9 marks)

2 With reference to named examples, explain how careful management can help to achieve sustainable development in cold environments. (25 marks)

Continuous   Discontinuous   Sporadic

Figure 2 The distribution of permafrost in the northern hemisphere

3 (a) Use Figure 2 to describe the distribution of permafrost in cold
       environments.   (4 marks)
  (b) Explain the weathering processes operating in permafrost areas
       in cold environments.   (6 marks)
  (c) Explain the impact of climate on vegetation in cold
       environments.   (6 marks)
  (d) With reference to one or more examples, explain how human
       activity in cold environments can destroy the fine balance of
       natural ecosystems and result in ecological change.   (9 marks)

4 With reference to named examples, explain how managing cold
  environments often requires a balance between socio-economic
  and environmental needs.   (25 marks)

Hot arid and semi-arid environments

Characteristics and processes

Key ideas

➤ Climatic and geomorphological processes give rise to the distinctive physical characteristics of hot arid and semi-arid environments.

➤ Climate, weathering, wind and water shape the landscapes of hot arid and semi-arid environments to produce distinctive landforms.

Classification and distribution of hot arid and semi-arid zones

Aridity is the ratio of average annual precipitation (P) to potential evapotranspiration (PET). The Food and Agriculture Organization (FAO) classifies 31% of the Earth's land surface as arid and semi-arid. It defines three arid zones: hyper-arid, arid and semi-arid (Table 4.1). Within this broad classification, hot arid and semi-arid environments occupy the arid zone in the tropics and sub-tropics (Figure 4.1).

Table 4.1 Classification of arid lands

	P/PET	Mean annual ppt (mm)	Area (%)
Hyper-arid	<0.03	<100	4.2
Arid	0.03–0.2	100–300	14.6
Semi-arid	0.2–0.5	300–600	12.2

In Köppen's climate classification (see Figure 3.1 on page 109), type BWh — hot, dry climates with a winter dry season — approximates the FAO's hyper-arid and arid climates. Type BSh climates — hot, dry with a summer dry season — correspond to the FAO's semi-arid climate.

Most arid lands occur between latitudes 20° and 35°. The hyper-arid and arid zone extends mostly across the Sahara (Figure 4.2), Arabian and Gobi deserts in the northern hemisphere. In the southern hemisphere, aridity is widespread in Australia, southwest Africa and Argentina. A feature of rainfall in arid lands is its inter-annual variability: typically 50–100%. Annual rainfall in Death Valley in California between 1887 and 1994 averaged 98 mm, but ranged from 54 mm to 171 mm (see Figures 4.3 and 4.4).

The semi-arid zone occurs polewards of hyper-arid and arid areas, and includes Mediterranean and Monsoon-type climates. Compared with the hyper-arid and arid zones, rainfall is higher, more reliable and more seasonal.

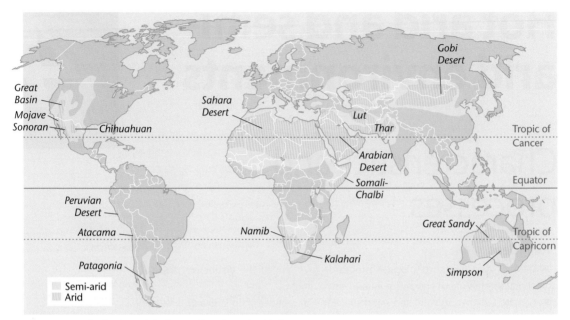

Figure 4.1 *Distribution of the hot arid and semi-arid climates*

Figure 4.2
Climate graph
for Marrakech,
Morocco

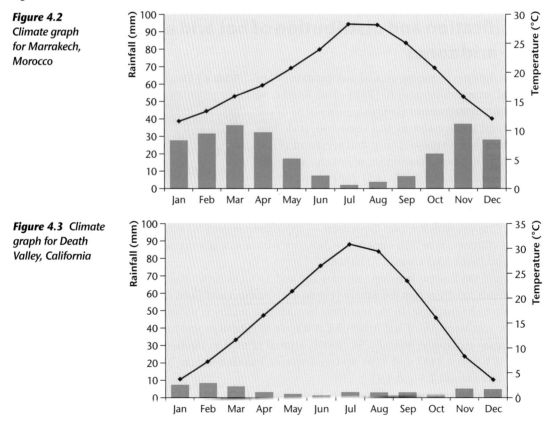

Figure 4.3 *Climate*
graph for Death
Valley, California

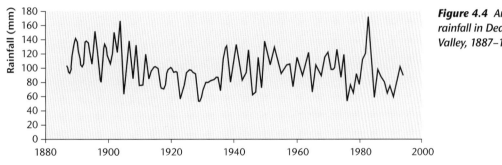

Figure 4.4 *Annual rainfall in Death Valley, 1887–1994*

Box 4.1 Aridity and rainfall effectiveness

All arid climates have comparatively low mean annual rainfall. However, what is more important for plant and crop growth is **rainfall effectiveness**; this means the amount of rain that reaches the root zone and is available to plants. Rainfall effectiveness is calculated thus:

$$\frac{\text{rainfall}}{\text{effectiveness}} = \frac{\text{actual}}{\text{precipitation}} - \text{evapotranspiration}$$

Several factors influence rainfall effectiveness.

■ **Rates of evaporation** — evaporation is determined by temperature and wind speed. In hot, dry climates, a large proportion of rainfall is lost to evaporation.

■ **Seasonality** — winter rainfall is more effective than summer rainfall. This is because evapotranspiration losses are lower in winter.

■ **Rainfall intensity** — rain falling in heavy convectional downpours results in rapid runoff, with little infiltration into the soil.

■ **Soil type** — clay soils may have limited capacity to absorb water and therefore cause additional runoff. In contrast, sandy soils are so porous that they are highly susceptible to drought.

The causes of aridity
Global circulation

The world's most extensive hot arid areas are found in the tropics and sub-tropics. They include the Sahara, Arabian and Australian deserts.

Aridity in these latitudes is determined by two large convective (Hadley) cells that control the circulation between the equator and the tropics in both hemispheres. The main features of the Hadley cells (Figure 4.5) are as follows:

➤ Intense insolation leads to surface heating, instability and convection around the Equator.

➤ Air, which is heated around the Equator, rises through the atmosphere to the tropopause, 10–15 km above the surface. This convection generates giant thunderstorm clouds and a zone of permanent low pressure at the surface.

➤ At the level of the tropopause, the air diverges and moves polewards.

➤ As it moves polewards, the air cools and eventually sinks back to the surface in the sub-tropics. A feature of sinking air is that it warms (due to compression) making the atmosphere cloud-free. The result is an area of permanent high pressure or anticyclone (the sub-tropical high) at the surface, and little likelihood of rain.

➤ The convection cell is completed by airflows from these sub-tropical highs near the surface returning towards the equator. These winds are the northeast and southeast trade winds. When they meet in the low-pressure area near the equator they form the inter-tropical convergence zone (ITCZ).

Figure 4.5
Hadley cells and the general circulation in the tropics and sub-tropics

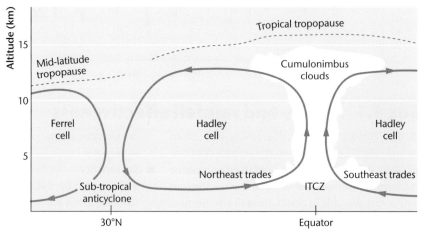

Topography

Mountain ranges create rain shadows and prevent moisture-laden air from entering some regions. Air rising across mountains cools, forming clouds and precipitation. On the lee side, the descending air is warmed and dried by compression. Thus the Mojave Desert in California is isolated from moist air masses originating from the Pacific Ocean by the coastal mountain ranges. Aridity in the Namib Desert of southwest Africa is partly due to the rain shadow effect of the Drakensberg Mountains of South Africa.

Cold ocean currents

Some of the driest places on Earth are associated with cold ocean currents. Cold ocean currents affect the western coastal margins of South America and southwest Africa where they form the Atacama and Namib Deserts respectively.

Cold ocean currents like the Humboldt current off the coast of northern Chile and Peru, and the Benguela current off Namibia, contribute to aridity. How does this happen? Local winds blow onshore bringing cool air from the ocean. This cool, dense air displaces the warmer air over the land and creates a **temperature inversion**. In these conditions, convection cannot take place and rain is unlikely. However, the land below the cool air is often shrouded in thick fog. Some plants and animals in the Atacama and Namib Deserts rely on fog water for their survival.

Prevailing winds

Even without this cold water offshore, the coastal regions of Namibia and Peru would be arid. This is due to: (a) prevailing southeast trade winds that blow from the dry continental interiors and (b) the rain shadow effect of the Andes in South America and the Drakensberg in South Africa.

Desert landforms and landscapes
Weathering processes

Hot arid and semi-arid environments generally experience slow rates of weathering. This is largely due to the lack of water, which means that the chemical breakdown of rocks is slow. Even so, chemical processes are more common than was once thought. Few deserts are absolutely dry. Occasional downpours penetrate pores and joints, weakening rocks by chemical action. Surface water also comes from dew and fog as air is chilled at night. **Hydration** — the absorption of water by minerals, which increase in volume and cause stress in rocks — is fairly widespread and leads to the flaking of rocks exposed near the ground surface.

Rock breakdown in hot arid and semi-arid environments is mainly due to physical weathering. This mechanical breakdown can be quite rapid, especially as the absence of soil and plant cover exposes bedrock over large areas (Photograph 4.1). There are three important physical weathering processes:

➤ freeze–thaw weathering
➤ salt weathering
➤ **insolation weathering**

Freeze–thaw weathering

Freeze–thaw weathering (described on page 110) is only possible where temperatures fluctuate above and below freezing and where there is sufficient moisture. These conditions are found in semi-arid, mid-latitude environments such as the Colorado Plateau. Moab, for example, situated 1200 m above sea level in Utah, has an average minimum temperature in January of $-8\,^{\circ}$C. At the same time, monthly precipitation averages 19 mm and snow is not unusual in winter (Figure 4.6 and Table 1.4 on page 34).

Michael Raw

Photograph 4.1
Rock fall in southwest USA

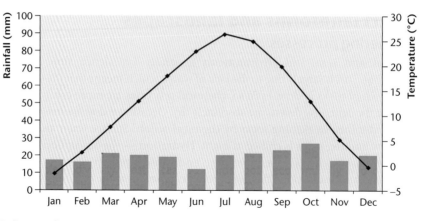

Figure 4.6
Climate graph for Moab, on the Colorado Plateau in Utah, USA

Salt weathering

Salt weathering occurs when salt in rocks crystallises out of solution. The growth of salt crystals stresses the rock, causing disintegration in a similar way to freeze–thaw weathering.

The importance of salt weathering is shown by the accumulation of salts such as sodium chloride, sodium sulphate and gypsum in desert environments. In more humid conditions they would be dissolved by rainwater and removed in solution by streams and rivers.

Insolation weathering

With cloudless skies and low humidity, surface temperatures in hot deserts can reach over 80°C during the day, and close to freezing at night. These temperature ranges cause rock minerals to expand and contract at different rates. In theory, these stresses could lead to rock disintegration. For many years scientists assumed that most weathered rock debris in desert environments could be explained by insolation weathering. The peeling of surface rock layers (known as **exfoliation**) and the rounding of boulders was also explained by this process. However, laboratory tests showed that rocks had little tendency to break down in the sort of temperature ranges found in hot deserts. But there was evidence of weathering when water was present. This suggests that insolation weathering could be a form of chemical weathering with water from dew, fog or rain acting as the trigger.

Weathering and past climates

Ten thousand years ago the climate of modern hot arid and semi-arid regions was cool and wet. Thus, some of the effects of weathering (and erosion) we observe in modern deserts are almost certainly due to past processes. Until the climate started to dry out 6000 years ago, weathering processes such as freeze–thaw, hydration and hydrolysis were far more active than today (see Photograph 4.11 on page 173).

Aeolian erosion and landforms

In modern deserts, wind is an important agent of erosion. Its main effect is the removal of loose fine-grained particles in a process called **deflation**. Wind is a far

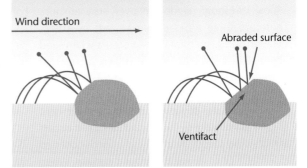

more effective erosional agent in deserts than it is in more humid environments. The sparse vegetation and soil cover increases the wind's effectiveness in desert regions. In more humid environments, plants reduce wind speeds close to the ground; and the sheltering and binding effects of plant stems and roots result in minimal erosion. But lack of vegetation cover is not the only factor that increases the wind's erosional power. Dry conditions mean that loose sand and dust are easily eroded and transported.

Aeolian abrasion, the sand-blasting effect of particles entrained and saltated by the wind, is less important as an erosional process than deflation. Although abrasion may polish rock surfaces, its overall effect is thought to be small. Because sand grains are relatively heavy, the effect of wind abrasion is confined to within 1–2 m of the surface.

Yardangs

Yardangs are streamlined wind-eroded ridges commonly found in hot arid and semi-arid environments. They are usually less than 10 m high and 100 m or more long, and are aligned with the prevailing wind. There is debate on the origins of yardangs and the extent to which they are wind-eroded features. However, their alignment with the wind and the fact that they are often undercut at the base (perhaps due to abrasion by saltating sand grains) suggests that wind erosion plays some part in their formation (Photograph 4.2).

George Steinmetz/SPL

Photograph 4.2
Yardangs in the Gobi Desert, China

Ventifacts

Ventifacts are faceted cobbles and pebbles that have been abraded or shaped by wind-blown sediment (Figure 4.7 and Photograph 4.3). The facets, formed in the direction of the prevailing wind, are separated from the protected lee side by a sharp edge.

Desert pavement

Deflation lowers the land surface through the removal of fine-grained particles by the wind. As a result, the coarser-grained particles are

Wind direction

Abraded surface

Ventifact

Figure 4.7 *Formation of ventifacts*

Michael Raw

Photograph 4.3
Ventifacts in the Sahara Desert

left as lag deposits at the surface. Eventually this produces extensive surfaces of coarse rocky particles that protect the underlying material from abrasion and deflation. Such a surface is called **desert pavement** (Figure 4.8). Stony deserts dominated by desert pavements are known as *reg* in the Sahara.

Figure 4.8
Formation of desert pavements

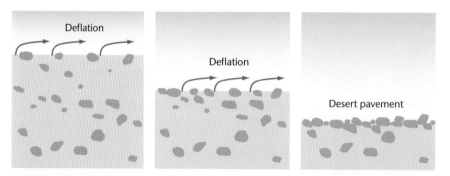

Box 4.2 Aeolian transport

Sand is transported when wind speeds exceed the critical threshold needed to overcome erosion. There are three types of movement: by creep, saltation and suspension. Creep occurs when sand grains slide and roll across the surface. It is caused by drag and by small differences in pressure, which create lift.

Saltation is the downwind bouncing movement of sand grains close to the ground surface. It occurs at high wind speeds. Normally saltation is confined to a metre or so above the ground surface. When saltating grains hit the surface they have a 'ballistic'

effect and set other grains moving in the direction of the wind.

Smaller dust particles entrained by the wind can be carried great distances by dust storms. The finest material (usually less than 0.2 mm in diameter) entrained by major dust storms may be transported in suspension beyond desert areas and deposited over the ocean.

In the UK, silt and clay particles originating in Saharan dust storms are sometimes washed out of the atmosphere as 'red rain'. Deposits of wind-blown dust are known as **loess**.

Aeolian depositional landforms

Around 20% of the Earth's hot arid and semi-arid area is covered with sand. Much of the sand collects in vast sheets or 'sand seas' which are known as *ergs* in the Sahara. Accumulation occurs in areas of reduced wind speed. Initially this could be a small surface depression or an obstacle such as vegetation. The latter can be seen when sand shadows develop in the lee of plants (Photograph 4.4).

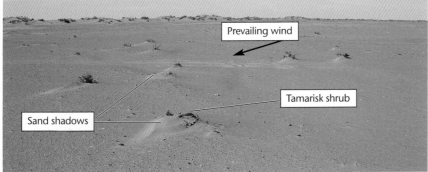

Michael Raw

Photograph 4.4
Sand shadows formed in the low wind zone to the lee of tamarisk shrubs

Sand seas contain distinctive landforms which range in size from sand ripples to sand dunes and mega dunes or **draa**.

Ripples

Sand ripples are small-scale features formed by the wind (Photograph 4.5). They consist of a succession of crests and troughs, which develop at right angles to the wind. The wavelengths and heights of the crests above the troughs increase with wind speed. Depending on the coarseness of the sand, heights vary from a few millimetres to 50 cm. Ripples develop through a combination of saltation and surface creep. Sand is moved from one crest to the next downwind as sand is eroded from the windward side and is deposited leeward of the crest. The coarsest sand tends to collect on the crests. Ripples migrate downwind while maintaining their spacing and wavelength.

Michael Raw

Photograph 4.5
Sand ripples — note the crests, troughs and regular wavelengths; the wind forming the ripples blew from left to right

Dunes

Dunes are accumulations of blown sand, which form a mound or a ridge (Photograph 4.6). Two conditions are needed for dunes to form:
➤ an adequate supply of sand
➤ winds strong enough and persistent enough to transport the sand

Carried by the wind, sand accumulates where there is a reduction in wind speed caused by an increase in surface roughness. Once formed, sand accumulations grow by positive feedback. Saltating grains entering a patch of sand are unable to rebound as on a rocky surface. The result is that sand is trapped, and the accumulation grows as it traps more sand.

Photograph 4.6
Desert dune showing windward slope, crest and steep slip face — the prevailing wind is from the left

Michael Raw

Thus areas of dunes are often fairly localised, forming sand 'seas' surrounded by alluvial plains, and stony and rocky deserts.

A typical dune formed by winds from a prevailing direction has a windward slope angle of 10–15°, a sharp crest, and a much steeper leeward or **slip face** of 30–35° (Figure 4.9). The slip face stands at the angle of repose, which is the maximum angle at which loose sand is stable. Sand is transported up the windward slope by creep and saltation. As sand piles up on the crest it eventually exceeds the angle of repose. Small sand avalanches occur on the slip face to restore equilibrium. In this way, dunes migrate in the direction of the prevailing wind.

Figure 4.9
Formation of desert dunes

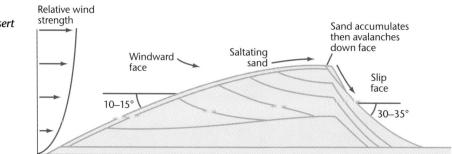

Dune height is limited by wind speed. As dunes increase in height, wind speed also increases until equilibrium between sand erosion and deposition is reached. Desert dunes are usually up to 30 m high.

Types of dunes

Dunes are classified according to their planform shape into four main types (Figure 4.10):

➤ crescentic (barchans and transverse dunes)
➤ linear (longitudinal)
➤ star
➤ parabolic

Several factors influence the type of dune that develops. Most important are sand supply, wind direction variability and vegetation cover.

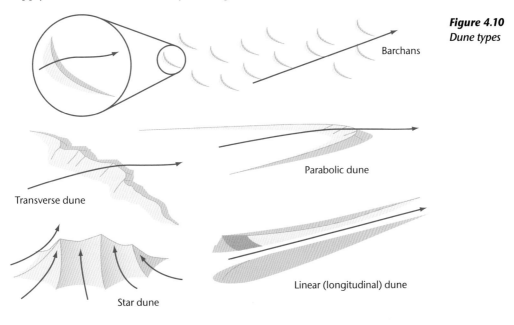

Figure 4.10
Dune types

Barchans

Parabolic dune

Transverse dune

Star dune

Linear (longitudinal) dune

➤ **Crescentic dunes** (also known as barchans and transverse dunes) are the most common type. They are wider than they are long, with a slip face on the dune's concave side and, in the case of barchans, horns that face downwind. These dunes form where winds blow predominantly from one direction. Crescentic dunes are highly mobile and have been known to move as much as 100 m in a year.
➤ **Linear dunes** (also known as seif or longitudinal dunes) are straight or slightly curved in planform. They are normally more than 100 km long, with slip faces on alternate sides, and occur as isolated ridges, or as a series of parallel ridges, separated by gravelly corridors. Linear dunes cover a larger area of desert than any other dune type.
➤ **Star dunes** are pyramidal sand mounds with slip faces on three or more arms that radiate from the high centre of the dune. They tend to form in areas where the wind is multi-directional (Photograph 4.7).

Photograph 4.7
A star dune in the Sahara Desert

➤ **Parabolic dunes** have U-shaped planforms with convex noses trailed by elongated arms. Although superficially similar to crescentic dunes, the arms of parabolic dunes, unlike crescentic dunes, extend upwind. This is because the arms are fixed by vegetation, while the main mass of dune migrates forward.

The work of streams and rivers

It may be a paradox, but many of the characteristic landforms of deserts are the work of streams and rivers (Photograph 4.8). Most desert streams and rivers are ephemeral: they only flow during and shortly after periods of steady rain or intense thunderstorms. However, in most hot arid and semi-arid environments, dry river beds, known as **wadis** in North Africa and **arroyos** in the USA, are impressive and familiar features. They remind us that although runoff may be short-lived, streams and rivers in dryland regions have considerable power.

Photograph 4.8
Death Valley, one of the driest places on Earth; the distant slopes, deeply eroded by runoff, together with water-transported rock particles in the foreground, underline the importance of water as a landscape-forming agent in the desert

Runoff in deserts often originates in surrounding mountains. There, convection and orographic uplift can trigger intense thunderstorms. However, high-intensity rainfall is only one of several factors responsible for high peak flows. Other factors promoting rapid runoff include:

➤ sparse vegetation cover, with minimal interception to slow the movement of surface water
➤ a ground surface often baked hard, which limits **infiltration**
➤ **rainsplash** on unvegetated surfaces, which quickly fills soil pores and reduces soil permeability
➤ shallow soils, which allow little water storage and **throughflow**

Desert streams and rivers transport exceptionally high sediment loads. Indeed, so high are the sediment loads that runoff from mountain catchments often takes the form of mudflows and **debris flows**. Large sediment loads are partly explained by powerful streams and rivers; and partly by large amounts of weathered rock debris, which, lacking a protective vegetation cover, is loose and easily eroded.

Fluvial landforms

The following landforms of hot arid and semi-arid environments owe their development, at least in part, to fluvial processes: alluvial fans, bajadas, playas, pediments and canyons.

Alluvial fans and bajadas

Alluvial fans are cones of sediment deposited by a river as it leaves a steep-walled valley in a mountainous area and enters an adjacent lowland (Photograph 4.9). Once in the lowland, the river is no longer confined and quickly loses energy, depositing alluvial sediments across a broad area (see Figure 1.16 on page 21). Where multiple canyons emerge along a mountain front, several alluvial fans may merge to form a continuous apron known as a bajada.

Michael Raw

Canyon

Alluvial fans

Pediment

Photograph 4.9
Alluvial fans merging to form a bajada at the foot of the Panamint Range in Death Valley, California

Playas

Many streams and rivers in hot arid and semi-arid environments drain to shallow inland basins where they form temporary lakes or **playas** (Photograph 4.10). Because salts tend to accumulate in areas of low rainfall, desert streams and rivers carry large amounts of salt in solution. With high temperatures and intermittent stream flow, playas soon evaporate, leaving behind soluble salts such as sodium chloride, sodium carbonate, sodium sulphate and gypsum. Many playas were the location of permanent lakes and marshes during the last glacial period when the climate in arid regions was more humid.

Photograph 4.10
Playa and salt deposits at Badwater, California

Michael Raw

Pediments

Pediments are gently sloping, concave rock platforms at the base of receding mountain fronts. They dominate slopes in hot arid and semi-arid environments and are usually covered with a thin layer of soil and alluvium. Isolated rocky hills known as **inselbergs** rise abruptly from pediment surfaces.

Pediments are formed by the parallel retreat of the steep slopes of a plateau or mountain front. As the upland retreats it leaves behind an extending, gentle-angled rock platform. Parallel retreat maintains more or less constant slope angles and lengths over time (Figure 4.11).The main cause of slope retreat is weathering. In areas such as Monument Valley on the Colorado Plateau, slope retreat is most effective where massive sandstone beds are underlain by less resistant shales. Weathering and erosion of the shales undermines the sandstone, leading to rockfall and parallel retreat (see also Photograph 4.1 on page 163).

Parallel retreat occurs because rock debris is removed as fast as it accumulates. In this way debris slopes cannot build up and modify the original slope profile. The agents of erosion and transport are water (runoff and surface wash) and wind (deflation). Their effectiveness is greatly increased by the lack of vegetation cover and the dry conditions.

On the Colorado Plateau, parallel retreat reduces the sandstone plateaux and tablelands to remnant **mesas**, **buttes** and **spires** (Photograph 4.11). Although

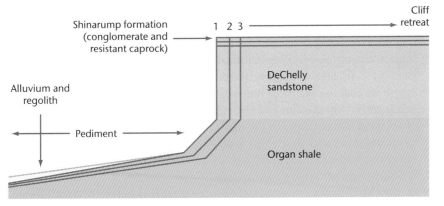

Figure 4.11
Parallel retreat, which leads to the formation of pediments and inselbergs (mesas, buttes and spires) in Monument Valley, Utah

these features are in different stages of **denudation**, they all have the same characteristic slope profiles, and confirm the reality of parallel retreat.

Photograph 4.11
Landforms created by parallel retreat in a semi-arid environment: Monument Valley, Utah

Canyons

Canyons or gorges are narrow river valleys with near-vertical sides cut into solid rock. They are a common feature of mountains and plateaux in hot arid and semi-arid areas (Photograph 4.12).

Canyons are the result of vertical erosion by streams and rivers. Abrasion due to the scouring action of coarse rock debris in transport is the dominant process. Erosion is vertical rather than lateral because the solid rock walls allow little lateral migration of river channels, which would otherwise widen out the valley.

Photograph 4.12 Canyon incised into sedimentary rocks in the Moroccan Anti-Atlas mountains

173

Although canyons and gorges are also found in humid and sub-humid environments, the best examples are in the desert regions of the southwest USA. Why is this?

➤ Intense downpours and rapid runoff create powerful flash floods in deserts (see page 170). High but short-lived peak flows give desert streams great energy.
➤ Sparse vegetation cover with little soil means that large volumes of loose rock debris are fed into streams and rivers during rainfall events. These are the 'tools' of abrasion and cut through the rock like a saw through wood.
➤ In upland areas, such as the Colorado Plateau and the Anti Atlas mountains in Morocco, recent tectonic uplift has meant that rivers have been continuously downcutting and incising their valleys.
➤ In more humid environments, slope processes such as soil creep, landslides and mudflows lower valley slope angles. This backwasting, which opens out the valley to a shallow V shape, depends on moisture and a soil and vegetation cover. In arid and semi-arid environments, these features are largely absent.

The shape of canyons in cross-profile is mainly determined by rock type. Where rocks are highly resistant and homogeneous, narrow **slot canyons** with vertical rock walls develop. Antelope Canyon, near Page in Arizona, is a classic slot canyon. Other canyons have stair-like sides. They form where rocks of alternating resistance crop out. The harder rocks form cliffs; the softer rocks support gentler slopes. The Grand Canyon is the best example of this stair-step type of canyon (see Photograph 1.17 on page 35).

Ecosystems in hot arid and semi-arid environments

Key ideas
➤ Hot arid and semi-arid environments are fragile and easily damaged.
➤ Climatic extremes lead to finely balanced ecosystems. Both flora and fauna can suffer as a result of change, and regeneration is difficult in the harsh conditions.
➤ Both physical and human factors make the hot arid and semi-arid environment vulnerable to change.

Hot arid and semi-arid regions are harsh environments for plants and animals. They have to adjust to the following extreme climatic conditions:
➤ low and unpredictable rainfall
➤ low humidity
➤ dry winds
➤ high summer temperatures

Soils impose further limits. Most are deficient in humus, lack essential plant nutrients (especially nitrogen and phosphorus) and have low water-holding capacity.

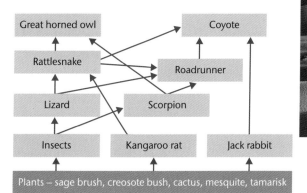

Moreover, high rates of evaporation create hardpans — solidified layers of calcium carbonate — and concentrate salts that are lethal to plants.

Given the extreme climatic and soil conditions, net primary production (NPP) and biomass are predictably low. NPP values range from $30\,g\,m^2\,year^{-1}$ to $200\,g\,m^2\,year^{-1}$. This compares with an average of $1800\,g\,m^2\,day^{-1}$ for tropical rainforest.

Desert food webs are complex because many animals are generalists. Sparse animal populations mean that few secondary and tertiary consumers are specialist carnivores. Most animals at higher trophic levels are omnivorous and take advantage of whatever food becomes available. The low biomass of desert ecosystems means that most food chains are relatively short, with just two or three trophic levels (Figure 4.12).

Figure 4.12 *Desert food web for southwest USA*

Soils of hot arid and semi-arid environments

These soils, known collectively as **aridosols**, are found over nearly one-third of the Earth's land surface. Because evaporation and transpiration greatly exceed rainfall, there is little leaching. This allows mineral ions to accumulate, causing high salinity or alkalinity. Low plant biomass means that organic content is low. Aridosols are predominantly mineral soils. Soils with a saline horizon are called **solonchaks** (Figure 4.13), and those with sodium carbonate are **solonetzes**. Most of the salt comes from rock weathering and inflowing rivers.

Plant and animal adaptations

Survival in the desert requires plants and animals to adapt to drought and high temperatures. Not surprisingly, relatively few plants and animals have been able to adapt and compete successfully for limited supplies of water. The outcome is high levels of endemicism (there are over 200 plant species found only in the Mojave Desert in southwest USA), and little biodiversity.

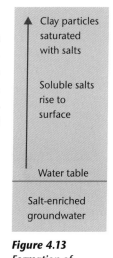

Figure 4.13 *Formation of solonchaks*

Plants

Desert plants have evolved a number of physiological adaptations to drought (Box 4.3). Plants that have altered their physical structure to survive drought are called **xerophytes**. They include **succulents** like cacti, which store water within their tissues, and **phreatophytes**, which have exceptionally long roots to tap water deep below the surface. Other plants survive in the desert through behavioural adaptation. Many perennial plants are dormant during long dry periods and spring to life only when water becomes available. Annuals are drought-evading. Their seeds germinate after rain and the plants complete their reproductive cycle and set seed within a few weeks.

Box 4.3 Some desert plants of southwest USA and their adaptation to water shortage and high temperatures

All photographs © Michael Raw

(a) Prickly pear

Prickly pear is a cactus. It stores water in its fleshy stems. Its waxy skin seals in moisture and prevents water loss by transpiration. Spines are modified leaves, which reduce water loss (through transpiration) and provide protection from animals. Prickly pear originated in the Americas, but is widespread in drylands in Africa, Australia, Asia and Europe.

(b) Joshua tree

Joshua trees are a type of yucca that are native to the Mojave Desert in southwest USA. The leaves have several xerophytic characteristics. Their needle-like shape helps to reduce moisture loss, leaf cells store water, and the leaves are covered with a thick, waxy cuticle to reduce transpiration loss.

(c) Creosote bush

The creosote bush is the most tolerant of all desert plants in southwest USA. It has several physiological adaptations to drought. Its long lateral taproots enable it to absorb soil water at a distance. In extreme drought it is able to extract soil moisture held so tightly in the soil that it is unavailable to other species. Its high surface-to-volume ratio and small leaves optimise the rate at which heat escapes and moisture is retained. The leaves of the creosote bush have stomata that close during the day to reduce water loss.

(d) Tamarisk

Tamarisk is a phreatophyte, with extremely long roots that extend deep into the sub-soil and close to the water table. It is also salt tolerant (an

alternative name is cedar salt). Tamarisk is a desert plant native to north Africa which has been introduced to the USA.

(e) Desert annuals
Desert verbena and desert paintbrush are two of hundreds of annuals found in the deserts of south-west USA. Annuals germinate after heavy seasonal rains and complete their life cycles very quickly. Within just a few weeks they flower, set seed and

die. The seeds remain dormant until the next rains. Annuals have no physiological adaptation to drought. They are simply drought evading.

(f) Halophytes
Salt often accumulates in deserts in enclosed basins. Halophytic plants are adapted to survival in environments where salt concentrations are high and toxic to other species. The saltbush is a common species on salt pans in the deserts of the US southwest.

Animals

Animals need to adapt to the extremes of temperature within hot arid and semi-arid environments as well as to the lack of water. Like plants, animal adaptation is both physiological and behavioural.

Physiological adaptations include: changes to body shape to dissipate heat, coloration and conserving moisture.

➤ Jack rabbits in North America, and bat-eared foxes in Africa, have evolved enormous ears. Circulating blood through thin ears dissipates unwanted body heat (Photograph 4.13).

➤ Animals often develop pale-coloured fur, scales or feathers to reduce heat absorption.

➤ Some animals, such as desert tortoises and turkey vultures, obtain all the moisture they need from their food.

➤ Birds and reptiles excrete wastes as uric acid — an insoluble white compound — wasting little water in the process.

➤ Kangaroo rats can recycle water from their own urine and reduce water loss from breathing by having special nasal cavities.

Photograph 4.13
Jack rabbits have enormous ears, which allow them to dissipate unwanted body heat

Other animals cope with heat and water loss by adapting their behaviour. Humming birds migrate in spring from the deserts of the US southwest to avoid the extreme temperatures of summer. Animals that live in the desert all year round often adopt a nocturnal habit. Being active at night eliminates the stress of high temperatures and reduces water loss. This is the strategy of reptiles such as rattlesnakes and gila monsters (a type of lizard), and mammals such as bats, foxes, skunks and small rodents. As heat falls quickly with depth below the desert surface, many animals burrow to escape high temperatures (some even block up burrow entrances to escape desiccating winds). Others, like the round-tailed ground squirrel, enter a state of hibernation (known as aestivation) at the onset of the hot season.

Fragility of hot arid and semi-arid ecosystems

Low rates of net primary production, limited biodiversity and slow recovery from damage are just some of the reasons why hot arid and semi-arid ecosystems are delicate and easily degraded by human activities. Even slight disruption can cascade through these ecosystems and cause irreversible change.

Cryptobiotic soil crusts

Cryptobiotic soil crusts (Photograph 4.14) are communities of cyanobacteria, green algae, lichen, fungi and mosses. They form a fragile ground cover just a few centimetres thick in hot arid and semi-arid ecosystems. It is no exaggeration to say that the health of these ecosystems depends on this delicate cryptobiotic layer remaining intact. In the deserts of the Colorado Plateau and southwest USA, cryptobiotic crusts account for more than 70% of the living ground cover.

Photograph 4.14
Cryptobiotic growth enriches soil for plants to grow

Cryptobiotic crusts perform several ecological functions:

➤ A dense network of filaments formed by blue-green algae sticks to rock surfaces and soil particles. As a result, loose soil material is bound together and protected from wind and water erosion.

➤ They increase soil infiltration and absorb and store rainwater. When moistened, filaments of blue-green algae can absorb up to ten times their volume of water.

➤ The roughened surface of the crusts slows runoff. This is important in arid environments where rainfall is sporadic and intense.

➤ They input organic matter to the soil and provide plants with essential nutrients such as nitrogen. Tiny clay particles cover the filaments. Nutrients such as calcium and potassium stick to the surfaces of the clays, where they are available to plants. Without the crust these essential nutrients would be leached from the soil.

➤ They are important nurseries for seedlings.

Human activities and cryptobiotic crusts

Cryptobiotic crusts are easily crushed and damaged by vehicles, mountain bikes, hikers and livestock. Damage is particularly serious because it can take 50–250 years for small areas to recover. Larger areas take even longer. This underlines the slow rates of growth in arid environments. Aridity causes other problems: sparse vegetation and dry soils makes ecosystems highly sensitive to the smallest changes in plant cover.

Many human activities threaten crypto-biotic crusts. They are thin, dry and brittle, and easily damaged by machinery and trampling by people and livestock. Damaged crusts contribute less nitrogen and organic matter to the soil and are more likely to be blown away by the wind. This in turn exposes soils to erosion. Blown soil then buries nearby crusts, stopping photosynthesis and causing further damage. Finally, motor vehicle and bicycle tracks create artificial channels for runoff, which accelerate rates of erosion by water. Once disturbed, large areas of crust, on which so many organisms depend, never recover. So fragile are hot arid and semi-arid ecosystems that their survival rests on a veneer of micro-organisms that form the cryptobiotic crust.

Key ideas

➤ Hot arid and semi-arid environments provide opportunities and challenges for development.
➤ Opportunities include resource exploitation, for example agriculture, and recreation and tourism.
➤ Challenges to development include environmental constraints, remoteness, development costs and conflicts with indigenous people.
➤ Managing hot arid and semi-arid environments is about balancing socio-economic and environ-mental needs to achieve a sustainable develop-ment.
➤ Hot arid and semi-arid environments can be exploited for short-term gains.
➤ Hot arid and semi-arid environments require careful management to ensure sustainable development.

Case study — The Draa Valley, Morocco

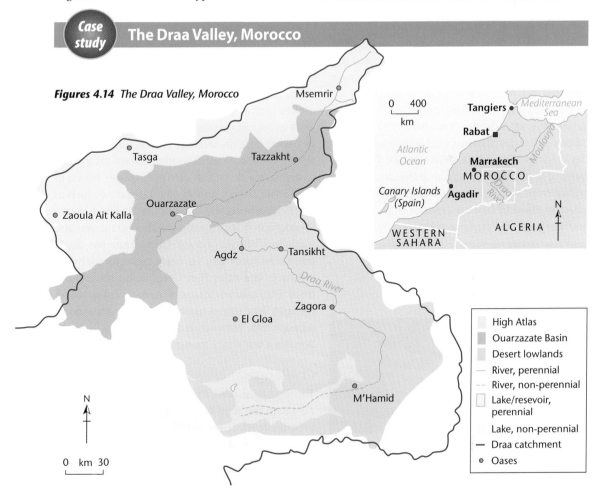

Figures 4.14 *The Draa Valley, Morocco*

Legend:
- High Atlas
- Ouarzazate Basin
- Desert lowlands
- — River, perennial
- -- River, non-perennial
- ☐ Lake/resevoir, perennial
- Lake, non-perennial
- — Draa catchment
- ⊙ Oases

The Draa River is one of Morocco's largest rivers (Figure 4.14). Its catchment covers nearly 35 000 km^2 and varies in altitude from 4071 m to 450 m. The Draa rises in the High Atlas mountains and drains to the arid lowlands of southeast Morocco and the Sahara Desert. The river has one of the most arid catchments in the world. As it flows away from the mountains, aridity increases. Aridity in the southeast of the country is due partly to the rain shadow effect of the High Atlas, and partly to the permanent sub-tropical high pressure over the Sahara. Mean annual rainfall downstream of Ouarzazate is barely 100 mm. Meanwhile in summer, daytime temperatures hit 40–45°C.

Resources and opportunities

The Draa River is the lifeblood of southeast Morocco. In total, 43 000 ha are irrigated in its catchment. Eighty per cent of irrigation water comes from the Draa and its tributaries. The rest is from groundwater. Water is diverted from the river into canals and irrigates land on the valley floor and on terraces high on the valley side (Photograph 4.15).

Thanks to the river, 225 000 people live in the Draa Valley. Most are subsistence farmers. They cultivate crops such as dates, barley, fruit and vegetables on tiny holdings of just one or two hectares. Traditional farming is based on a type of **polyculture** where annual crops such as barley and vegetables are cultivated on the same plot beneath tree crops like citrus and date palms. For centuries this oasis cultivation has

Photograph 4.16 *Draa Valley oasis, with* ksour *and* kasbah.

allowed local populations to prosper despite the fragility of the environment (Photograph 4.16).

Where irrigation stops, the desert begins. The surrounding desert is mainly rocky *hamada* plains and stony *reg*. Beyond M'Hamid, the sixth and last oasis in the Draa Valley, there are dunes and sand seas.

In recent years, tourism has provided alternative employment for local people. Around 8% of the economically active population works in tourism. Formal sector tourism supports jobs in hotels, restaurants, supermarkets and filling stations in larger centres such as Ouarzazate and Zagora. People also work as tourist guides; in handicrafts and bazaars geared to foreign tourists; and as informal street sellers. The Draa Valley's tourism attractions include its dry, sunny climate, its date palm groves, access to the Sahara Desert, and its cultural features such as mudbrick architecture, *kasbahs* (fortified houses (see Photograph 4.16)), *agadirs* (fortified granaries) and traditional villages (*ksours*). Ouarzazate has developed as an important, if unlikely, centre for the movie industry. The Atlas Film Corporation has studios there. They take advantage of the excellent quality of the light, guaranteed sunshine of the desert and low labour costs. Meanwhile the film studio itself has become a significant tourist attraction.

Challenges

The Draa River owes its existence to snowpacks and rainfall in the High Atlas mountains created by the orographic effect. But in the past 15 years, precipitation in the High Atlas has declined. At the same time, water demand for irrigation and tourism has been

Photograph 4.15 *Oasis in the Draa Valley, with palm groves and irrigation canal*

increasing by up to 3% a year. A number of environmental, economic and demographic challenges therefore face the Draa Valley oases.

Environmental challenges

Since 1972 water resources on the Draa River have been regulated by the Mansour Eddahbi dam near Ouarzazate. In recent years both inflows and outflows to and from storage have been well below average (Figure 4.15). Water shortages seem inevitable in future as climate change and reduced rainfall take hold, and water demand continues to rise. One estimate suggests that water resources are set to decrease by 4% between 2000 and 2020. Water quality declines downstream from the Mansour Eddahbi dam. It is poorest in the southern irrigated zones between Agdz and M'Hamid due to high salinity.

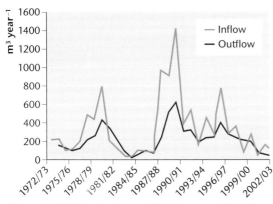

Figure 4.15 *Water balance of the Mansour Eddahbi from 1972/1973 to 2002/2003*

Already, many parts of the Draa Valley rely on groundwater. However, the increased use of mechanised pumps has caused over-exploitation and a fall in the water table of between 3m and 6 m. Over-use of groundwater has triggered salinisation of aquifers in the southern oases. So far there has been little or no management of groundwater.

Salinisation of farmland has become an urgent environmental problem (Figure 4.21, page 188). Its cause is over-irrigation, which results in a rise in the water table. Salts dissolved in soil water are then drawn to the surface by high temperatures

where evaporation deposits them as a saline crust. Salinisation is a type of **land degradation**. When it is severe, farmers have no option but to abandon their land. Other problems include soil erosion, sand encroachment on oases and the loss of genetic biodiversity among cultivated plants. Soil erosion has resulted in increased sediment loads on the Draa and its tributaries, causing a 25% reduction in the capacity of the Mansour Eddabhi reservoir. In the reservoir's catchment, soil erosion averages 35 t ha year^{-1}.

Demographic challenges

Rates of population growth in the Draa Valley are high: around 2.5% a year. Three factors account for this increase: youthful age structure; high fertility among the rural population; and relatively low mortality. Demographic pressure on natural resources is destabilising the ecosystem leading to the over-exploitation of water resources and farmland and ultimately to **desertification** (see page 185).

Economic challenges

The Draa Valley is one of Morocco's poorest regions. Average incomes are barely $300 a year, well below the average for the country. Nearly two in every five people live in poverty. Differences in wealth are most obvious between the majority rural population, and the urban dwellers in prosperous towns like Ouarzazate and Zagora.

Conclusion

There is no doubt that the Draa Valley faces severe environmental, social and economic challenges. Because of aridity, farming is only possible in oases, fed by water from the Atlas mountains. As the climate begins to dry out, these water resources decline. Meanwhile the demand for water continues to rise in response to rapid population growth. Increasing reliance on groundwater has led to overpumping and a fall in the water table; and over-irrigation has caused localised salinisation of soils. Already there are signs that the unsustainable use of soil and water resources is responsible for land degradation, increased poverty and out-migration to towns and cities.

Arches National Park: tourism in a semi-arid environment

The Arches National Park in southeast Utah is a high desert environment on the Colorado Plateau (Figure 4.16). Its altitude varies from 1245 m to over 1700 m. The climate statistics for Moab, located just outside the park boundaries, are summarised in Figure 4.6 (see page 164). Rainfall averages around 230 mm a year. Summers are hot, with maximum temperatures often exceeding 40°C. Winters are cold. Rainfall is sufficient to support sparse vegetation, including dwarf pinyon pine and juniper in open woodland in the more humid higher areas.

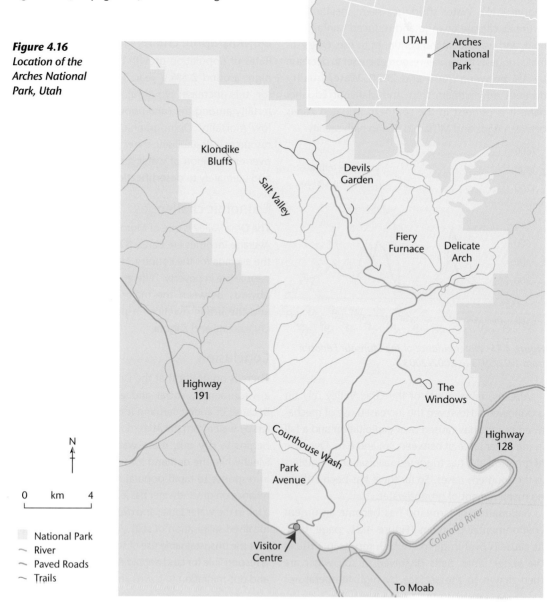

Figure 4.16
Location of the Arches National Park, Utah

Opportunities

The Arches was designated a National Park by Congress in 1971. It is one of the smallest parks in the USA, occupying just over 300 km². And yet this small area has the highest concentration of natural stone arches in the world (over 2000). The arches, sculpted from red Entrada sandstone, are the major visitor attraction (Photographs 4.17 and 4.18, and Box 4.4).

In 2006 the park received 833 000 visitors (Figure 4.17), two-thirds of them between May and September. Most visitors access the park by car and use the park's 60 km of paved roads. The main activities are sight-seeing, hiking, biking, climbing and camping. The National Park Service operates a visitor centre at the park entrance and a large camp ground; maintains the road network, turn-outs and lay-bys, and trails; and provides a ranger service. The park is on federal land. There are no permanent settlements and economic activities inside the park, which is reserved for conservation and recreation. Unlike national parks in the UK, visitors pay a fee for entrance.

Challenges

The main problem is overcrowding and congestion at peak times. Cars have to queue to enter the park; popular attractions such as Delicate Arch, Garden Wall and The Windows reach capacity, and trailheads become congested. Cars parked along road shoulders often damage soil and vegetation. The park plans to implement a new transport strategy by 2008. This might include reserved parking at key attractions, closing roadside pull-off areas and controlling illegal parking. There are no immediate plans to follow the Grand Canyon and Zion approach — to close the park to private vehicles and introduce a shuttle bus system.

There is also concern over damage to the fragile cryptobiotic crust (see page 178) caused by bikers and walkers who follow popular trails. As we have seen, the crust is a fragile but crucial component of the desert ecosystem.

Michael Raw

Photograph 4.17 Double Arch, Arches National Park

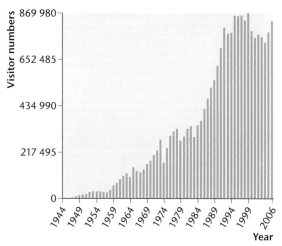

Michael Raw

Photograph 4.18 Landscape Arch, Arches National Park

Figure 4.17 Arches National Park visitor numbers, 1947–2006

Conclusion

The high desert of the Colorado Plateau is a valuable economic resource, which attracts millions of visitors a year. Similar tourist attractions in the semi-arid lands of Utah include Monument Valley tribal park, and the national parks at Bryce Canyon, Canyonlands and Zion. In addition, there are numerous smaller conservation areas designated national monuments. The appeal of the desert to visitors is the unique landscape and scenery, the experience of wildness, exotic wildlife, and high summer temperatures with guaranteed sunshine.

Box 4.4 Formation of natural arches

Most natural arches on the Colorado Plateau are formed in 'fins' or narrow ridges of massively bedded sandstone. A possible sequence of events in their formation is as follows:

- The Arches area of eastern Utah is underlain by extensive salt deposits. Under the pressure of hundreds of metres of sandstone, these salt deposits are unstable. As they are squeezed together they push the overlying sandstone into a dome. This process creates extensive parallel and vertical jointing in the sandstone.
- Over millions of years these joints are widened by weathering and erosion to leave residual vertical fins of sandstone (Photograph 4.19).
- A combination of factors reduces the fins to arches: (a) weathering (e.g. salt, solution, hydration, freeze–thaw) and erosion (e.g. surface wash, wind abrasion) concentrated at the base of the fins where water is available; (b) force of gravity on the standing rock (which increases towards the base owing to the greater mass of rock above); and (c) massively bedded sandstone of uniform structure and few bedding planes. When rockfall occurs, large sections of rock are likely to collapse; for example, in 1991 a 200 t section of Landscape Arch collapsed.
- Rockfall on opposite sides of the fin may expose a window, which slowly enlarges to form an arch. The characteristic rounded arch at the top of the opening is a strong and durable shape, held in place by compressive forces from the surrounding rock.

Michael Raw

Photograph 4 19 *Sandstone fins and pinnacles, Arches National Park*

Desertification

Desertification describes the degradation of formerly productive land to the point where desert-like conditions prevail. There is a progressive loss of biological and economic activity as water, soil and vegetation resources are degraded. Desertification results from both natural processes and human activities (Figure 4.18). Drought often triggers desertification, but the immediate causes are poverty and the consequent over-exploitation of natural resources. **Overcultivation**, overgrazing and excessive irrigation all contribute to land degradation.

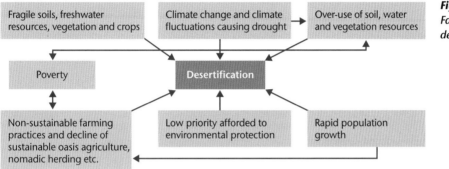

Figure 4.18
Factors forcing desertification

It is estimated that one-third of the world's land area, and one-quarter of the global population, are at risk of desertification. Although the most severely affected areas are hot arid and semi-arid environments in LEDCs, desertification is by no means confined to sub-tropical drylands and LEDCs (Figure 4.19). It is also widespread in MEDCs such as the USA and Spain, and in sub-humid climates in mid-latitudes (Figure 4.20). However, the environmental fragility of hot arid and semi-arid regions makes them particularly vulnerable.

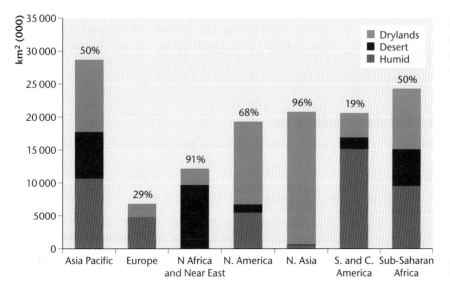

Figure 4.19
Regional aridity and risk of desertification (%)

Source: Food and Agriculture Organization

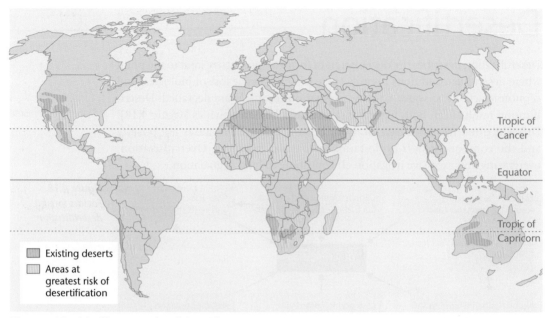

Existing deserts

Areas at greatest risk of desertification

Figure 4.20 *Risk of human-induced desertification*

Box 4.5 Desertification

- According to UNESCO, desertification directly affects over 250 million people and threatens the lives of some 1.2 billion people in 110 countries.
- Most people affected by desertification are poor and rely on farming for their livelihood.
- One-third of the Earth's land surface — over 4 billion hectares — is threatened by desertification.
- In the less economically developed world, the total land area affected by desertification is between 6 million km^2 and 12 million km^2.

- Desertification and drought cause an estimated $42 billion in lost agricultural production worldwide every year.
- Annually, an estimated 1.5–2.5 million hectares of irrigated land, 3.5–4 million hectares of rain-fed agricultural land, and about 35 million hectares of rangeland lose all or part of their productivity due to land degradation.
- In Africa, 36 countries are affected by desertification or by land degradation, and an estimated 75% of the continent's farmland is rapidly losing the basic nutrients needed to grow crops.

Land degradation

There are several forms of land degradation in hot arid and semi-arid environments:

➤ soil erosion
➤ salinisation of water and soils
➤ deforestation

All reduce the productive potential of farmland and impoverish the lives of millions of people. In extreme cases, land degradation may create food shortages and cause irreparable damage to soil, water and vegetation.

Dennis Cox/Alamy

Photograph 4.20
Eroded hills on the loess plateau near the Yellow River, China

Soil erosion

Soil erosion usually follows the destruction of the vegetation cover that prevents the topsoil being removed by runoff and wind. In hot arid and semi-arid environments, deforestation as a result of overgrazing, or deliberate clearance for fuelwood and timber, often trigger erosion. Overcultivation has similar effects. Exhausted soil lacking organic material loses its structure and is easily removed by wind and water.

Soil erosion also causes problems elsewhere. Blown soil can damage crops by sandblasting and burial; runoff on slopes can carve deep gullies across fields; and soil, washed away in streams and rivers, causes problems of silting in irrigation canals and reservoirs. The scale of soil erosion can be huge. In the drylands of the loess plateau in central China, soil losses average $100\,t\,ha\,year^{-1}$ (Photograph 4.20).

Salinisation

Salinisation is widespread in hot arid and semi-arid environments. The process involves the accumulation of chloride, sulphate and carbonate salts of sodium, calcium and magnesium in the soil and occurs when the water table is close to the surface. When salts build up in the soil they seriously affect crop production. Not only do salts reduce the soil's capacity to hold air and nutrients, they are also toxic to many plants.

Most salinisation of cropland is due to mismanagement (Figure 4.21). When farmers irrigate land without adequate drainage or apply excess irrigation water, the water table in the soil rises. Salty water may then reach the root zone of crops, or worse, be drawn to the surface. There, high temperatures and evaporation create a salt crust. In extreme conditions, farmers may have no choice but to abandon the land.

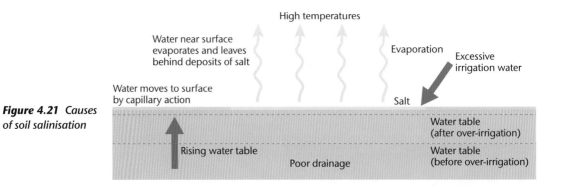

Figure 4.21 *Causes of soil salinisation*

In semi-arid environments in southern and western Australia, deforestation causes soil salinisation. Under the natural vegetation cover, deep-rooted trees suck water from the soil, keeping the water table well below the surface. Deforestation in the twentieth century, and the replacement of trees with shallow-rooted annual crops, allowed groundwater levels to rise and bring salts to the surface.

Deforestation

Deforestation contributes to desertification and land degradation in many hot and semi-arid regions in the economically developing world. Pressures on woodland are particularly acute in the transition zones from dry to more humid environments. The demand for firewood for cooking and lighting is a major cause of desertification in the African Sahel, in countries like Burkina Faso and Niger. In some areas, virtually all trees and shrubs have been removed within a 2–3 km radius of each village. Overgrazing by domestic livestock also prevents the regeneration of woodland. Deforestation exposes soils to erosion by wind and water.

Case study   **Land degradation in Nara, Mali**

Nara is a semi-arid region in the landlocked west African state of Mali (Figure 4.22). Even by African standards Mali is poor. The UN's human development index for 2006 ranks Mali as the 175th poorest country in the world out of 178.

Mean annual rainfall in Nara is 378 mm and potential evapotranspiration is four to five times higher. Rainfall follows a seasonal pattern. There is a wet season between June and October. The rest of the year is dry. Despite its seasonality, rainfall is highly variable and often unpredictable (Figure 4.23). Drought is an all too common characteristic of the climate. There are no permanent rivers and the natural vegetation is grass and woody scrub.

The native people of Nara divide into two economic groups. The agro-pastoralists such as the Sarakolé are sedentary. They rely on direct rainfall (not irrigation), and grow crops such as millet, cowpeas and sorghum. At the same time, they keep cattle, sheep, goats and donkeys. Nomadic pastoralists such as the Fulani form the second group. Their economy is based on the continual movement of livestock in search of pasture and water.

Causes of desertification

Desertification is neither a sudden nor a new problem in Nara (Figure 4.24). Local people believe that it can be traced back to the severe drought that hit the region between 1969 and 1973. Since then, rainfall has dropped by 30%. At the same time, explosive

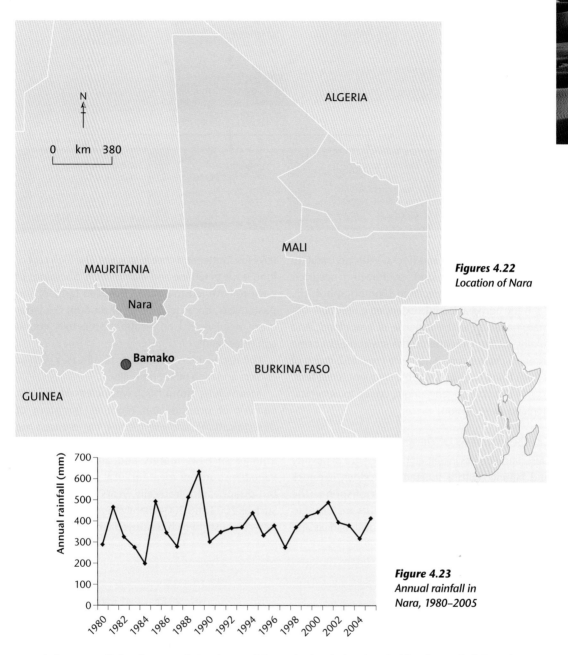

Figures 4.22
Location of Nara

Figure 4.23
Annual rainfall in Nara, 1980–2005

population growth has increased the demand for food, animal feed and firewood. Drought and population growth have combined to cause deforestation, soil erosion and desertification. Degraded croplands and pasturelands have lowered yields, creating poverty and food shortages. Thousands of people have become environmental refugees: forced to quit the land, they headed for the capital, Bamako. As a consequence, its population has grown from 800 000 to 2 million in the past 20 years.

Despite significant out-migration, Nara's population grew from 120 000 in 1976 to over 190 000 in 1996. This expansion had predictable results. First, both the agro-pastoralists and nomads

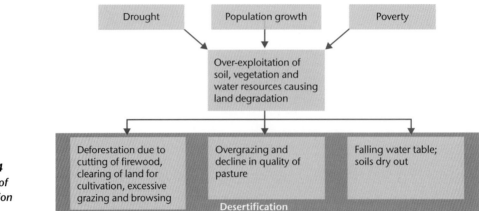

Figure 4.24
The causes of desertification in Nara

increased their herds and flocks. With no tradition of managing pastureland, overgrazing occurred and pasture quality declined (Photograph 4.21). Then the agro-pastoralists extended cultivation into marginal areas at the expense of woodland. And finally, further pressure on the environment came through people collecting more firewood, much of it from living trees and shrubs. Frequent forest fires, mainly of anthropogenic origin, added to deforestation and wind erosion.

Consequences of desertification

Desertification has increased the incidence of poverty and famine. With a shortage of fodder, livestock produce less milk and have fewer offspring. The economic effects are acute. Pastoralists are forced to sell their animals at lower prices in local markets and have less butter and cheese to trade. The high cost of food leads to famine and malnutrition. Shortages of pasture have led to conflict between farmers and pastoralists, because in times of drought the latter graze their livestock on the more fertile soils around cultivated lands.

Polluted water is responsible for diseases such as cholera and high infant mortality.

Meanwhile, droughts have increased the salt content of groundwater (another symptom of desertification), and overgrazing has reduced the vegetation cover and plant and animal biodiversity. Wildlife such as rabbits and antelope, once a valuable source of meat for local people, have all but disappeared. Ironically, years of plentiful rain such as 2003 and 2004 merely triggered plagues of desert locusts, which destroyed crops.

Photograph 4.21
In Nara, pasture quality has declined due to overgrazing and no tradition of managed pastureland

Frans Lemmens/Alamy

Conclusion

Nara, situated between the savanna and the Sahara Desert, is part of the Sahel: a vast parched region stretching across north Africa from Senegal to Eritrea. This is a delicate environment where plant and animal life, and human economies, are finely balanced. In the past, indigenous people like the Sarakolé and Fulani have exploited the ecosystem's resources sustainably. These societies were resilient: they could cope with drought and the Sahel's erratic and unpredictable rainfall.

Present-day desertification in Nara is a sign that this balance no longer exists. Two things have changed: rainfall has dropped by 30% and droughts are more prolonged and more frequent. At the same time, population growth has been rapid and unchecked. Thus, while environmental resources shrink, the demands on these resources are greater than ever. The result is desertification. This means falling groundwater levels, increasing salinity, deforestation, the degrading of pastures and, ultimately, the erosion of the soil by wind and water. As the natural wealth degrades, famine, death, societal instability and out-migration take hold.

Tackling desertification

Desertification causes serious environmental damage, often depleting resources such as soil and water over large areas. Reversing this process is not easy. In this section, we look at two ambitious attempts to combat desertification. First, through a massive afforestation programme in northern China; and second, through the reclamation of salinised farmland in northern Pakistan.

Case study **China's Great Green Wall**

The desertification problem

Environmental degradation leading to desertification is a major problem in China. It affects one-third of the country's total land area. The most seriously affected areas are the arid, semi-arid and sub-humid regions of northern China. The environmental costs are startling. Every year China loses 5 billion tonnes of topsoil to erosion. Meanwhile, poorly managed irrigation has created nearly 1 million km^2 of saline land in China.

Combating desertification

In 1978, China began an ambitious programme to tackle desertification in its northern provinces. Popularly known as the 'Great Green Wall', it is the largest afforestation scheme in the world. Its purpose is to establish 350 000 km^2 of shelterbelt and plantation forests across the entire region of northern China by 2050. So far over 130 000 km^2 have been planted. The programme has three main objectives:

- to protect farmland and settlements from wind and water erosion
- to improve land management
- to stabilise sand dunes and reclaim degraded lands

Korqin Sandy Lands

The Korqin Sandy Lands of northern China cover nearly 42 000 km^2, an area about the size of Denmark (Figure 4.25). In this warm, semi-arid environment rainfall averages 300–500 mm a year. But high temperatures and strong winds raise potential evapotranspiration two to three times higher than rainfall. Problems of water shortage are made worse by sandy soils, which are highly permeable. In addition, being loosely structured with little organic material,

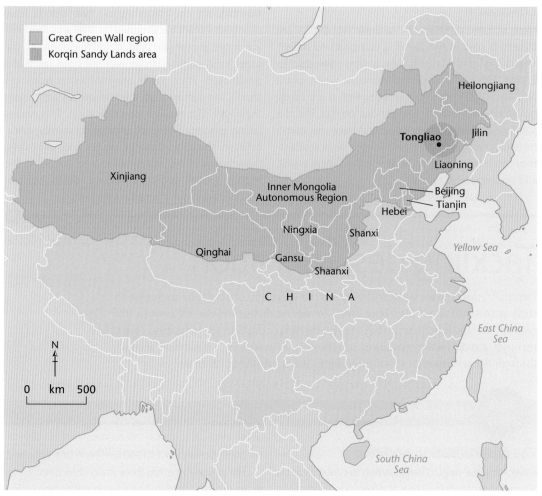

Figure 4.25 *China's 'Great Green Wall' and the Korqin Sandy Lands project area*

they are highly susceptible to wind erosion. Today little remains of the original grassland and open woodland that once covered the region (Figure 4.26).

The Korqin Sandy Lands, inhabited by farmers and herdsmen, include some of the most degraded land in China. Desertification, due to inappropriate farming practices and population pressure, has accelerated in the past 100 years. Its immediate causes are overgrazing (by cattle, goats, sheep, camels and horses), clearing of land for agriculture, and the removal of trees and shrubs for timber. Recently, increased demands for water for irrigation, domestic

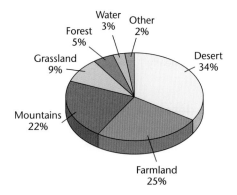

Figure 4.26 *Land use in the Korqin Sandy Lands*

use and industry, have lowered the water table, and accelerated deforestation. Soils in the Korqin are fragile and overcultivated. Soil fertility has declined as residues from crops, formerly used as manure, are removed for fuel and fodder. Furthermore, where drainage is poor, salinity becomes a problem. Very strong winds, which occur on 25–40 days per year, are the chief agents of desertification and produce violent duststorms.

The Great Green Wall programme in Korqin is financed jointly by the governments of China and Belgium and by the Food and Agriculture Organization (FAO) of the UN. The Korqin project aims to:
- protect cultivated land against soil erosion
- restore soil fertility
- improve the economic well-being of the region's inhabitants
- provide the local population with a sustainable source of timber

Most of the emphasis is on afforestation. Plantations and shelterbelts have been established using native poplars, which are drought and frost resistant. Mechanised afforestation techniques (e.g. fast planting machines and aerial seeding) suitable for large-scale planting have been developed. However, the project is more than just afforestation. There is, for example, an emphasis on appropriate cultivation techniques, especially recycling organic material in the soil; integrating tree crops with pasture and cash crops (agro-forestry); and planting tree species that provide fodder for grazing animals and improve soil fertility. Controlled management of grazing lands is being introduced for the first time.

Box 4.6 Shelterbelts and soil conservation

A shelterbelt is a barrier of trees or shrubs. Shelterbelts:
- reduce soil erosion by wind
- increase moisture for crop growth by reducing evaporation
- reduce wind damage to crops
- increase crop yields
- provide valuable wildlife habitats

Shelterbelts modify microclimates downwind. Most importantly, they reduce wind speed for a distance approximating 20 times the height of the shelterbelt. Thus, a shelterbelt 10 m high will provide protection for soils and crops for a distance of 200 m downwind. Shelterbelts even reduce wind speeds on the upwind side, to a distance of three to five times their height (Figure 4.27).

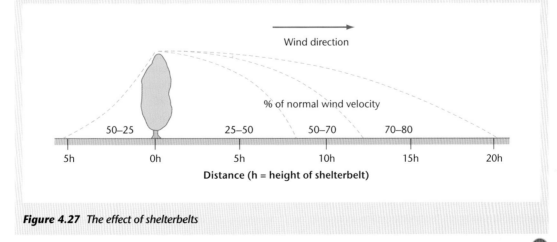

Figure 4.27 *The effect of shelterbelts*

Case study

Khushab salinity control and reclamation project

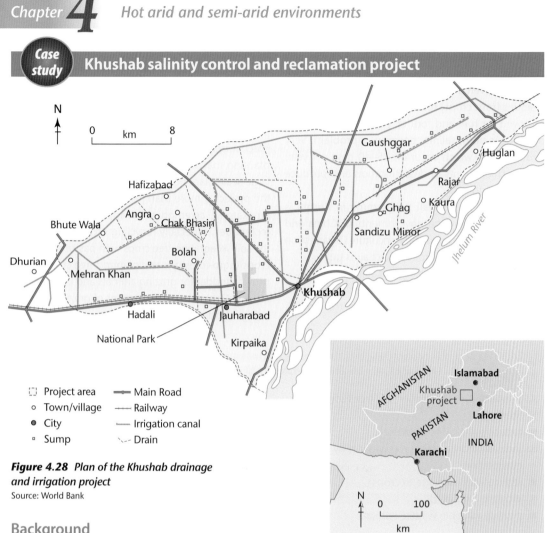

Figure 4.28 *Plan of the Khushab drainage and irrigation project*
Source: World Bank

Legend:
- Project area
- Town/village
- City
- Sump
- Main Road
- Railway
- Irrigation canal
- Drain

Background

The Khushab project is located in northern Pakistan on the north bank of the Jhelum River (Figure 4.28). It occupies a small part of the vast alluvial plain of the Indus River system. Annual rainfall averages around 400 mm, and maximum daily temperatures exceed 40°C from May to July.

In this hot, semi-arid environment cultivation relies on irrigation. However, by the late 1980s, over-irrigation had caused severe waterlogging and soil salinity problems. Reductions in crop yields and land abandonment meant high unemployment and acute poverty for most of the area's 8000 farming families. A range of techniques are available to reclaim and manage degraded and desertified land. They are listed in Table 4.2.

The project

The Khushab project, financed by the World Bank, was a high-cost scheme ($69 million) to reduce waterlogging and salinisation on 360 km² of cultivated land (Figure 4.28). Successful land reclamation and rehabilitation would increase agricultural production, create more jobs, and raise farm incomes. Waterlogging and salinisation were tackled by installing field underdrainage using PVC pipes, constructing new surface water drains, and lining irrigation canals to reduce water losses through seepage. In addition, demonstration farms and centres educated local farmers on sustainable water management.

Impact

The project, completed between 1989 and 1994, has been highly successful. Thanks to effective drainage, groundwater levels have fallen significantly, lowering soil salinity and reducing waterlogging. Indeed, the waterlogged area halved within the first 2 years of the project.

The project has brought considerable economic benefits to local farming families. Per capita incomes have increased from $46 in 1989 to $195 in 2005. This is a considerable achievement. It means that incomes for an average family in Khushab are now 34% above the official poverty level. Without the project, the World Bank estimates that average incomes would have continued to decline to around $30. All of this has been made possible by improvements in land quality, which have increased the production of crops such as rice, wheat and sugar cane. Drainage has also resulted in fewer waterborne diseases and less damage to homes from land subsidence.

Clearly the significant achievements of poverty reduction and the reclamation of desertified land fully justify the Khushab project. However, the project also demonstrates how once land has been degraded by salinisation, reclamation is both a costly and a complex process.

Table 4.2 Reclaimation and management of degraded and desertified lands

Land degradation	Management responses
Soil erosion (water)	• Terrace hillslopes • Afforestation to hold soil in place, increase interception and reduce runoff • Build check dams in gulleys to intercept soil washed from fields • Strip cropping to ensure some crop cover throughout the year • Agro-sylviculture: integration of tree crops with arable farming • Contour ploughing on slopes to reduce the energy of runoff
Soil erosion (wind)	• Shelterbelts and plantations to reduce wind speed • Maintain soil fertility and structure by adding organic matter to the soil • Leave the stubble and residues of previous crops in fields to reduce wind speed close to the ground • Strip cropping • Agro-sylviculture • Stabilise dunes by afforestation • Prevent overgrazing of rangeland and destruction of vegetation cover
Salinisation	• Remove salinised surface layers of the soil • Leach salt from the soil by applying large amounts of water (water table must be lowered first) • Install artificial underdrainage to lower water table • Line drainage ditches and irrigation canals to prevent seepage • Lower the water table by pumping and/or planting trees • Water management and prevention of over-irrigation
Deforestation	• Reafforestation — trees provide shelter, fodder, fuelwood and prevent soil erosion
Overgrazing	• Controlled grazing • Fencing and rotation of grazed areas • Fencing of heavily grazed areas around wells and waterholes • Reduce stocking densities • Reseeding and re-establishing vegetation cover

Examination-style questions

Figure 1

1 **(a)** Use Figure 1 to describe the main features of the vegetation in hot arid and semi-arid environments. (4 marks)

(b) Explain the limiting effects of climate on ecosystems in hot arid and semi-arid environments. (6 marks)

(c) In what sense are hot arid and semi-arid environments 'fragile'? (6 marks)

(d) With reference to one or more named examples, explain the opportunities for development in hot arid and semi-arid environments. (9 marks)

2 With reference to named examples, explain how planning for development in hot arid and semi-arid environments is often about balancing socio-economic and environmental needs. (25 marks)

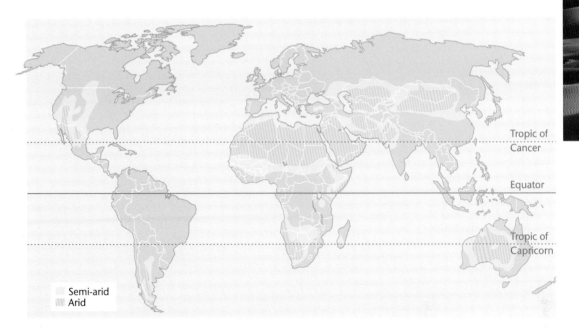

Tropic of
Cancer

Equator

Tropic of
Capricorn

Semi-arid
Arid

Figure 2 *The world's hot arid and semi-arid environments*

3 (a) Describe the distribution of the world's hot arid and semi-arid
environments in Figure 2. (4 marks)

(b) Explain the distribution of the world's hot arid and semi-arid
environments. (6 marks)

(c) Explain the formation of one named landform that occurs in hot
arid and semi-arid environments. (6 marks)

(d) With reference to one or more named examples, outline the
opportunities for, and the problems created by, agriculture in
hot arid and semi-arid environments. (9 marks)

4 With reference to named examples, explain how careful management is
needed to ensure sustainable development in hot arid and semi-arid
environments. (25 marks)

Unit F762

Managing Change in Human Environments

Managing urban change

The characteristics of urban areas

Key ideas

➤ Urban areas have a variety of functions, processes and distinct patterns of land use.

➤ The range of functions found in urban areas include industrial, commercial, residential and recreational activities.

➤ Patterns of urban land use are influenced by a number of factors that vary from place to place.

➤ Social, economic, political and environmental factors influence urban land-use patterns.

Defining towns and cities

There is no simple or internationally agreed definition of towns and cities. The UK census describes a town or city as:

> …a free-standing built-up area with a service core with a sufficient variety of shops and services…to make it urban in character. It has administrative, commercial, educational, entertainment and other social and civic functions, and in many cases evidence of being historically well established. A local network of roads and other means of transport focus on the area and it is a place drawing people for services and employment from surrounding areas.

According to this definition, towns and cities have four essential characteristics. They:

➤ are built up

➤ provide a range of services and employment for residents and people in the surrounding area

➤ act as focal points for local transport networks

➤ are free standing

However, not all towns and cities are free standing. In the UK, as towns have grown, many have merged with neighbouring towns to form continuously built-up areas known as conurbations. Examples include Greater Manchester and West Yorkshire. Others, such as Shinjuku in Greater Tokyo, have developed as satellite centres in the suburbs.

For the purposes of national censuses, urban definitions must be simple and practical. Table 5.1 lists some national definitions. The most widely used criterion is population size. Other criteria include population density, average distance between buildings, and employment in non-agricultural activities. Variable definitions of 'urban' reflect differences in economic and social conditions between countries. For this reason, the UN does not use a standard definition when compiling its statistics. Thus, any general statements about urban populations at a global scale must be viewed with caution.

| Country | Criteria used for defining urban populations | | | |
	Population size	Employment	Contiguity of building	Density
Botswana	5000+	75% workforce in non-agricultural activities		
France	2000+		In contiguous housing with <200 m between houses	
Iceland	200+			
India	5000+	75%+ male workers in non-agricultural activities	Pronounced urban characteristics	Not less than 390 km^2
Israel	2000+	Less than one-third workforce employed in agriculture		
Japan	50 000+	60%+ engaged in manufacturing, trades and other urban businesses	60%+ of houses located in main built-up area	
Mexico	2500+			
Senegal	10 000+			

Table 5.1 Some national census definitions of urban populations

Source: UN Demographic Yearbook

Urban functions

Towns and cities perform a varied range of functions for their own residents and for the population in the surrounding area. We group these functions into several broad categories, such as residential, retailing and commercial (Table 5.2). In geographical terms, each urban function translates into a specific type of land use. The resulting mosaic of land uses makes up the built area that we call a town or a city. Each land-use type has a number of distinctive characteristics such as morphology, density, extent and location.

Table 5.2 *Urban functions and land use*

General functions	Land use
Residential	Housing types (morphology): detached, semi-detached, terraced, apartments, maisonettes Housing types (tenancy): owner-occupied, rented (private, public), illegal (e.g. squatters)
Commercial	Retailing, warehousing, offices, hotels
Administrative	Offices: central/local government (e.g. town hall); public utilities
Other public services	Schools, hospitals, swimming pools, sewage works, cemeteries, crematoria, landfill sites
Transport	Roads, railways, airports, canals
Industrial	Manufacturing (light/heavy), energy supply, mining, quarrying
Recreational	Parks, playing fields, allotments, woodland
Non-functional	Derelict land, wasteland

Urban land-use patterns

Every town and city has its own unique land-use geography. The distribution of land use within cities reflects the influence of factors often operating over several decades or centuries. Among these factors are:

➤ transport technology — the speed and efficiency of urban transport affects the size of an urban area, and the opportunities for commuting. Cities in Europe, which rely on public transport, are more compact than US cities, which depend heavily on private (car) transport and urban freeways.

➤ historic growth — in Europe, the Middle East and Asia, large parts of the urban structure relate to past historic growth. In contrast, cities in North and South America have a more recent origin.

➤ competition between land uses — in a free market, land-use patterns are often the outcome of competition between land users. Theory says that retailing, other services and offices dominate the central areas of towns and cities because they are the most profitable functions and can afford the high rents.

➤ topography — the distribution of land uses will be influenced by coastlines, river valleys, altitude and slopes.

➤ social distance — where strong social, ethnic and racial differences exist between groups, segregation often occurs. Segregation is facilitated by the distribution of housing types.

➤ transport routes — railways, airports and motorways increase accessibility and so may attract manufacturing industries, warehousing and other commercial activities, and commuters.

➤ traditions, values, culture — land-use patterns reflect differences in culture. For example, the urban land-use patterns in cities in Europe and North America are very different from those in the economically developing world.

➤ local economic system — cities that specialise in economic activities such as tourism and heavy industry carry a strong imprint of these activities in their land-use patterns.

➤ local climates — prevailing winds and the development of temperature inversions in valleys often influence the type, quality and distribution of urban housing in both MEDCs and LEDCs.
➤ planning — before the twentieth century, most cities grew organically, with little formal planning. In the UK, the introduction of government planning from the 1930s has had the greatest influence on the land use and internal structure of cities. Some urban settlements, such as new towns, owe their form entirely to the planning process.

Urban structure models

The distribution of types of land use within towns and cities is not random. Pattern and order in urban land use was first recognised in the 1920s. Intrigued by these patterns, geographers and other social scientists devised a number of general land use or structure models to describe urban land use. The early models focused on North American cities. Later models were adapted to describe the structure of cities in LEDCs (Figures 5.1–5.3).

1 Central business district
2 Wholesale light manufacturing
3 Low-class residential
4 Medium-class residential
5 High-class residential
6 Heavy manufacturing
7 Outlying business district
8 Residential suburb
9 Industrial suburb
10 Commuters' zone

Zonal model

The zonal model represents urban land use as a series of concentric rings or zones. The assumption is that the city has grown outwards in all directions from a central core. Each growth period adds a new zone of urban development. As a result, the urban fabric gets younger with increasing distance from the centre. The width of each zone depends on the density of the built area and the efficiency of urban transport. The zonal model, based on Chicago in the 1920s, describes an expanding city due to massive in-migration. Physical expansion of the built area is explained by the process of **invasion and succession**. Immigrants first settled in cheap housing near the city centre, displacing existing residents who moved out to the next zone. This process had a ripple effect which resulted in new growth zones being added around the edge of the city.

Figure 5.1

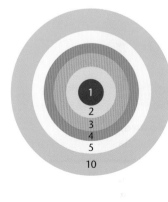

(a) Zonal model

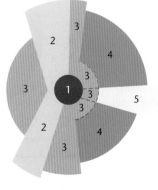

(b) Sector model

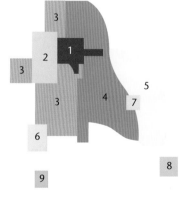

(c) Multiple-nuclei model

Sector model

The sector model describes urban land use as a series of wedges or sectors that radiate from the city centre. Sectors develop along transport corridors where accessibility is high. Unlike zonal growth, sectoral growth is directional and often segregates different land uses (e.g. industry from housing) and different ethnic and income groups.

In the sector model, residential areas develop by **filtering** rather than by invasion and succession. The process starts when new housing is built for high-income groups. They vacate their old residences which are occupied by the next income group down. In this way, the housing stock filters down the economic and social hierarchy over time.

Multiple-nuclei model

Most large cities do not grow around a single central business district. The multiple-nuclei model describes cities that have a loose structure, with growth concentrated around several nuclei. The nuclei comprise outer business districts, industrial concentrations and residential areas. The model acknowledges that some activities repel each other due to negative externalities (e.g. polluting industry and high-quality residential areas) and others attract (e.g. a port facility and manufacturing industry).

Pre-industrial model

Many contemporary cities in LEDCs have a pre-industrial structure in their central core. Pre-industrial cities had a feudal social hierarchy. The wealthy elite occupied the city centre – the highest status area. The lower the status of any social group, the more peripheral would be their location. Thus an economic and social gradient extended from the city centre, with the poorest groups living on the edge of the city or even outside its walls. Foreign and ethnic minority groups were segregated into distinctive quarters of the city (e.g. a Jewish quarter).

Figure 5.2 *Pre-industrial model*

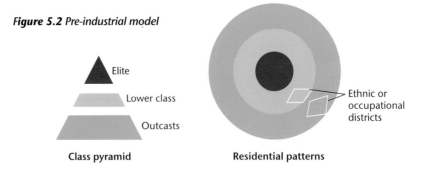

Elite

Lower class

Outcasts

Class pyramid

Ethnic or occupational districts

Residential patterns

Latin American city model

Colonialism left a strong imprint on Latin American cities. The Spanish and Portuguese adopted similar city plans: a central square with a major church or cathedral, with the main administrative area and residences of the colonial elite nearby. A grid-iron street pattern then spread out from the centre. Modern Latin

American cities often have a commercial spine that extends out from the central business district. Adjacent to the commercial spine, giving easy access to shops and cultural services, are the homes of high-income groups. Social and economic status tends to decline with distance from the centre. The zones of maturity are either areas of elite housing that have filtered downmarket, or self-built housing that has been upgraded. Housing in the zone of accretion is more modest and with inferior infrastructure. The periphery is the location of squatter settlements. This is also a zone of disamenity, where industry and environmentally polluting activities occur.

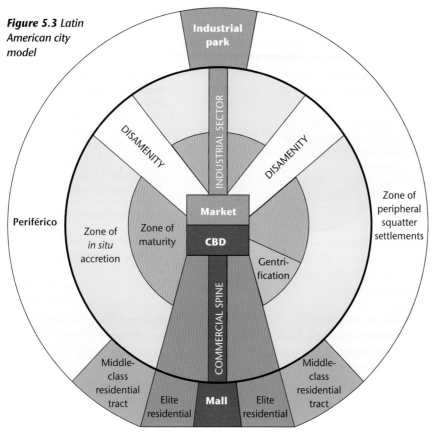

Figure 5.3 *Latin American city model*

Urban structure models suggest that spatial patterns of land use in towns and cities have a clear order and that similar types of land use tend to cluster in three basic forms: **zones**, sectors and nuclei. No single model fits any one city, but despite their simplicity, elements of the structure models are found in most large cities.

The zonal, sector and multiple-nuclei models were based on North American cities in the period from 1920 to 1950. In 1965, Mann devised a structure model for a medium-sized British city (Figure 5.4). Based on zones and sectors, it gives more insight into the land-use patterns that are typical of British cities, incorporating local authority housing and a climatic factor. Its main features are as follows:

➤ High-income residential areas (A) form the western suburbs, upwind of, and on the opposite side of the city from, the industrial sector (D).

➤ Low-income residential areas including local authority (council) housing (C) are located close to the industrial zone.

➤ Lower-middle-class housing (B) is peripheral and adjacent to the high-income residential area (A).

➤ A central business district (CBD) surrounded by a transitional zone of small terraced houses (sectors C and D), old larger houses in sector B, and large houses in sector A; post-1918 and post-1945 houses in zone 4 on the periphery; and the commuter zone in 5.

Figure 5.4
Mann's structure of a British city

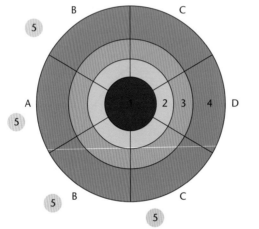

1 City centre
2 Transitional zone
3 Zone of small terraced houses in sectors C and D, bye-law houses in sector B, large old houses in sector A
4 Post-1918 residential areas with post-1945 development mainly on periphery
5 Commuting-distance villages

A Middle-class sector
B Lower-middle-class sector
C Working-class sector (and main municipal housing areas)
D Industrial and lowest working-class areas

Box 5.1 Bid-rent model

The bid-rent model provides an alternative, economic explanation for the zonation of urban land use. In a free-market system, urban land use is determined by a process of competitive bidding. Thus, in the absence of planning controls, those users making the highest bid will gain control of the land.

Each land user has a unique bid-rent curve, i.e. the price or rent they are prepared to pay to secure a particular location. These bid-rent curves are the outcome of the trade-off between accessibility and land rent (or price). In the model, the city centre is assumed to be the most accessible location and therefore commands the highest rent. High levels of demand and shortages of space are reflected in high-density development and the concentration of multi-storey buildings in the CBD. As distance from the city centre increases, demand falls and rents or land values decline; so too do building heights and building densities.

For commercial functions such as retailing, financial and legal services, the city centre is often the most attractive location in the city, giving access to the largest number of customers. Thus, under normal circumstances, these functions outbid other users and dominate the central area. For other land users, proximity to the centre may be less important than access to motorways, the countryside or extensive sites. In Figure 5.5 this is evident in the more gently sloping bid-rent curves for housing and industry. The result of competitive bidding is a series of concentric land use zones around the city centre.

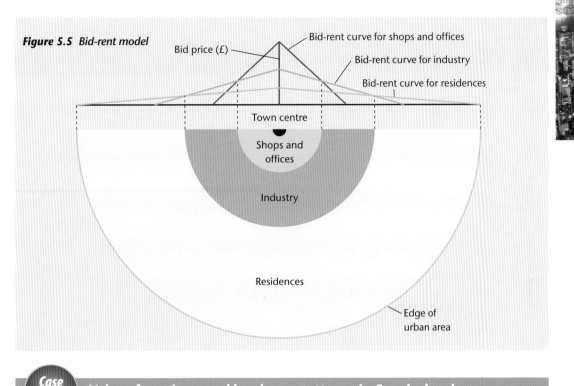

Figure 5.5 *Bid-rent model*

Bid price (£)

Bid-rent curve for shops and offices

Bid-rent curve for industry

Bid-rent curve for residences

Town centre

Shops and offices

Industry

Residences

Edge of urban area

Case study — Urban functions and land-use patterns in Sunderland

Sunderland is a port and free-standing city located on the coast in northeast England. The total population within the Sunderland metropolitan district in 2001 was 280 000.

Site

A 'site' is the area occupied by a settlement. Sunderland's site has had an important influence on the city's structure. Expansion to the east is limited by the coastline. Meanwhile, the site is bisected by the River Wear. At Sunderland the river has cut a deeply incised valley through the limestone of the East Durham Plateau. Settlements on the north and south banks of the River Wear developed separately until they were joined by the Wearmouth Bridge, opened in 1796.

Industrialisation

Sunderland's basic layout and structure were established in the nineteenth century when industrialisa-tion transformed the city. Like other industrial cities in northern England, Sunderland experienced massive population growth during this period. Between 1801 and 1901, its population grew from 12 400 to 146 000. Industrialisation created an economic boom and migrants flocked to the city to find work in its shipbuilding, coal and glass industries. As population expanded, so too did the built area.

The CBD, located on the south bank, was the focal point around which the city has developed (Figure 5.6). An inner city zone of high-density, low-quality terraced housing developed on both sides of the river as the urban area expanded outwards from the city centre. A sector of nineteenth-century terraced housing also developed southeast of the CBD, following the coastline and docks in Hendon. Although the worst slum housing was cleared in the 1950s, much of the fabric built between 1870 and 1914 survives today in Southwick, Roker and Hendon (see Photograph 5.1).

Figure 5.6
Sunderland:
urban structure

Source: Robson, B.
(1969) *Urban Analysis*,
Cambridge University
Press

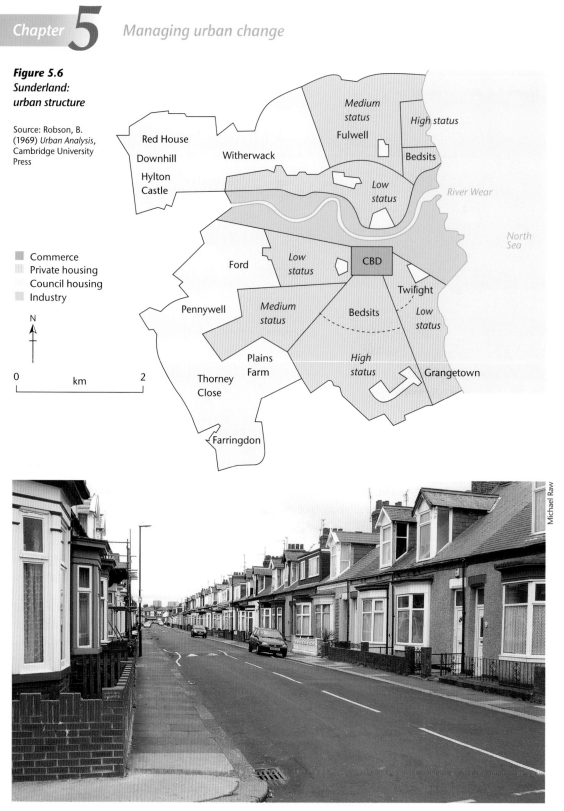

■ Commerce
▥ Private housing
☐ Council housing
▥ Industry

N

0   km   2

Photograph 5.1 *Terraced housing in Hendon*

The nineteenth-century terraces housed workers employed in nearby shipbuilding and coal industries that lined the riverside and quaysides. Because industries needed access to the river and docks, the main industrial areas developed as two sectors radiating from the centre. One followed the Wear Valley. The other extended south of the river along the coast and included the docks at Hendon. Thus, by 1862, when the first large-scale Ordnance Survey map of Sunderland was published, the modern urban structure of the city had already been established.

Suburbanisation

The city continued to expand in the twentieth century. Most of the growth was sectoral, following the major roads that radiated from the city centre. Sectoral growth made access of essential infrastructure such as roads, water and sewerage easier and cheaper. Suburban growth was low density and reflected rising living standards among the middle class. During the inter-war period, large tracts of private semi-detached and detached suburban housing were built in districts such as Fulwell and Grangetown. If the main driver of urban growth before 1939 was economic, in the 1950s and 1960s political factors played an increasing role. The local

authority tackled problems of housing shortages and slum housing by building large suburban council estates such as Pennywell, Thorney Close and Downhill. Thus, by the end of the 1970s, Sunderland's built area had extended westwards as far as the A19.

Deindustrialisation and regeneration

Until the late twentieth century, Sunderland retained its Victorian legacy of heavy industries such as shipbuilding and coal mining. Already in decline, these industries were hit hard by foreign competition in the 1980s. Deindustrialisation ravaged the city's economy. Shipbuilding ended in 1988, and the last colliery closed in 1993, leaving vast swathes of derelict land along the river.

However, since the 1990s, much of the river has been regenerated, creating new jobs, new land uses and a new urban morphology. Former industrial land at the mouth of the river is the site of the St Peter's Wharf project — a £55 million investment in luxury apartments, pubs, clubs, restaurants and bars (Photograph 5.2). Alongside is the new National Glass Centre. On the south bank directly opposite, the Echo project will create 179 waterside apartments. Upriver, the old Vaux brewery site is being regenerated with offices and apartments, while on the opposite bank,

Photograph 5.2
Regenerated waterfront at the mouth of the River Wear, Sunderland

Michael Raw

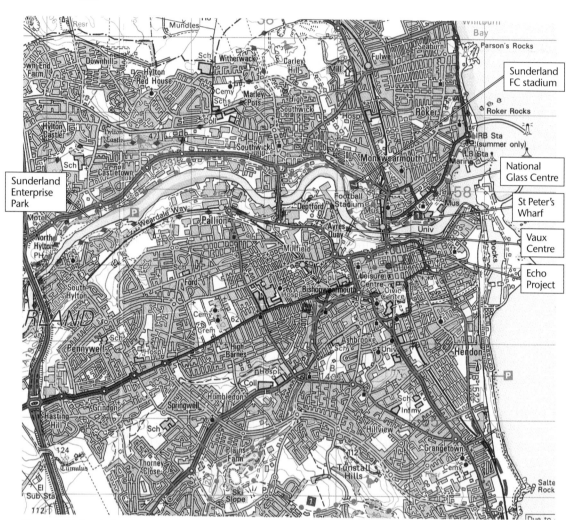

Figure 5.7 *Sunderland: regeneration schemes*

adjacent to Sunderland FC's new stadium, there is a major leisure-led development. Further west on the north bank, the Sunderland Enterprise Park occupies 30 ha of former brownfield land.

In the space of 20 years a large part of the zone of heavy industry and derelict land has been transformed into a thriving cityscape of waterside apartments, offices and leisure activities.

Case study Urban functions and land-use patterns in Buenos Aires

Buenos Aires, the capital of Argentina, is a **mega city** (i.e. a metropolitan area with a population of more than 10 million people). In 2001, the population of the Buenos Aires metropolitan area (Figure 5.8) was 12.5 million, which according to the UN makes the city the tenth largest in the world. Within the federal area, the population was 2.78 million. One-third of Argentina's population lives in the Buenos Aires metropolitan region. Not surprisingly, Buenos Aires is much bigger than any other city in the country.

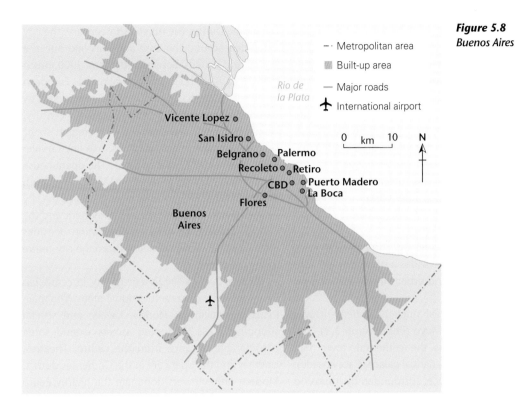

Figure 5.8
Buenos Aires

Key:
- ·· Metropolitan area
- ▨ Built-up area
- — Major roads
- ✈ International airport

Rio de la Plata

Vicente Lopez ○
San Isidro ○
Belgrano ○ Palermo ○
Recoleto ○ ○ Retiro
CBD ○ ○ Puerto Madero
○ ○ La Boca
Flores ○
Buenos Aires

0 km 10 N

Córdoba, Argentina's second city, has a population less than one-eighth the size of Buenos Aires. This makes Buenos Aires a **primate city** (i.e. the largest city in a country which is more than twice as big as the second city), dominating the settlement hierarchy as well as the economic and political life of Argentina.

History

The city was established in 1580 by Spanish colonists after an earlier unsuccessful attempt in 1537. Its site, on the western shore of the Rio de la Plata (see Figure 1.27, p. 29), is flat, extensive and gives direct access to the Atlantic Ocean. The city grew rapidly during the nineteenth century following Argentina's independence from Spain in 1816. Immigrants flooded into the city, mainly from Italy and Spain. As a result, its population grew from 90000 in 1850 to 1.3 million in 1910 (Table 5.3). By 1895, 70% of the city's inhabitants were foreign-born. As the population grew, the city expanded outwards from its centre. Key to this expansion was the flat site and

radial rail network. In the late nineteenth century and the twentieth century this pattern of radial growth was reinforced by the tram and bus networks. Although Buenos Aires has a subway system, this does not extend far into the suburbs.

Table 5.3 Population of the Buenos Aires metropolitan area and Argentina, 1869–2001

Year	Buenos Aires (BA)	Argentina	% of Argentina's population in BA
1869	181 000	1 830 000	9.9
1895	671 000	4 045 000	16.5
1914	1 973 000	7 904 000	25.0
1947	4 643 000	15 894 000	29.2
1960	6 750 000	20 014 000	33.7
1970	8 353 000	23 364 000	35.8
1980	9 766 000	27 949 000	34.9
1991	10 887 000	32 423 000	33.6
2001	12 550 000	37 916 000	33.1

Buenos Aires benefited because its location on the Rio de la Plata gave access to Europe and to the interior along the Parana River system. A further advantage was its proximity to the vast agricultural wealth of the Pampas. It was the natural outlet for the export of wheat and meat products to Europe. Agricultural products from its hinterland also supported a vast food processing industry in the city. Thus, Buenos Aires became a classic gateway city, articulating trade between Europe and Argentina, Uruguay, Paraguay and southern Brazil.

Central area

The urban structure model for Latin American cities shown in Figure 5.3 provides a useful insight into patterns of land use and urban structure in Buenos Aires.

The original colonial nucleus settlement was around the Plaza de Mayo (Photograph 5.3). The historic core contains the cathedral, town hall (Cabildo), and the presidential palace (Casa Rosada). It is a large public space, surrounded by imposing buildings. During the nineteenth century, the city expanded around the core and was laid out in a formal grid pattern. Between 1870 and 1900, much of this area was rebuilt. The inspiration was European architecture, especially central Paris, remodelled by Baron Hausmann in the mid-nineteenth century. Neighbourhoods were rebuilt with elegant six or seven-storey apartment buildings, tree-lined boulevards, plazas and formal gardens. The opera house (Teatro Colón) dates to this time. As in other South American cities, elite social groups occupied the city centre, giving easy access to employment and the cultural facilities of the city. Population densities remain high and decline steeply from the city centre to the periphery.

Because Buenos Aires is a mega city, its centre has geographically discrete functional areas. The main focus of retailing is Florida, Lavalle and several shopping malls. Shopping streets extend some considerable distance from the centre. Theatres, cinemas and the opera are in the Corrientes district. Modern office towers dominate the nearby Retiro

Photograph 5.3 *Plaza de Mayo and the colonial town hall (Cabildo)*

Michael Raw

Photograph 5.4 *Avenida 9 de Julio — the main commercial spine of Buenos Aires*

quarter north of the centre. Planners have excluded modern office towers from the old central areas of the city. Government functions occupy the Plaza de Mayo and the Avenida de Mayo axis (Photograph 5.3).

Two spines cut through the central parts of the city. One, the Avenida de Mayo, is the main processional way for state occasions, linking the National Congress building with the Casa Rosada. Its intersection with a second spine — the Avenida 9 de Julio (Photograph 5.4) — is marked by the Obelisco, commemorating the first 100 years of Argentina's existence as a sovereign state. Commercial activities such as banks, five-star hotels and transnational company headquarters, as well as luxury apartments, cluster along the Avenida 9 de Julio spine.

A sector of industry originally dominated the nine-teenth-century Puerto Madero waterfront to the east of the centre. Much of this area has been regenerated since the early 1990s. Warehouses have been converted to luxury flats, restaurants, bars, offices and a university. A former dock is now a marina.

Similar change is occurring in La Boca, a rundown dockside area to the south of Puerto Madero.

The suburbs

The social and economic status of residents in the suburbs of Buenos Aires generally declines from north to south. This spatial pattern is reflected in the urban structure. Low-density northern suburbs such as Belgrano and Palermo (and some in the west such as Flores), and outlying municipalities like San Isidro and Vicente Lopez, have tree-lined streets, large areas of gardens, parks, country clubs and golf courses. These suburbs are comparable to high-income neighbourhoods in European and North American cities.

However, most of suburban Buenos Aires is a vast urban sprawl of low-quality, high-density housing mixed with industry. Laid out on the same grid plan as the city centre, there are few open spaces and services are often poor. Street lighting is dim, roads are badly maintained, and much of the housing, built with minimal planning control, is rundown. Self-

Michael Raw

Photograph 5.5 *Squatter settlements* (villas miserais) *in the inner suburbs of Buenos Aires*

improvement of homes is common, with improvised extensions and additional storeys. These suburbs, comprising older, conventional housing, correspond to the zone of maturity in the Latin American city model (see Figure 5.3, page 205).

A similar urban structure is found in the more distant suburbs or zone of accretion. This zone has a more uniform residential land use. Services are fewer, the inhabitants poorer, and planning is largely absent.

The periphery

The periphery is the main zone of squatter settlements. In Buenos Aires these settlements, known as *villas miserais*, are occupied by the poorest groups — mainly migrants of mixed Indian and European race *(mestizos)* from the northern provinces of Argentina (Photograph 5.5). However, squatter settlements are by no means confined to the periphery. Clusters of unserviced, temporary shacks are found along railway tracks and beneath motorway bridges close to the city centre — anywhere that gives access to vacant land and employment.

Since the mid-1990s, there has been a huge expansion of gated communities in municipalities in the northern periphery of the metropolitan area, such as San Isidro and Vicente Lopez. High-income groups are deserting the centre for a North American suburban lifestyle, with free-standing houses, gardens, safe play areas for children, golf clubs and country clubs. The construction of urban freeways has opened up the periphery to commuters prepared to travel 20–30 km to the city centre, but high-income enclaves have to be gated because they are often surrounded by squatters, who find unoccupied land on the edge of the city easy to settle on. The physical separation of poor from rich in gated communities highlights the massive inequalities found in cities like Buenos Aires in the less-economically developed world.

Social and economic issues associated with urban change

Key ideas

➤ Urban growth and decay give rise to a variety of social and economic issues.

➤ A large proportion of urban dwellers suffer social and economic deprivation.

➤ The characteristics of urban deprivation include low levels of economic well-being, poor housing and environmental quality, and poor social conditions.

➤ There are problems of managing the growing demand for services such as health, education and public transport in urban areas.

➤ Urban change creates problems of managing the growing demand for services such as water and sanitation.

Deprivation

Deprivation refers to the material poverty associated with low incomes. It is predominantly (though not exclusively) an urban problem in the UK. In England the most severe multiple deprivation is geographically concentrated in large northern cities and conurbations, especially Merseyside and Greater Manchester (Table 5.4).

Issues of poverty, inequality and deprivation have intensified in urban areas in the past 20 years. In the UK, the most disadvantaged groups live in cities. Poverty leads to **social exclusion**. People living in poverty and with other disadvantages lack the resources

	Number of SOAs
Merseyside	41
Greater Manchester	27
West Yorkshire	5
Tyne and Wear	5
Teesside	5
Nottingham	3
Hull	3
West Midlands	3
Bristol	2
Coventry	2
Great Yarmouth	1
London	1
NE Lincolnshire	1
Sheffield	1

Table 5.4 *Distribution of the hundred most deprived super output areas* (SOAs — middle level) in England*

* SOAs are the small area units used for the first time in the 2001 census of England and Wales. There are two scales of SOAs: 'middle level', and the smaller-scale 'lower level'.

Box 5.2 Index of multiple deprivation (IMD)

In the UK, the IMD is used as an objective measure of poverty. It is derived from seven components or domains which contribute to poverty and deprivation. The components and their weightings are: income (22.5), unemployment (22.5), health/disability (13.5), education (13.5), skills/training (9.3), housing (9.3) and the living environment/crime (9.3).

The IMD ranges from 1 (least deprived) to 100 (most deprived). The 2000 IMD scores are available for England's 8184 wards and parishes. In 2004, the IMD was applied to the smaller super output areas (SOAs). There are 32 482 SOAs in England. The IMDs are published as tables or maps either as index scores or as rank values from 1 to 32 482.

Figure 5.9 *Poverty and multiple deprivation*

to achieve acceptable standards of well being that would allow them to take part in the customary activities of society.

Poverty is associated with a range of social and economic dysfunctions, which together constitute multiple deprivation (Figure 5.9). For example, poor people suffer worse health than the better-off. Levels of education and skill are low among poor people and are themselves major drivers of deprivation and poverty. Unemployment, due to lack of skills, education and opportunities, clearly influences poverty. Where poverty and deprivation are concentrated, rates of crime also tend to be higher.

The main cause of deprivation is economic. Poorer people in employment earn low wages. This is due to lack of skills, and the fact that much employment is part time. More often, poverty is linked to unemployment. Many people, and whole families, have never worked and depend on state benefits. Often the long-term unemployed suffer poor health and physical disability, and are more likely to be single parents.

A number of problems stem directly from poverty such as crime. These include poor housing, ill-health and lack of access to services such as shops selling fresh food. Moreover, in cities in the UK, these problems tend to be spatially concentrated in two specific areas: the inner city and peripheral estates. This polarisation further accentuates the effects of poverty and deprivation.

In this section we shall look at two contrasting examples of urban deprivation. First, in part of Leeds, a prosperous city in West Yorkshire; and second, in Kibera, a suburb of Nairobi, and notorious as Africa's largest slum.

Case study **Deprivation and urban decay in east Leeds**

The east area of Leeds comprises the inner-city suburb of Harehills and Gipton and the outer suburb of Seacroft and Killingbeck, (Figure 5.10).

In 2001, this area had a total population of 71 250 living in 30 500 households. Both areas suffer deprivation and urban decay (Table 5.5).

Table 5.5
Comparison of Leeds inner east with the Leeds metropolitan district

	Inner east (%)	Leeds metro average (%)
Owner-occupied households	38	62
Rented from council	41	21
Black and ethnic minorities	17	8
Households with children <5 years	14	11
Households without central heating	38	20
Muslim population	8	3
Households without a car	55	34

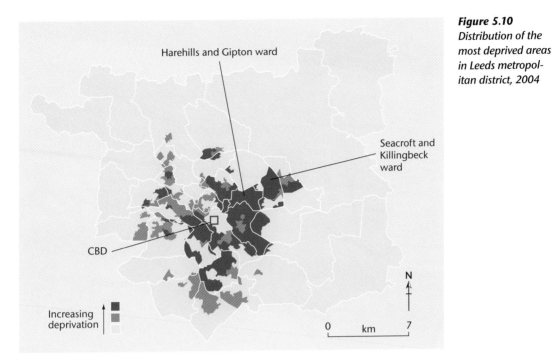

Figure 5.10
Distribution of the most deprived areas in Leeds metropolitan district, 2004

Harehills and Gipton ward

Seacroft and Killingbeck ward

CBD

Increasing deprivation

N

0   km   7

Harehills: inner-city deprivation and decay

Harehills forms part of the inner city of Leeds and is located 1–2 km east of the CBD. The suburb, built between 1870 and 1914, still retains much of its original back-to-back terraced housing. Harehills is the most densely populated ward in Leeds (Photograph 5.6).

DaeSasitorn/www.lastrefuge.co.uk

Photograph 5.6
Harehills Road, inner-city Leeds showing late-nineteenth-century terraced housing

Figure 5.11 *Inner-city Harehills: location of SOAs 048 and 053*

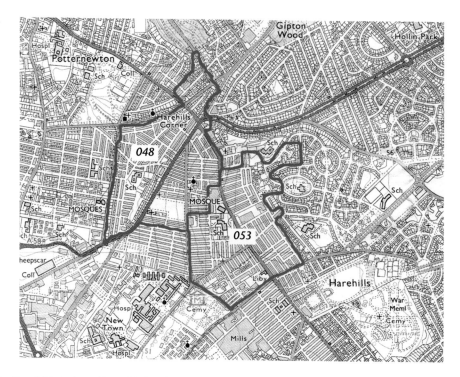

Housing quality in Harehills is low. Two-thirds of housing is rented from the council, social landlords such as housing associations and private landlords. Low-cost housing attracts low-income groups, including significant ethnic minorities of Pakistanis, Bangladeshis and African-Caribbeans (Table 5.6).

Social and economic issues

A large proportion of the residents of Harehills experience multiple deprivation. Measured by the IMD, in 2000 Harehills ward was the 429th most deprived in England. This placed it in the worst 5%. The situation had hardly improved by 2004, when all 16 SOAs in Harehills were among the most deprived 10% in the country. Two in five households receive council benefits, compared with one in ten in the leafy outer suburbs.

Several social and economic factors combine to create multiple deprivation in Harehills. First, unemployment is high: in 2006 it was 8% — nearly twice the Leeds average. In the age group 16–74 years, only 57% of Harehill's population was economically active, nearly 10% less than for Leeds as a whole. High levels of unemployment are related to poor

Table 5.6 *Ethnic composition and population density in two inner-city SOAs in Harehills and two SOAs on peripheral estates in Seacroft, east Leeds**
* See Figures 5.11 and 5.12.

SOAs	Ethnic composition %			Density: persons ha^{-1}
Harehills	White	Black	Asian	
048	28.3	10.1	54.4	125.6
053	59.3	6.1	26.6	120.4
Seacroft				
040	92.9	1.6	3.0	44.4
050	96.7	0.6	1.0	46.2

levels of education and skills, ill-health and ethnicity.

Forty-five per cent of the adult population of working age in Harehills have no educational qualifications, compared with 30% in Leeds as a whole. Less than one-third of 16 year olds achieved five GCSE passes at A* to C. Poor levels of educational attainment exclude most adults from well-paid employment, a factor that explains why average household incomes in Harehills are less than half

Photograph 5.7
Back-to-back terraced housing in the inner city, Leeds

those of the wealthiest wards in Leeds. As well as being badly paid, most jobs requiring minimal qualifications and skills are insecure.

At the last census, 12.1% of the residents of Harehills stated they were not in good health, a proportion that is significantly higher than the Leeds average. Health is also measured by life expectancy. Average life expectancy for males in Leeds in 2006 was 75.5 years, but in Harehills it was just 71.7 years. Death rates from cancer are nearly twice as high as in some of the more prosperous wards in Leeds.

A number of economic and lifestyle factors explain the poor health of people living in Harehills. Diet is one factor. People on low incomes cannot afford to eat healthily, a situation often made worse by an absence of local shops that sell fresh food. Lack of education and awareness of healthy eating adds to the problem.

Sub-standard housing also contributes to poor health. Most residential areas in Harehills comprise uniform blocks of terraced houses, many of them back-to-back, built over a century ago. Lack of investment characterises the area. As a result, population densities are high: typically between 120 and 130 persons per hectare. Owner occupation is typically around 20%, with the majority renting houses from private landlords, housing associations and the local

authority. The combination of low incomes, ill-health, poor diet and inadequate housing pushes the ward's infant mortality rates well above the average for Leeds.

Harehills has a diverse ethnic make-up. Asians (particularly Bangladeshis) are the largest ethnic minority group. Meanwhile, one-quarter of the ward's population was born outside the UK. Poor language skills limit access to the job market, especially for immigrants and those for whom English is not a first language. In common with other cities in the UK, unemployment is particularly high among young Asian men.

There are strong links between unemployment, poverty, low educational attainment and crime. Compared with the most prosperous outer suburbs of Leeds, reported crime is four times higher. Domestic burglary, vehicle crime and criminal damage are all two to four times higher.

Seacroft: deprivation and urban decay on a peripheral estate

Seacroft, on the outskirts of east Leeds, is a huge post-war housing development (Photograph 5.8). Its purpose was to re-house people displaced by inner-city slum clearance schemes in the 1950s, and to tackle the post-war housing shortage. At the time it was the biggest council estate in Europe. Most of the

Photograph 5.8
1960s run-down local authority housing in SOA 50A, Seacroft

Michael Raw

suburb is relatively low density, comprising mainly semi-detached family homes with gardens. In the 1960s, several high-rise apartment blocks were built, together with a new district shopping centre. The centre became a target for vandalism and was demolished in the late 1990s and completely re-built. With a population of around 90 000, 97% of which belongs to white ethnic groups, Seacroft is the equivalent of a medium-sized town but lacks comparable service provision.

Economic issues

In the UK, the social and economic problems of peripheral council estates are just as severe as those of the inner city. In terms of deprivation, Seacroft ranks in the 5% of most deprived wards in the country. In fact, Seacroft has a lower IMD ranking than inner-city Harehills. It also includes the most deprived SOA (lower level) in the Leeds metropolitan area — SOA 50A (Figure 5.12 and Table 5.7). This SOA is the 78th most deprived out of 32 482 SOAs in England.

Figure 5.12
Seacroft: peripheral post-war estate showing SOAs 040 and 050

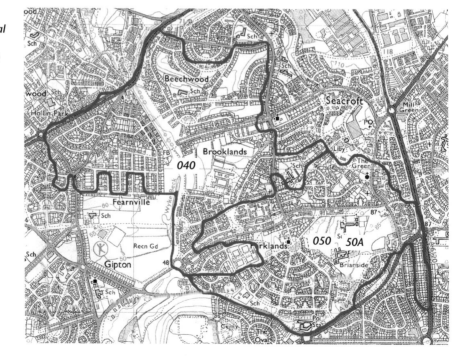

	Seacroft (SOA 050)				Harehills (SOA 053)			
	50A	50B	50C	50D	53A	53B	53C	53D
IMD	78	1115	5697	275	1631	2989	1902	2117
Income	237	3333	10113	348	2254	4060	2951	2511
Health	831	2121	7373	1939	6462	7318	4116	5435
Skills/training	4	198	4935	25	1181	1509	4509	4193
Crime	416	459	1944	941	1177	2470	289	873

Table 5.7
Rankings* of SOAs (lower level) in SOAs (middle level) for Harehills (053) and Seacroft (050)

In the lowest 5% of SOAs in England
In the lowest 10% of SOAs in England

* Rankings are for all SOAs (lower) in England, where 1 is the most deprived and 32 482 is the least deprived.

While large council estates like Seacroft are among the most run-down areas in England, this has not always been the case. Whereas between 1961 and 1971 fewer than half those in council housing in the UK were the poorest 40% of the population, by 1991 the proportion had risen to 75% (Pacione, M. (2005) *Urban Geography* (2nd edition), Routledge). Since the 1970s, Seacroft has become increasingly occupied by people on low incomes.

Multiple deprivation and social exclusion are widespread in Seacroft. The incidence of low incomes and youth unemployment are well above the city and national averages; benefit dependency is high — over 40% of the residents receive council benefits; educational achievements and home ownership levels are low.

In 2003, nearly one in two households in Seacroft did not own a car. A good public transport system is therefore essential if residents on peripheral estates are to access jobs and essential services such as food shops and health care. Hitherto, the public transport system, based on bus services, has been inadequate and has contributed to high levels of unemployment. Plans to build a supertram network in Leeds, which would have given Seacroft a direct link with the city centre, were abandoned in 2006, making Leeds the largest city in western Europe without a tram or rapid-transit system.

Social issues

Recorded crime in Seacroft is high, with criminal damage rates nearly twice the city average. Anti-social behaviour among young people, associated with drugs and gang culture, is a serious problem (Figure 5.13). In 2005, 15 anti-social behaviour orders (ASBOs) were in force in Seacroft. Some of these issues are made worse by the ward's relatively youthful population. But despite the numbers of young people, mortality rates and ill-health in Seacroft are high. High levels of teenage pregnancy are an important contributor both to child poverty and above-average levels of infant mortality. Deaths from lung cancer are 30% higher than the Leeds average, and coronary heart disease deaths are 16% higher.

Managing the growing demand for services in east Leeds

Both Harehills and Seacroft are part of the east and southeast Leeds (EASEL) regeneration project. This £1 billion investment over 20 years aims to revitalise east and southeast Leeds. EASEL is a partnership programme between Leeds City Council, developers, employers and various agencies. A distinctive feature of the scheme is close consultation with residents. In addition to EASEL, the poorest SOAs in Harehills and Seacroft also benefit from the Neighbourhood Renewal Fund. This Fund, in 2007–08 worth nearly £15 million, aims to improve the quality of life and employment prospects in the most disadvantaged areas. Eligible areas are SOAs that are among the most deprived 3% in the country.

Harehills includes two priority housing areas. Both areas comprise nineteenth-century terraces and back-to-backs. The emphasis is on housing improvement, demolition of the worst housing, and environmental improvements. Some back-to-backs in

'I'm frightened to death' said Mrs Parras, looking out at the empty boarded-up homes that surrounded her. She's alone in the last lived-in house in a block of council homes waiting for the bulldozer. All along South Parkway in Seacroft, east Leeds, stretch the rows of empty council houses destined for demolition. Here and there, an occupied house stands in the middle of a steel-sheeted derelict block. The last residents are desperately looking for a transfer so they can get out of the community that is now a ghost town.

Mrs Parras explains: 'It's really bad. There are gangs around now every night. There were 50 in the garden next door last night. I daren't go out. They pulled the neighbours' windows out. I've had bricks at my windows and my shed torn down. The house three doors up was firebombed. It could have been me.' Six hundred system-built council houses in Seacroft are scheduled for demolition because of the too-high cost of bringing them up to decent standard. This is the first phase of the EASEL regeneration programme, a huge 20 year multi-million pound flagship scheme to bring about the transformation of east & southeast Leeds. The scheme will bring economic and environmental improvements to the area and over 25 per cent of all new housing built will be classed as 'affordable' family homes, available to current residents. However to make space for new housing, up to 5000 council homes may need to be demolished during the lifetime of the project.

'It's a total nightmare' said Christine Page. She lives in a street that is not immediately due to be demolished but is already desolate and near-derelict. The street lights are smashed and thieves broke into the empty home next door and stole the lead water pipes, flooding her home, she says. In the demolition zone, what was once a community has become a wasteland. Drunken gangs and drug users find shelter among the empty homes; mice infest the houses.

Figure 5.13 *Extract from a local news report on crime in Seacroft*
Source: Home@Leeds, Spring 2007.

Harehills are being knocked through to create larger family homes. A new housing scheme is also planned in north Seacroft.

Health-care services will be improved to tackle the high rates of ill-health and mortality. Primary health care will be upgraded, with new GP surgeries, health centres and clinics. A new children's unit at St James's Hospital in Harehills will enhance the provision of secondary health care. Meanwhile, sexual health services will be extended and more focus placed on reducing teenage pregnancy.

Improvements in educational services are essential if young people are to gain access to the job market. Extensions will be made to existing primary schools; more nursery places will be available for young children; and parenting support and family outreach services will be strengthened. Seacroft is the location of a new city academy. This is targeted at local secondary school pupils, and aims to raise educational standards in the most deprived area of Leeds.

A good range of neighbourhood retail services selling a variety of fresh and healthy food is essential to improving the quality of life and the health of local people. In Harehills, retail provision will be improved by upgrading the Harehills Corner shopping centre.

In the late 1990s, the purpose-built Seacroft Centre, opened in 1964, was demolished after years of neglect, decay and crime. It was replaced by a new centre. A Tesco superstore was the anchor tenant and provided local residents with much-improved shopping services. This in itself was unusual, because large supermarkets had in the past preferred locations in more prosperous suburbs. The Tesco store was used as a catalyst for regeneration. In a unique partnership scheme, Tesco pledged to reserve most of the new jobs in the store for local people. In total, the company recruited 320 people who lived within 1 km of the store and who previously were unemployed. New employees were drawn from the most disadvantaged groups such as lone parents, young people aged 16–24 years, and those over 50. As a partnership scheme, other companies provided training in basic skills, as well as child care and benefit advice.

Improved transport services are also needed if residents are to get employment. Tesco has introduced a free 'hail and ride' scheme. It gives access to retail services in the Seacroft Centre and training courses for local residents.

Case study

Rapid growth and urban decay in Kibera, Nairobi

Huge social and economic differences are found within cities in LEDCs. Nairobi, Kenya's capital and largest city, exemplifies this inequality (Figure 5.14). Slums house 60% of the city's population. Kibera, situated 7 km southwest of Nairobi's city centre, and with an estimated 700 000 inhabitants, is Africa's largest slum (Figures 5.15 and 5.16). Adjoining Kibera, a golf course occupies approximately the

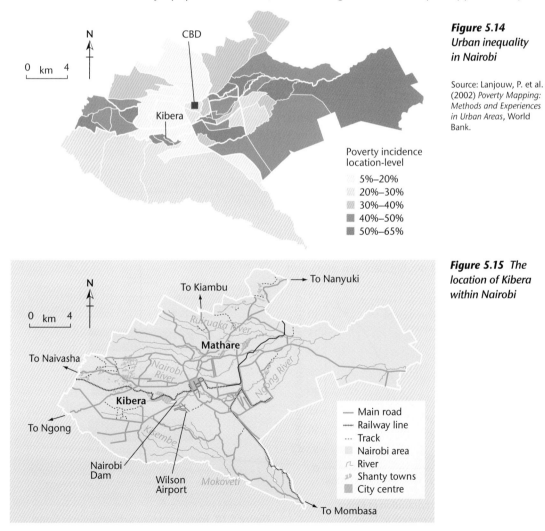

Figure 5.14
Urban inequality in Nairobi

Source: Lanjouw, P. et al. (2002) *Poverty Mapping: Methods and Experiences in Urban Areas*, World Bank.

Poverty incidence location-level

- 5%–20%
- 20%–30%
- 30%–40%
- 40%–50%
- 50%–65%

Figure 5.15 *The location of Kibera within Nairobi*

Legend:
- Main road
- Railway line
- Track
- Nairobi area
- River
- Shanty towns
- City centre

Figure 5.16 *Kibera*

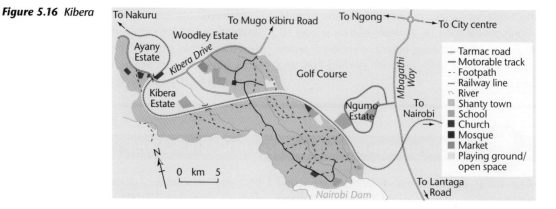

same area as the settlement. Underlining the inequality, the golf course has irrigated greens, while Kibera's residents have barely sufficient water to provide for their basic needs. The vast majority of Kibera's residents live in poverty and in the most appalling conditions.

Urbanisation in Kenya

The key to understanding informal settlements like Kibera is the rapid rate of urbanisation that has occurred in Kenya since 1950, and the equally rapid growth of the capital, Nairobi (Figure 5.17). Urbanisation continues to gather pace. Kenya is urbanising faster than Africa as a whole. Between 1982 and 2002, Kenya's urban population increased at an average rate of 6.3% a year — more than double its national population growth. At this rate, Kenya's urban population will double between 2005 and 2015, by which time half of Kenya's population will be urban dwellers.

Urbanisation and urban growth in Kenya are due to both rural–urban migration and natural population growth in towns and cities. A combination of push and pull factors, from drought and declining agricultural productivity to inter-tribal clashes, explains the migration from the countryside to urban areas (Figure 5.18). Nairobi is by far the most attractive destination for Kenya's rural migrants.

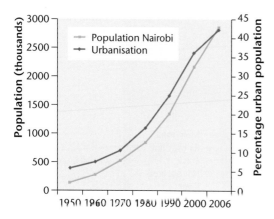

Figure 5.17 *Urbanisation in Kenya and population growth in Nairobi*

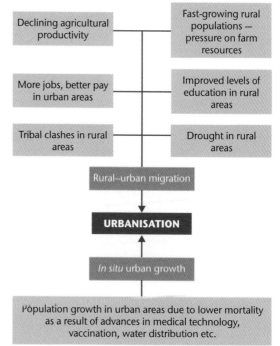

Figure 5.18 *Factors causing urbanisation in Kenya*

Social and economic issues

The existence of informal settlements like Kibera reflects the inability of the Kenyan government to provide basic housing needs, essential services and effective governance. Currently, 60% of Nairobi's population lives in informal settlements on just 5% of the city's land area. Two factors explain the growth of informal settlements: the lack of resources to invest in essential infrastructure and the pace and scale of urbanisation, which has overwhelmed Kenya and most other countries in sub-Saharan Africa.

The most serious social and economic issues in Kibera are connected to deprivation and environmental quality. They include:

- economic deprivation
- poor housing and overcrowding
- poor infrastructural services such as water supply, roads, waste management, sanitation and drainage
- poor health
- unemployment

Economic well-being

The residents of informal settlements such as Kibera have one thing in common: poverty. Four out of five residents do not live in Kibera out of choice; poverty simply gives them no other option. According to a UN survey, only 44% of households have a regular income, and 80% of regular earners are poor to very poor. Table 5.8 shows that half of all households

Daily income (US$)	% of households
<1.5	1
1.5–6	14
6.1–10.5	35
10.6–15	26
>15	24

Table 5.8
Daily household income in Kibera

survive on less than $10.5 a day. Extreme poverty means that even the most basic needs cannot be met. For example, 40% cannot afford on a daily basis to buy sufficient food, or food of adequate quality.

Unemployment in Kibera could be as high as 50%. Around 70% of those in work are in wage employment. Most wage employment consists of unskilled, casual work in Nairobi's main industrial zone situated close by. Self-employment accounts for a quarter of all jobs. The most popular businesses are selling vegetables, selling second-hand clothes, hair salons and kiosks.

Housing

Kibera's residents list the main housing problems as poor roofing, poor walls, overcrowding and high rents. The physical condition of housing in Kibera is so poor that the entire settlement is one huge slum (Photograph 5.9). Most houses are built from rudimentary materials such as mud, timber, polythene and corrugated iron. Mud is the most common building material; only 1% of houses are built from

Box 5.3 Measuring poverty

There is no simple measure of poverty. Although poverty is mainly thought of in material terms, for example the provision of basic needs like food, water and shelter, it also encompasses areas such as health care, education and opportunities for the poor to improve their circumstances.

In most societies, the distribution of benefits is uneven. Thus, where there is poverty, there is inequality. Inequality is found at all scales: from the global scale and the division between rich and poor countries, to the local scale and the sharp contrast between prosperous and poor districts of cities.

In the absence of any precise measure of poverty, the World Bank has adopted a simple indicator. It defines a poverty line that is set at US$1 or US$2 per person per day. The measure includes purchasing power parity (PPP) to reflect local differences in the cost of living. According to the World Bank, in 2001 20% of the world's population lived on less than US$1 a day, and about half lived on less than US$2 a day.

Photograph 5.9
Slum housing in Kibera

brick or stone. Corrugated iron sheets are the universal roofing material. Forty-three per cent of houses have floors made from natural earth.

Adding to the slum conditions is chronic over-crowding. Kibera is one of the most densely popu-lated settlements in the world. Densities exceed 90 000 persons per square kilometre and, due to in-migration and high natural increase, are rising. Most houses consist of a single room, occupied on average by five people. Overcrowding contributes to ill-health and the spread of infectious diseases such as tuberculosis (TB).

Most of Kibera's residents are tenants, and most are squatters with no legal title to the land they occupy. As a result, they have no security and there-fore little incentive to improve their homes. Rents charged by absentee 'slum landlords' (who may own as many as 1000 shacks) are high, and estimated at 15% of household incomes.

Social conditions

Investment in infrastructure and provision of services are essential for the development and sustainability of human settlements. But providing and main-taining infrastructure and services requires huge capital sums, which Kenya can ill-afford.

Kibera does have a range of services and ameni-ties such as schools, health facilities, government offices, water points and telephones. But much of this infrastructure is either inadequate or in a poor condition. Roads and pathways are made of natural earth and vehicles cannot access most households. The absence of paved roads forces most commuters to walk to and from work.

Environmental conditions

Eighty-three per cent of households have water within 100 m, though most is sold by private dealers and is costly. The poorest households are forced to rely on water from the highly polluted Ngong River and the Nairobi Dam (Figures 5.15 and 5.16).

Sanitation and drainage are major problems in Kibera. Ninety-five per cent of households have inad-equate sanitation facilities, and 56% are without any means of excreta disposal. Few households have proper toilets. Pit latrines, the main means of sewage disposal, pose a significant threat to human health. It is not unusual for a single latrine to be used by 75 people. Human faeces are often disposed of in drains, rivers and garbage heaps, creating further health risks such as diarrhoea and intestinal worms.

Waste water and storm drainage run in open earth canals. Much of the drainage system is inade-quate, leading to stagnant polluted waters, which provide perfect breeding grounds for mosquitoes and flies. During the rainy season, runoff in open drains collects garbage, including human waste, and drains become open sewers.

Charlotte Thege/Alamy

Photograph 5.10 *Squalid environmental conditions in Kibera*

Few households in Kibera are connected to electricity supplies. Charcoal, kerosene and firewood are used for cooking; candles and hurricane lamps are used for lighting. These forms of fuel are highly polluting, especially in poorly ventilated and cramped housing, exposing occupants to high levels of carbon monoxide as well as to serious fire risks.

A settlement the size of Kibera generates huge volumes of solid waste. Waste collection is the responsibility of Nairobi City Council (NCC). However, the system is on the verge of collapse and only manages to collect 5% of the solid waste produced by the whole city each day. And because the NCC does not recognise informal settlements, there are no waste collection services in Kibera.

As residents cannot afford private waste collection, waste is dumped everywhere: in open trenches; in the Ngong River and Nairobi Dam; and along roads and

Box 5.4 The informal economy

Employment in many economically-developing world cities is dominated by the so-called informal economy. The informal sector is unregulated, untaxed and unmonitored by governments. Workers are self-employed, non-wage earners and are not protected by labour codes. Being labour-intensive, the informal sector is easy to access and 'soaks up' millions of workers who otherwise would be unemployed. Jobs in the informal sector include street selling, recycling, repairing cars and cycles, odd jobs (e.g. car cleaning) and so on.

In 2001, Kenya's informal sector accounted for around one-quarter of the country's non-agricultural GDP and 75% of national employment. It is dominated by small enterprises, most of which are one-person businesses. The informal sector plays a vital economic role in LEDCs because the formal sector (which is capital-intensive and requires formal skills and qualifications) is both difficult to access and cannot satisfy the demand for employment.

pathways. Dumping sites attract houseflies, disease-carrying vectors and rodents. The sites occupy a lot of space and are aesthetically and socially undesirable.

Health

Poverty, lack of proper sanitation and solid waste management all contribute to ill-health among Kibera's residents. Malaria and AIDS are the most urgent health problems. Other common illnesses are typhoid, TB and diarrhoea. Malaria is the number one killer disease in Africa. It affects 20 million people in Kenya, and contributes to poverty by causing the loss of millions of working days every year. In Kenya, AIDS is responsible for over 500 deaths a day.

Meanwhile poor drainage systems and irresponsible waste disposal create ideal conditions for typhoid, while TB, an infectious disease, thrives in Kibera's overcrowded slums. Diarrhoea is a persistent health problem and will remain so until sanitary arrangements improve. It is hardly surprising that infant mortality rates in Kibera are as high as 200 per 1000.

Managing Kibera's slums: the growing demand for services

Sixty per cent of Nairobi's inhabitants live in slum conditions and the city's population is increasing by 200 000 a year. Nairobi City Council and the Kenyan government face massive problems of slum housing and inadequate services in the capital. Nowhere is the scale of the problem worse than in Kibera.

In the past, the government refused to recognise informal settlements that it considered illegal. As a result, no provision was made to upgrade services, and periodically the slums would be demolished and their inhabitants evicted. But demolition failed to stop the growth of informal settlements, and with the government unable to provide low-cost housing for the poor, policy changed. In 1996 the government abandoned slum demolition and instead opted to work with the slum dwellers, community-based organisations and non-governmental organisations to improve housing and basic services.

A new water distribution system was built in Kibera in 2000. Meanwhile, the Kibera Urban Environment and Sanitation Master Plan has been completed but not yet implemented (Table 5.9). This major upgrade is financed jointly by the United Nations (UN-HABITAT) and the Kenyan government. Its total cost is $11 billion. The plan provides a coherent approach to development: too often in the past improvements have been uncoordinated and piecemeal. Surprisingly, not everyone is in favour. Some residents who will suffer temporarily relocation to allow contractors to build new homes are opposed to the plan. Slum landlords who own most of Kibera's shacks and who rent them out, and rent collectors, are also unhappy. Although planning was largely completed by 2005 and funds have been established, 2 years later work on the ground had still not started.

Table 5.9 Kibera upgrading master plan	Upgrading
Physical infrastructure	Sewerage system, water supply and sanitation, access roads, storm water drainage, electricity, street lighting
Social infrastructure	Schools, health centres, community centres, recreational facilities, open spaces
Housing	Security of tenure, new housing, housing improvements, cooperative housing
Environment and solid waste management	Garbage collection and treatment; clean-up of River Ngong
Employment	Establish markets, shops, kiosks, shopping centres, micro-finance and credit schemes
HIV/AIDS	Education awareness programmes, counselling, test centres, dedicated HIV clinics

Table 5.9 Kibera upgrading master plan

Environmental issues associated with urban change

Key ideas
➤ Urban change puts increasing pressure on the environment.
➤ Urban change creates problems of managing traffic congestion, atmospheric pollution, water pollution, urban dereliction and solid waste disposal.

Unsustainable urban growth has created severe environmental problems such as air pollution, land dereliction and traffic congestion in cities throughout the world. In this section we look at the impact of urban change on the physical environment through case studies of Santiago de Chile and London, and at some of the efforts made to tackle them.

Case study | Urban-environmental problems in Santiago de Chile

Figure 5.19 *Location of Santiago de Chile*

Santiago, with a population of 5.43 million, is the seventh-largest city in Latin America and dominates Chile's urban hierarchy (Figure 5.19). Like its Argentine neighbour Buenos Aires, Santiago is a primate city, seven times larger than Valparaiso, Chile's second city. The agglomeration accounts for 42% of Chile's urban population. Santiago has experienced rapid population growth in the past 50 years (Table 5.10). Between 1960 and 2005 its population

Table 5.10 *Population growth (millions): Santiago agglomeration, 1960–2005*

1960	1970	1980	1990	2000	2005
1.509	2.731	3.651	4.311	5.493	5.737

increased almost fourfold — a rate of increase that is twice as fast as the national average. This massive growth has placed huge pressures on the physical environment of the city and its surroundings.

Atmospheric pollution

Santiago vies with Mexico City and São Paulo as the city with the most atmospheric pollution in Latin America (Table 5.11). Despite action by the government to tackle the problem, pollution levels still exceed safe limits set by the World Health Organization (WHO).

Table 5.11 *Comparison of atmospheric pollution in Santiago and other cities*

	Suspended particles (ppm)	Sulphur dioxide (ppm)
Santiago	210	38
Mexico City	100–500	80–200
São Paulo	50–85	35–62
Tokyo	51	20
Los Angeles	46–115	0–10
Mumbai	140	23

Causes

The main pollutants are nitrous oxides (NO_x), sulphur dioxide (SO_2), carbon monoxide (CO), ozone (O_3) and small particulates. The main sources of pollution are motor vehicles and industries such as smelters and power plants. Particulates also come from dust from streets and eroded hillsides. Motor vehicles emit three-quarters of all nitrous oxides and half of all organic compounds. A cocktail of pollutants interact with sunlight to form ozone, which exceeds world health standards for, on average, 150 days a year.

Atmospheric pollution is aggravated by Santiago's location in a broad valley, surrounded by the Andes to the east and the coastal ranges to the west (Figure 5.20). During the winter months, cold air sinks into the central valley from the surrounding mountains. Warm air is then displaced above, forming a temperature inversion. In this situation, pollutants are trapped near the surface and form a vast pollution dome over the city (Photograph 5.11). Dispersal is further hindered by the city's dry climate and light winds.

The primary cause of atmospheric pollution in Santiago is economic growth and the enormous increase in vehicular traffic. Average car ownership increased from 320 cars per 1000 households in 1977 to 560 in 2001. In the same period, the number of motorised trips went up by 69% and the average length of trips increased as well. Although public transport is good by South American standards, the city relies heavily on an aged fleet of 11 000 diesel buses, which are highly polluting (Photograph 5.12).

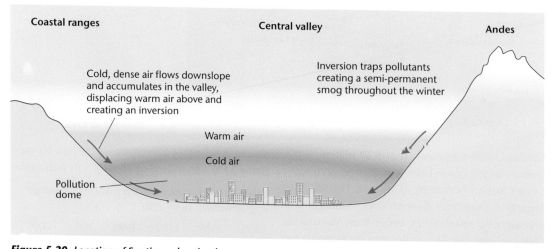

Figure 5.20 *Location of Santiago showing how temperature inversion traps pollutants to create a pollution dome*

Photograph 5.11 *Santiago: pollution dome and smog trapped by the temperature inversion in mid-winter*

Photograph 5.12
Public transport in Santiago relies heavily on a large fleet of old and polluting buses

Impact

High levels of airborne pollutants affect the health of Santiago's inhabitants and their quality of life. Atmospheric pollution increases rates of morbidity (ill-health) and mortality. Annual costs of traffic-generated pollution exceed $500 million. Winter is the critical period when air pollution is at its worst and rates of respiratory infection rise steeply. Studies have shown how pollution by small dust particles in the atmosphere causes increases in respiratory illnesses among children in Santiago, and higher rates of mortality.

Water pollution

The Mapocho River flows west from the Andes and through downtown Santiago (Photograph 5.13). It should be an environmental attraction. Instead it is an open sewer contaminated by sewage and a cocktail of chemicals, which flows in a concrete box. High levels of coliform bacteria occur downstream of

Photograph 5.13
The Mapocho River, Santiago

Michael Raw

sewage outfalls and hazardous chemicals and heavy metals, such as lead, copper and chrome, are routinely discharged into the Mapocho by industries. These pollutants are potential health hazards, with heavy metals in particular known to cause neurological damage and cancer. Heavy metals are also washed into the river from tailings in abandoned copper workings in the mountains. Elsewhere in Santiago, open drainage canals polluted by sewage run through the city.

Santiago's inadequate sewerage system is typical of other cities in Chile, where at best only 15% of sewage effluent is treated, and the rest flows directly into rivers and the sea. However, there are plans for a $300 million clean-up. Nearly 30 km of sewerage pipes will, from 2009, intercept untreated sewage that currently flows into the Mapocho and transfer it to a new treatment plant. Domestic sewage will be separated from industrial effluent and the treated sewage effluent will then be discharged into the river downstream from Santiago. This should finally transform the Mapocho River into an environmental attraction rather than the environmental hazard that it has presented for the past 50 years.

Traffic congestion

Economic growth and the relentless urban sprawl have resulted in a doubling of vehicles in Santiago in the past 20 years. These have in turn created a

second environmental problem: traffic congestion. Santiago's public transport system deteriorated between 1981 and 2001. The proportion of journeys made by bus fell from 60% to 42% while private car journeys increased from 18% to 38%. There was also a small drop in the proportion of subway journeys.

An inefficient bus system is a major cause of traffic congestion. The city's bus industry is fragmented and informal. Private bus operators compete for passengers on the streets of the capital. Bus drivers get commission on the number of passengers carried. As a result, buses race to pick up passengers with little thought for the safety of other road users and pedestrians. In 2002, over a quarter of all road accidents in Santiago involved buses. There is no coordination between bus services and other transport systems, while the duplication of services and oversupply during off-peak periods result in excessive numbers of buses on the roads. They add significantly to congestion as well as to pollution. Most bus routes maximise passenger potential by running through the city centre, using the main axial roads, which become heavily congested.

Managing atmospheric pollution and traffic congestion in Santiago

The government's 2000–10 Urban Transport Plan, Transantiago, aims to improve the quality of life, provide better traffic flows and reduce inequalities in

Santiago by:

- reducing average journey lengths
- improving air quality through reduced emissions of air pollutants
- improving access to public transport
- improving mobility

Among the specific investments proposed by the plan are:

- expansion of the metro system — extensions to the metro, which already carries 2.5 million passengers a day, will increase the network by 31 km to 105 km by 2009
- three new suburban rail services
- 15 segregated busways
- reform of the public bus system
- reform of the taxi system and conversion to compressed natural gas (CNG) fuel
- a $700 million programme to improve the road network
- road pricing
- coordination of land-use and transport policies to reduce average trip lengths

Improvements in the road network are already well advanced. Four modern urban freeways have been built covering the central areas of the Santiago metropolitan area. The north–south freeway is typical: a four-to-six lane highway built at a cost of $440 million, it can handle 140 000 vehicles a day. With minimal toll booths it allows the free flow of traffic across the city in less than 30 minutes. The improved flow of traffic will reduce both congestion and air pollution from vehicle emissions.

The Transantiago plan will radically improve transport in general, and bus services in particular, by 2010. Bus services that operate on the city's five main axial routes will be put out to tender, together with services in ten local areas that transfer passengers to the metro or to axial bus services. Sixty-five transfer stations will provide transport interchanges, linking bus routes with the metro. Two transfer terminals will provide more extensive connections between bus services, the metro and taxis. The result should be an integrated system that is more efficient for passengers, less polluting, and which reduces traffic congestion.

Action to improve urban transport has already been taken. Bus lanes have been created along seven radial avenues in central Santiago. For example, the ten-lane O'Higgins thoroughfare in downtown Santiago has six lanes reserved for buses. These simple measures have, at low cost, reduced noise pollution, congestion and journey times. Bus occupancy rates have increased, and particulate pollution has fallen by 14%.

In the longer term, Santiago plans to reduce greenhouse gas emissions (GHG) from ground transport and improve air quality by encouraging more sustainable and less polluting forms of transport. Bicycles will be promoted, especially in suburbs of high car ownership, by building over 40 km of cycle tracks. Not only will the bus system be overhauled, but the city's bus fleet will gradually be renewed with clean technologies such as hybrid diesel-electric and CNG vehicles.

Road pricing is also being studied as an option. Pricing could help to reduce traffic volumes and generate finance for transport improvements.

Problems of managing waste in London

Case study

Major cities throughout the world, whether in rich or poor countries, face similar environmental challenges. However, the urgency and scale of these challenges vary from city to city. While Santiago de Chile's priorities are to tackle pollution and traffic congestion, the most urgent problems facing London are the disposal of ever-increasing volumes of solid waste, and land dereliction in the inner city.

Solid waste

London is a wealthy city. The relatively affluent lifestyle enjoyed by most of its residents generates

Table 5.12 *Solid waste production by London 2005*

Types of waste	Tonnes
Hazardous waste	0.4
Municipal household waste	4.4
Construction/demolition	6.1
Commercial/industrial	6.4

4.4 million tonnes of municipal household waste (MHW) a year (Table 5.12). Disposing of this waste is a huge headache. London's waste is collected daily by approximately 500 collection vehicles, barges, containers and specialist transporters. It is then transported to 18 landfill sites, two incinerators, 23 recycling centres, two compost centres, and two energy-from-waste plants. The volume of solid waste is so great that it easily exceeds the capacity of London's own landfill sites. As a result, 76% of London's MHW is exported by road, rail and barge to sites in southeast England (Photograph 5.14). Some of these sites are situated more than 120 km from the capital.

The biggest landfill sites for MHW are Calvert in

louise murray/Alamy

Photograph 5.14 *Landfill site at Mucking*

Buckinghamshire, Stewartby in Bedfordshire and Appleford in Oxfordshire (Figure 5.21). Calvert is a typical landfill site. It occupies a disused clay quarry previously owned by the London Brick Company. This is a secure site because clay forms an impermeable barrier that prevents toxins leaking into the environment. The site receives nearly 2000 t of MHW a day, delivered in containers by rail from London. Methane, extracted from the landfill, fuels a small power station, which generates enough electricity to

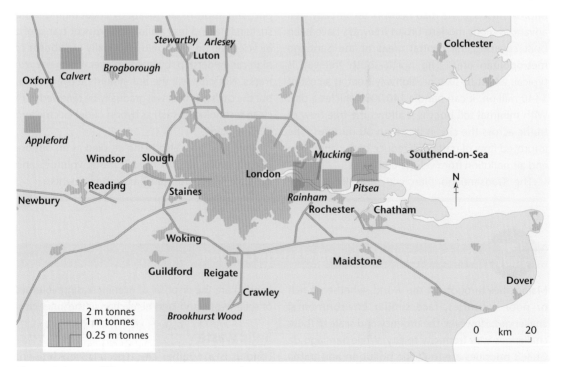

Stewartby Arlesey
Luton
Brogborough
Oxford Calvert
Appleford
Windsor Slough Mucking Southend-on-Sea
Reading London Pitsea
Newbury Staines Rainham N
Rochester Chatham
Woking
Maidstone
Guildford Reigate Dover
Crawley
Brookhurst Wood

2 m tonnes
1 m tonnes
0.25 m tonnes

Colchester

0 km 20

Figure 5.21 *Landfill sites in southeast England for London's solid waste (industrial and household), 2005–06*

supply 4000 homes. Solid waste from all sources (i.e. industry, construction, household) is transported to a total of nine landfill sites around London.

Landfill is an environmentally unsatisfactory method of solid waste disposal. First, pollution caused by leakage from landfill sites is always a possibility. Second, landfill accounts for one-quarter of methane production in the UK — a potent greenhouse gas, which adds to global warming and climate change. Third, landfill takes up precious land — something the overcrowded southeast of England can ill afford.

Running out of space

London is failing to deal sustainably with its own waste problem and a crisis is rapidly approaching. The capital's MHW is expected to increase from 4.4 million tonnes in 2005 to 6.5 million tonnes by 2020. This is mainly due to population growth:

between 2005 and 2016, an extra 800 000 people will be added to London's population.

Without urgent action, London and the southeast of England will simply run out of landfill space early in the next decade. Today there are only four landfill sites in London and one of them will be full by 2012 (Figure 5.22). The situation is hardly better in the counties around the capital. In 2005, the east of England region had only 3 years' landfill capacity remaining; and the southeast region had just 6 years' capacity left.

Exporting London's solid waste outside the capital is undesirable. It extends the capital's ecological footprint (Box 5.5), and damages environmental resources elsewhere. This footprint includes the environmental cost of transport as well as the impact on landscapes, watercourses and wildlife in the immediate area of the landfill sites.

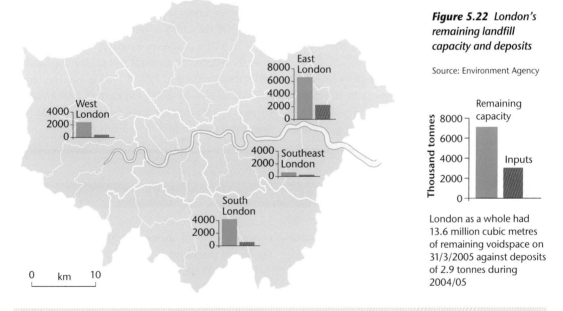

Figure 5.22 *London's remaining landfill capacity and deposits*

Source: Environment Agency

London as a whole had 13.6 million cubic metres of remaining voidspace on 31/3/2005 against deposits of 2.9 tonnes during 2004/05

Box 5.5 Ecological footprint

'Ecological footprint' is defined as: '...the amount of productive land and water a given population requires to support the resources it consumes and the absorption of its wastes'.

Thus, ecological footprint is a concept that describes the impact of a country, a city or an

individual on **renewable resources**. The size of the ecological footprint will suggest whether resource use is sustainable.

A place's or person's ecological footprint is measured in units of global hectares (gha). A gha is 1 ha with an annual biological productivity equal to the world average. Currently, the biosphere comprises 11.2 billion gha of which 8.8 billion are terrestrial ecosystems and 2.3 billion are marine ecosystems, which in global terms averages out at 1.8 gha per person. However, actual usage per person is almost 2.2 gha. In 2004, the estimated global usage was equivalent to 13.5 billion ha, representing an overshoot of 20%. In the long term, such an overshoot is unsustainable. It is only possible through an annual drawdown of natural capital, which results in a depletion and a degrading of renewable resources.

The ecological footprint idea is useful because it provides a general indication of the impact of people on the environment. It is not, however, a precise measure of sustainability. It is based only on renewable resources. Moreover, the concept of gha ignores productivity, which in specific locations is very different from the global average.

The production, management and disposal of municipal waste is part of London's ecological footprint. Currently, around 49 000 000 global hectares (gha) are required to produce and dispose of all the energy and matter needed to support London and its 7.5 million inhabitants. This averages out at 6.63 gha per person, or three times the global average. It is 42 times greater than its biocapacity and 293 times its geographical area. This is roughly an area the same size as Spain!

Tackling London's mountain of waste

One approach to London's solid waste problem is to extend recycling schemes and reduce the amount of waste going to landfill. But so far, London's record on recycling is not good. Five of the 12 local authorities with the lowest recycling records in the UK are London boroughs.

London currently landfills most of its MHW. To meet landfill targets, London needs to achieve six times its current levels of recycling. The Mayor of London has proposed a London Single Waste Authority to be responsible for the treatment and disposal of all of London's MHW. At the moment, London's boroughs are failing to invest enough in recycling and new technology and are not meeting their MHW recycling targets. An EU directive adds urgency to the problem. By 2010, local authorities have to reduce the amount of non-biodegradable MHW they produce to 75% of 1995 levels. This target extends to 35% by 2020. On current performance, London will fail to meet these targets and could face fines totalling hundreds of millions of pounds.

Case study — Urban dereliction in the Lower Lea Valley, east London

Large tracts of east London, some barely a kilometre or so from the City, are blighted by dereliction. Derelict land is the legacy of deindustrialisation, factory closures and the decline of the docks in inner London. In the 1970s and 1980s, globalisation led to massive deindustrialisation and the collapse of large sectors of the UK's manufacturing industry. Along with deindustrialisation went huge job losses and the creation of large swathes of derelict land in inner London. Nowhere was the problem of land dereliction greater than in the Lower Lea Valley. Today the borough of Newham, which includes a large part of the Lower Lea Valley (Figure 5.23), contains 42% of inner London's brownfield or previously used land.

Brownfield sites on former industrial land in the Lower Lea Valley have been vacant for 20–30 years. Three factors explain the unattractiveness of brownfield sites for developers:

- Much of the land is fragmented and divided into hundreds of small plots.
- Some sites are contaminated by pollutants from former industrial use such as oil refineries, landfill and infilled reservoirs.
- The area is criss-crossed by overhead power lines, waterways, sewerage, roads and rail lines.

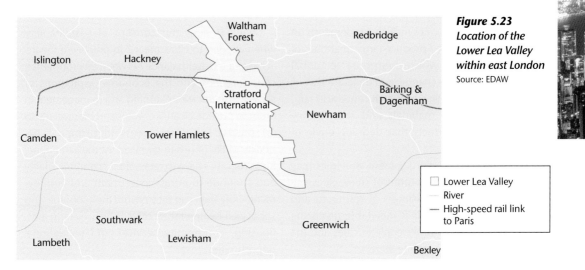

Figure 5.23
Location of the Lower Lea Valley within east London
Source: EDAW

Legend:
☐ Lower Lea Valley
— River
---- High-speed rail link to Paris

All of these factors make land regeneration in preparation for the 2012 London Olympic Games difficult and expensive (see the case study on page 238). The journalist Will Hutton described dereliction in the Lower Lea Valley (*Observer*, 30 July 2006) as 'a disgrace...which makes the dereliction in parts of the north of England and Scotland look tame'.

Managing and planning for sustainable urban living

Key ideas
➤ The sustainable development of urban areas requires detailed planning and management.
➤ The sustainable development of urban areas requires a careful balance between socio-economic and environmental needs.

Solving the environmental problems of urban areas will require a more sustainable approach to management and planning. Although achieving fully sustainable cities remains a long way off, the concept of the sustainable city has begun to take root. The case studies that follow describe the transformation of London's East End for the 2012 Olympic Games, and China's ambitious attempt to create the world's first fully sustainable eco-city at Dongtan, near Shanghai.

Box 5.6 Sustainable urban development

The UN defines sustainable development as 'development which aims to meet the needs of the present without compromising the ability of future generations to meet their own needs'.

We have seen that cities make huge demands on the environment. They produce large quantities of greenhouse gases, which contribute to global warming and climate change, and generate nitrous oxides and sulphur dioxide, which cause acid rain. By consuming raw materials and energy they produce waste products that degrade environmental systems.

While sustainable management strategies may reduce the ecological footprint of cities, cities will continue to be net consumers of resources and producers of waste. This is inevitable given the massive concentrations of people in cities and the intensity of economic activity there.

So what does the concept of sustainability when applied to cities mean? In practice it means achieving a better balance between environmental considerations and the economic aspirations of society. This involves planning and management in order to provide clean air, water and biodiversity to (a) conserve natural resources and (b) improve the quality of life of urban dwellers. At the same time, however, cities have to retain their economic vitality and continue to attract investment and employment. Only then can they ensure the economic and social well-being of their citizens by providing jobs, housing, community services and recreational opportunities.

Case study: Land reclamation and the sustainable use of urban land in the Lower Lea Valley

The Lower Lea Valley, which includes parts of the boroughs of Hackney, Newham, Tower Hamlets and Waltham Forest, is the largest regeneration project in the UK. It aims to transform nearly 6 km² of London's most stressed urban landscapes into a high-quality, sustainable environment. By 2020, the project should deliver 30 000 to 40 000 new houses, 50 000 jobs and an attractive urban environment of canals, wetlands, open space and riverside developments. The Lower Lea Valley is also part of the Thames Gateway strategy. This is a much larger sub-regional scheme, which extends along both sides of the Thames estuary from east London to Kent and Essex. Thames Gateway is expected to provide 120 000 new homes for Londoners by 2016.

The 2012 Olympic Games and urban regeneration

The site for the 2012 London Olympic Games is located in the heart of the Lower Lea Valley (Figure 5.24 and Photograph 5.15). It covers 312 ha and includes some of the worst examples of urban dereliction in inner London. The Olympic Games are behind the drive to revive a large part of the Lower Lea Valley, and east London.

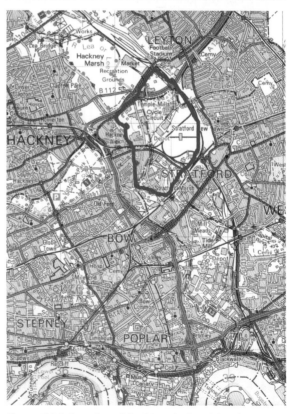

Figure 5.24 Location of the Olympic site within the Lower Lea Valley, east London

London 2012

Photograph 5.15 *A computer-generated image of the Olympic Park*

The Olympic Village will include accommodation for 16 000 athletes, the main stadium, two 50 m swimming pools, four indoor arenas, a velo park and a hockey centre. Apart from new sports stadia, there will be investment in new transport infrastructure and housing. Meanwhile, the largest new urban park in Europe in the past 150 years will be created. The Games will transform one of the most deprived parts of the capital, helping to tackle poverty, unemployment, poor housing and poor health as well as land dereliction. They will also provide the UK with world-class sporting facilities and integrate east London into the fabric of the capital. The legacy of the games for local communities will be considerable, ranging from affordable homes and parks to new schools and family health services. Stratford will have its own international station on the high-speed rail link to Paris. There will be a new business park and the infrastructure for a new university.

The aim is to ensure that the Olympics provide a sustainable and lasting legacy to east London.

Construction of the Olympic site must meet a number of sustainability principles:
- Zero waste will go to landfill for the entire Olympics, including the preparation period, the games themselves and the legacy phase.
- There will be 90% reuse and recycling of demolition materials.
- Reused or recycled materials must account for 20% of the value of materials used in the permanent venues, and 35% of the venues and infrastructure.
- Fifty per cent of the construction materials for the Olympic Park must be carried to the site by rail or river.
- Homes in the Olympic village must meet sustainable standards.
- Twenty per cent of electricity demand will be met from renewable sources, and all buildings will be energy efficient.
- The following will be cleaned up: 3000 m of river courses, 3800 m of canals and 3500 m of river bank.

Urbanisation and its environmental consequences in China

China's urbanisation and economic development has been relentless in the past 30 years. The country already has 90 cities with more than a million inhabitants and it is estimated that between 2005 and 2035 another 400 million people will migrate from the countryside to the cities. However, economic success has placed severe pressure on the environment. According to the World Bank, China has 20 of the world's 30 most polluted cities. Half its cities suffer chronic air pollution and acid rain, mainly caused by coal-burning power stations and millions of motor vehicles.

Sustainable cities

There is increasing concern in China that its current industrialisation, which has caused widespread environmental degradation, is unsustainable. As a result, China is leading the way in developing the world's first fully sustainable eco-city. It will be located on Chongming, a large alluvial island situated in the Yangtze River delta (Figure 5.25). The project, just 15 km from China's largest city Shanghai

Figure 5.25 *The location of Dongtan*

Photograph 5.16 *The skyline of Shanghai*

(see Photograph 5.16), provides a model for sustainable urban living in the twenty-first century. The new eco-city is called Dongtan: it will be carbon-neutral and have an ecological footprint (see Box 5.5 on page 235) that is only a fraction of conventional cities.

Dongtan — the master plan

Dongtan occupies an area of newly reclaimed land at the eastern end of Chongming Island (Figure 5.26). The eco-city is designed by a British company — Arup. Backing the $1.3 billion project is the Shanghai Industrial Investment Corporation, a state-controlled developer that was given the newly reclaimed Dongtan site in 1998.

The first phase of the scheme, due for completion in 2010, will house 25 000 residents. This will rise to 80 000 in 2020, and to 500 000 by 2030. The total urban area will cover one-fifth of Dongtan's 86 km^2 and will consist of three village-style neighbourhoods separated by forests, organic farms, lakes and tourist attractions. The aim is to develop new urban lifestyles. Unlike Shanghai's 100-storey tower blocks, the residents of Dongtan will be accommodated in low-rise developments. Housing densities will be 75 dwellings per hectare (more than twice typical urban densities in the UK), but much lower than in a conventional Chinese city.

Dongtan is planned as a compact, largely car-free city, where people can cycle or walk to shops, schools, work and services. A network of footpaths and cycling tracks will help achieve zero vehicle emissions; and public transport will be highly accessible — no more than 500 m from each home. Despite its high density, there will be generous provision of public green space, adding significantly to the quality of urban living. Each inhabitant will have on average 27 m^2 of green space, compared with 20.5 m^2 in London, and 6.6 m^2 in Los Angeles. Public transport will include solar-powered water taxis on Dongtan's canals, and buses powered by hydrogen cells, which generate no harmful emissions.

Dongtan will be self-sufficient in energy and water and will generate almost no carbon emissions. Overall the new eco-city will be a quiet place, allowing residents to open windows for natural ventilation in summer rather than switching on their air conditioning.

Energy will be generated from renewable resources using wind turbines, photovoltaic cells and biofuels from household and agricultural waste. Most of the city's solid waste and sewage will be recycled and there will be no landfill. Meanwhile, green building technologies will reduce the amount of energy needed to heat and cool buildings by 70%. Grasses will grow on rooftops, and rainwater will be purified and stored in Dongtan's canals and water features.

A new expressway, including a 9 km tunnel and several new bridges, will link Dongtan with down-

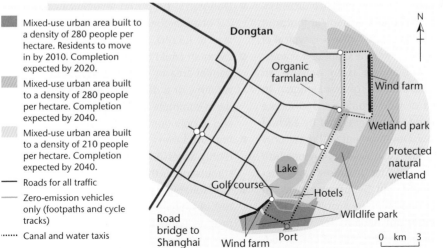

Key:
- Mixed-use urban area built to a density of 280 people per hectare. Residents to move in by 2010. Completion expected by 2020.
- Mixed-use urban area built to a density of 280 people per hectare. Completion expected by 2040.
- Mixed-use urban area built to a density of 210 people per hectare. Completion expected by 2040.
- Roads for all traffic
- Zero-emission vehicles only (footpaths and cycle tracks)
- Canal and water taxis

Dongtan
Organic farmland
Wind farm
Wetland park
Protected natural wetland
Lake
Golf course
Hotels
Wildlife park
Road bridge to Shanghai
Wind farm
Port
0 km 3
N

Figure 5.26 Master plan for Dongtan on Chongming Island

Table 5.13 *Dongtan: a sustainable, eco-friendly city*

	Dongtan eco-city	Conventional city
Residents	80 000	50 000
Jobs	51 000	19 000
Ecological footprint	2.2 gha person^{-1}	5.8 gha person^{-1}
Water consumption	16 500 t day^{-1}	29 000 t day^{-1}
Waste water	4300 t day^{-1}	29 000 t day^{-1}
Agricultural production	No loss of production	Loss of 1000 ha productive land
Energy demand	600 GWH year^{-1}	1650 GWH year^{-1}
Carbon dioxide emissions from power/heat	None	350 000 t year^{-1}
Waste management: landfill	5000 t year^{-1}	30 000 t year^{-1}
Daily travel distance	4.2 million km	6 million km
Carbon dioxide emissions from transport	None	400 000 t year^{-1}
Average trip length	24 km	56 km

town Shanghai, reducing journey times from 2 hours to 20 minutes. By improving access and infrastructure, Dongtan will also become a major tourism attraction. Already, Dongtan is arousing international interest. The Mayor of London recently visited Shanghai to investigate the scheme. The intention is to build a sustainable eco-city in the Thames Gateway region, east of the capital. It would accommodate some of the 800 000 population increase that is forecasted for London between 2005 and 2016.

Ecological footprint

The ecological impact of China's massive urbanisation will be huge. Shanghai's ecological footprint (see Box 5.5, page 235) — 6.5–7 gha — is typical of urban China and is four times the Chinese average.

The aim of the planners is to achieve an ecological footprint of around 2 gha for Dongtan. In other words, 2 ha of land would accommodate the consumption and waste generated by each of Dongtan's residents. Development will make only a limited impact on the countryside. Only one-fifth of Chongming Island will be urbanised; and one-quarter of the island will be protected as an ecological buffer. Chongming's valuable wetlands, which provide important habitats for migrating cranes, swans and spoonbills, will be conserved.

The wetlands are internationally important and have protected status as Ramsar sites. At Dongtan, the planners will preserve the wetlands and create a 4 km-wide wildlife park separating the new city from the wetlands.

Dongtan: a truly sustainable city?

While everyone agrees that the environmental impact of Dongtan will be much less than a conventional city, several commentators have questioned the sustainability of the project. They make the following points:

- Dongtan's proposed ecological footprint of 2.2 gha is higher than the theoretical sustainable level of 1.9 gha.
- Dongtan could become merely an exclusive residential area or weekend retreat for Shanghai's wealthy, or a dormitory town from which residents commute to Shanghai. Commuting would add to pollution.
- Improved transport links will make Chongming highly accessible, pushing up land values and stimulating further development.
- The suitability of the Dongtan model for the rest of China is doubtful. Initially, Dongtan will provide leisure activities for affluent visitors from the mainland. However, this is only feasible

because it is situated next to Shanghai, one of China's wealthiest cities.

- It is not clear how affordable the scheme would be elsewhere in China. The vast majority of Chinese could not afford to live in Dongtan, where the cost of a single solar panel is equal to a year's income

for a peasant farmer. The cost of electricity generated by wind turbines will be four times that from coal-fired power stations. People with low incomes cannot support this type of eco-technology.

- Chongming's migrant birds could be threatened by wind turbines and population growth.

Examination-style questions

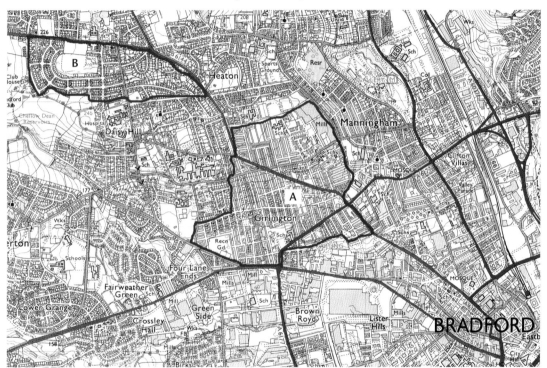

Figure 1

1 **(a)** Using the evidence of the OS map extract of Bradford shown in Figure 1, describe the main differences between the housing areas A and B. (4 marks)

  (b) Suggest two possible reasons for the differences between housing areas A and B. (6 marks)

  (c) With reference to one named example, describe how urban growth can cause social and economic problems in urban areas. (6 marks)

  (d) With reference to one or more named urban areas, examine the ways that problems of inadequate service provision are being managed. (9 marks)

2 With reference to named examples, describe and explain how planning and management can enable urban areas to become more sustainable.

(25 marks)

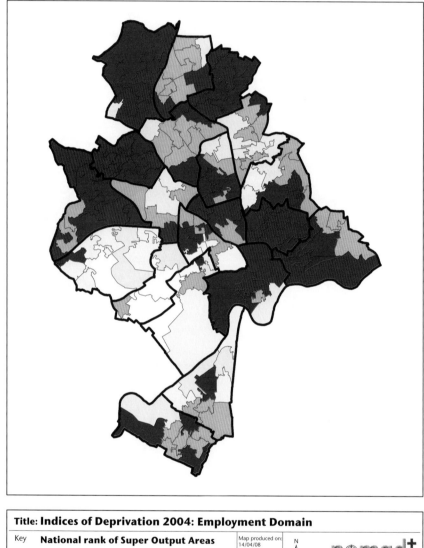

Figure 2 *Employment deprivation in Nottingham*

3 (a) Describe the pattern of employment deprivation in Nottingham shown in Figure 2. (4 marks)

  (b) Suggest two possible reasons for the pattern of employment deprivation in Nottingham. (6 marks)

  (c) With reference to one or more examples, outline the causes of atmospheric pollution in urban areas. (6 marks)

  (d) With reference to a named urban area, examine the problems of managing increasing volumes of waste. (9 marks)

4 With reference to a named example, describe and explain the attempts by planners and managers to tackle the problem of urban dereliction. (25 marks)

Chapter 6

Managing rural change

The characteristics of rural areas

Key ideas
➤ Rural areas have distinctive characteristics and a variety of functions, processes and opportunities.
➤ The range of functions and opportunities in rural areas is influenced by economic, social, political and environmental factors.

Defining rural areas

There is no internationally agreed definition of rural areas. However, national censuses use a range of criteria to define urban areas, which reflect local social and geographical circumstances (Box 6.1). In this context, rural areas are, by default, non-urban. Figure 6.1 shows a government classification of types of rural population and rural settlement for England and Wales.

Box 6.1 Some census definitions of urban areas

- Botswana — an agglomeration of more than 5000 people and where 75% of inhabitants are engaged in non-agricultural activities.
- Senegal — an agglomeration of more than 10 000 people.
- Japan — a settlement of more than 50 000 people, where at least 60% of houses are in the main built-up area and at least 60% of the population work in manufacturing, trade

and other business activities.
- India — a settlement of at least 5000 people, where more than 75% of the male population works in non-agricultural activities and with an average population density of at least 400 persons per square kilometre.
- Denmark — a coherent built-up area with at least 2000 inhabitants and where the average distance between each building does not exceed 200 m.

Figure 6.1 *Classification of rural areas in England and Wales*

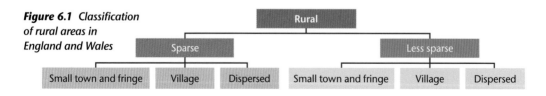

The social characteristics of rural communities

Rural communities have a number of characteristics that distinguish them from their urban counterparts. Compared with urban communities, rural communities are:

➤ closer-knit, with everyone knowing and interacting with everyone else
➤ socially and ethnically more homogeneous
➤ more family centred (many extended families)
➤ more conservative
➤ less mobile, both geographically and socially

Functions, opportunities and development in rural areas

Rural areas provide a range of opportunities based on local resources. As we shall see through case studies of Wensleydale and Västernorrland, realising these opportunities depends on a number of economic, social, political and environmental factors.

Case study   Wensleydale

Wensleydale is a rural district in North Yorkshire drained by the River Ure and its tributaries (Figure 6.2). It covers an area of around 900 km².

In many ways, Wensleydale is a microcosm of the geography of rural Britain. The lower parts of the dale resemble eastern England with gently rolling countryside, dominated by intensive arable farming. Much of the farmland in this area is highly productive

grade 2 and grade 3 (Figure 6.3). Lower Wensleydale is also highly accessible, with fast road and rail links to nearby towns and cities such as Leeds, York and Harrogate. According to the most recent classification of rural areas in England and Wales (2005), lower Wensleydale is a 'less sparsely populated sub-region of small towns and villages'.

Moving upvalley, Wensleydale's climate and relief

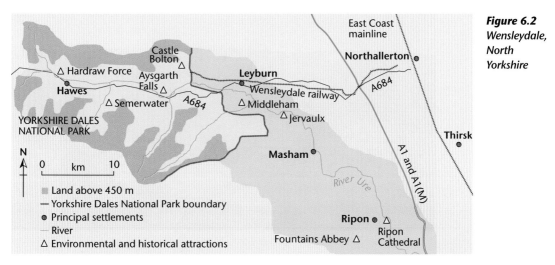

Figure 6.2
Wensleydale, North Yorkshire

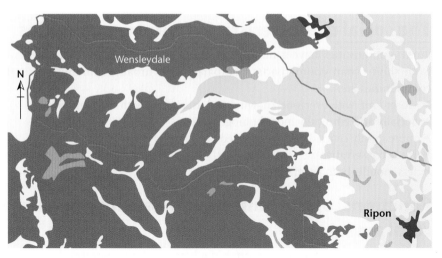

Figure 6.3
Land-use quality in Wensleydale

Legend:
- Grade 1
- Grade 2
- Grade 3
- Grade 4
- Grade 5

Increasing quality

- Non-agricultural
- Urban

⌒ Wensleydale boundary

change dramatically. Upstream from Leyburn we enter highland Britain. At the head of the valley, on the high Pennine watershed, Great Shunner Fell rises above 700 m. This is a rugged environment of high rainfall, steep slopes, acid soils and hill sheep farming. Although undeniably beautiful and protected by the Yorkshire Dales National Park, upper Wensleydale is as remote as it gets in England. In some parishes, commuter journeys average more than 40 km a day, and the nearest supermarket is 26 km away. Unlike the lower dale, this is a sparsely populated rural region, dominated by isolated dwellings and dispersed settlements.

The total population of Wensleydale is around 31 000. Just over half live in Ripon. Population density averages 35 persons per km² (17 per km² excluding Ripon). This compares with an average density for England of 322 persons per km². Such low densities are typically rural.

Ethnically, societies are generally more homogeneous in rural areas. Wensleydale is no exception. In most parishes, 95% to 100% of the population is white and British born. This compares with 87% in England as a whole. Rural populations also tend to be older than urban populations. Whereas the average age for England is 38.6 years, in Wensleydale it is 42.8. However, there are wide variations at the parish scale: from 35.2 to 50.4 years.

Photograph 6.1
Wensleydale landscape

Topfoto

Rural characteristics of Wensleydale

Functions

Rural land use dominates Wensleydale, underlining the importance of farming to the local economy. Improved pastures occupy the main valley floor and lower valley slopes. Arable land is more common in the lower parts of the dale where it merges with the Vale of York. Meanwhile, rough grazing and moorland occurs everywhere above 400 m.

All settlements, with the exception of Ripon, are rural. They comprise isolated dwellings, hamlets, villages and small towns such as Hawes, Leyburn and Masham, with populations of between 1000 and 3000. Ripon, with a population of 16 000, has a full range of shops, schools, hospital and other services, and is the main service centre in Wensleydale.

Employment

The rurality of Wensleydale is less obvious in terms of employment. Declining employment in agriculture means that only a small minority of the rural population now works in farming. Agriculture is no longer the driver of the rural economy. Most rural dwellers work locally in service activities such as wholesaling, retailing and tourism.

In Wensleydale, many villages and small market towns have substantial retired populations. In the less remote lower dale, commuting to Harrogate, Northallerton and Ripon is popular. Home working provides an increasing number of jobs in the countryside.

Opportunities for rural development

A range of resources and opportunities exist for economic and social development in Wensleydale. These resources are geographical, environmental, economic and cultural.

Accessibility

Much of Wensleydale is attractive for economic investment because of location. The lower and middle parts of the dale are within 25 minutes' drive time of the A1 and A1(M), which give rapid access to

major urban concentrations in West Yorkshire and northeast England. The train stations at Northallerton and Thirsk give access to the east coast mainline, and provide direct links to York, Leeds, Newcastle, Edinburgh and London.

Access to nearby urban centres such as Ripon, Northallerton and Harrogate is good. For this reason, many villages such as Burton Leonard and Kirkby Malzeard have developed commuter functions.

Opportunities in the upper dale are limited by poor accessibility. The only main road from the east — the A684 — between Leyburn and Hawes is slow and inconvenient. Access from the west, across the Pennine Hills, is even more difficult. Overall there is a sense of remoteness in this part of the dale.

Quality of life

The quality of life in Wensleydale is high. Its rural character, attractive villages, wildlife and scenic landscapes have made it a popular retirement area as well as a magnet for commuters. Most of the middle and upper dale lie within the Yorkshire Dales National Park. Given the environmental quality of this area and its recreational opportunities, it is not surprising that many dwellings have become second homes and holiday homes. In the upper dale, one in six dwellings is a second home or holiday home, and in Higher Abbotside parish, the proportion is over one-third.

Physical and historic environments

Wensleydale's most important resources are its high-quality physical environment and its many outstanding cultural features. They provide opportunities for recreation and tourism. West of Leyburn, virtually the whole of Wensleydale is in the Yorkshire Dales National Park (see Figure 6.2). This area attracts hill walkers and sightseers. Among its spectacular physical features are Semerwater, one of only two natural lakes in the Dales, Aysgarth Falls on the River Ure (Photograph 6.2), and the smaller Hardraw Force waterfall. Areas of moorland in the extreme southeast of the Ure catchment, which fall outside the Yorkshire Dales National Park, are protected by the Nidderdale Area of Outstanding Natural Beauty.

Photograph 6.2
Aysgarth Falls

Michael Raw

The middle and lower parts of the dale are rich in historical interest. Several sites are of national and international importance. Fountains Abbey near Ripon is a World Heritage Site; Jervaulx, like Fountains, is a ruined Cistercian abbey; Ripon has a large medieval cathedral; and there are castles at Middleham and Bolton. The re-opening of the picturesque rail line between Redmire and Leeming Bar to passengers provides a further attraction and improves accessibility to the middle dale.

Employment figures underline the importance of recreation and tourism in rural regions such as Wensleydale. While agriculture accounts for just 5% of employment, nearly 20% of the active population works in hotels, restaurants and other services for visitors.

Resources for primary activities

Farming is the traditional economic activity in Wensleydale, and auction marts survive in Hawes and Leyburn. The physical environment provides varying opportunities for farming. Most of the upper dale comprises windswept moorland. High rainfall, a short growing season, steep slopes and acidic soils support only low-intensity hill sheep farming. This activity is in decline and its survival depends on government subsidies. The best land is in the valley.

Dairy cattle and sheep farming are more prosperous. Down the valley, the dale widens out and the climate becomes less severe. **Mixed farming** starts to appear in mid-Wensleydale. In lower Wensleydale it is possible to grow a full range of temperate arable crops such as wheat, barley and oilseed rape on fertile soils derived from glacial deposits.

Other opportunities, so far little developed, exist in the upper dale. The potential for wind power on the hills above the dale is considerable, though in conflict with the area's designation within the National Park. Afforestation could be greatly increased, both for economic and amenity reasons. Water remains a resource that has yet to be exploited. The Ure catchment, unlike the heavily reservoired Nidd catchment to the immediate south, is one of the few 'wild' rivers left in northern England.

Political factors and rural development in Wensleydale

The economic viability of farming in the upper dale is strongly influenced by the EU's Common Agricultural Policy (CAP). Without subsidies, livestock farming, which in the past has been the mainstay of the local economy, would be scarcely viable.

Today's CAP has two strands. The first and more traditional one provides income support to farmers;

the second, which has assumed greater importance in recent years, has a broader focus on rural development. This includes retraining farmers and farm workers, encouraging new rural enterprises aimed at diversifying incomes and the rural economy, and helping farmers to invest in new buildings and new technologies. In its present form, the CAP is as much about sustainable rural development and environmental protection as it is about food production.

Box 6.2 Government schemes in rural areas

The CAP and the Single Payment Scheme

Major reform of the CAP in 2005 meant that subsidies for crops, numbers of livestock and production were to be phased out. They have been replaced by a Single Payment Scheme for each hectare farmed. Payments depend on the quality of the land farmed. Upper Wensleydale, classed as a severely disadvantaged area (i.e. moorland upland), qualifies for payments of £20–40 ha year[-1]. Mid-Wensleydale farmers will receive £110–130 ha year[-1], and the best farming areas in the lower dale £210–230 ha year[-1]. However, there are 'cross-compliance rules' that farmers must fulfil in order to qualify for payments. These include repairing walls and hedges, ensuring that pastures are not overgrazed, using less artificial fertiliser and so on.

The new system has several advantages. It uncouples subsidies from production and thus reduces the incentive to farm more intensively. This is good for the environment. It should also reduce production, and encourage farmers to grow crops that the market wants. Already there is evidence that upland farmers, no longer receiving payments for each animal, are keeping fewer livestock on the high pastures and moors.

Environmental Stewardship

The Environmental Stewardship (ES) scheme, operated by the UK Department of Environment Food and Rural Affairs (DEFRA), was introduced in 2005. ES encourages environmental management and enhancement by farmers. There are three levels of entry: entry, organic entry and higher. For the entry level scheme, farmers are paid £30 ha year[-1] in the lowlands, and £8–30 ha year[-1] in the uplands. These payments depend, for example, on the protection and management of the rural environment.

Case study Västernorrland, northern Sweden

Background

Västernorrland is a rural county in central northern Sweden (Figure 6.4). In the context of the European Union (EU), Västernorrland is a disadvantaged region, its development hindered by a combination of geography, environment and socio-economic factors.

Geography

Västernorrland has a similar area to Wales, but is much more sparsely populated. With a total population of just 240 000 in 2006, its average density (11 persons per km^2) is one of the lowest in Europe (Photograph 6.3).

Pixonnet.com/Alamy

***Photograph 6.3** Västernorrland*

Figure 6.4
Västernorrland

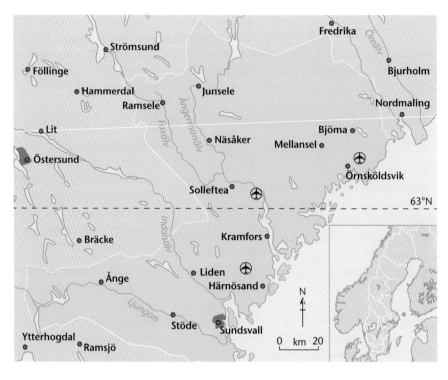

Ninety-eight per cent of Västernorrland's land area is rural and here population densities average only 2 km² (Figure 6.5). Three-quarters of the population is concentrated in urban centres, with 40% living in the three largest towns: Sundsvall, Örnsköldsvik and Härnösand (see Figure 6.4). Interior Västernorrland is particularly remote and inaccessible, while in relation to the EU, the region is as peripheral as southern Spain, Greece and western Ireland.

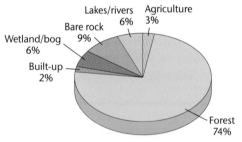

Figure 6.5 *Land use in Västernorrland*

Physical environment

Västernorrland has a harsh climate. This is due to two factors: its high latitude (62°N to 64°N) and the influence of the Kjølen mountains, which isolate northern Sweden from the warming influence of the North Atlantic Ocean. Winters are long and cold. Temperatures can fall as low as −30°C and sea ice forms along the Bothnian coast in winter.

Other factors contribute to the harshness of the environment. Soils are shallow, sandy and boulder strewn; 9% of the land area is bare rock; and 6% is wetland (see Figure 6.5). As a result, only 3% of the land area is cultivated.

Socio-economic conditions

The combination of Västernorrland's remoteness, low population density and harsh physical environment has created a number of socio-economic problems. Out-migration of young people over the past 50 years has created an ageing population, which has resulted in **natural decrease** and population decline (Figure 6.6 and Table 6.1). Meanwhile, traditional industries such as forestry (timber, pulp and paper) are over-represented, limiting the diversity of the local economy. A further weakness is the heavy dependence on jobs provided in public services (Figure 6.7).

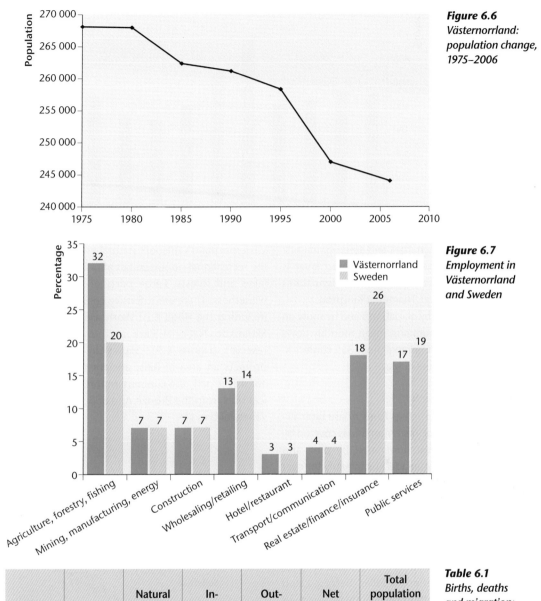

Figure 6.6
Västernorrland: population change, 1975–2006

Figure 6.7
Employment in Västernorrland and Sweden

	Births	Deaths	Natural change	In-migration	Out-migration	Net migration	Total population change
	16 455	21 808	−5353	44 884	44 858	+26	−5327

Table 6.1
Births, deaths and migration: Västernorrland 2000–06

Range of functions

Västernorrland's economy relies heavily on the region's natural resource base, especially its forests, rivers and minerals. Forestry, farming, HEP production, mining and quarrying, and forest-based industries account for nearly 40% of total employment.

Hydroelectricity

Twenty-two large HEP stations are located on the region's three main rivers: the Ångerman, Indals and Ljungan. Between them they produce 8% of Sweden's electricity. Rivers like the Ångerman are ideal for HEP generation:

Figure 6.8 *Mean monthly discharge for the Ångerman River at Sollefteå*

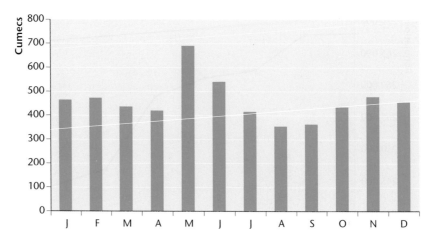

- They have large discharges and steep gradients: the mean discharge of the Ångerman River is 469 cumecs (Figure 6.8) — almost eight times greater than the River Thames at Kingston.
- Flows are regulated by glacial lakes and by snow on the high Kjølen mountains: mean monthly flows on the Ångerman River range from 355 cumecs in August to 691 cumecs in May.

Forestry and related industries

Traditional industries such as forestry are typically resource based. Most of Västernorrland is covered by dense coniferous forest dominated by pine and spruce. These forests, managed sustainably for over a century, provide timber for local sawmills and for the manufacture of pulp and paper. Sustainability does not only mean that annual timber growth exceeds the amount harvested: since the early 1990s, sustainability has included the promotion of forest biodiversity and encouraging multiple uses of forest resources (e.g. recreation, wildlife, berry picking etc.). Forestry contributes significantly to Sweden's economy. Sweden is currently the world's third-largest exporter of sawn softwood timber, pulp and paper. The raw material, softwood timber, is primarily sourced from its northern forests.

Tourism

Tourism is an important and expanding sector of the Västernorrland's economy. In 2005, visitors spent £250 million. The main visitor attraction is Västernorrland's unspoilt natural environment and the recreational opportunities afforded by its rivers, lakes and forests. Large parts of the region are wilderness. There are extensive conservation areas, including the Höga Kust World Heritage Site, the Skuleskog National Park and over 100 nature reserves (Figure 6.9). Skuleskog National Park protects an area of hills, ancient forests and sea coast. The park also contains important archaeological sites from the Bronze Age and supports a rich variety of bird life.

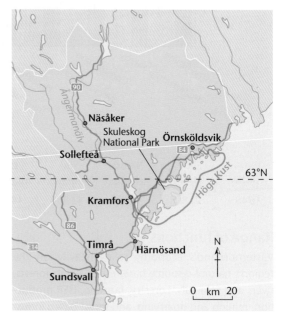

Figure 6.9 *The Höga Kust World Heritage Site*

Opportunities

We know that Västernorrland suffers disadvantages because of its peripheral location within Sweden and the EU, its relative isolation, its harsh physical environment, its low population density and its dependence on a narrow range of resource-based industries. Depopulation has compounded these problems. Västernorrland's population declined by 9% between 1970 and 2005, the result of out-migration and a steady ageing of the population.

Although Västernorrland is relatively prosperous, the unique problems of geography that affect it, and the whole of northern Sweden, explain its designation as an Objective 1 area under the EU's regional policy. This qualified the region for maximum financial assistance from the European Regional Development Fund (ERDF) between 2000 and 2006. While Objective 1 is gradually being phased out, the region will retain assisted status under the EU's new Cohesion Policy, 2007–13.

Natural and cultural environment

Apart from its timber and HEP resources, Västernorrland's biggest asset is its unspoilt natural environment. This sparsely populated region on the periphery of Europe is a place where human activities have made little impression on the environment. Opportunities for the expansion of recreation and international tourism in this wilderness, based on the region's lakes, forests and cultural history, are enormous. At the moment, however, only 6% of visitors are from outside Scandinavia.

Pointing the way to future development is the unique Höga Kust World Heritage Site. The Höga Kust is a stretch of coastline that has experienced the world's greatest isostatic uplift — 285 m — in the past 10 000 years. The coast also has cultural and archaeological importance because the old shorelines attracted a succession of prehistoric settlements. A museum, currently under construction,

Leslie Garland Picture Library/Alamy

Photograph 6.4 *Prehistoric rock carvings at Näsåker on the Ångerman River*

should boost the area's popularity. Another site of international importance is at Näsåker on the Ångerman River (see Figure 6.9 and Photograph 6.4). Here there are over 2000 prehistoric rock carvings, some over 6000 years old.

Transport and communications

Modern and fast transport and communications are valuable assets to Västernorrland. They provide opportunities for inward investment and development of the region's recreation and tourism potential. While transport and communications between the coast and interior Västernorrland are poor, the transport corridor along the Bothnian coast is fast and efficient. Major road and rail routes — the E4 and the main east-coast rail line — link Västernorrland to Stockholm and southern Sweden. A new rail link between Umeå and Nyland will further improve journey times along the east-coast route, which will be upgraded to a high-speed line in the next few years. The E14 is the only significant east–west road link to Östersund and Trondheim (Norway).

Västernorrland has three small airports with frequent flights to Stockholm, while 95% of the population has access to broadband internet connections.

Factors influencing rural development

There are many factors that influence rural development in Västernorrland (Figure 6.10). These factors, which are geographical, social, economic, environmental, demographic and political, explain the lack of rural development. At the same time they also provide opportunities for future development and growth.

Västernorrland lags behind most of Sweden and the core regions of the EU. The main reasons are its harsh physical environment and the location remote from the main hub of economic activity in Sweden and western Europe. However, the region has rich and varied natural resources which provide opportunities for future sustainable development. Least exploited is the near-pristine wilderness of Västernorrland's forests and lakes. The value of such environments in a densely populated continent like Europe, and the scope for international tourism, are immense. Meanwhile further improvements in transport and communications will make the region increasingly accessible and attractive for investment. With an expansion in job opportunities there is every chance that the flow of young people from the region will be stemmed and that depopulation will be reversed for first time in half a century.

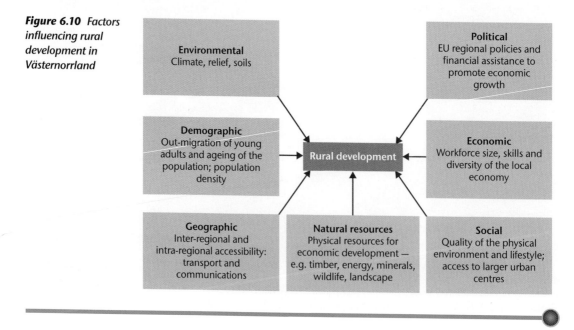

Figure 6.10 *Factors influencing rural development in Västernorrland*

Rural change

Key ideas

➤ A number of social and economic issues are associated with rural change.
➤ Structural changes can lead to social and economic differences within and between rural areas.
➤ Lack of economic opportunities in rural areas can lead to depopulation and decline.
➤ Economic and social problems occur in areas of rural decline.
➤ Economic and social problems are associated with growth and development in rural areas.

Economic and social change in rural areas often has two opposite effects. In some rural regions it leads to a decline that creates a raft of social and economic problems such as unemployment, loss of services and out-migration. Elsewhere, rural change often results in rapid growth which can be equally problematical. The problems of rural growth and rural decline will be illustrated in this section with two case studies from the USA: Nebraska on the Great Plains and Chester County in Pennsylvania.

Case study Rural decline in Nebraska

Nebraska is a US state at the centre of the Great Plains (Figure 6.11). Roughly the size of England and Wales combined, Nebraska is an immense flat land (Photograph 6.5). Relief rises gradually over 400 km from east to west: from around 500 m in the Missouri Valley to over 1500 m along the border with Wyoming.

Nebraska

Great Plains

Figure 6.11
Location of Nebraska and the Great Plains

Photograph 6.5
Landscape of the Great Plains, Nebraska

Nebraska's climate is dominated by its position in the continental interior. Winters are cold, with average minimum temperatures in January falling to −11.7°C at Scottsbluff. Summers are hot: average maximum temperatures in July in the east reach 33°C. Rainfall decreases towards the west where the rain-shadow effect of the Rockies is most pronounced. Western areas receive barely 400 mm a year. Nonetheless, 94% of Nebraska is farmland — this despite the fact that much of the state is semi-arid and the growing season lasts for just 130 to 170 days a year.

Population change in Nebraska

Although Nebraska's population grew by over 8% between 1990 and 2000, this overall growth conceals massive **rural depopulation** (Box 6.3) at the county scale. Fifty-three of the state's 93 counties lost population between 1990 and 2000: part of a slow demographic collapse in rural areas that has lasted for the past 70 years (Figure 6.12). Almost all the state's population growth has been concentrated in two areas: the eastern metropolitan counties, especially in Omaha, Sioux Falls and Lincoln; and in the Interstate 80 (I-80) corridor (Figure 6.13).

Figure 6.12
Population change in Nebraska, 1950–2000

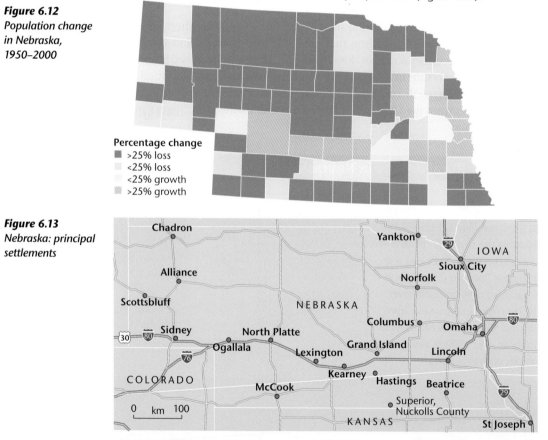

Percentage change
■ >25% loss
  <25% loss
□ <25% growth
▨ >25% growth

Figure 6.13
Nebraska: principal settlements

Box 6.3 Rural depopulation

Rural depopulation is an absolute decrease of population in a rural area. It is most common at the small scale of parishes and townships. Sometimes rural depopulation affects entire regions such as the

Great Plains of the USA. Occasionally, depopulation hits entire countries. This happened during the potato famine in Ireland between 1845 and 1850 and is happening today in southern African countries such as Botswana and Lesotho, which are devastated by AIDS.

Rural depopulation is most often caused by a combination of natural population decrease and migration. It starts when young people migrate from rural areas in search of employment. This affects the demography of rural areas in three ways:

■ It immediately reduces the population.
■ It reduces the number of births that are likely in future.

■ It increases the average age of the population.

An ageing population leads to fewer births and more deaths, increasing the likelihood of natural decrease.

Rural depopulation also occurs in the absence of migration when mortality is exceptionally high, for instance due to famine or disease. Equally it can occur in areas of natural increase where heavy **net migration** loss takes place.

The causes of rural decline

Demographic

Rural depopulation is driven primarily by demographic and economic factors. As we shall see, they are closely connected, with demographic change forcing economic change and vice versa.

We can explain demographic change by the interaction of three variables: births, deaths and migration. Depopulation in most rural counties is caused

by all three. An excess of deaths over births produces **natural decrease**. At the same time, out-migration exceeds in-migration resulting in a **net migrational loss**. Superior, Nuckolls County in south Nebraska has the typical demographic profile of an area suffering prolonged depopulation (Table 6.2). It also has two other characteristics typical of depopulating counties on the Great Plains: its small total population; and the small size of its largest town — Superior (2100) (Figure 6.14).

Table 6.2 *Demographic causes of population change in Nuckolls and Douglas counties, 1990–2000*

County	Type	Total population	Births	Birth rate per 1000	Deaths	Death rate per 1000	Net migrational change	% population change
Nuckolls	Rural	5057	510	10.1	794	15.7	−455	−12.6
Douglas (Omaha)	Urban	463 585	70 563	15.2	35 010	7.6	+11 588	+10.2

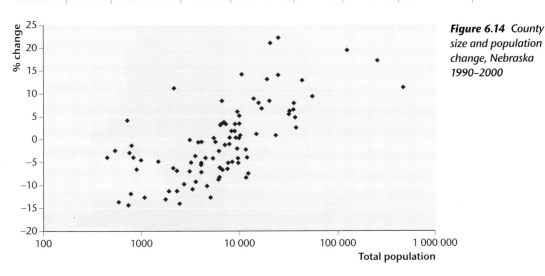

Figure 6.14 *County size and population change, Nebraska 1990–2000*

Nuckolls County has experienced continuous depopulation since 1940 and the most recent figures show an accelerating trend (Figure 6.15). Table 6.2 shows that this depopulation is the result of both natural decrease and net migrational loss. Natural decrease reflects the out-migration of young adults aged 20 to 35 years: the group most likely to have children. Overall, 455 more people left Nuckolls County between 1990 and 2000 than moved in. The effect on the county's age structure is startling (Figure 6.16). Its population pyramid has a 'pinched' appearance in the age groups 20 to 30 years. Meanwhile, the loss of young people gives rise to an ageing population, which in turn pushes up the death rate.

The median age of Nuckolls' population is 44 years. Compare this with the relatively youthful age structure of metropolitan Omaha where the median age is 33 years (Figure 6.17).

Depopulation has continued in the twenty-first century. By 2005, Nuckolls County's population had slumped to 4743. Forecasts for 2010 suggest a population of around 4500.

Economic

We know that the basic cause of demographic change in Nuckolls County is out-migration of young adults. But what causes young people to leave in the first place? Out-migration is mainly due

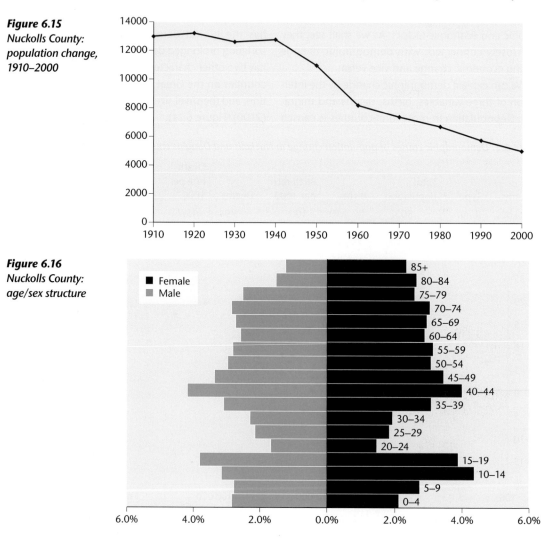

Figure 6.15
Nuckolls County: population change, 1910–2000

Figure 6.16
Nuckolls County: age/sex structure

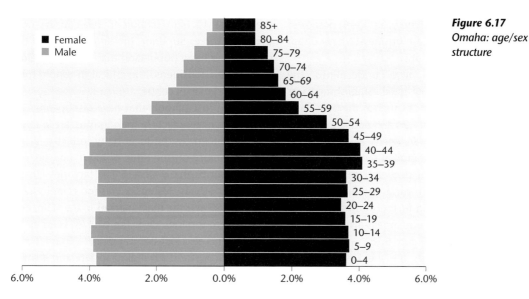

Figure 6.17
Omaha: age/sex structure

Legend:
■ Female
■ Male

Age groups: 85+, 80–84, 75–79, 70–74, 65–69, 60–64, 55–59, 50–54, 45–49, 40–44, 35–39, 30–34, 25–29, 20–24, 15–19, 10–14, 5–9, 0–4

Axis: 6.0% 4.0% 2.0% 0.0% 2.0% 4.0% 6.0%

to economic factors and it is not difficult to see why. The median family income in Nuckolls is just under $25 000 a year. In metropolitan Omaha, median incomes are more than double at $55 000. Indeed rural poverty is widespread in Nebraska, which has 7 of the USA's 12 poorest counties.

Out-migration is also caused by lack of employment opportunities in rural areas. Agriculture has always been the mainstay of the rural economy and even today it supports one in four jobs, either directly or indirectly. However, for the past 50 years employment in agriculture has been declining. Small farms have declined in number, replaced by highly mechanised large-scale **agribusiness** (Photograph 6.6). With few employment opportunities outside agriculture, many people have been forced to leave.

But it is not just employment in agriculture that has contracted. As farms have become bigger, they have outgrown the hundreds of small businesses

Photograph 6.6 *Wheat harvesting, Nebraska*

that used to provide machinery, fertilisers, pesticides and livestock feed. As these businesses have disappeared, so too have the jobs.

Rural depopulation also undermines the threshold requirements of retail establishments as well as government agencies such as the police and fire services, schools, hospitals and public transport. A rural county in the USA needs at least 10 000 people to support a full range of services and infrastructure. The impact of declining services is, of course, to make small rural towns even less attractive, thus triggering further out-migration to metropolitan areas. The outcome is a spiral of rural decline, summarised in Figure 6.18.

Although push factors are the key to understanding rural–urban migration in Nebraska, the complementary attraction of large metropolitan areas such as Omaha and Lincoln is important too. These areas offer greater economic diversity, a wider range of job opportunities and higher incomes. Their presence fuels rural–urban migration, which is bringing about the increased geographical concentration of population in Nebraska and other states on the Great Plains.

The social and economic problems of rural decline in Nuckolls County

As a result of falling numbers of students in Nuckolls County, two schools closed in 2003. Thirty years ago there were 10 high schools in the county; now there are three. Superior, the largest place in the county; now has a population that has fallen below 2000, often considered the critical threshold for a functioning market centre.

It is not just schools that have disappeared. In Superior, a cheese factory making mozzarella using milk produced by the local dairy industry, a big cement factory on the edge of town, and dozens of small shops, have closed. The factories closed because southeast Nebraska was too remote from Interstate-80 and the main markets in the state, and profits were too low. Over the past 20 years or so Superior has also lost two car dealers, four clothes shops, a drugstore, a building society and a small department store. Shops closed because depopulation meant fewer customers.

Meanwhile, competition from large superstores such as Wal-Mart at Hastings (see Figure 6.13 on page 258), 90 km distant and close to I-80, was also to blame. The impact of a powerful retailer such as Wal-Mart on a small market centre is particularly severe. The resultant closure of small stores in Superior meant that the local newspaper lost about 40% of its advertising revenue.

As these economic functions shut down, jobs disappear, forcing more people to move out. Most jobs are tied to farming, although the hospital remains the biggest single employer with 148 workers.

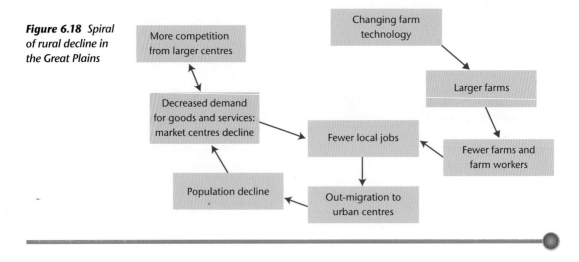

Figure 6.18 *Spiral of rural decline in the Great Plains*

Case study — Chester County: growth and development in a rural area

Chester County, Pennsylvania, is situated 40 km southwest of Philadelphia and 18 km west of Wilmington in the peri-urban zone. Apart from being a rural county, Chester County has little in common with Nuckolls County in Nebraska, 1500 km further west. Unlike Nuckolls, it has experienced strong population growth and development in the past 50 years. This growth is part of a wider trend in the USA and the developed world, known as **counterurbanisation** (Box 6.4).

However, as we shall see, counterurbanisation has brought its own problems. They include:

■ the loss of countryside to urban sprawl
■ soaring house prices and shortages of affordable homes
■ longer commutes
■ more traffic congestion

Background

Chester County's population in 2006 was just over 480 000, with an average of 160 persons per km². In spite of its high population density, most of the county has a rural character. Forty-four per cent of its area is used for agriculture and 30% is woodland. However, prolonged economic growth, particularly in southern Chester County, has led to uncontrolled urban sprawl. This has placed huge pressure on the rural environment, threatening its distinctly rural character.

Problems associated with growth and development

Chester County's population more than doubled between 1960 and 2006 (Figure 6.19). Rapid development has seen farmland and woodland replaced with low-density housing, business parks, large superstores and shopping strips.

Box 6.4 Counterurbanisation

Counterurbanisation describes the dispersal of population from urban areas to rural areas that has taken place in MEDCs since around 1970. It has resulted in an increase in the proportion of rural dwellers.

Counterurbanisation is a dramatic turnaround from the urbanisation trend that dominated the first half of the twentieth century in MEDCs. It is due primarily to urban–rural migration, especially of middle- and upper-income groups, dominated by families and retirees.

Most counterurbanisation takes place in peri-urban areas, i.e. in rural and semi-rural hinterlands within commuting distance of cities. In the process, many villages and rural market towns acquire dormitory functions. In the UK, this type of counterurbanisation is exemplified by rural counties such as Cheshire and Warwickshire, adjacent to conurbations and large cities.

Migration to rural areas is caused by:

■ a desire for rural living
■ a perceived better quality of life
■ lower house prices
■ opportunities to work from home
■ better services, such as state schools

Retirement migration also contributes to counterurbanisation. Favoured destinations are more distant rural regions with high amenity value such as Provençe, the Algarve and Cornwall.

Many remote rural regions, such as the Highlands and Islands of Scotland, and counties in Idaho, Wyoming and Colorado in the US Rocky Mountains, have also experienced a population revival. Migrants are usually willing to trade off the higher incomes and standards of living they enjoyed in urban areas for a higher quality of life and preferred lifestyle in rural communities.

Figure 6.19
Population change in Chester County, 1960–2006

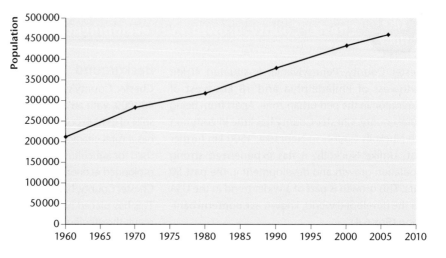

Eastern Chester County has developed as a commuter belt for Philadelphia and Wilmington.

The 2000 census records 10 000 residents commuting to Philadelphia; 43 000 to the adjacent Delaware and Montgomery counties (covering much of the Philadelphia metro); and 13 000 to Wilmington and New Castle County (Figure 6.20). Huge increases in commuting, with 90% of journeys made by car, has caused chronic traffic congestion on main routes west to Philadelphia and adjacent counties. People are also commuting longer distances and journey times are increasing. Public

Figure 6.20
Commuter flows into and out of Chester County

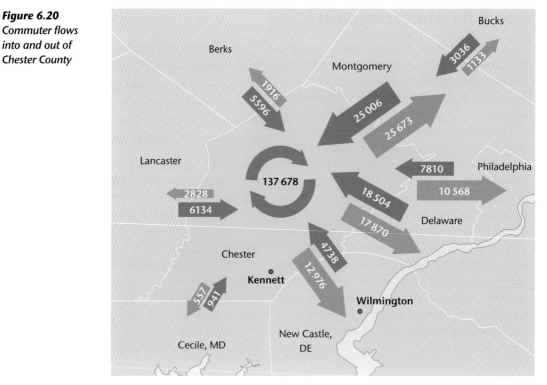

transport accounts for only 3% of commuter journeys. The dispersed, low-density development in Chester County illustrates the problem of serving communities in the peri-urban zone with public transport.

At a smaller scale, Kennett Municipality, on the southern edge of Chester County, provides an insight into the pressures and problems of rapid development in a peri-urban zone. Kennett, part of a traditional rural area, is still dominated by farmland and open spaces. Population grew by one-quarter between 1990 and 2000 as a large number of migrants moved into Kennett. Most development has comprised low-density single family houses, many occupying large plots of land. Some 'mini-mansions' occupy plots of up to 0.5 ha.

Affordable housing

As demand for housing has grown, soaring housing costs have led to shortages of affordable housing. The problem has been aggravated by the large influx of highly paid managers and executives attracted by the many high-tech firms, financial services and corporate headquarters located along Route 202. This has driven up house prices in the most affluent areas such as Kennett in the southern part of the county. Kennett has a highly educated workforce

with 46% of residents aged 25 and over holding a university degree.

The rising demand for housing has also been driven by societal changes. These include higher divorce rates, later marriage and more old people living alone. The outcome has been a massive increase in house building since 1980 (Figure 6.21).

Lack of affordable housing forces many workers to live in surrounding counties and commute to Chester County. This increases the length of journeys to work and adds to congestion and pollution.

Hispanics who work in farming have the most difficulty finding affordable housing. They and other low-income groups are effectively locked out of the housing market, especially in areas like Kennett where most housing developments have targeted higher income groups. Median house prices in Kennett are $248 000, compared with $182 000 in Chester County.

Other groups who have difficulty affording houses in Kennett include university graduates born in the area and who want to return home, and young high school graduates who are forced to move because of prohibitive house prices. There is a widespread belief that this generational out-migration could in future damage the demographic balance and sense of community in Kennett.

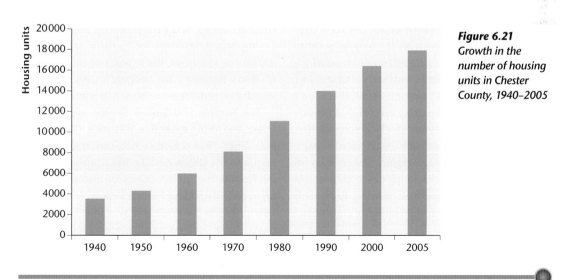

Figure 6.21
Growth in the number of housing units in Chester County, 1940–2005

Environmental issues and rural change

Key ideas

➤ Rural change is often associated with environmental issues.

➤ The changing use of rural areas can put increasing pressure on the environment, creating problems of traffic congestion and increasing the use of rural areas for recreation and leisure, and for building developments. These also cause land degradation and rural dereliction, and there is a need to manage these problems.

We saw in the previous section how rural change can have economic and social impacts. Rural change also has an environmental impact. Much of this is due to changes in farming, changes that themselves are a response to economic, demographic and political factors. These shifts have been far reaching, causing widespread land degradation, pollution, and damage to wildlife and landscapes. In this section, the environmental dimension of rural change is illustrated with case studies of East Anglia and the Fens. See also the case study on land degradation in Nara, Mali (page 188) and the Korqin Sandy Lands section of the China's Great Green Wall case study (page 191).

Case study: Environmental issues and rural change in East Anglia

For the purposes of this case study, East Anglia is defined as Norfolk and Suffolk (Figure 6.22). This is a relatively remote region with a distinctly rural character. Norwich and Ipswich are the only large urban centres. The next tier in the settlement hierarchy is occupied by medium-sized towns such as King's Lynn, Bury St Edmunds and Thetford. Below them are a large number of small market centres that provide local services and employment for local communities.

East Anglia (together with the adjacent Fens) is the UK's leading agricultural region. Seventy-two per cent of the region is cropland, devoted to arable farming, horticulture and fruit growing. Favourable climate, relief and soils sustain intensive cultivation.

The increasing use of rural areas for recreation and leisure

Rural tourism is an important feature of East Anglia's economy. In total it contributes around £3.5 billion

to the economy of the east of England.

The farmed landscapes of East Anglia, with their cultural heritage and natural beauty, are themselves an important resource for tourism and outdoor recreation. Moreover, the region's open landscapes of fields bounded by hedgerows and scattered woodlands provide a mosaic of rich wildlife habitats.

The Norfolk and Suffolk Broads are England's finest and most extensive wetlands (Photograph 6.7). Since 1988 they have had conservation status similar to the UK's national parks. Large stretches of the Norfolk and Suffolk coasts are also protected as Areas of Outstanding Natural Beauty. Mudflats and saltmarshes in the Wash and along the East Anglian coast have international importance and are protected as Ramsar sites, and there are hundreds of nature reserves and Sites of Special Scientific Interest. The Breckland is the UK's largest area of lowland heath, an internationally scarce resource. Although

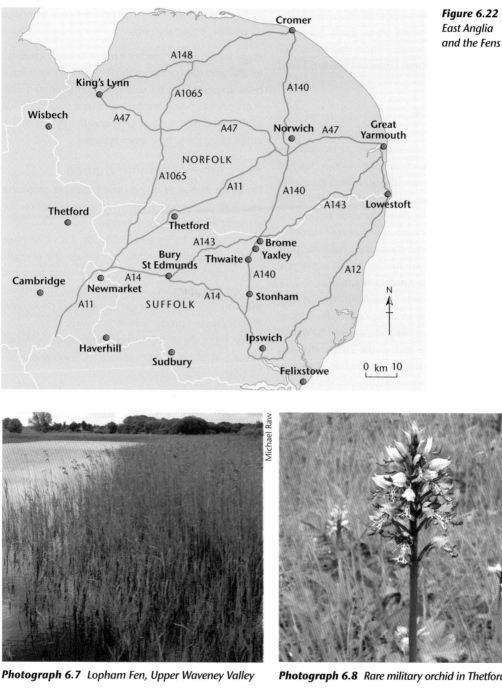

Figure 6.22
*East Anglia
and the Fens*

Photograph 6.7 *Lopham Fen, Upper Waveney Valley*

Photograph 6.8 *Rare military orchid in Thetford Forest*

much of the heath has been lost to afforestation since the 1930s, large tracts survive and support rare species such as stone curlews, nightjars and military orchids (Photograph 6.8).

East Anglia's rich cultural and historic heritage is also a significant attraction for visitors. The region has major historic buildings such as Norwich Cathedral, Framlingham Castle and Blickling Hall; and hundreds of large parish churches originally funded by the prosperous medieval wool trade. Even older are archaeological sites such as Sutton Hoo in Suffolk (Anglo-Saxon) and Grimes Graves in the Breckland (Neolithic).

Protected environments

The flooded areas of the valleys of the Yare, Bure, Waveney and Wensum are known as the Norfolk and Suffolk Broads. The Broads are shallow pits, formed by peat extraction between the ninth and thirteenth centuries, and subsequently flooded. With 190 km of navigable waterway, the Broads provide opportunities for boat-based recreation as well as bird watching and fishing. The Broads' status as a national park reflects the need to manage its fragile ecological resources and plan for a sustainable future.

Pressures on the Broads come from two sources: climate change and the growing demands of recreation and leisure. Rising sea levels caused by global warming will increase salt water incursions and threaten wildlife and habitats. Meanwhile, with over 1 million visitors a year, pressure on the Broads is considerable. One in five visitors is boat-based and with 13 000 pleasure boats, overcrowding is a problem in the peak summer months.

Specific environmental problems in the Broads include the following:

- Water quality is deteriorating. Originally the water was clear; today it is cloudy and turbid. This is due to algal growth caused by nutrient enrichment of the water, and turbulence from power boats. The effect is to destroy shallow-water aquatic plants that rely on sunlight.
- Nutrient-rich water from the runoff of nitrates from farmland and phosphates from sewage lead to algal growth and eutrophication (i.e. water is depleted of oxygen).
- Disruption to food chains has led to large increases in the number of small fish. They feed on water fleas that would otherwise eat the algae and keep the water clear.
- Bank erosion is caused by the wash from powerboats (despite speed restrictions of 5–9 kph). This leads to siltation and problems of navigation.

- Noise and wash from boats causes disturbance to wildlife, especially birds.

Huge investments have been made to improve water quality and navigation on the Broads. Nutrients have been stripped from the water; silt contaminated with nutrients has been dredged; and reed swamps, vital to top predators such as pike and the health of the entire ecosystem, have been restored.

The causes of farming change

Nowhere else in England have intensive cropping and agricultural policies had a greater impact on the environment than in East Anglia.

During the 1970s and 1980s, the EU's CAP gave farmers financial incentives to increase the production of arable crops like wheat, barley, sugar beet and oilseed rape. Farmers, understandably, maximised their output in order to get the biggest payments. They increased production in two ways:

- by intensification, using more agrochemicals such as nitrate and phosphate fertilisers and pesticides
- by increasing the total area under cultivation

Meanwhile, farm amalgamation continued. Hundreds of small farms, unable to achieve economies of scale, were absorbed by large agribusiness enterprises. They farmed on an industrial scale, automating production and making full use of agrochemicals to raise production and profits.

Other changes in farming practice also affected the countryside. These included a marked reduction in the area of spring-sown cereals, the introduction of simpler rotations and greater concentration on specialist arable farming at the expense of mixed farming.

The impact of farming change on the environment

Hedgerow removal

Farm amalgamation, farm economies of scale and increasing arable specialisation have resulted in the loss of thousands of kilometres of hedgerow. The decline of livestock farming has also made stock-proof

Box 6.5 Changes in arable farming since 1950 and their effect on bird populations

Increasing mechanisation

The use of combine harvesters and more efficient harvesting meant there was less food for seed-eating birds. Ground-nesting birds were at greater risk of losing their nests and chicks.

Fertiliser and pesticide usage

The use of inorganic chemical fertilisers (e.g. nitrates and phosphates) on arable land increased in the 1970s and 1980s. This reliance on chemical fertilisers was at the expense of farmyard manure. The result was faster-growing crops and fewer suitable habitats for ground-nesting birds such as skylarks and lapwings. Chemical fertilisers also reduced the need for livestock to produce manure. Thus, mixed farming, which offers a wider range of food resources, feeding sites and nesting sites for farmland birds, declined. Since the 1950s, the use of pesticides has increased. These chemicals destroy weeds that provide important foods for invertebrates and farmland birds. By controlling disease,

pesticides have also contributed to the decline of traditional rotations and, hence, of mixed farming.

Reduction of spring sowing

Since 1970 there has been a decline in spring-sown cereals. The move towards late summer and autumn sowing has reduced the area of winter stubble and winter-feeding opportunities for seed-eating birds. Today, cereal crops grow throughout the winter. By the spring, young crops are often too tall and dense for ground-nesting birds.

Simplification of rotations and reduction in mixed farming

Farming has become more specialised, with arable dominating East Anglia. Within arable systems, pasture has become scarce and rotations simplified. Often cereals are grown continuously in the same field for several years. One outcome is that the countryside has become more uniform, providing fewer food resources and habitats for birds.

hedges redundant. Hedgerow removal peaked in the 1960s. Its main purpose was to accommodate more automation and the use of bigger farm machines, but it also provided more land for cultivation.

Hedgerow removal has transformed the rural landscape on the clay lands of Norfolk and Suffolk.

Small fields bounded by hedgerows and trees have been converted to bleak prairie-like landscapes (Photograph 6.9). The use of pesticides has caused a drastic reduction in biodiversity.

Hedgerows are a vital ecological resource in lowland farm landscapes. They provide shelter, food

Michael Raw

Photograph 6.9
Modern farming has changed the character of the rural landscape on the clay lands of Norfolk and Suffolk; hedgerow removal has created open landscapes and destroyed valuable habitats for wildlife

and breeding sites, and corridors for movement for insects, mammals and birds. They are also a refuge for wild plants unable to survive in intensively cultivated arable fields. Hedgerow destruction has caused a loss of biodiversity and led to the fragmentation of wildlife habitats.

Loss of ancient woodland, lowland heath and wetlands

The intensification and specialisation of agriculture between 1960 and 1990 reduced the area of ancient woodland, lowland heath and wetland. Like hedgerows, these semi-natural habitats require careful management. Maintenance of wetlands such as the Broads and Upper Waveney Valley rely on controlled grazing and management of water levels. Even today, rising demand for groundwater and the pollution of surface water by agrochemicals continue to threaten lowland fen environments.

As recently as the 1980s, farmers around the Wash were converting inter-tidal saltmarshes to arable land, destroying habitats for birds and invertebrates (see Box 6.5, and earlier case study on Freiston Shore, page 100).

Water pollution

Chemical fertilisers and pesticides are a major source of water pollution in East Anglia and the Fens. Leaching removes nitrate and phosphate fertilisers from the soil, polluting groundwater and watercourses. These pollutants have toxic effects on aquatic plants. Nutrient enrichment also leads to eutrophication, which kills fish and aquatic invertebrates, and contaminates public water supplies. The cost of treating drinking water polluted by farm chemicals amounts to £225 million a year in the UK.

Land degradation

Several soil types in East Anglia and the Fens are prone to erosion by wind and water. Light soils, including the peaty soils of the Fens, the sandy soils of the Breckland and the chalky soils of the clay lands are most at risk. Soil erosion is a form of land degradation and is usually associated with unsustainable farming management.

Erosion has increased in recent years as a result of:

■ the popularity of winter cereals. Ploughed land may be left without any crop cover for several weeks, especially if sowing is late.
■ the use of tramlines and wheelings to access fields to apply fertilisers and pesticides. Tramlines and wheelings create artificial channels for runoff.
■ the creation of fine, flat seed beds to help to establish crops; and the removal of hedgerows, which provide shelter and reduce wind erosion. Hedgerow removal also increases the length of slopes and the volume of runoff water.
■ growing maize for silage rather than grass. Grass provides continuous plant cover and reduces erosion.
■ the increase in arable land at the expense of live-stock and pasture
■ the trend to plough up pastures and re-seed them. This is particular problematic on slopes
■ locating outdoor pig farms, which involves the complete removal of plant cover, often on unsuitable sites (e.g. sloping, very light sandy soils)
■ the reduction in inputs of organic fertiliser (e.g. manure) and the increasing reliance on chemical fertilisers damages soil structure. Soil particles are less able to bind together, making the soil more prone to erosion.

Managing farming changes and the environment

The CAP and agri-environment policies

Over many centuries, farming has shaped Britain's rural landscape. In doing so it has also created a wide range of semi-natural habitats. Much of the UK's wildlife depends for its survival on farmers maintaining these habitats.

Today the CAP affords environmental concerns greater priority and aims to promote a more sustainable agriculture. Indeed, since the reform of the CAP in 2000, the sustainable development of rural areas has become one of the CAP's two central 'pillars'.

Recent reforms of the CAP have replaced the old system of subsidies and guaranteed prices with Single Payments (see Box 6.2 on page 251). This benefits wildlife because it takes away the incentive to intensify production and increase output. It was this policy that caused so much environmental damage in East Anglia and other arable regions in the 1970s and 1980s. Now farmers receive subsidies only if they comply with minimum environment standards. This principle is known as **cross-compliance**. It includes, for example:

➤ limits on stocking levels for sheep on upland pastures
➤ limits on the volumes of fertiliser used
➤ reduced inputs of pesticides
➤ leaving strips around the margins of arable fields uncultivated
➤ taking steps to minimise soil erosion

Where farmers deliver an environmental service beyond the level required by cross-compliance, they receive extra payments. Examples of practices that attract additional payments are: the preservation of features such as hedgerows and stone walls, organic farming and the conservation of habitats such as wetlands and ancient woodlands.

Set-aside

Set-aside is an EU policy introduced in 1992. Its main aim was to reduce massive overproduction of food crops in the 1970s and 1980s. It currently accounts for around 5% of arable land in the east of England (Photograph 6.10).

Photograph 6.10 *Land recently entered into set-aside*

Set-aside has always been controversial, not least because farmers are paid for leaving their land fallow (i.e. doing nothing). The scheme allows farmers to set-aside a certain proportion of their arable land. In compensation for lost production they get a fixed payment for every hectare they set-aside. To qualify for set-aside, farmers must adhere to a number of regulations. On set-aside land they must:

➤ grow a green cover crop such as grass, or allow natural vegetation to establish itself
➤ leave the land untouched between January and mid-July
➤ not use any agrochemicals

There is no denying that set-aside has considerable environmental benefits. Cover crops provide food and habitats for insects and birds. As the land is not ploughed until mid-July at the earliest, ground-nesting birds are not disturbed. The RSPB reports that many farmland birds such as lapwings, grey partridges and skylarks have benefited from set-aside.

Table 6.3 The UK government's agri-environment schemes in England

Environmentally Sensitive Areas (ESAs)	Set up in 1987, ESAs are the most successful agri-environment scheme. There are 22 ESAs in England, covering around 10% of the agricultural area — nearly 6000 km². The scheme, now closed to new areas, has been succeeded by Environmental Stewardship (ES). Farmers in ESAs enter an agreement to farm in an environmentally friendly way. In return they receive grants to compensate them for loss of income. The aim is to safeguard and enhance parts of the country with high landscape, wildlife and historic value. ESAs include areas such as the Pennine Dales, the Lake District and the Suffolk Valleys.
Environmental Stewardship (ES)	ES was established in 2005 and replaced earlier ESAs and Country Stewardship. Essentially it rewards farmers for conservation and environmental enhancement of the countryside. A new agency — Natural England — is responsible for the ES programme. Under ES, farmers and other land managers get funding if they deliver 'effective environmental management'. This can mean: using farming and management methods that conserve wildlife and biodiversity; protecting historic environments and natural resources; and maintaining and enhancing the quality and character of the landscape.
Farm Woodland Premium	Farmers entering this scheme are paid to convert agricultural land to woodland. The environmental gain is the creation of new habitats for wildlife, greater biodiversity, and improvements in the quality and character of the countryside. Annual payments compensate farmers for loss of agricultural income. Payments are made for 10 years for conifer woodlands, and for 15 years for deciduous woodlands. A similar scheme known as Woodland Grant is operated by the Forestry Commission.

Nitrate pollution

The excessive use of chemical fertilisers by arable farmers is responsible for 70% of the nitrates in surface water and groundwater. Farming is also the major contributor to the pollution of water supplies by phosphates, pesticides and manure.

In 1991, the EU issued its Nitrates Directive to prevent and reduce nitrate pollution of water by agriculture. The UK responded by setting up a number of

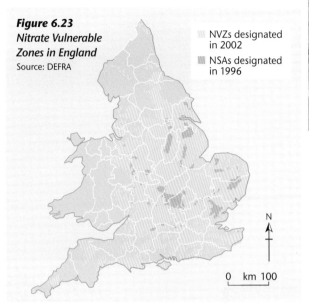

Nitrate Sensitive Areas (NSAs) where farmers applied smaller amounts of nitrate and received financial compensation for lower yields and lower incomes. In 2002, NSAs were replaced by Nitrate Vulnerable Zones (NVZs) (Figure 6.23). These were far more extensive, covering 55% of England. Farmers in NVZs were compelled, as part of cross-compliance, to follow an action programme to reduce the leaching of nitrate. This action programme required farmers to:

➤ limit nitrate applications to crop requirements

➤ limit organic manure applications to a maximum of 210 kg ha year^{-1}

➤ keep records on their use of nitrates and make them available for inspection

Figure 6.23
Nitrate Vulnerable Zones in England
Source: DEFRA

NVZs designated in 2002

NSAs designated in 1996

0   km   100

Case study

Changes on Langton Grove Farm, Eye, Suffolk

Tom Baldwin farms 223 ha near Eye in Suffolk (Figure 6.24). Langton Grove Farm is an arable enterprise growing sugar beet, winter wheat, winter barley and oilseed rape (Figure 6.25). Yields for all crops are 10–20% above the national average. These high yields reflect the favourable growing conditions. Land quality is good — grade 2 and grade 3 — with few physical limitations to arable cultivation. Climatic conditions are ideal for temperate arable crops, with warm summers, a long growing season and a mean annual rainfall around 600 mm. Apart from himself, Tom employs just one full-time worker.

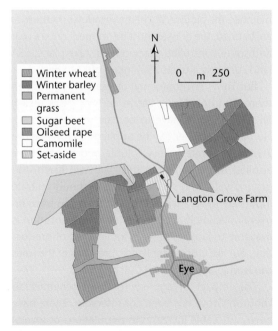

Winter wheat
Winter barley
Permanent grass
Sugar beet
Oilseed rape
Camomile
Set-aside

0   m   250

Langton Grove Farm

Eye

Figure 6.24 *Layout of Langton Grove Farm*

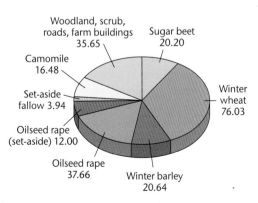

Woodland, scrub, roads, farm buildings 35.65

Camomile 16.48

Set-aside fallow 3.94

Oilseed rape (set-aside) 12.00

Oilseed rape 37.66

Winter barley 20.64

Sugar beet 20.20

Winter wheat 76.03

Figure 6.25 *Langton Grove Farm: land use (ha)*

Photograph 6.11
*Langton Grove
Farm*

Michael Raw

Set-aside

Eight per cent of Langton Grove's arable area — nearly 16 ha — is in set-aside. Three-quarters of this is planted with oilseed rape. This is possible under CAP regulations because the oilseed crop is used for non-food production — in this case, to make biodiesel fuel. The remaining 4 ha of set-aside are left fallow. Set-aside currently attracts an area payment of around £92 ha^{-1}. CAP payments for non set-aside land are £182 ha^{-1}. In 2012 these payments will be replaced by a single payment of approximately £175 ha^{-1}.

Farming and the environment

In order to get maximum area payments from the CAP, Tom must comply with a range of environmental regulations. For example, there are limits on pesticide usage and spraying around the margins of fields. Under cross-compliance, steps must be taken to prevent soil erosion and hedgerows cannot be cut between 1 March and 31 July, to protect nesting birds and other wildlife. In addition, Tom must leave a 2 m-wide grass margin for wildlife around every field.

In 2005, Tom joined the ES scheme. ES is worth £30 ha^{-1}. To qualify for the payments Tom has to:
- leave field corners uncultivated
- leave 6 m buffer strips around fields with streams and ditches

- sow wild bird seed mixes on the strips
- cut hedges once every 3 years to a minimum height of 2 m
- clean ditches out only occasionally

Langton Grove also has 5 ha of meadows in the Upper Waveney Valley, which is part of the Broads ESA. This semi-natural wetland is an important habitat for wildfowl, waders and amphibians. Only low-input farming is allowed in the meadows. To maintain the biodiversity of the meadows, herbicides are banned, the grasses must be 'topped' once a year and some controlled grazing must take place. ESA land currently attracts a premium of £140 ha^{-1}.

But Tom's environmental obligations do not end there. Langton Grove lies in an NVZ. As a result, all nitrate inputs have to be carefully monitored. No nitrate fertiliser can be applied to crops before 1 March (nitrate is very soluble and most nitrate applied to crops before this date will leach into groundwater and surface water). Although nitrate inputs are lower than in the past, there has been no overall decline in crop yields. No compensation is available to farmers in NVZs for any loss of production, but like cross-compliance, breaches of the rules can lead to a reduction in CAP payments.

The impact of agri-environment schemes on Langton Grove has been considerable. There have been noticeable increases in populations of several bird species such as grey partridges, skylarks and lapwings. Brown hare numbers have also increased. Less welcome have been the big increases in rook, roe deer and muntjac deer populations.

Farm diversification

In 1996, Langton Grove diversified its operations when Tom's wife, Frances, opened a children's nursery in redundant buildings attached to the farm. The business was an immediate success. As a result, new buildings were added, including an indoor swimming pool and a pets' corner. Today the nursery provides places for 60 children a day and employs 19 staff, of whom 14 are full time. It serves a rural catchment that includes Eye and the nearby market town of Diss. Langton Grove was the first children's nursery in Eye. It provided a service that exploited a latent demand for child care, releasing parents to return to work full time. It also attracted funding from the EU's Objective 5b programme, which between 1994 and 1999 assisted economic development in areas like rural east Suffolk, heavily dependent on declining employment sectors such as agriculture. The nursery also received a rural development grant from DEFRA.

Conclusion

Langton Grove Farm exemplifies the socio-economic and environmental changes that have occurred in large parts of rural Britain in the past 30 years. These include:

- the declining importance of agriculture as a major employer in rural areas. Although Langton Grove is a relatively large farm, automation and its specialisation in arable crops means that it provides full-time employment for just two people.
- the rising importance of employment in service activities in the countryside. The children's nursery at Langton Farm employs nearly ten times more workers than the farm itself. Most of these jobs are for women (farming, in contrast, has always relied on a predominantly male workforce), and most live locally.
- the importance of rural development and the need for farming to diversify into other, non-agricultural activities
- the rising demand for child-care facilities in rural areas. This suggests that rural dwellers are today disconnected from the rural economy and increasingly find employment in local market towns and nearby urban areas.
- the reduction in the intensity of farming and the use of agrochemicals, and the move away from EU subsidies based on production
- the shift to more environmentally friendly and sustainable farming supported by EU and UK government money, with a variety of agri-environment schemes

Environmental issues associated with building developments in rural areas

Population growth and societal changes, such as increases in life expectancy and more single-person households, have created a rising demand for housing in the UK. One result has been to put more pressure on rural environments, especially in southern and eastern England. For example, the draft plan for eastern England says that nearly 500 000 new houses must be built in the region between 2005 and 2021.

Although most new homes will be in urban areas, some rural settlements in commuter hinterlands, close to centres of employment, will have to accommodate growth. In these settlements, new building development will result in some loss of countryside and amenity, and will be controversial.

Case study Felixstowe and the Trimleys

Felixstowe in Suffolk is the UK's biggest container port (Figure 6.26). It has grown rapidly since the 1970s and further expansion is likely in future. This growth will fuel the demand for more housing. So too will national trends such as the ageing population, international migration and more single-person households. The demand for housing cannot be met solely by redeveloping brownfield sites and other vacant land in Felixstowe.

Suffolk Coastal District Council (SCDC) is looking to accommodate some of the proposed housing development outside Felixstowe. It has selected the villages of Trimley St Mary and Trimley St Martin as sites for 1900 new houses to be built by 2021. The

plans also include provision for a supermarket, sports facilities, a health centre, a village hall and a primary school. To accommodate the development, 1400 ha of agricultural land, currently owned by Trinity College, Cambridge, will be released. The plan is controversial and has aroused considerable opposition from residents in the Trimleys.

The residents have organised a local protest group to oppose the scheme. They argue that the development is inappropriate because:

■ it is out of scale with the area
■ brownfield sites in Felixstowe should absorb the planned housing
■ it will wreck the rural character of the two villages

Figure 6.26
The Felixstowe peninsula and the Trimleys

- it is on greenfield land and is close to the Suffolk Coast and Heaths Area of Outstanding Natural Beauty, which would be lost
- it will generate increased traffic flows and congestion
- it could mean that the Trimley villages will merge physically with the built area of Felixstowe

The SCDC has rejected the local pressure group's arguments. It counters by saying that:

- it has to meet its obligations under the government's east of England draft plan
- brownfield sites in Felixstowe could accommodate a maximum of 300 new houses

- large housing estates built in the Trimleys in the 1970s and 1980s, together with a combined population of more than 4500, mean that the villages no longer have a rural character. For example, between 1971 and 1996 the number of houses in Trimley St Martin increased by 88%, and by 140% in Trimley St Mary.
- geography severely limits the opportunities for new sites for housing in the Felixstowe peninsula, which is bounded to the north by the Deben estuary, to the south by the Orwell estuary and to the east by the North Sea. Moreover, many areas that might otherwise be suitable are close to sea level and at risk from flooding.

Traffic problems in rural areas

The A140 links East Anglia's two largest cities, Norwich and Ipswich (see Figure 6.22 on page 267). It runs north–south through the heart of rural East Anglia and it is strategically important to the regional economy. The A140 is one of East Anglia's busiest roads, yet in Suffolk it is single carriageway for all but 3 km and is badly congested. In 2004, traffic flows averaged 15 500 vehicles a day, of which 15% were lorries. Traffic levels are forecast to increase in future, especially with the expansion of the port of Felixstowe.

The A140 passes directly through several villages such as Stonham, Thwaite, Yaxley and Brome. None of the villages on the A140 in Suffolk has a bypass. Heavy traffic has a detrimental effect on these village environments. It causes air pollution and noise pollution, severs village facilities on opposite sides of the road, and generally reduces the quality of life for residents. Safety is another issue. Seventy-six deaths and 58 fatal accidents occurred on the Suffolk section of the A140 between 1980 and 2005. This has prompted a local protest group

Photograph 6.12
The A140 in Suffolk

Michael Raw

to campaign for improvements such as the upgrading of the road to dual carriageway and the construction of bypasses for some of the larger villages like Stonham.

Unfortunately for village residents, Suffolk County Council has no plans for large-scale investment to upgrade the A140. In recent years, improvements designed to increase road safety include imposing lower speed limits and installing speed cameras. A £6 million scheme to bypass Stonham, which was supported by three-quarters of the village's residents, has been abandoned. The council argued that although it would improve the quality of life for residents living on the A140, it would have an adverse impact on the landscape, and increase carbon dioxide emissions and the number of accidents.

Management, planning and the sustainable use of rural areas

Key ideas

➤ The sustainable use of rural areas requires a careful balance between socio-economic and environmental needs.

➤ Planning and management can enable rural areas to become increasingly sustainable.

The sustainable use of resources in rural areas requires careful management. In MEDCs, management is needed to maintain rural services, provide affordable housing and to maintain populations. In LEDCs, management is needed to tackle severe environmental problems such as desertification and land degradation. Examples of rural management and planning are provided by the following case study of St Edmundsbury in Suffolk. See also the Korqin Sandy Lands section of the China's Great Green Wall case study (page 191) and the case study of the Khushab salinity control and reclamation project (page 194).

Case study **Rural management and planning in St Edmundsbury, Suffolk**

St Edmundsbury borough in Suffolk is a predominantly rural district (Figure 6.27). Its total population is around 100 000, of whom 43% are rural dwellers. Economic, social and environmental changes in the past decade or so have created a number of difficult rural problems. Among the most urgent are poor access to key services, housing shortages and the affordability of rural housing. Rural areas throughout England have suffered a decline in community services and facilities, with shops, post offices, garages and public houses being hardest hit. All of this threatens the sustainability of rural communities. Decline is likely to continue as a result of increasing competition from large supermarkets in market towns and cities. Access to services is a major problem for low-income families without transport and for old people. A recent survey in St Edmundsbury showed that most rural communities lack essential services (Table 6.4).

Government policy is to resist the closure of services such as shops, pubs, post offices and community buildings, and to create sustainable rural communities. Currently food shops, post offices, pubs, petrol stations and village stores qualify for a mandatory 50% rate relief, which can, at the discretion of the council, be extended to 100%.

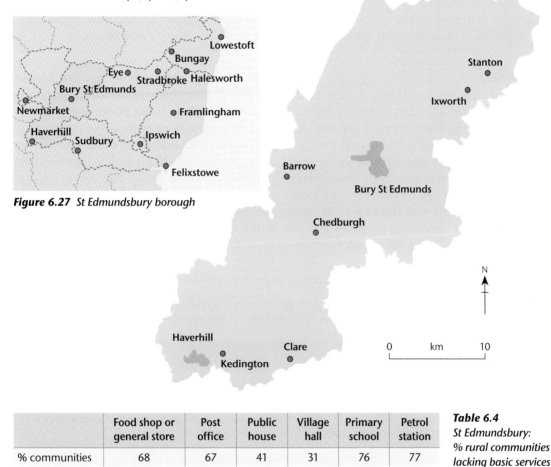

Figure 6.27 *St Edmundsbury borough*

	Food shop or general store	Post office	Public house	Village hall	Primary school	Petrol station
% communities	68	67	41	31	76	77

Table 6.4
St Edmundsbury:
% rural communities
lacking basic services

Box 6.6 Key settlements and rural planning

During the past 50 years, a cornerstone of rural planning in the UK has been to concentrate services, employment and new housing in market towns and larger villages. These centres chosen for development are known as **key settlements**. As well as being a focus for development, key settlements are also service centres and hubs for surrounding rural hinterlands. Key settlements remain a national policy, which continues to have a strong influence on rural planning at regional and local scales.

The logic of key settlement policy is that for services and small businesses to be viable, they need access to a critical mass of people known as the **threshold**. Thresholds are most likely to be achieved in larger centres. Concentrating development and services also promotes sustainable development by strengthening market towns and villages, protecting open countryside and reducing the need to travel.

However, recent research casts some doubt on the way rural settlement hierarchies function. The view that most rural dwellers work and do most of their shopping in their local market towns is questionable. Improvements in personal mobility due to high levels of car ownership and falling costs of private motoring, mean that most people are more mobile than ever. Many rural residents no longer base their lives around their nearest market town. Journeys to work and shopping trips (especially shopping for durable goods) are often to a range of destinations, including more distant cities and supermarkets on the edge of town.

Housing

Rural planning in St Edmundsbury is the responsibility of the local authority. It follows national guidelines issued by the government, and strategies developed in the Suffolk County Structure Plan.

Major new housing developments are confined to the two largest urban places in St Edmundsbury — Bury St Edmunds and Haverhill. In rural areas, new housing will be concentrated in six large villages capable of sustaining a minimum range of essential services. These key settlements, which will meet the needs of their local areas, are: Barrow, Chedburgh, Clare, Ixworth, Stanton and Kedington (Figure 6.27). Only minor developments will be allowed outside these centres. The planners will continue to exercise careful control on development in the countryside, which is regarded as a long-term resource.

A lack of affordable housing, either rented or owner occupied, is a concern in St Edmundsbury, as it is throughout rural Britain. It, too, threatens to undermine the sustainability of rural areas.

Table 6.5 *Schemes for the sustainable management of village shops, post offices and pubs*

Rate rebate	Food shops, post offices, pubs, petrol stations and village stores qualify for a mandatory 50% rate relief, which can at the discretion of the council be extended to 100%
Rural Shops Alliance	National trade association, which represents the interests of 7200 independent village shops and lobbies on their behalf
Enterprise Development	Encourages and supports local businesses; low-interest loans of up to £10 000 available
Rural Enterprise Network Support	Opposes the closure of rural services and supports the development of independent shops, post offices, pubs, restaurants, garages and cafes
LEADER	An EU initiative to help rural communities improve their quality of life; makes funds available for development projects such as farmers' markets
Sainsbury's Assisting Village Enterprises (SAVE)	Association between village shops and the supermarket giant, Sainsbury's, whereby rural shops are able to stock and sell Sainsbury's products; 71% of SAVE stores are rural post offices that sell a small range of convenience goods; similar partnership schemes have been set up between other large supermarkets and village shops, e.g. Tesco and local village shops in south Norfolk
Village Shop Development	Local authorities such as mid-Suffolk operate a rural services scheme to fund and give advice to rural businesses; grants are available towards new projects; the scheme also extends to community services such as the maintenance of village halls and child care

In St Edmundsbury, house prices have inflated due to the decentralisation of population from southeast England and influxes of commuters. Many incomers are higher earners than local people. Price inflation has put even modest dwellings beyond the reach of many young families on average and below-average incomes. Under current guidelines, developers must allocate land within sites to ensure that 40% of new dwellings comprise affordable housing.

Services

The local authority's policy is to resist the closure of village services such as shops, post offices, pubs and community buildings. Despite this, many village shops, post offices and public houses have closed in the borough in the past decade (see Table 6.4). Closures often have an enormous impact on rural communities, especially on the old and those without transport. A large number of schemes are available that aim to support sustainable services, and give financial help and advice to rural shops and small businesses (Table 6.5).

There is also a commitment to improve public transport services in rural areas. They include more rural bus services, more community-based transport schemes, encouraging more people to cycle and walk, and reducing the impact of traffic in villages. Access to public transport is vital if old people and people on low incomes are not to suffer social and economic exclusion.

Regenerating Suffolk's market towns

The East of England Development Agency (EEDA) has supported a £2 million project to regenerate Suffolk's market towns. Funding is from the UK's Single Regeneration Budget. The project, which started in 2000, aims to revitalise the market towns of Bungay, Eye, Framlingham, Halesworth and Stradbroke. The key to achieving sustainable rural communities in future is the vitality of market towns.

The central problem is the remoteness of rural Suffolk with low levels of access to essential services, and limited opportunities for jobs, training, child care, public transport, leisure and shopping. As a result, young people have tended to leave the countryside and drift to larger settlements outside the region. The scheme, comprising a partnership between public funding and private capital, has helped to provide new jobs, skills training and rural development in east Suffolk.

Second homes and holiday homes in north Norfolk

At the 2001 census, 7.2% of all households in north Norfolk were classed as second homes and holiday homes. North Norfolk, along with south Devon, Cornwall and south Lakeland, is one of the most popular areas in England for second homes and holiday homes.

Within north Norfolk there are hotspots such as the picturesque coastal villages of Cley-next-the-Sea (Photograph 6.13) and Blakeney. There, roughly one in four households are second homes and holiday homes (Figure 6.28). The huge demand for housing in these villages has grossly inflated house prices. North Norfolk, just 3 hours' drive from London, has become a magnet for well-off Londoners seeking a weekend retreat. In 2007, typical prices for two-bedroomed terraced cottages in Cley and Blakeney were between £300 000 and £400 000.

Photograph 6.13 *Cley-next-the-Sea, Norfolk*

Figure 6.28 *Second homes and holiday homes in north Norfolk, 2004*
Source: National Statistics

Local people can no longer compete in the housing market. To get onto the property ladder, first-time buyers must move at least 6–7 km inland to places like Holt. Even there, two-bedroomed homes start at £200 000.

The influx of wealthy incomers explains why Cley's two general stores have long since closed. Second homes are empty during the week or rented out to tourists. This situation threatens the economic and social fabric of rural communities.

Where a large proportion of houses in a village are second homes, there is a loss of community. The village may be deserted for much of the year. Without a large permanent population, local services such as shops, post offices, primary schools and public transport struggle and eventually close. The whole fabric of rural life can be undermined. On the positive side, local builders often do well renovating many semi-derelict properties; specialist services catering for weekenders such as restaurants may flourish; and the physical fabric of the village may improve.

In environmentally attractive parts of England, large numbers of second homes contribute significantly to local housing shortages and to problems of housing affordability. As part of a sustainable management strategy, since 2004, local authorities in these areas have increased the council tax on second homes from 50% to 90%. However, this has done little to quell demand. Local authorities are looking at other ways of tackling the second-home problem. Some of the suggestions include levying a separate tax on second homes, and preventing the sale of permanently occupied properties as second homes.

Examination-style questions

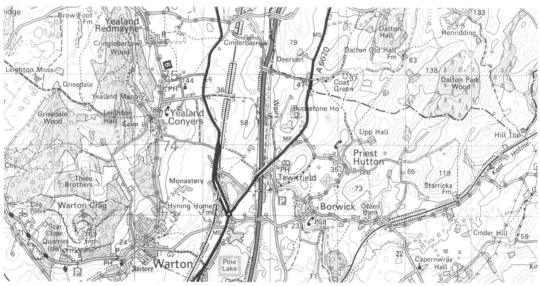

Figure 1

1 **(a)** Using evidence from the OS map extract shown in Figure 1, compare and contrast the rural land uses to the west and east of the motorway (M6). (4 marks)

 (b) Using evidence from the OS map extract, suggest two reasons for the differences in rural land use between the areas west and east of the motorway. (6 marks)

 (c) With reference to one named rural area, outline the factors that have led to the area's decline. (6 marks)

 (d) With reference to one or more named rural areas, examine the impact of social and economic decline on rural communities. (9 marks)

2 With reference to named examples, describe and explain attempts to manage rural areas sustainably. (25 marks)

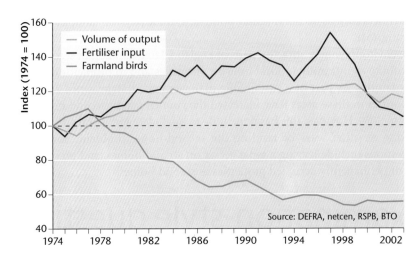

Figure 2 *Agricultural output, fertiliser input and farmland bird populations, 1974–2002*

3 **(a)** Describe the changes in farm output, fertiliser input and farmland bird populations shown in Figure 2. (4 marks)

(b) Explain how changes in farming in MEDCs in the past 40 years have put increasing pressures on the countryside. (6 marks)

(c) With reference to a named rural area, examine the causes of rural population decline. (6 marks)

(d) With reference to one or more named rural areas, examine the economic and social issues associated with population growth and development. (9 marks)

(e) With reference to named examples, explain why the sustainable development of rural areas requires careful planning and management. (25 marks)

The energy issue

Global energy sources

Key ideas
➤ The global energy mix comprises both finite (non-renewable) and renewable sources.
➤ Renewable and non-renewable energy resources vary in their availability both geographically and historically.
➤ Physical, economic and political factors influence the global pattern of energy supply both geographically and historically.

Finite and renewable and energy sources

There is a simple division of energy sources into finite and renewable types (Figure 7.1). Most **finite energy** comes from the three principal fossil fuels: coal, oil and natural gas. They provide 80% of the energy that drives the modern world economy. Unlike renewables, fossil fuels take millions of years to form and are finite. Once used, they are irreplaceable on timescales that are meaningful to society.

Renewable energy is either recyclable, like HEP and biofuels, or inexhaustible, like solar and geothermal energy. Because of these qualities, renewables can be exploited sustainably. However, renewables supply relatively small amounts of energy to the global economy. Figure 7.2 shows that in 2005, renewables accounted for less than 13% of world energy production.

Nuclear energy is also finite or non-renewable because it depends on uranium, an element that is available in limited quantities. Although uranium occurs widely in seawater and in the Earth's crust, it is found in commercial concentrations in relatively few locations. In theory, uranium could be recycled and used sustainably.

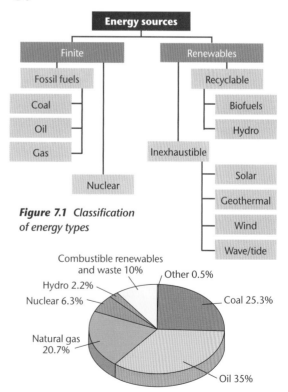

Figure 7.1 Classification of energy types

Figure 7.2 World energy production, 2005

Until advances are made in nuclear technology, however, nuclear energy, like fossil fuels, will remain non-renewable.

Finite energy sources: fossil fuels

Coal production

At the global scale coal has a wide geographical distribution (Figure 7.3). With the exception of South America, all continents have substantial coal reserves. In 2006, coal supplied one-quarter of the world's energy. Although this proportion has fallen steadily over the past 20 years, world production actually increased by just over 60% between 1986 and 2006 (Figure 7.4). Coal production increased everywhere except Europe, with Asia (including China) recording the fastest growth.

Figure 7.3 *World coal production*

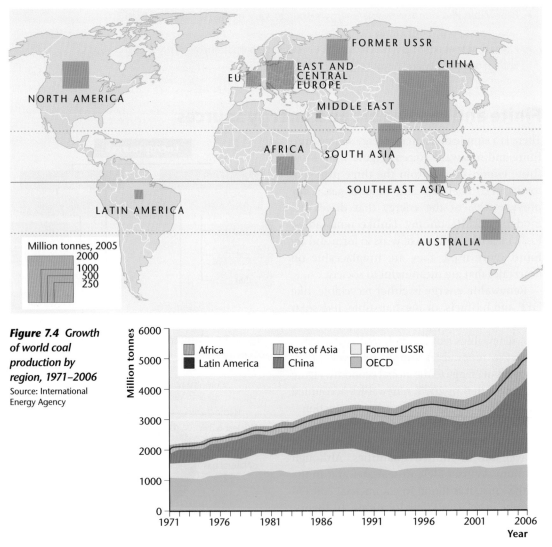

Figure 7.4 *Growth of world coal production by region, 1971–2006*

Source: International Energy Agency

However, the largest coal-producing countries are not confined to one region — the top five producers are China, the USA, India, Australia and South Africa (Table 7.1). Growth has been most spectacular in China (Figure 7.5). Since 1981 its output has increased fourfold. Today, China accounts for 46% of the total world hard coal production. Global coal reserves, estimated at 910 billion tonnes in 2006, should at current rates of production last for another 150 years.

Table 7.1 *Leading hard coal producers, 2006*

Producers	Hard coal (million t)
China	2481
USA	990
India	427
Australia	309
South Africa	244
Russia	233
Indonesia	169
Poland	95
Kazakhstan	92
Colombia	64
World	**5370**

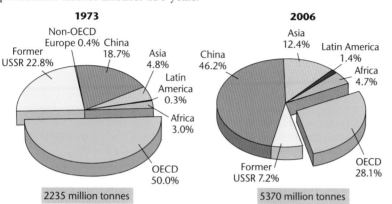

Figure 7.5 *Geography of world coal production, 1973 and 2006*
Source: International Energy Agency

Unlike other fossil fuels, only a small fraction of world coal production — just 16% — enters international trade. Most is consumed domestically in the country of production. This is particularly true of China, India and the USA. Coal is less transportable than oil and gas because:
➤ it contains a larger proportion of waste
➤ it has lower calorific value than oil and gas
➤ it is a solid and less transportable than liquids and gases
➤ it is less versatile than oil, having little value for the transport industry

Photograph 7.1
Open cast coal mining in New South Wales, Australia

Physical (geology)	Coal seams that are thick and close to the surface are cheapest to exploit. Shallow seams can be extracted by open-cast mining, which has lower production costs than deep mining. Seams displaced by faulting and folding are expensive to work. Coal also varies in quality. High carbon-content coals (e.g. anthracite, coking coal) are most valuable.
Physical (geography)	Geographical location often influences development. Some locations may be isolated (e.g. Amazonia) and difficult to access; elsewhere, climate conditions and environmental sensitivity may limit development (e.g. regions of permafrost, extreme arid environments). Access to markets (e.g. eastern China) and to the coast (e.g. northwest Australia) for exports is often critical.
Economic	Production depends on demand and the cost of coal compared with other fuels. The cost of coal is affected by geological conditions, geographical location, methods of production, labour and transport.
Political	Most coal production is for domestic markets. Governments may encourage supply by sub-sidising domestic production and placing tariffs on imports. The promotion of coal production is often for reasons of energy security, i.e. to reduce reliance on imported energy and maintain a diverse energy mix. Some governments may discourage the use of coal for environmental reasons and impose carbon taxes on coal-burning industries (e.g. in California).

***Table 7.2** Factors influencing coal supply*

Coal mining depends crucially on production costs. Costs are influenced by geological conditions such as the depth of coal deposits, the thickness of coal seams, the quality of coal and the degree of faulting (Table 7.2). They are lowest where coal occurs near the surface and can be mined by open-cast methods (Photograph 7.1). In contrast, deep mining is more expensive and allows the recovery of little more than half of all reserves. Thanks to cheap open-cast mining and low freight rates, Australia, the world's leading coal exporter, is able to ship coal half-way around the world to Europe and easily undercut the price of locally produced coal.

Oil production

Global oil production was nearly 4 billion tonnes in 2006. This represents a fairly modest increase of 37% on 1973 production levels and suggests that oil reserves are more limited than coal. Oil production at the global scale is geographically less dispersed than coal (Figure 7.6). Seventy per cent of production originates in the Middle East, the OECD countries (mainly the USA) and the former USSR (Figure 7.7). Output is relatively small in Australia and the Pacific, south Asia and Europe. This spatial pattern of production remained more or less unchanged in the period 1973 to 2006.

Several of the largest oil producers such as the USA and China cannot satisfy domestic demand from their own production, and rely on huge oil imports (Table 7.3). Other major oil importers such as the EU and Japan have minimal resources of their own. Oil exports are dominated by the Middle East, especially Saudi Arabia, Iran, the UAE and Kuwait. Between them, these four countries account for nearly one-third of oil exports. Russia, Nigeria, Norway, Mexico and Venezuela are important exporters outside the Middle East. Because crude oil is shipped in huge tankers, transport costs per tonne are low and distance from markets has little influence on production. For example, the typical cost of transporting crude oil from the Middle East to the USA works out at only 0.5 cents per litre.

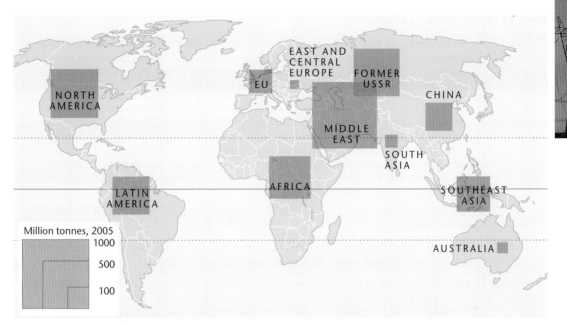

Figure 7.6 *World oil production*

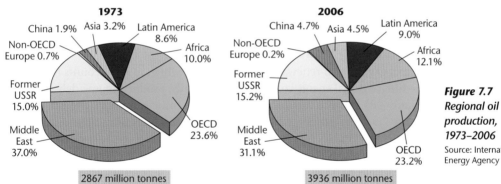

1973

China 1.9%   Asia 3.2%   Latin America 8.6%
Non-OECD Europe 0.7%
Africa 10.0%
Former USSR 15.0%
OECD 23.6%
Middle East 37.0%

2867 million tonnes

2006

China 4.7%   Asia 4.5%   Latin America 9.0%
Non-OECD Europe 0.2%
Africa 12.1%
Former USSR 15.2%
OECD 23.2%
Middle East 31.1%

3936 million tonnes

Figure 7.7
Regional oil production, 1973–2006
Source: International Energy Agency

Photograph 7.2
Oil production is usually more expensive offshore than onshore

Ingram

Table 7.3 Factors influencing oil supply

Physical (geology)	Simple geological structures such as anticlines, with little faulting, create oil traps that lower production costs. The size of these structures will influence the amount of reserves and the unit costs of production (i.e. cost per barrel). Large oilfields such as those in Saudi Arabia have lower unit costs than small fields like those in the North Sea.
Physical (geography)	Oil production is usually more expensive offshore than onshore (Photograph 7.2). Offshore production costs are largely influenced by the depth of water. For example, oilfields in the northern North Sea in depths of more than 200 m are more expensive to exploit than those in shallower waters further south. In Alaska and Siberia, production costs are increased because of the severe climate and the need to preserve the permafrost layer (see page 147). Environmental conservation and the need to minimise disruption to animal migration and damage to tundra ecosystems may also add to costs. Remoteness requires extra investment in infrastructure (e.g. roads, pipeline), which adds to production costs.
Economic	The world price of oil determines which oilfields are profitable. Many small fields in the North Sea are only profitable when oil prices are high, e.g. over $60 a barrel.
Political	Oil prices are sensitive to political conditions in oil-producing regions. Prices quadrupled following the Israeli–Arab conflict in 1973. Other notable increases followed the Iranian revolution in 1979 and the Gulf War in 1991. Economic sanctions against Iraq reduced its oil exports in the late 1990s, and the Iraq war in 2003 greatly reduced oil production from Iraq. Oil-importing countries may be reluctant to rely on oil imports from unstable geopolitical regions such as the Middle East.

Natural gas production

Natural gas is a non-renewable, finite resource which today accounts for around one-fifth of global energy consumption. Globally, production is widely dispersed (Figure 7.8) and production has increased significantly since the early 1980s (Figure 7.9). Compared with other fossil fuels, gas is cleaner and more environmentally acceptable. Natural gas reserves are large. Despite almost a doubling of gas production between 1982 and 2006, the reserve-to-production ratio hardly changed (Figure 7.10). At 2006 rates of production, reserves were sufficient to last for 63 years. This underlines how the discovery of new gas reserves is keeping pace with rising demand. Indeed the industry is confident that there are substantial reserves yet to be discovered. As well as being plentiful, gas reserves are widely distributed. Russia has the largest reserves, followed by the Middle East.

Until the twentieth century, the development of gas resources was hindered by problems of transport and storage. Natural gas remains complex to transport and requires large investments in pipelines, liquefied natural gas (LNG) carriers and storage facilities. In addition, many gas resources such as those in Siberia and North Africa are far from consuming centres. As a result, only around one-quarter of gas production is traded internationally. Of this, 21% is in the form of LNG. Moreover, the construction and management of international pipelines in remote or environmentally sensitive areas presents major logistical problems. Pipelines are also vulnerable to war and terrorism in regions of political instability like the Middle East.

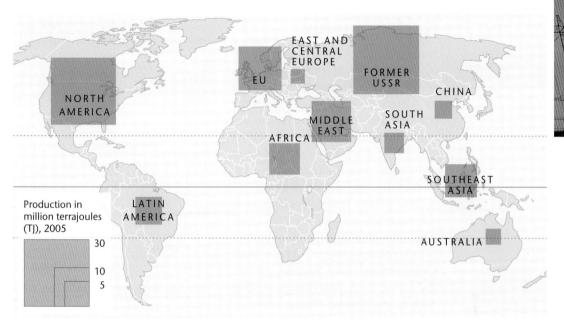

Figure 7.8 *World natural gas production*

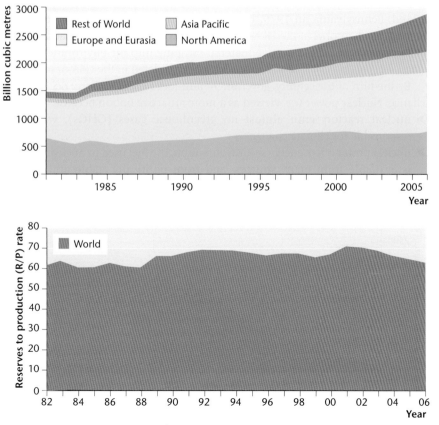

Figure 7.9 *Natural gas production by area, 1981–2006*
Source: BP

Figure 7.10 *Natural gas reserves-to-production ratios, 1982–2006*
Source: BP

Nuclear energy

Nuclear power produces just over 6% of the total world energy and 15% of the world's electricity. Because of its advanced technology and high cost, nuclear power generation has mainly been concentrated in MEDCs (Table 7.4). Countries such as France and Japan, with limited resources of fossil fuels, have invested heavily in nuclear power. Today, France has 59 nuclear reactors supplying 78% of its electricity. Meanwhile, nuclear power is expanding in several LEDCs. Both China and India are building reactors and expect to increase their generating capacity several times over by 2015.

Producers	Terrawatt hours (TWh)	% world total
USA	911	29.2
France	452	16.3
Japan	305	11.0
Germany	163	5.9
Russia	149	5.4
South Korea	147	5.3
Canada	92	3.3
Ukraine	89	3.2
UK	82	3.0
Sweden	72	2.6
Rest of world	406	14.7
World	**2868**	**100.0**

Table 7.4 Nuclear power production, 2005

During the 1960s and 1970s, the nuclear energy industry expanded rapidly and was seen as the answer to the world's energy problems. Then two serious accidents dented confidence and sent the industry into decline. The first at Three Mile Island, Pennsylvania, in 1979, caused a partial melting of a reactor core. The second, at Chernobyl in the Ukraine, in 1986, was far more serious and resulted in large amounts of radioactive material escaping into the environment. Since 1986, no new nuclear power stations have been ordered in the USA or in the UK.

By the turn of the century, government attitudes in MEDCs were beginning to change. Nuclear power was viewed as a more attractive option because:

➤ nuclear reactors emit almost no greenhouse gases (GHGs), which are responsible for climate change
➤ nuclear power offers energy security: uranium, the fuel used in nuclear reactors, is available from many sources, and from politically stable and friendly countries such as Canada and Australia (Figure 7.12)

Figure 7.11
Nuclear electricity production by region, 1971–2005

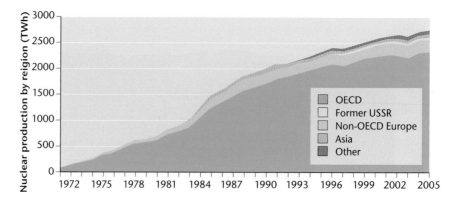

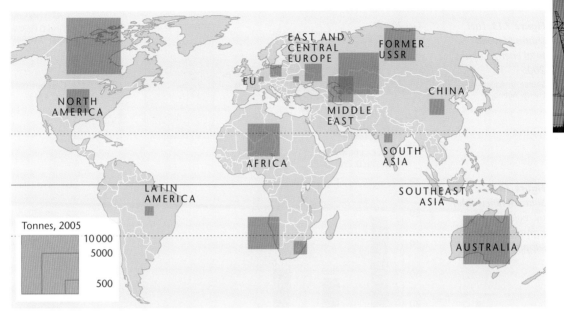

Figure 7.12 *World uranium production*

➤ nuclear technology and new designs for nuclear plants are more efficient and reliable than 30 years ago

Even so, nuclear energy has a downside. It is still expensive — nuclear power stations can take billions of dollars to build. Nuclear plants also produce toxic waste, which remains radioactive for thousands of years. So far no country has built a final disposal site for high-level radioactive waste. Some countries, including the UK, reprocess spent nuclear fuel. However, this is controversial. Reprocessing produces plutonium, the basic ingredient of nuclear weapons, raising concerns about safety and nuclear weapons' proliferation.

Renewable energy sources

In 2005, renewables accounted for 13% of world primary energy production. Eighty per cent of this energy came from combustible renewables (mainly wood for cooking and heating) consumed in LEDCs, and 17% from hydro-power (Figures 7.13 and 7.14). Rates of increase in the production of renewable energy have been similar to the overall growth of energy production since 1970. The growth of 'new' renewables such as wind, tide, geothermal (see Photograph 7.3) and solar power has, however, increased more rapidly. Wind energy, with an annual growth rate of 48%, has the highest increase; but high rates of growth in 'new' renewables are from a very low base. Altogether, wind, tide, geothermal and solar energy's contribution to total world energy production is just half of one per cent (Figure 7.13).

Figure 7.13 *Fuel shares of world total energy supply, 2005*
Source: International Energy Agency

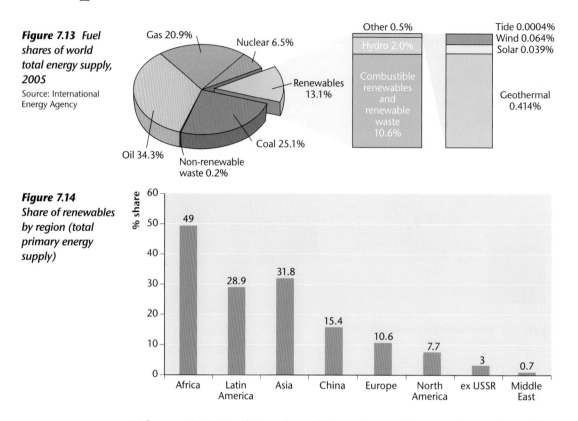

Gas 20.9%

Nuclear 6.5%

Renewables 13.1%

Coal 25.1%

Oil 34.3%

Non-renewable waste 0.2%

Other 0.5%

Hydro 2.0%

Combustible renewables and renewable waste 10.6%

Tide 0.0004%
Wind 0.064%
Solar 0.039%

Geothermal 0.414%

Figure 7.14 *Share of renewables by region (total primary energy supply)*

% share

Africa	49
Latin America	28.9
Asia	31.8
China	15.4
Europe	10.6
North America	7.7
ex USSR	3
Middle East	0.7

Rich countries in North America and Europe have a disproportionate share of the world's hydro-power and 'new' renewables, such as wind, solar and geothermal energy (Figure 7.15). But like nuclear power, the development of these energy resources is limited by their high capital costs and sophisticated technologies.

Photograph 7.3 *A geothermal power station in northern Iceland*

eye35.com/Alamy

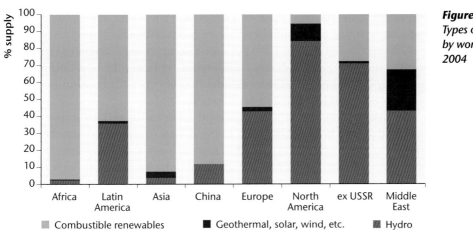

Figure 7.15
Types of renewable by world region, 2004

Energy use and economic development

Key ideas

➤ As economies develop the demand for energy increases.
➤ There are significant differences in energy use between MEDCs and LEDCs.
➤ There are significant differences in energy mix between MEDCs and LEDCs.

Figure 7.16 shows, for 124 countries, the relationship between development, measured in US$ as GDP per capita, and energy usage, measured in kilograms of oil equivalent per person. Even though the scales are logarithmic, the trend is clear: as wealth and development increase, so too does energy consumption. In

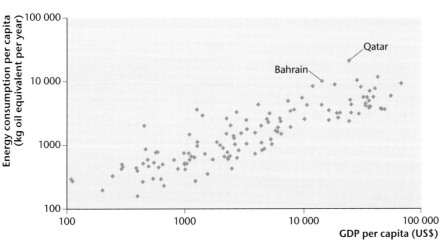

Figure 7.16
GDP per capita versus energy consumption per capita in selected countries

this example, the relationship gives a correlation coefficient of 0.66, suggesting a moderately strong association between the two variables.

Although in Figure 7.16 GDP per capita occupies the *x*-axis, suggesting that wealth causes increases in energy consumption, in reality the relationship works both ways. It is just as valid to assume that energy consumption per capita contributes to rising wealth and development.

The distribution of points on the scattergraph in Figure 7.16 shows a trend, but one that is far from perfect. Some points deviate considerably from the general trend. The main anomalies are oil-rich states such as Bahrain and Qatar. An abundance of cheap oil allows energy usage to be high, even though GDP per capita is moderate.

Explaining the relationship between energy demand and development

It is no surprise that energy consumption rises with economic development. Most residents in MEDCs enjoy lavish lifestyles that depend on massive amounts of cheap energy. The USA, for example, consumes six times more energy than India, and 23 times more per capita. Energy is needed to manufacture consumer goods, to construct buildings, for transport, to produce food, for space heating (and air conditioning) in homes, offices, schools and hospitals, and for cooking.

Why is energy consumption in LEDCs like India low? The simple answer is poverty. People depend on goods and services produced locally. They cannot afford to buy expensive manufactured goods that require lots of energy to make; nor can they afford to own cars, and in rural areas often rely on animals for transport. Cooking and heating depend on biofuels like wood, and crops are produced using human labour and animals, rather than machinery powered by diesel and petrol engines. Finally, most people in LEDCs have little if any income left after satisfying basic needs. Thus, international air travel, which is extremely energy intensive, is not an option for the bulk of the world's population.

Case study — **Sweden's energy use and energy mix**

Sweden is one of the world's most developed countries. In 2006, Sweden's GDP per capita was the eighth highest out of 184 countries, while the UN's human development index (HDI) ranked it fifth out of 177 countries. The high standard of living and a high quality of life enjoyed by Swedes is made possible by a sophisticated post-industrial economy. This in turn is only possible through the consumption of large quantities of energy per person. High energy dependence gives Sweden and other MEDCs a distinctive energy profile (Table 7.5).

Table 7.5 *Energy use in Sweden*

Sector	Total use (1000 tonnes oil equivalent)	% use
Industry	12 549	37.3
Transport	8 564	25.4
Residential	7 152	21.3
Commercial/ public services	4 561	13.6
Other	827	2.4

Box 7.1 Energy mix

Energy mix is the combination of energy types used to power a country's economy. Several factors can influence a country's energy mix:

- Indigenous energy resources — the energy resources available within a country are often cheaper than imports and supply is more reliable. Thus, China and India, with abundant reserves of cheap coal, have energy economies geared to this fuel.
- Energy security — a country may opt for a diversified energy mix to avoid excessive dependence on imported energy. This is an important factor where export regions are politically unstable and supplies may not be secure (e.g. oil exports from the Middle East). Energy security is often an

important reason why governments aim to develop their own indigenous energy resources.

- Levels of development — whereas MEDCs rely on fossil fuels, nuclear energy and some renewables to power their industrial and post-industrial economies, LEDCs have large traditional economic sectors that still depend on fuelwood, crop residues and animal dung.
- Environment — many countries are trying to reduce their consumption of fossil fuels in order to reduce GHG emissions and meet international obligations on climate change. This trend is exemplified in the growth of renewables such as wind power in Germany and Denmark, and the revival of interest in nuclear energy since the late 1990s.

Energy resources

Sweden's energy economy relies heavily on nuclear power, renewables (especially HEP) and imported oil and petroleum products. Because of the relatively small quantities of fossil fuels used in Sweden, the country has low carbon dioxide emissions. The government, with a keen concern for the environment, sees a low-carbon economy as an important objective. Even so, electricity consumption in Sweden is one of the highest in Europe, due in part to the government's promotion of electricity for space heating.

Sweden's reliance on nuclear energy and renew-

ables is above the EU average. The country ranks third in the EU for nuclear energy production. Renewable energy (mainly HEP) accounts for nearly 30% of Sweden's total energy supply and 50% of total electricity supply. This compares with EU averages of just 5.8% and 15.5% respectively (Figures 7.17 and 7.18).

Sweden's energy mix

Sweden's energy mix reflects its limited resource base. Northern Sweden has significant HEP resources. Power plants are concentrated on large rivers such as the Luleälv and the Umeälv, which

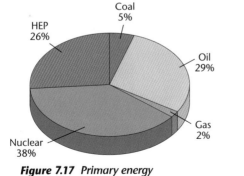

Figure 7.17 *Primary energy supply in Sweden*

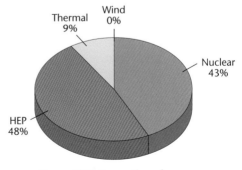

Figure 7.18 *Generation of electricity in Sweden*

drain to the Gulf of Bothnia (Figure 7.19). Most of this potential has now been harnessed. Although HEP potential remains, public opinion is against further expansion because of environmental dis-benefits. Moreover, surviving wild rivers in northern Sweden such as the Torneälv, Kalixälv, Vindelälv and Piteälv are protected from development by law.

Sweden's northern rivers provide ideal conditions for HEP generation. The rivers drain large catchments, have high discharge, and flows are regulated by natural lakes. These lakes store peak flows in the spring and autumn. Waterfalls, such as those at Harsprånget and Porjus on the Luleälv, provide ideal sites for HEP stations (Photograph 7.4). The Luleälv alone generates around 10% of Sweden's electricity; Harsprånget, with a capacity of 939 MW, is Sweden's largest HEP plant.

Nuclear energy

Sweden's geology is dominated by ancient metamorphic rocks. As a result, the country has virtually no indigenous fossil fuels. This in part explains Sweden's decision in the mid-1960s to develop nuclear power and generate electricity by nuclear fission. The decision was also influenced by considerations of energy security and the need to avoid excessive reliance on imported oil, coal and gas.

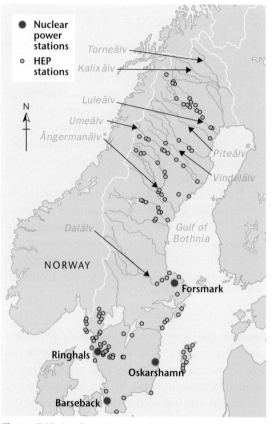

Figure 7.19 *Nuclear plants and HEP stations operated by Vattenfall AB*

Photograph 7.4
Hydroelectric plant at Porjus on the Luleälv

Hans Blomberg

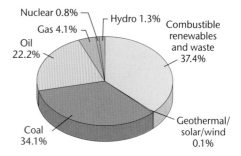

Today Sweden has ten nuclear reactors that supply about half its electricity. The reactors are located at four sites: at Ringhals, Forsmark, Oskarshamn and Barseback (Figure 7.19). Following a public referendum in 1979 it was decided not to build any more nuclear plants and not to replace existing plants at the end of their normal operating life. Following the closure of the first reactor at Barseback in 1999, the second reactor, which was a cheap and highly effective source of electricity, was shut down permanently (and controversially) in 2005.

In recent years, public opinion towards nuclear power has become more positive. Only 10% of the population is now in favour of phasing it out. Other environmental issues, such as climate change and protecting Sweden's remaining unspoilt rivers from HEP development, have assumed greater importance.

Sweden's progress in limiting carbon emissions is due in part to the importance of nuclear power in its energy economy.

Case study — India's energy use and energy mix

With a population of over 1 billion and a rapidly industrialising economy, energy is vital to India's development. However, energy consumption in India is very different from Sweden (compare Tables 7.5 and 7.6). Despite its huge economy and rapid economic growth, India remains a poor country. Its per capita income in 2006 was just $802, placing it 126th out of 177 countries. Its HDI, based on social as well as economic criteria, gave India an even lower ranking — 136th out of 184 countries. Like other LEDCs, India's population is overwhelmingly rural with a heavy dependence on agriculture. At the last census in 2001, there were 880 million rural dwellers living in nearly 600 000 villages.

Energy resources

India is the world's third-biggest coal producer and consumer after China and the USA. Coal is India's most abundant energy resource and the primary fuel that drives the country's industrial economy (Figure 7.20). With huge coal reserves, coal will remain the leading fuel for the foreseeable future. Mining is concentrated in the northeast and central regions in Chhattisgarh, Orissa, Jharkhand and West Bengal, and is used for electricity generation and in heavy industries such as steel making, chemicals and cement (Figure 7.21).

Compared with coal, India's oil and gas reserves are small. Most reserves are located offshore around Mumbai and Assam. In addition to fossil fuels, India

Table 7.6 Energy use in India

Sector	Total use (1000 tonnes oil equivalent)	% use
Industry	95 479	25.3
Transport	36 319	9.6
Residential	229 963	61.0
Commercial/ public services	5 418	1.4
Other	9 937	2.7

Nuclear 0.8% — Hydro 1.3% — Combustible renewables and waste 37.4%
Gas 4.1%
Oil 22.2%
Coal 34.1%
Geothermal/ solar/wind 0.1%

Figure 7.20 Share of total primary energy supply in India, 2004

has developed some of its HEP resources in the northern mountains, and renewables such as wind and solar power have growth potential. India already has several nuclear power stations and a programme for expansion. It also has the world's largest resources of thorium, the raw material for fast-breeder nuclear reactors. However, their exploitation will depend on future advances in nuclear technology.

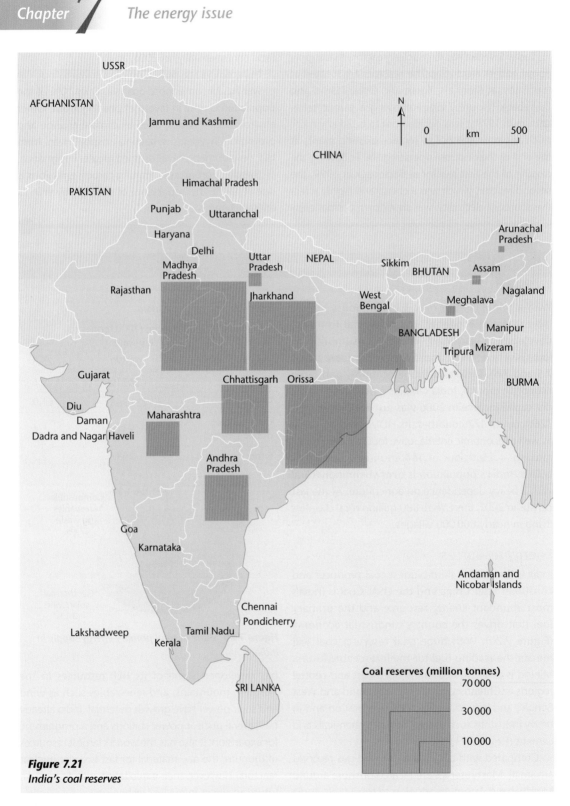

Figure 7.21
India's coal reserves

Coal reserves (million tonnes)
70 000
30 000
10 000

Photograph 7.5 *A coal-fired power station in India; coal generates most of the electricity used by industry*

Energy mix

India's energy mix reflects the dual nature of the Indian economy. The modern, industrial economy relies on electricity, mainly generated from coal. Coal provides 55% of the energy consumed by this sector (Photograph 7.5). Nuclear energy capacity is just 3800 MW and accounts for 3% of electricity production. However, by 2025 its contribution is set to double. India's domestic oil reserves supply only one-third of demand, hence its reliance on imports from the Middle East and Africa. Oil is mainly consumed in the transport sector.

The outstanding feature of India's energy mix compared with MEDCs such as Sweden, however, is the importance of the traditional rural economy. Sixty-one per cent of India's energy consumption occurs in rural areas (see Table 7.6). In rural India, most people rely on biomass resources such as fuelwood, crop residues and animal dung (Photograph 7.6). These are collected locally and at zero cost.

Fuelwood is collected from commonlands, reserves and protected areas, and privately owned lands, mainly by women and children. Its principal use is for cooking and it is burnt on inefficient clay

Photograph 7.6 *Cow dung cakes drying (an example of a biomass resource)*

stoves, often in poorly ventilated kitchens. Liquefied petroleum gas (LPG) and kerosene provide less than 2% of the energy consumed in rural areas. Sixty-two per cent of households use kerosene for lighting. Although rural electrification is widespread, there are still 80 000 villages in India without electricity. Large amounts of electricity and diesel fuel are used in agriculture to power pump sets for irrigation. Small manufacturing enterprises, many of them in rural areas, contribute 40% of India's industrial output. Just over one-third rely on traditional fuels such as wood and charcoal.

For many years, the production and consumption of fuelwood has outstripped the regenerative capacity of India's woodlands. This unsustainable exploitation of natural woodland has led to serious deforestation and land degradation throughout rural India.

Issues associated with the increasing demand for energy

Key ideas

➤ The exploitation of energy resources brings both opportunities and problems for people and the environment.

➤ The social and economic opportunities created by the exploitation of energy resources include employment, community development and economic sustainability.

➤ The problems created by the exploitation of energy include conflicts with indigenous people, economic issues and environmental degradation.

In this section we shall investigate economic, social and environmental issues associated with the exploitation of energy resources. Two contrasting examples will be used to illustrate the opportunities and problems created by the exploitation of energy: the massive Three Gorges Dam HEP scheme on the Yangtze River in central China; and the oil- and gas-rich lower Niger Delta, in Nigeria, west Africa. (See also pages 148–150 on the Arctic National Wildlife Refuge in Alaska and the impact of oil production on the environment and indigenous people.)

Case study   **The Three Gorges Dam, China**

In central China, the Three Gorges stretch of the Yangtze River is the location of the world's biggest and most controversial HEP scheme (Figure 7.22). The Yangtze is China's longest river and, after the Amazon and the Nile, the third longest in the world. It rises in the Kunlun Mountains in southwest China and flows eastwards across central China to its mouth in the east China Sea, just north of Shanghai. Four hundred million people (nearly one in every three Chinese) live within the Yangtze drainage basin.

Opportunities created by the Three Gorges Dam (TGD) project

The TGD project (Figure 7.23 and Photograph 7.7) will bring significant economic and environmental benefits to China.

Economic

The TGD will provide much needed electricity to meet China's soaring demand for energy. In the past 20 years, China's industrialisation has surged ahead, with economic growth reaching 10% a year or more. In order to fuel this growth, China has become by far the world's largest producer and consumer of coal, and the second-largest oil importer. Demand for energy will continue to grow in future but meeting it will not be easy. Already, electricity shortages lead to widespread and frequent power cuts and threaten economic growth. Disruption of energy supplies is of particular concern in the Yangtze Delta and Shanghai, the engine that drives the Chinese economy.

When fully operational in 2009, the TGD will provide 18 200 MW of HEP. This represents around

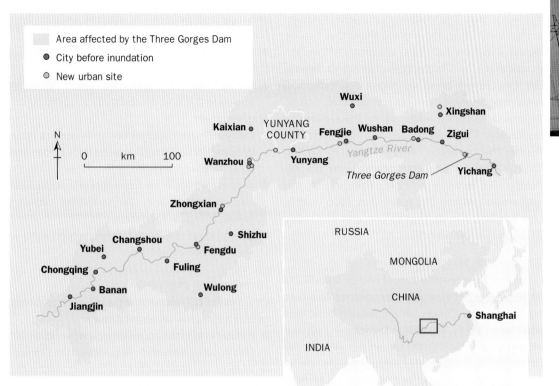

Figure 7.22 *The location of the Three Gorges Dam, China*

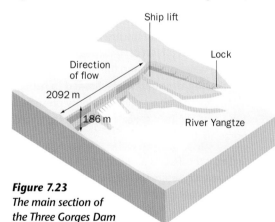

Figure 7.23
The main section of
the Three Gorges Dam

Photograph 7.7 *The Three Gorges Dam on the Yangtze River, China*

20% of all HEP generated in China, and 4% of electricity produced from all sources. According to government statements, electricity from the TGD will create 'millions of new jobs' and generate up to $65 billion in additional industrial activity.

The Yangtze is an important transport route and trade artery into central China. The TGD and its reservoir will improve navigation on the river,

allowing 10 000-tonne vessels to navigate from Shanghai as far as Chongqing. Vessels will negotiate the dam through a two-way lock and a lift system.

Community development: flood control

The TGD has other benefits. It will greatly reduce the risk of flooding in the lower Yangtze valley. The 660-kilometre long reservoir behind the TGD is large enough to store the floodwaters of a 100-year flood event (statistically, the highest flood that can be expected in every 100 years) and protect 15 million people and 1.5 million hectares of farmland. Taming the Yangtze will bring significant economic and social opportunities to China in general, and to thousands of communities on the lower Yangtze floodplain. The benefits are hard to overstate. During the twentieth century, flooding on the Yangtze River and its tributaries caused over 325 000 deaths. As recently as 1998, flooding in the area around Wuhan City resulted in 3000 deaths, cost $24 billion in damage to property and made 14 million people homeless.

Sustainability and climate change

HEP is a clean, renewable form of energy. If the TGD's 18 200 MW of electricity were generated by coal-fired power stations, China's carbon dioxide emissions would increase by 100 million tonnes per year, and nitrogen oxide by 370 000 tonnes per year. At the same time, sulphur dioxide outputs would rise by 2 million tonnes per year, adding to the problem of acid rain. That said, any environmental gains will soon be wiped out by China's massive on-going investment in coal-burning power stations.

Problems of the TGD project

Set against the economic and environmental opportunities created by the TGD are a range of disadvantages. These disadvantages are social, economic and environmental.

Resettlement of indigenous people

The reservoir created by the dam will flood an area of 1045 km^2, including 300 km^2 of farmland. Estimates of the number of people displaced and forcibly resettled are startling: they vary from 1.2 million to 1.9 million. These people lived in 1200 villages and towns, which since 2002 have slowly disappeared below the rising waters behind the dam.

The government promised cash compensation and new homes for those displaced. So far it has built 13 new towns, while 1500 factories and 70 waste treatment plants have either closed or moved. However, many indigenous people are deeply unhappy and believe the scheme violates their human rights. They complain of:

- inadequate levels of compensation for their loss of homes, land and livelihoods
- land offered in compensation being inferior in quality to the land compulsorily acquired by the government
- the resettlement budget being diverted to other unrelated infrastructure projects such as road and hotel building
- widespread fraud and corruption among local officials, with money earmarked for ordinary people failing to reach them
- thousands of displaced families being forced to live in squalid conditions

Environmental degradation

Critics of the TGD argue that the project has already caused major environmental damage:

- Pollutants leached from waste dumps and landfill sites in flooded towns have poisoned the Yangtze.
- Water in the reservoir behind the dam is now too slow-moving to flush out pollutants.
- Nutrient enrichment from pollution has resulted in algal blooms and reduced levels of dissolved oxygen in the river and the reservoir. This has had severe knock-on effects on aquatic ecosystems.
- Declining water quality and the transformation of a free-flowing river into a lake has led to habitat loss. The Yangtze River dolphin is now presumed extinct and 47 fish species indigenous to the Yangtze are threatened.

Like all dams, the TGD is a sediment trap. The river's entire suspended sediment load is deposited in the reservoir. Water exiting the reservoir is both sediment-free and cold. This has changed the ecology of the Yangtze downstream from the TGD and has contributed to habitat loss. The sediment-free water has also led to accelerated erosion of the channel bed and banks.

In the area flooded by the reservoir, rising water levels have caused erosion of valley sides, leading to slope collapse and landslides. There is also a risk of earthquakes and seismic activity caused by the weight of the dam and the reservoir.

Social and cultural problems

Flooding such a large area has meant the loss of hundreds of cultural, archaeological and historic sites. Although some historic relics have been moved to higher ground, many stone sculptures, petroglyphs and tombs have disappeared beneath the reservoir.

The 660-kilometre long reservoir will also destroy much of the natural beauty and character of the three gorges — Qutang, Wuxia and Xiling — that give the region its name. The Three Gorges is the most impressive section of the Yangtze River and a major attraction for Chinese tourists and foreign visitors (Photograph 7.8)

Economic problems

The economic outcomes of the TGD project are not entirely beneficial. The most obvious losers are farmers. Flooding has resulted in the loss of 30 000 ha of productive farmland behind the dam. Furthermore, sediment trapped by the dam no longer reaches the floodplain of the lower Yangtze. Because floods are a thing of the past, natural fertilisation of fields by silt deposited during floods no longer occurs. This means that farmers in future will have to rely on costly chemical fertilisers.

The impact of sediment depletion is also felt at the mouth of the river. Reductions in the amount of river sediment reaching the East China Sea has had two effects. First, by reducing nutrient inputs, inshore fish

Panorama Media (Beijing) Ltd/Alamy

Photograph 7.8 *The Three Gorges section of the Yangtze River is a major tourist attraction*

catches have fallen by around 1 million tonnes per year. Second, the loss of sediment has destabilised the Yangtze delta, eroding mudflats, saltmarshes and wetlands.

Finally, flooding has meant the permanent loss of coal and metal ore mines and hundreds of industrial activities that once lined the river banks.

Case study — Oil in the Niger Delta

Nigeria is Africa's leading oil producer. Nearly all of the country's oil (and gas) reserves are concentrated in the Niger Delta and offshore in the Gulf of Guinea (Figure 7.24). The scale of the delta's oil and gas resources has attracted most of the world's leading oil companies. The largest, Shell, accounts for nearly half of Nigeria's annual oil production.

In 2005, oil production was 131 million tonnes. Of this, all but 5 million tonnes was exported, making Nigeria the world's fourth-largest oil exporter. Oil represents over 90% of Nigeria's exports by value.

While oil is vital to the country's economy, Nigeria's dependence on such a narrow export base is a potential economic weakness.

Significant reserves of natural gas occur in association with oil. Natural gas production in 2005 was equivalent to 18.5 million tonnes of oil; 60% was exported as liquefied natural gas.

The Niger Delta ecosystem

The Niger Delta supports important and diverse ecosystems. It contains Nigeria's largest surviving areas

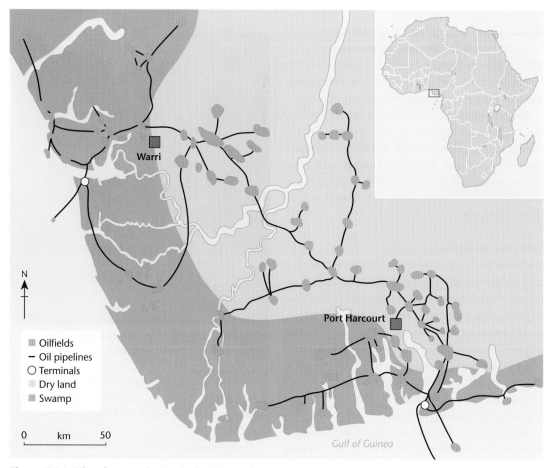

Figure 7.24 *Oil and gas production in the Niger Delta*

of rainforest and the third-largest mangrove forest in the world. Aquatic and marine ecosystems support over 150 species of fish, and spectacular animals including primates, manatees, hippos and otters.

Dominating the delta are its mangrove forests. Mangroves are assemblages of tropical trees and shrubs adapted to tidal flooding and salinity. They provide vital habitats and food sources for plant and animal communities. At various times they are also breeding areas and nurseries for fish and inverte-brates such as crustaceans and molluscs. Sixty per cent of west Africa's fish stocks spawn in the swamps, creeks and tidal inlets along the delta coast. Many birds use mangroves for refuge, nesting and feeding. Despite their diversity, the delta's ecosystems are fragile and highly sensitive to change.

The delta and traditional economies

For thousands of years local people have used the resources of the Niger Delta sustainably. Traditional ways of life have depended on fishing, subsistence farming, gathering forest products and crafts based on local materials. Today an estimated 23 million people live in 2000 communities in the six states that make up the Niger Delta.

The impact of oil and gas production
Environmental degradation and conflict with indigenous people

Economic development and the specific impact of the oil and gas industries have caused widespread envi-ronmental damage in the Niger Delta, and have undermined traditional economies and culture. Over

reportage/Alamy

Photograph 7.9 *Oil spillage in the Niger Delta forest*

4000 oil spills have been recorded since production started in 1958. So bad is the situation that in 2006 the World Wide Fund for Nature (WWF) described the Niger Delta as one of the five most polluted places on the planet. In total, 500 million tonnes of crude oil have been lost to spillage, and the current cost of leaks is around $10 million a day. These spills have severely degraded the environment, destroying wildlife, ecosystems and the livelihoods of local people.

Environmental degradation is worst in Ogoniland in the southernmost part of the delta (Photograph 7.9). This region alone has 100 oil wells, two oil refineries, a petrochemical complex and a fertiliser plant. An oil spill in 2001 at the Ogoni village of Yaata, a traditional farming and fishing community, was described by UN observers thus: '...dying vegetation in various shades of ochre stretched as far as the eye could see, poisoned by soil turned soggy and greasy since oil began seeping through over a month ago.'

Further spills and explosions caused fires, releasing poisonous gases, and crude oil swamped farmlands, forests, rivers and people's homes. The fires burned for 3 months. After the spillage stopped,

the village was uninhabitable. Crops, livestock and fish were dead and drinking water contaminated for miles around.

A local fisherwoman from the village of Bille in Ogoniland described the devastation:

'When oil spills here, those of us who go to the mangrove forest to harvest periwinkles and other sea foods suffer. The crude oil affects the growth and development of the mangrove forest resources such as periwinkles, oysters and crabs. When the river is polluted they all die.'

In addition to oil spills, the routine flaring of gas has for many years been of major concern to local residents (Photograph 7.10). Flaring pollutes the air, creates gas fogs and acid rain, and releases carcinogenic particles into the environment. Villagers claim that flaring damages their crops and is responsible for respiratory illness and cancer.

The causes of environmental degradation

The oil industry's ageing network of 6000 km of high-pressure pipelines criss-cross the Niger Delta.

Friedrich Stark/Alamy

Photograph 7.10 *Environmental pollution is caused by burning off gas from oil production in the Niger delta*

This network is above ground and corrodes quickly in the hot, humid climate, increasing the risks of spillage. It is not uncommon for pipelines to cross farmers' fields, gardens and village. Thus any significant leak or spillage can have devastating consequences. Local people and environmentalists accuse the oil companies of negligence and failure to maintain and replace rusty pipelines, which are in many cases 40–50 years old, and blame them for the pollution that has caused an environmental disaster.

However, the problem of spillage is more complex. While accepting blame for some of the spillages, the oil companies say that most are due to local people illegally tapping oil from pipelines, and to sabotage. One estimate suggests that 10% of Nigeria's oil is stolen by illegal tapping. As a result, the oil companies are often reluctant to compensate local people for spillages which they regard as acts of vandalism or terrorism.

It would be simplistic to place all the responsibility for environmental degradation solely on the oil and gas industries. Other influences have been significant. Not least is the huge increase in Nigeria's population in the past half-century. In 1958, when oil was first developed, Nigeria's total population was 38 million. By 2007, this had soared to 135 million. For much of this period, population growth rates exceeded 3% a year. This huge population growth alone has placed acute pressure on environmental resources, triggering widespread deforestation and loss of habitat in the Niger Delta.

Accompanying rapid population growth has been massive urbanisation and the development of major cities and industries in the south, such as Port Harcourt and Warri. Domestic and industrial waste discharges from these cities have added to pollution and environmental degradation in the Niger Delta.

Economic issues

The people of the delta (and especially in Ogoniland) have derived few benefits from Nigeria's oil wealth, despite suffering most of the costs. When Nigeria achieved independence in 1960, it was agreed that revenues from the country's natural resources would be split evenly between the central government and the regions. This has not happened. In the past, the Niger Delta region has received as little as 1% of the oil and gas revenues. Although this figure has now risen to 13%, it is still a long way from parity. Local people continue to lack the most basic services: most have no electricity, no running water, no access to health care and few functioning schools. In the past there have been few projects or initiatives aimed at benefiting local people. They also see natural gas being flared, which could generate the electricity they so badly need.

The oil industry has come to dominate the economic base of the delta to the exclusion of other economic activities. Traditional activities such as agriculture and fishing have been gradually squeezed out and this has served to increase economic inequalities in the region.

Managing energy supplies to ensure sustainability

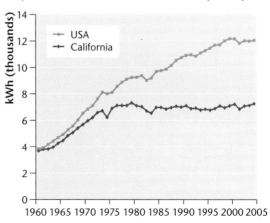

Key ideas

➤ Managing energy supply requires detailed planning and balancing of socio-economic and environmental needs.
➤ Energy demand can be satisfied in an increasingly sustainable way.
➤ The development of renewable energy resources is an important goal of sustainable energy policies.

Although finite energy reserves such as oil and coal cannot be managed sustainably, much can be done to reduce their consumption and to use them more efficiently. At the same time, renewable energy such as wind and solar power can be developed. In this section we shall see how California has made significant progress towards a more sustainable energy future.

 Case study | **California: planning a sustainable future**

California is the most populous state in the USA, with 36.5 million residents in 2007. In economic terms, however, California is far more important than its population suggests. It is the richest US state: were it an independent nation, California's economy would be the sixth largest in the world, comparable in size with those of France or the UK.

Until recently, California's wealth and the high standards of living were supported by an energy consumption that was both extravagant and heavily dependent on fossil fuels.

However, in the past 20 years there has been a huge increase in environmental awareness among Californians. Today, California is a world leader in innovative and sustainable energy policies. While the US federal government has shown little interest in energy sustainability, California's government has forged ahead with its green agenda. It has intro-duced radical legislation that aims to:

- reduce energy consumption
- increase the efficient use of energy
- expand renewable energy resources
- cut GHG emissions

Developing a more sustainable energy economy

California's per capita electricity consumption remained static between 1975 and 2005 (Figure 7.25). This performance easily outstripped that of the USA as a whole. Its attempt to reduce carbon dioxide outputs was even more remarkable: per capita

Figure 7.25 Comparison of per capita electricity consumption in the USA and California
Source: California Energy Commission, 2005

Figure 7.26
Comparison of per capita carbon dioxide emissions in the USA and California
Source: Oak Ridge National Laboratory

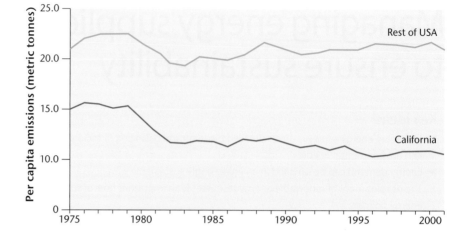

carbon dioxide production fell by nearly a third between 1975 and 2005. Meanwhile, the rest of the USA recorded hardly any change (Figure 7.26). California has made these advances through policies focusing on the transport, electricity production, energy efficiency and renewable energy industries. The California state government's most recent targets, set in 2006, include a cut in GHG emissions to 1990 levels by 2020, rising to an 80% cut by 2050.

Transport

California has 26 million motor vehicles, which emit over 40 million tonnes of carbon dioxide a year (Photograph 7.11 and Table 7.7). Emissions of carbon dioxide and other GHGs by motor vehicles contribute to global warming and climate change, and lower air quality in large urban areas such as Los Angeles. To tackle the problem, California has introduced tough laws forcing auto manufacturers to introduce cleaner technologies and cut vehicle exhaust emissions. Thus by 2009, the auto industry must reduce exhaust emissions by 25% for cars and light trucks, and by 18% for heavy trucks and sports utility vehicles. The state government will also promote the use of non-petroleum fuels such as LNG, biodiesel, electricity and hydrogen, to increase fuel economy. The target is for non-petroleum fuels to take 30% of the market by 2030.

Tom Uhlman/Alamy

Photograph 7.11 *Heavy traffic on an interstate highway in Los Angeles, California*

Table 7.7 *Carbon dioxide emissions by economic sector in California*

Sector	Carbon dioxide output (million tonnes)
Transport	40.7
Agriculture and forestry	8.3
Industry	20.5
Electricity generation	22.2
Others	8.3

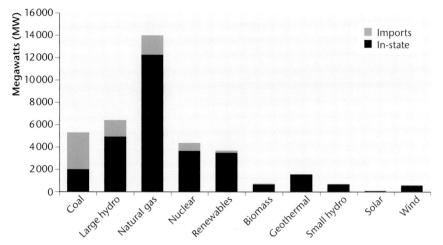

Figure 7.27
Fuel sources for electricity production in California in 2006

Coal-fired power stations

Since 2005, electricity companies in California have been assigned a money cost to their GHG emissions. Carbon dioxide costs the companies $8 per tonne, increasing by 5% a year. This means that investment in dirty coal-fired plants, which emit twice as much carbon dioxide as gas-fired alternatives, has become less attractive. At the same time, this initiative boosted the position of renewable energy resources that emit virtually no GHGs. The government has also banned electricity companies from signing long-term contracts with coal-fired power stations, encouraging them to buy from cleaner sources.

Energy efficiency

Over the past 30 years, California has invested heavily in energy efficiency programmes, including building efficiency. The result has been a saving of 12 000 MW of electrical generating capacity. The latest targets for energy efficiency will save a further 2800 MW and avoid the need to build five new power stations in the next 10 years. This is equal to a saving of carbon dioxide emissions of 11 million tonnes per year.

Developing renewable energy resources

Because of its lack of coal and heavy industry, California has always been a relatively clean state. It already generates more electricity from renewable sources than any other US state. In 2006, 12% of its electricity came from geothermal, wind, solar power, biomass, and small HEP schemes (Figure 7.27). A further 19% came from large-scale HEP schemes, some of which are located outside California, mainly in the Pacific northwest.

California's interest in renewable energy dates back to the global oil crises of the 1970s and the introduction of state and federal tax incentives to promote renewables. The state has ambitious plans to increase the proportion of electricity it generates from renewable resources. The New Renewables Program provides a subsidy for each unit of electricity produced by new solar, biomass and wind energy schemes. By 2010 the target is to produce one-fifth of the state's electricity from renewables (excluding large-scale HEP), rising to one-third by 2020. However, present performance suggests that these targets will be hard to achieve.

Geothermal energy

Steam from hot rocks below the surface can be used to make electricity in geothermal power plants. California, a tectonically active region located on the Pacific Ring of Fire, has 25 geothermal resource areas (Figure 7.28). Geothermal power plants produce nearly 5% of California's electricity and about 40% of the world's geothermally generated electricity. The most developed geothermal resource area is Geysers, located north of San Francisco. Other major geothermal locations include the Imperial Valley east of San Diego, Coso Hot Springs near Bakersfield, the Mammoth Lakes area, and the Lassen Volcanic

Figure 7.28
Principal geothermal, wind and solar power resources in California

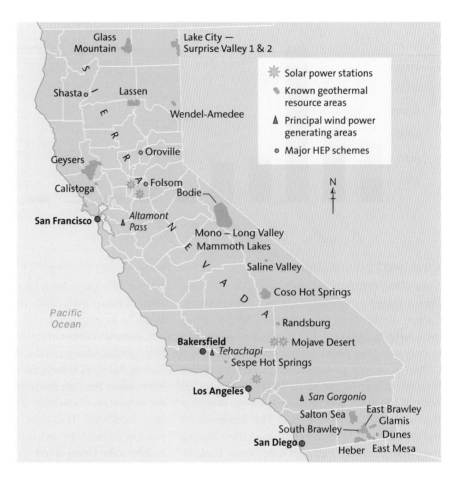

National Park. Current production is 1900 MW, with a potential for an additional 4000 MW.

Apart from supplying electricity, geothermally active areas also provide hot water for space heating, swimming pools and greenhouses.

Wind power

California has around 14 000 wind turbines. Despite the numbers, their combined electricity output is only 1800 MW, providing just 1.5% of the state's electricity. Many turbines are small, old and in need of re-powering.

Ninety-five per cent of California's wind-generating capacity is located in three regions: Altamont Pass, Tehachapi and San Gorgonio (Photograph 7.12). Wind power resources vary seasonally: three-quarters of all annual wind power output is produced during spring and summer.

Production is highest in the hot summer months.

Under the New Renewables Program, 1000 MW of new capacity will be added between 2004 and 2010. Larger and more advanced turbine designs, which are replacing the older generation of turbines, are able to match the electricity prices from coal and nuclear plants. However, wind farm development raises a number of environmental issues:

■ It requires large tracts of land (a typical wind farm needs 7 ha to generate 1 MW of electricity).
■ The installation of wind turbines, transmission systems, sub-stations and roads in environmentally sensitive areas, such as deserts, can lead to erosion.
■ Wind turbines are a visual intrusion.
■ There is disturbance to wildlife habitats and bird mortality occurs due to collisions with wind turbines and transmission lines.

Michael Raw

Photograph 7.12 *Wind turbines near San Gorgonio, California*

Solar power

Solar power provides 1% of California's electricity, while 0.5 million households in the state use solar water heaters. Electricity is produced from solar energy in two ways: by thermal solar generation and by using photovoltaic (PV) cells. Since 1985, nine solar thermal power stations have been in operation in the Mojave Desert, ranging in size from 14 MW to 80 MW. They comprise huge rows of solar mirrors that focus the sunlight to boil water. Steam can then be used to drive turbines to make electricity. Alternatively, electricity is produced directly and on a smaller scale from arrays of PV cells.

Conditions for generating solar energy in commercial quantities are ideal in California's Mojave Desert (Photograph 7.13). This region has 360 days of sunshine a year and just 150 mm of rainfall. Even so, solar energy is still in the early stages of development. There are, however, big plans to expand production in the Mojave Desert. For example, the Mojave Solar Park, occupying 250 ha of desert and due for completion in 2011, will increase capacity by 553 MW.

In 2006, California's state government, as part of its policy to promote renewable energy, introduced its Solar Initiative.

David R. Frazier Photolibrary Inc/Alamy

Photograph 7.13 *Solar energy plant in the Mojave Desert, California*

The plan gives $3.2 billion in refunds to investors in solar power. These incentives should provide for a 3000 MW expansion in solar energy, roughly the power equivalent of six gas-fired power stations. In addition, subsidies will be available for solar projects on existing residential buildings, public buildings, industrial premises, offices and agricultural facilities.

HEP

HEP is a long-established renewable energy source in California. Development peaked in the 1960, but today most cost-effective sites have been exploited. Most HEP developments pre-date California's environmental protection laws that were enacted in the 1970s. As a result, HEP has caused significant environmental stress. These stresses, which have had adverse impacts on river ecosystems and aquatic plants and animals, include:

- modifying runoff patterns and river flow
- removing water for electricity production
- temperature changes in rivers downstream from dams
- blocking the movement of migrating fish
- rapid changes in water levels in reservoirs in response to the demand for electricity

California's HEP plants generate around 16% of the state's electricity. Imported electricity produced by HEP, mainly from the Pacific northwest, accounts for a further 5% (see Figure 7.27). Large-scale dams such as Shasta, Oroville and Folsom, located in the Sierra Nevada, are responsible for the bulk of home production (see Figure 7.28). These schemes are multipurpose: as well as producing HEP they control flooding, provide recreational amenities and are a source of water for irrigation and drinking.

Biomass energy

Biomass energy produces 1% to 2% of California's electricity. There are 28 small plants with a combined output of 550 MW. However, under California's renewable energy plan, biomass sources will contribute an additional 2000 MW in the next 10 years. Biomass energy can play a small but significant role in the fight to reduce GHG emissions: every tonne of biomass fuel used saves 0.4 tonnes of carbon dioxide from gas-fired power stations. However, in the past, biomass energy has not received the tax credits to give it parity with other new technologies such as geothermal and solar power.

Because biomass fuel contains less energy per tonne than fossil fuels, its transport to power plants is expensive. This problem is being met by building small power plants in areas of biomass production near forests and plantations. Large quantities of fuel can be sourced from dead wood that accumulates within overgrown forests. Removing this material will also improve forest health and greatly reduce the risk of wildfires that threaten many communities in California.

Box 7.2   Biomass energy

Biomass fuels such as small trees, wood residues and forest litter (i.e. dead tree stems, branches, leaves etc.) are **carbon neutral**. Fast-growing trees such as willow saplings are planted and harvested by farmers and foresters. The production of electricity from biomass sources releases the same amount of carbon as the trees absorbed through photosynthesis during their growth. Thus, unlike the burning of coal, oil and gas, biomass energy involves no net increase in GHGs.

Biomass energy is generated through burning wood in a power boiler. Combustion produces steam, which drives a turbine and a generator to make electricity.

Energy derived from biomass has been widely used for years by sawmills and pulp and paper industries to provide electricity to power other mills and factories. Some larger biomass plants also supply excess power back to the electricity grid.

Examination-style questions

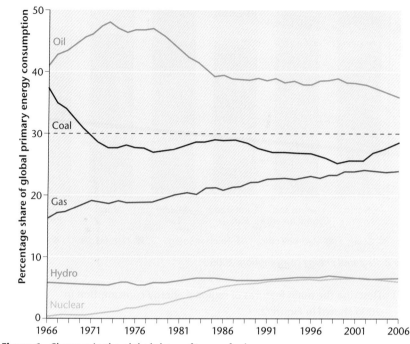

Figure 1 *Changes in the global share of types of primary energy*

1 (a) Describe the trends in primary energy consumption between 1966 and 2006 shown in Figure 1. (4 marks)

(b) Suggest reasons for the trends described in 1(a). (6 marks)

(c) Explain the relationship between energy use and level of economic development. (6 marks)

(d) With reference to one or more named examples, explain how the exploitation of energy resources can create problems for indigenous people and the environment. (9 marks)

(e) With reference to named examples, explain how energy demand can be satisfied in an increasingly sustainable way. (25 marks)

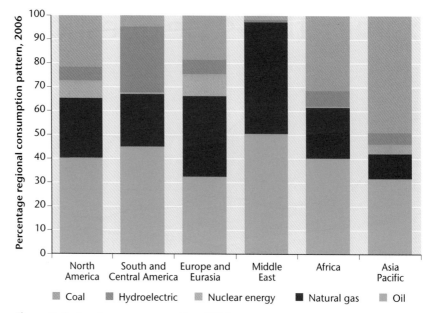

Figure 2 *Regional energy consumption, 2006*

2 (a) Describe the main features of regional energy consumption in 2006 shown in Figure 2. (4 marks)

(b) Suggest reasons for the variable pattern of regional energy consumption shown in Figure 2. (6 marks)

(c) Explain how the exploitation of energy resources can damage the natural environment. (6 marks)

(d) With reference to one or more named examples, show how the exploitation of energy resources can create opportunities for local communities. (9 marks)

(e) With reference to named examples, describe and explain the contrasts in energy mix between countries with highly developed economies and those at the lower end of the development spectrum. (25 marks)

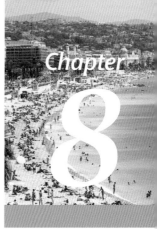

The growth of tourism

The changing pattern of global tourism

The World Tourism Organization defines tourism as: 'The activities of persons travelling to, and staying in, places outside their usual environment for leisure, business and other purposes.' However, this chapter focuses exclusively on tourism related to recreational and leisure activities.

Measuring international tourism

International tourism occurs when tourists cross political boundaries from one country to another. There are two common measures of international tourism:
➤ the number of foreign visitor arrivals
➤ the receipts from international tourists, usually measured in US$

Foreign visitor arrivals is the simpler measure. Using this measure, France is the leading destination for international tourists, followed by Spain and the USA (Table 8.1). The main drawback with foreign visitor arrivals is its tendency to inflate the importance of international tourism in parts of the world where there are many small countries. For this reason, Europe dominates international tourism in terms of numbers of foreign visitor arrivals. For example, tourists travelling relatively short distances, say from Germany into Switzerland, are classed as international tourists. In contrast, In North America, New Yorkers holidaying in California are not recorded as international tourists,

Table 8.1 *International visitor arrivals and international tourism receipts, 2006*

Top 10 countries	Visitor arrivals (million)	Top 10 countries	Receipts ($ billion)
France	79.1	USA	85.7
Spain	58.5	Spain	51.8
USA	51.1	France	46.3
China	49.6	Italy	38.1
Italy	41.1	China	33.9
UK	30.1	UK	33.5
Germany	23.6	Germany	32.8
Mexico	21.4	Australia	17.8
Austria	20.3	Turkey	16.9
Russia	20.2	Austria	16.7

even though they have travelled nearly 5000 km. Only when Americans cross the border into either Canada or Mexico do they become international tourists.

When we measure international tourism in terms of receipts, we see a rather different pattern. Now the table of top tourist destinations is led by the USA (Table 8.1). This is explained by the USA's greater share of high-spending, long-haul tourists compared with Europe. Clearly receipts from international tourism are a more accurate measure of tourism's economic importance to a country than simple foreign visitor counts.

Types of tourism

There are many typologies of tourism based on criteria such as its purpose (e.g. recreation, business, education, health), scale, location and sustainability. Perhaps the most important distinction is between **mass tourism** and alternative types of tourism (Photograph 8.1).

Mass tourism caters for very large numbers of visitors. It is highly organised by the travel industry, with a network of tour operators, travel agents, hotel chains, airlines and so on. The result is huge concentrations of tourists in popular resorts such as Torremolinos on the Costa del Sol and El Arenal in Mallorca. Mass tourism is usually based around natural resources such as beaches, snow and climate. Because of its scale, it is often environmentally damaging and therefore unsustainable. With mass tourism, contact between tourists and local people, culture and the natural environment is often minimal.

Ecotourism and **green tourism** are alternatives to mass tourism, though neither term has a precise definition. They usually describe small-group tourism based around special interests such as sport, wildlife, trekking and historic or cultural features. However, alternative tourism often uses the same infrastructure of mass tourism.

Unlike mass tourism, alternative tourism is small scale, involves local people and has a preference for remote places. An example would be trekking holidays in the foothills of the Himalayas and the Andes. The environmental, social and economic impact of small group tourism is less than mass tourism, and ecotourism and green tourism aim to be sustainable. However, it is debatable how far this is possible unless the use of natural resources is on a very small scale. Moreover, the environments popularly sought for small-scale group tourism, such as mountains and deserts, are often fragile, have very low carrying capacities and are easily degraded (see pages 152–56 and 182–84).

Photograph 8.1 Mass tourism on the Côte d'Azur, southern France

Tourism: the world's biggest industry?

The global value of tourism in 2006 was $680 billion. To put this in perspective, the value of tourism to the world economy exceeds all global oil exports and the international trade in cars and transport equipment. In the EU, tourism and other related activities account for 12% of GDP and support 20 million jobs.

Tourism is economically important because it:
- ➤ makes a huge contribution to the balance of payments of so many countries
- ➤ is highly labour intensive and creates jobs
- ➤ provides opportunities for small businesses such as farming, fishing, handicrafts that supply products, and services to tourists
- ➤ attracts inward investment, helping to upgrade infrastructure and modernise the economies of many LEDCs
- ➤ helps to reduce poverty — international receipts from tourism for LEDCs will soon pass $250 billion a year
- ➤ is the main source of foreign exchange for many countries, including 46 of the 49 least-developed countries in the world

Trends in international tourism

Since the end of the Second World War, tourism has developed into a global industry. This globalisation has two outstanding features: first, its strong and continuous growth; and second, its relentless geographical expansion.

The growth of international tourism

Figure 8.1 shows the upward trend in international tourism in terms of visitor arrivals. According to the World Tourism Organisation, in 1950 there were approximately 25 million international tourist arrivals. By 1990 this figure had reached 441 million and by 2006 was 842 million. The growth of international tourism in the UK underlines the global trend. In 1998, British residents, for the first time, took more foreign holidays (29 million) than holidays at home. Then in the space of just 7 years the number of foreign holidays had soared to 44 million.

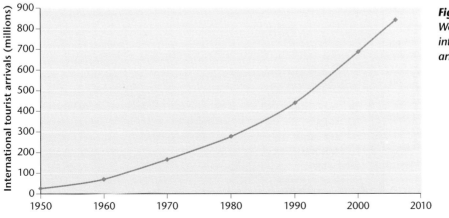

Figure 8.1
World growth of international tourist arrivals, 1950–2006

The outstanding feature of the growth of international tourism has been its consistency. Despite economic downturns such as the quadrupling of oil prices in the 1970s, and political crises like the Iraq war in 2003, the growth of global tourism has been unstoppable. Between 1950 and 2005 the average annual growth rate was 6.5%. Although a slowing occurred between 2000 and 2005 due to terrorism and political instability in the Middle East, by 2006 growth had recovered to over 6%.

The geographical expansion of international tourism

An important feature of international tourism in the past 50 years has been its ever-increasing geographical expansion. In 1950, the top ten countries for international tourist arrivals claimed 88% of the market. By 2004 there had been a dramatic change. The top ten's share had fallen to 48% as more countries became tourist destinations (Figure 8.2). Although international tourism is still dominated by Europe, the region's relative importance has declined as new destinations, particularly in Asia-Pacific (e.g. China and Australia) and more recently in north Africa, have developed (Figures 8.3 and 8.4).

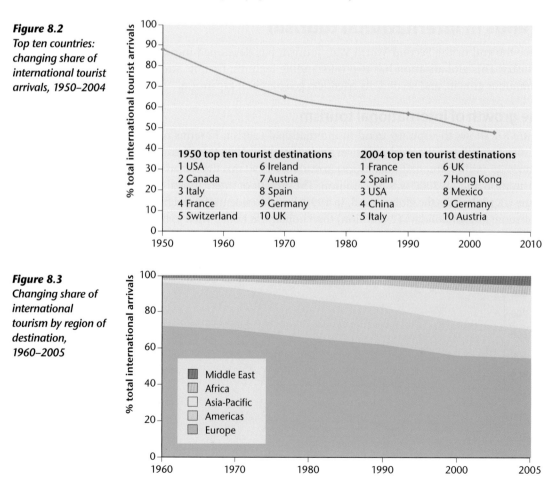

Figure 8.2
Top ten countries: changing share of international tourist arrivals, 1950–2004

1950 top ten tourist destinations
1 USA
2 Canada
3 Italy
4 France
5 Switzerland
6 Ireland
7 Austria
8 Spain
9 Germany
10 UK

2004 top ten tourist destinations
1 France
2 Spain
3 USA
4 China
5 Italy
6 UK
7 Hong Kong
8 Mexico
9 Germany
10 Austria

Figure 8.3
Changing share of international tourism by region of destination, 1960–2005

Middle East
Africa
Asia-Pacific
Americas
Europe

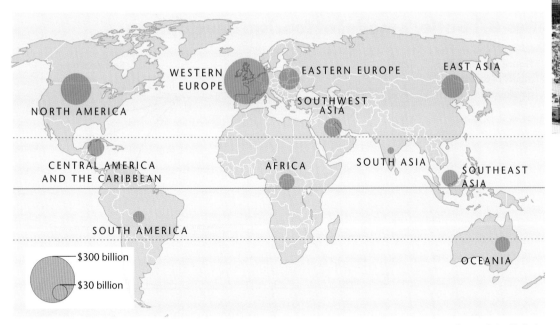

Figure 8.4 *Global tourism: receipts by region in 2005*

International tourism in Europe

In 2005, Europe accounted for 55% of all international tourist arrivals and 51% of all international tourism receipts (Figure 8.5). Yet despite its dominance, the geographical distribution of tourism within Europe is very uneven. Eight out of ten tourist arrivals are in southern Europe, the Mediterranean and western Europe. Within southern Europe, western areas (i.e. Portugal to Italy) are more popular than eastern areas such as Greece and Turkey. This is largely due to the longer history of tourism in the west (Box 8.1). Elsewhere in Europe, levels of international tourism are much lower. For example, central and eastern Europe accounts for just 6% of tourist arrivals.

Figure 8.5 *International tourism in Europe, 2005*
Source: World Tourism Organization

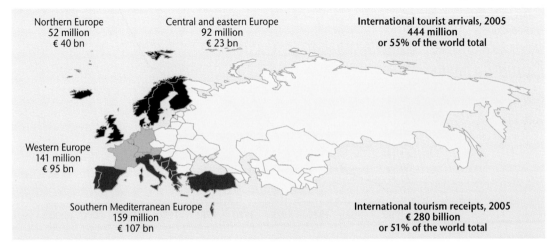

Box 8.1 Butler's model of tourism development

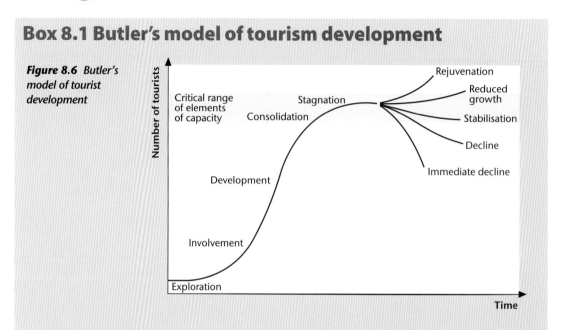

Figure 8.6 *Butler's model of tourist development*

Butler's model suggests tourist areas develop through a number of stages, which are shown in Figure 8.6.

- The initial development of a tourist resort, often exclusive to a social and economic elite, is slow (e.g. Mallorca before 1950).
- As the resort becomes more accessible and more widely known, development accelerates (e.g. Mallorca in the 1960s and 1970s).

- Tourism reaches maturity and the resort's popularity stagnates or declines (e.g. Mallorca in the latter part of the 1990s, Figure 8.7).
- The future of tourism in the resort depends on the response to stagnation. Some resorts enter

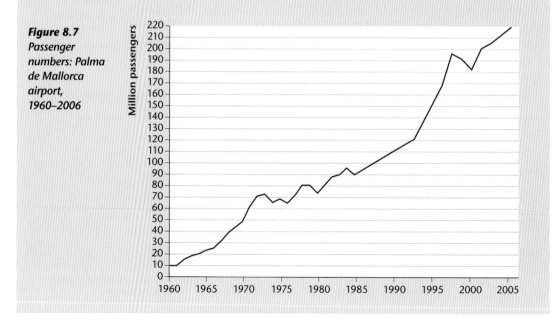

Figure 8.7 Passenger numbers: Palma de Mallorca airport, 1960–2006

terminal decline (e.g. British seaside resorts such as Seaton Carew and New Brighton). Others reinvent themselves, invest in new attractions (e.g. conference facilities in Torquay) or appeal to a different segment of the market (e.g. Mallorca's move away from mass tourism in the twenty-first century towards fewer but higher-spending tourists).

This pattern of change in Butler's model is driven by a number of factors: the desire by tourists for new places and novel experiences; changes in transport technology; and changes in economic status and lifestyle. Recent modifications to the model include environmental limitations to growth. On a small island like Mallorca, future growth may be severely constrained by water shortages.

The main flow of tourists within Europe is from north to south. International tourists from the UK, Germany, Scandinavia and the Low Countries converge on the Mediterranean basin, particularly Spain, southern France, Italy and Greece. Spain is the most popular destination for EU residents, followed by Italy and France. In winter, tourists flock to the snowfields in the Alps. This explains the prominence of countries such as Austria and Switzerland in international tourism rankings.

Important flows of tourists occur in all seasons to major cities of historic and cultural importance such as Paris, London, Rome, Barcelona and Milan. The market for urban tourism, especially short breaks to major European cities, grew by nearly 40% between 2000 and 2006, fuelled mainly by the expansion of low-cost airlines.

Factors influencing global tourism

The rapid growth of international tourism is due to a range of economic, social and political factors.

Air transport

One of the most important economic factors promoting international tourism has been the development of affordable commercial air services and jet passenger aircraft. The massive increase in international tourism in the past 50 years correlates closely with the growth in air passenger numbers. Affordability is partly explained by the introduction of wide-bodied aircraft in the 1970s, which lowered the real cost of air travel. Today even the most exotic and distant tourist destinations are no more than 24 hours' flying time away. At the same time there is no doubt that the absence of tax on aircraft fuel has boosted international air travel.

However, while air transport dominates inter-continental tourist traffic, travel within Europe is particularly dependent on road and rail communications. The continent's modern motorway infrastructure, Alpine road tunnels, the Channel Tunnel, high-speed trains, and the relatively small size and mosaic of countries, accounts for the lower-than-average importance of air travel.

The development of scheduled low-cost airlines in the 1990s acted as a further boost to international tourism. Not only did companies such as Ryanair and easyJet lower the cost of flying, they also stimulated international travel by opening up many new routes. The success of low-cost airlines is apparent in their current ranking: of the 12 leading airlines based in the UK, 10 are either low-cost carriers or charter companies (Figure 8.8). Some, such as First Choice and Thomas Cook, belong to tour operators that provide travel agents, package holidays and currency exchange for their customers.

Figure 8.8 *Leading UK airlines, 2006*

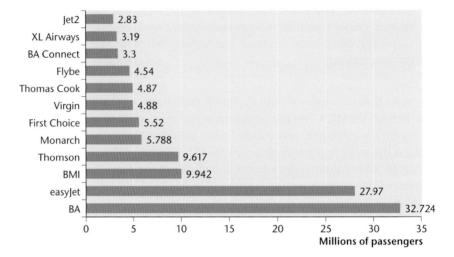

Airline	Millions of passengers
Jet2	2.83
XL Airways	3.19
BA Connect	3.3
Flybe	4.54
Thomas Cook	4.87
Virgin	4.88
First Choice	5.52
Monarch	5.788
Thomson	9.617
BMI	9.942
easyJet	27.97
BA	32.724

Low-cost airlines reduce the costs of flying by:
➤ operating many services to and from smaller regional airports
➤ promoting on-line booking and ticketing
➤ operating tight schedules with rapid turn-rounds
➤ providing few in-flight services

Leeds-Bradford in West Yorkshire is a typical example of a regional airport that has promoted low-cost airlines and boosted international tourism in the Yorkshire

Photograph 8.2
Ryanair is a leading budget airline

Steven May/Alamy

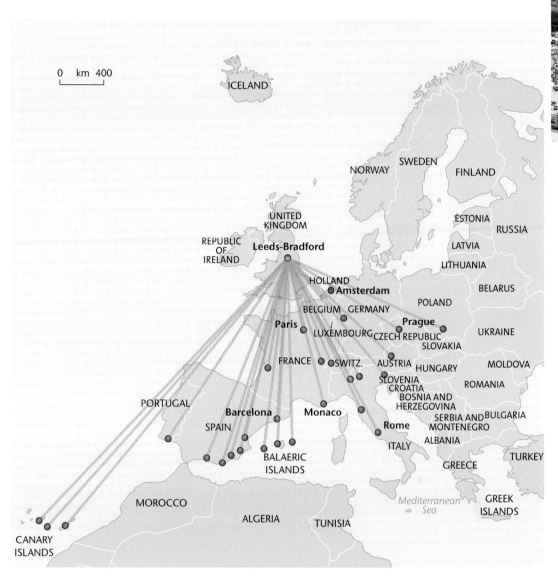

Figure 8.9
Destinations of low-cost airline scheduled flights from Leeds-Bradford

region. Three low-cost airlines operate from the airport — Jet2, Ryanair and Flybe. In 1995, before the introduction of low-cost airlines, passenger numbers were steady at around 900 000 a year. By 2006 numbers had reached 2.8 million. Today the low-cost airlines account for over half of all passengers.

The vast majority of passengers are tourists jetting to holiday destinations in the Mediterranean, the Canary Islands, the Alps and European city breaks in Paris, Amsterdam, Venice and so on. Jet2, the largest low-cost airline operating from Leeds-Bradford, began services in 2002. Between 2003 and 2006, passenger numbers leaped by 60%. International destinations now available from Leeds-Bradford are shown in Figure 8.9. Growth is likely to continue. A doubling of passengers to over 5 million is forecast by 2015.

Travel industry

The massive growth of international tourism since the 1960s would not have been possible without the development of a mature travel industry. Tour operators such as Thomson and Thomas Cook provided all-inclusive packages which were the catalyst to the growth of international tourism after 1960. Tourists bought their holidays through high street travel agents. The travel agents not only advertised and sold foreign holidays, they also booked flights, arranged transport between airports and hotels, and organised accommodation for customers.

Most packages comprised budget hotels and self-catering apartments. Tour guides liaised between visitors and hosts and arranged visits and evening entertainment. However, in the past 15 years, the package holiday market has declined. Today's international tourists are more confident, better educated and more experienced. Whereas in 1995, 54% of all foreign holidays taken by UK residents were package deals, 10 years later the proportion was 43%. Increasing numbers of people book their flights and arrange their own accommodation and car rental on-line. This trend will continue in future, putting high street travel agents under even greater pressure.

Inevitably many tourists want the freedom to travel when they get to their holiday destination. The result has been a big expansion in car rental businesses operated by international companies such as Hertz and Avis. Car rental services are now available at even the smallest international airports.

Economic

Two economic trends in MEDCs have boosted international tourism. Everywhere in the economically more developed world in the past 50 years incomes have risen and people have become better off (Figure 8.10). The proportion of income that is left after essentials have been paid for (e.g. housing, food, clothing, taxes) is known as **disposable income**. People can decide how they want to spend this 'surplus' income. As disposable incomes grow, many people opt for more holidays and foreign travel. In the UK, thousands of people on higher incomes have invested in holiday homes in France, Spain and Portugal, which they visit several times a year.

Figure 8.10 Per capita disposable real income per year: USA, 1959–2006

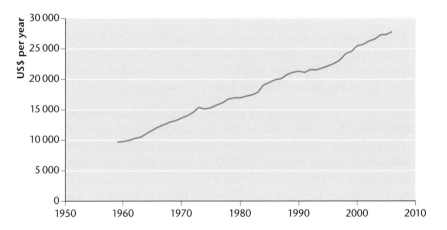

Social

As people in MEDCs have become better off, they have also been working shorter hours and receiving more paid holidays (Figure 8.11). Thus they have the time as well as the means for international travel. For many this means two or more foreign holidays a year.

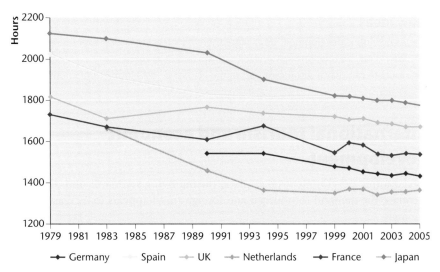

Figure 8.11
Average annual working time
Source: IZA *Facts and Figures*

Foreign travel has also become easier for a number of social reasons. Higher levels of education have smoothed the growth of international tourism. Foreign languages are more widely spoken both by tourists and hosts; more highly educated consumers have a better knowledge of places and seek out new locations and new experiences. Modern electronic communications such as e-mail and mobile phones make it easier for tourists to remain in contact with work and home; and credit cards and ATMs make money transactions easier. Finally, international hotel chains such as Marriott and Holiday Inn offer standardised accommodation and familiar food, reducing any sense of dislocation.

Political

Within Europe, the absence of any major international conflict since 1945 has created stability and confidence in international travel. The importance of a stable geopolitical background was evident in the wake of the 9/11 terrorist attacks (2001). In the USA it was not until July 2004 that air passenger levels recovered to their pre-9/11 peak.

At a national scale, as we shall see later, governments can encourage domestic tourism industries. Tourism is used as a strategy for development, modernisation, job creation and reducing poverty. Eighty per cent of the world's poor live in 12 countries: and in 11 of these, international tourism is signficant and growing. Governments are the key players. They can create an attractive economic climate for inward investment, provide security for foreign tourists and remove obstacles to international travel.

Tourism and economic development

International tourism and economic development

As economic development takes place, raising living standards and disposable incomes, the demand for tourism and foreign travel appears to increase proportionately.

Figure 8.12 shows the relationship between spending per person per year on tourism and development in individual countries measured by the United Nations' HDI. HDI, based on economic, social and demographic measures, is the most accurate indicator of development (Box 8.2).

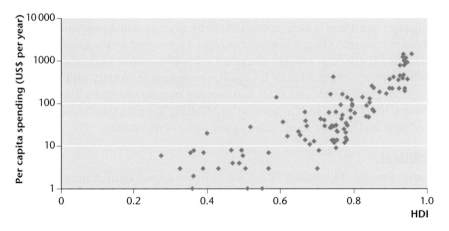

Figure 8.12
Economic development and international tourist expenditure per capita, 2005

Box 8.2 Human development index

The HDI is a composite and comparative measure of economic and social development. UN member states are ranked each year from 1st to 177th. The index ranges from 0 (least developed) to 1 (most developed). In 2007/8 Iceland was ranked 1st; Sierra Leone was ranked 177th.

The HDI is based on three variables: life expectancy at birth, literacy and GDP per capita at purchasing power parity (PPP) in US$. All three variables are weighted equally.

Example: life expectancy index for Argentina in 2006

$$\text{Index} = \frac{x - x_{min}}{x_{max} - x_{min}}$$

Life expectancy in Argentina, 2006 (x) = 76.1 years

Maximum life expectancy for any country, 2006 (x_{max}) = 80.5 years

Minimum life expectancy for any country, 2006 (x_{min}) = 32.6 years

$$= \frac{76.1 - 32.6}{80.5 - 32.6}$$

$$= 0.908$$

The overall index (HDI) is obtained by making similar calculations for literacy and GDP per capita and averaging the three results.

The world's poorest countries, with HDIs of less than 0.5, have minimal demand for international tourism. Out of the ten countries with the lowest spending on international tourism, five are in sub-Saharan Africa (Table 8.2).

People in the world's least developed countries are excluded from international tourism because of poverty, low levels of education and isolation. Countries with medium levels of development (according to the UN, countries with HDIs between 0.5 and 0.8) have a higher demand for tourism. However, demand remains low, with an average spending per person of just US$30–40 a year.

Top 10 countries				Bottom 10 countries			
	Per capita spending (US$)	HDI	HDI world rank (out of 177)		Per capita spending (US$)	HDI	HDI world rank (out of 177)
Norway	1464	0.956	1	Bangladesh	1	0.509	137
Austria	1441	0.934	14	Myanmar	1	0.551	130
Denmark	1234	0.932	15	Ethiopia	1	0.359	170
Ireland	1199	0.936	4	Angola	2	0.361	161
Belgium	1179	0.942	13	Cambodia	3	0.568	129
Switzerland	1008	0.936	9	Kyrghystan	3	0.701	110
Sweden	918	0.946	5	Malawi	3	0.388	166
Netherlands	900	0.942	10	Nepal	3	0.504	138
UK	798	0.936	18	Rwanda	3	0.431	158
Germany	785	0.925	21	Sudan	3	0.505	141

Table 8.2 Per capita expenditure on international tourism and level of development, 2005 (HDI)

Even so, the situation in many LEDCs is far from bleak (Table 8.3). Some LEDCs emerged as tourism 'hotspots' between 1990 and 2005 and experienced spectacular growth. China, for example, had over 40 million international arrivals in 2005, and in nearby Laos and Vietnam growth rates were over 1000%.

The overwhelming message in Figure 8.12 is that international tourism is dominated by the world's richest countries, with HDIs of 0.9 and above (Figure 8.13). Moreover, the demand for international tourism increases geometrically in the later stages of development (see log scale in Figure 8.12). Norway tops the list (Table 8.2): on average, Norwegians spend nearly US$1500 on foreign tourism a

Table 8.3 *Tourism hotspots in LEDCs, 1990–2005 (thousand international arrivals)*

	1990	1995	2000	2005	% change 1999–2005
Laos	14	60	191	236	1 586
Vietnam	250	1 351	2 140	2 972	1 089
Myanmar	21	117	208	242	1 052
South Africa	1 029	4 684	6 001	7 518	631
Cuba	327	742	1 700	2 017	517
Nicaragua	106	281	486	615	480
Nigeria	190	656	813	962	406
El Salvador	194	235	795	966	398
Madagascar	53	75	160	229	332
China	10 484	20 034	31 229	41 761	298
Peru	317	541	1 027	1 208	281
Tanzania	153	285	459	566	270
Costa Rica	435	785	1 106	1 453	234
Panama	214	345	479	621	190
Dominican Republic	1 305	1 776	2 977	3 450	164
Indonesia	2 178	4 324	5 064	5 321	144

year. In fact European countries fill the top ten places in terms of per capita spending (Table 8.2). This is partly explained by their high levels of development. But the absence of countries such as the USA, Canada and Australia from the list also points to other influences. These include geographical isolation: residents in Canada and Australia, for example, need to travel long distances to reach other countries. Equally because these countries are so large, they provide ample opportunity for tourism without international travel.

Figure 8.13
The relationship between per capita tourist receipts and economic development

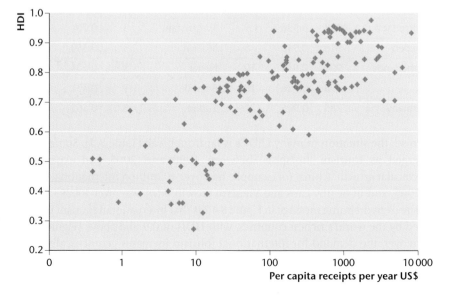

Case study   Thailand

Thailand has a total population of 65 million and is roughly the same size as France. During the past 30 years it has developed as a major destination for international tourism. International visitor numbers — 11.5 million in 2006 — are higher than in any other country in the Asia-Pacific region except China. In 1969, international tourists numbered just 469 000; by 2005 this figure had grown to just over 11.5 million. In 2005, 62% of international tourists came from Asia (principally from Malaysia, Japan and China), with 25% from Europe. The growth of tourism increased consistently after 1970, though there was a dip in the late 1990s when the country experienced a financial crisis. More recently, international terrorism, the 2004 tsunami, bird flu and SARS have slowed down rates of international tourist arrivals.

In general terms, the rapid growth of Thailand's international tourism industry is explained by two factors: rising levels of income in MEDCs and in neighbouring Asian countries, and reductions in the real cost of international air travel. But other more specific factors have also played a part in this growth:

■ The rising costs of competing destinations such as Spain and Italy have made Thailand more affordable.

■ The search for newer, more exotic locations in the past 30 years has benefited Thailand, as well as making tourism a truly global industry.

■ The diversity of special features in Thailand, including its beaches, western-style resorts (e.g. Phuket), nightlife and Buddhist temples, attracts tourists to the country (Photograph 8.3).

Tourism has played a significant part in the economic development of Thailand. There is a strong correlation between the rise of international tourism in

Photograph 8.3 *Wat Phra Keo temple Bangkok, Thailand*

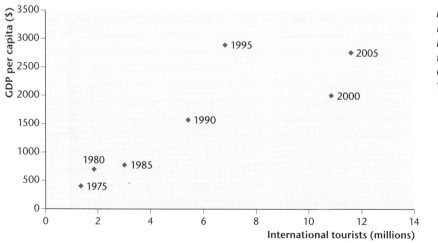

Figure 8.14 Relationship between international tourism and GDP per capita: Thailand, 1975–2005

Thailand and the growth of its GDP per capita (Figure 8.14). Thus, while the number of international tourists increased ninefold between 1975 and 2005, GDP per capita rose sevenfold over the same period.

Even so, Thailand's economy is not excessively dependent on tourism. The government targeted manufacturing industry for investment between 1986 and 1996, and today this sector contributes 35% to Thailand's GDP. Tourism's contribution, by comparison, is relatively small, amounting to just 7%. However, this measure understates the economic significance of tourism for three reasons:

- Tourism is the country's top earner of foreign currency.
- It is extremely labour intensive and creates substantial employment.
- Tourism generates spin-off benefits, stimulating employment in related industries such as catering, entertainment, transport, souvenir industries and even agriculture.

The combined direct and indirect employment attributed to tourism was around 1.5 million in 2005.

Case study Iceland

Iceland is a large volcanic island in the North Atlantic with a small population comparable in size to cities like Leicester or Bradford. Icelanders enjoy one of the highest standards of living in the world, with high incomes, a clean environment and excellent services such as health care and education.

Iceland also has a small but highly successful ecotourism industry. In 2006, 364 000 tourists visited Iceland — more than the country's entire population — attracted by the island's dramatic volcanic scenery, rugged coastline, glaciers and wildlife (Table 8.4). Whale watching alone attracts 72 000 people a year. Between 1995 and 2005, tourism was one of the fastest-growing sectors of Iceland's economy (an average growth of 7.2% a year) and an important earner of foreign currency. During this period, tourism receipts increased by 30%. Overall, tourism supports 6900 jobs directly and accounts for 5% of Iceland's GDP.

Visitors to Iceland are generally well-off: the cost of living is high and there are no budget airlines that fly to Reykjavik. Iceland's successful tourism industry is geared to a niche market: relatively wealthy Europeans and North Americans with an interest in and concern for the environment and wildlife. Similar groups of ecotourists can be found in places like Alaska, Patagonia, Costa Rica and the Himalaya. Given the relatively modest scale of tourism in Iceland and the country's rugged landscapes, the ecological footprint

UK	210 350
Germany	193 318
USA	139 508
Denmark	90 514
France	82 660
Sweden	76 520
Norway	71 537
Netherlands	56 875
Italy	49 237
Spain	37 019

Table 8.4
Origin of foreign visitors to Iceland: number of overnight stays, 2006

of tourism is small and the industry is sustainable.

Iceland's tourism industry is mainly concentrated in the southwest, in and around the capital, Reykjavik (Figure 8.15). In recent years tourism has boosted economic development in this area. Reykjavik has also benefited from its reputation as a chic centre for nightlife, the large number of hotels and guest houses, and its proximity to Iceland's only international airport at Keflavik (30 minutes' drive from Reykjavik), where 98% of foreign visitors enter the country. This part of Iceland also has several star attractions including: the Blue Lagoon (Photograph 8.4), warmed by waste water from a nearby geothermal power station; Gullfoss, a magnificent waterfall; the Strokkur geyser; and Thingvellir, a stunning rift valley and the site of the world's first parliament.

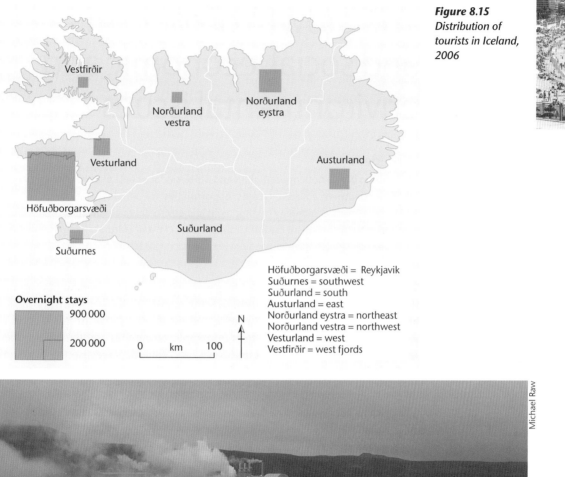

Figure 8.15
Distribution of
tourists in Iceland,
2006

Höfuðborgarsvæði = Reykjavik
Suðurnes = southwest
Suðurland = south
Austurland = east
Norðurland eystra = northeast
Norðurland vestra = northwest
Vesturland = west
Vestfirðir = west fjords

Overnight stays

900 000

200 000

0   km   100

N

Photograph 8.4 *The Blue Lagoon, a major tourist attraction in the Reykjanes peninsula, southwest Iceland*

Michael Raw

The growth of tourism and social, economic and environmental issues

Key ideas

➤ Tourism brings both opportunities and problems for people and the environment.

➤ The growth of tourism creates opportunities for employment, infrastructure improvement, community development and environmental protection.

➤ The growth of tourism creates problems of social and cultural change, inequality, seasonality of employment and environmental degradation.

We have seen that tourism is used by governments as an instrument of economic development. Yet while we cannot deny the opportunities that tourism brings, it also creates problems for local people and the environment. In this section we shall look at the impact of tourism on people, economies and the environment through case studies of St Kitts and Nevis, and Tenerife. (See also the case study on Spain's concrete coast, page 92.)

Case study: Tourism and economic development in St Kitts and Nevis

St Kitts and Nevis is a small island nation in the eastern Caribbean (Figure 8.16). Although tourism is a mature industry in most Caribbean countries, in St Kitts and Nevis development is still in its early stages. Nonetheless, by the start of the twenty-first century tourism had already become the islands' leading economic sector.

Physical background

St Kitts and Nevis is part of the Lesser Antilles island chain of the eastern Caribbean, which stretches from Sombrero in the north, to Grenada in the south. The Lesser Antilles form a classic island arc and represent the eastern boundary of the Caribbean plate. The islands have formed by the subduction of the North American plate beneath the Caribbean plate. Altogether there are thought to be 18 active volcanoes in the Lesser Antilles, including Mount Liamuiga on St Kitts (Figure 8.16).

The most recent eruption, on Montserrat, started in 1995 and is still ongoing.

Economic background

The two-island federation of St Kitts and Nevis covers just 275 km^2 and has a population of 48 000. As former British colonies, St Kitts and Nevis achieved political independence in 1983. For the past 200 years the islands' economy has depended on sugar production. Plantations covered most of the land area below 30 m. Ninety per cent of the inhabitants are descended from slaves brought from west Africa to work in the sugar plantations in the eighteenth and early nineteenth centuries. However, from the 1980s, the sugar industry became increasingly uneconomic, its survival dependent on government subsidies. This situation was unsustainable and the last plantation closed in 2005. Today large areas of St Kitts and Nevis are covered by overgrown cane fields

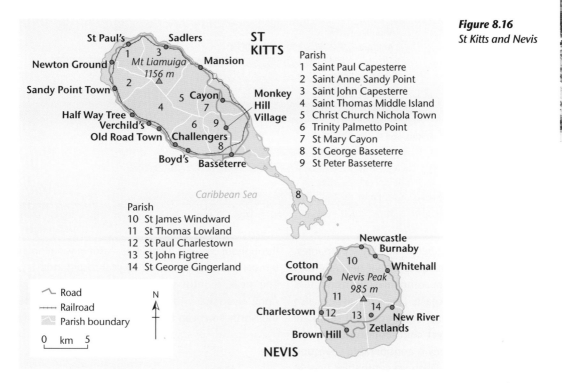

Figure 8.16
St Kitts and Nevis

St Paul's   Sadlers   **ST KITTS**

Newton Ground   Mt Liamuiga   Mansion
1156 m

Sandy Point Town

Half Way Tree   Cayon   Monkey Hill Village

Verchild's   Challengers

Old Road Town

Boyd's   Basseterre

Caribbean Sea

Parish
1 Saint Paul Capesterre
2 Saint Anne Sandy Point
3 Saint John Capesterre
4 Saint Thomas Middle Island
5 Christ Church Nichola Town
6 Trinity Palmetto Point
7 St Mary Cayon
8 St George Basseterre
9 St Peter Basseterre

Parish
10 St James Windward
11 St Thomas Lowland
12 St Paul Charlestown
13 St John Figtree
14 St George Gingerland

Newcastle   Burnaby
Cotton Ground   Whitehall
Nevis Peak
985 m

Charlestown   New River
Brown Hill   Zetlands

NEVIS

Road
Railroad
Parish boundary
N
0   km   5

(Photograph 8.5). Now the government has to decide how this land is to be used in future, and how to resolve the problem of unemployment among thousands of former sugar cane workers. Additional economic problems include the high price of imported oil, the country's large national debt which in 2006 was nearly twice as large as its annual GDP,

and recovery from severe hurricane damage suffered by the islands in the late 1990s.

Given its micro-scale territory and small population, the natural resource base of St Kitts and Nevis is negligible. However, small independent states often promote financial services, and St Kitts and Nevis is no exception. Over 17 000 businesses, including

Michael Raw

Photograph 8.5
St Kitts: abandoned sugar cane fields and rainforest on the lower slopes of Mount Liamuiga

Figure 8.17
Eastern Caribbean islands: tourism receipts, 2005 (US$ million)

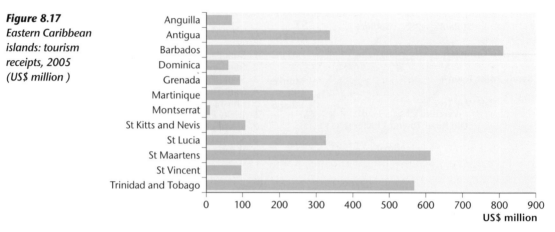

offshore banks and limited liability companies, operate from Nevis. The government gets revenues from the registration of companies, licensing, fees and renting of office space. Financial services also provide jobs and foreign exchange, and stimulate construction. The direct contribution of financial services to the economy is considerable — around 15% of total income. Offshore companies benefit from a tax-friendly regime, which gives exemption to several types of company tax, and legislation that guarantees confidentiality and secrecy.

Small island states such as St Kitts and Nevis are often over-dependent on a single economic activity. In the past, sugar dominated the country's exports. Now sugar production has ended, only to be replaced by an equally narrow specialism — international tourism (Figure 8.17).

Resources for tourism

Natural resources

Tourism on St Kitts and Nevis, and throughout the eastern Caribbean, is based largely on natural resources (Figure 8.18). The principal natural resources are the tropical climate, sandy beaches, and the warm water of the Caribbean Sea and the Atlantic Ocean.

Situated 17° north of the equator, St Kitts is a tropical island with a warm, humid climate all year round. It is surrounded by ocean, and average annual maximum temperatures are around 25°C, varying from 22°C in February to 30°C in August. Prevailing onshore trade winds moderate temperatures throughout the year. With little seasonal variation in temperature, tourism is an all-year-round industry. The peak months are between November and April, when many tourists visit the island to escape the North American and European winter. The only

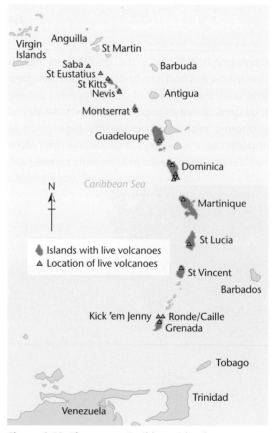

Figure 8.18 *The eastern Caribbean islands*

downside to the climate is occasional hurricanes. For example, in 1999 hurricane Lenny caused considerable damage to St Kitts's beaches and infrastructure.

St Kitts, like the other islands in the Lesser Antilles, has a volcanic origin. Sand for beaches is therefore in limited supply, particularly on the Caribbean coast. Hurricanes and the mining of sand for construction have also led to beach erosion along this coast. However, there are several extensive beaches on both the Atlantic coast, such as Frigate Bay and Halfmoon Bay, and on the southeast peninsula (a group of small islands linked by tombolos), which are major tourist attractions. Coral reefs are found on both the Caribbean and Atlantic coasts and they, together with crystal clear waters, provide excellent conditions for scuba diving and snorkelling. Other water sports include windsurfing, canoeing, sailing and jet skiing.

Although there are no historic records of any volcanic eruption, Mount Liamuiga on St Kitts is considered to be active. Any eruption would pose considerable risks to the northern part of the island. Covered in montane rainforest, the summit crater reaches 1155 m. Both the volcanic crater and the rainforest are major attractions for hikers and eco-tourists.

Even so, large parts of St Kitts have little attraction for tourists. Much of the Caribbean coast is rocky, has limited access and few beaches. Away from the mountains, the original forest vegetation was replaced by a monoculture of sugar cane. Today the former sugar plantations are abandoned and derelict. The government, which owns most of this land, faces a major challenge as to how to use and rehabilitate it

in future. Meanwhile, the island's biodiversity has suffered from forest clearance and the introduction of alien species such as rats, mongooses, pigs and vervet monkeys.

Cultural resources

St Kitts has a small number of historical tourist sites. Brimstone Hill, a fortress perched on a volcanic cone, is one of the finest examples of British military architecture in the world. It is the only World Heritage Site in the eastern Caribbean. Bloody Point marks the site where 2000 Carib Indians were massacred in 1626 by English and French militia. A narrow-gauge railway, which originally served the sugar plantations, encircles the northern part of the island and is now a popular tourist attraction. There are many eighteenth-century sugar estate houses which have been converted to hotels, artist studios, galleries and private residences. The island's capital, Basseterre, has a colonial character, and some of the best examples of Georgian architecture in the Caribbean. Its quayside market and duty-free shops are major attractions for cruise ships' passengers.

The growth of tourism

Tourism has replaced sugar production as the leading economic sector on St Kitts and Nevis. Between 1990 and 2000 growth in international tourism was steady. The fragility of international tourism was evident in 2002, when, following 9/11, numbers declined. Since then there has been a strong recovery, due partly to the opening of the 648-room Marriott hotel resort in 2002 (Figure 8.19).

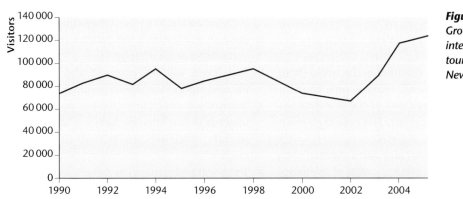

Figure 8.19
Growth of international tourism: St Kitts and Nevis, 1990–2005

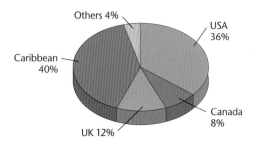

Figure 8.20 *St Kitts and Nevis: origin of international tourists*

With massive investment planned in the islands' tourism infrastructure, stay-over visitor numbers are forecast to reach 200 000 by the end of the decade. In 2005, tourism contributed US$107 million directly to the country's economy. However, the spillover effects of tourism are considerable. Indirectly, tourism accounts for nearly two-thirds of the islands' GDP. With few other resources, the growth of tourism has been vital to offset the decline of the sugar industry. Visitor numbers grew by nearly 13% between 2000 and 2005. Of the 280 000 tourists in 2005, 40% were stay-over visitors. The remaining 60% were visitors on cruise ships.

International stay-over visitors from outside the Caribbean come almost exclusively from the USA, Canada, UK, France and Germany (Figure 8.20). To a large extent, the origins of North American and European stay-overs is related to the availability of direct flights to and from St Kitts' international airport. The introduction of a twice-weekly direct service from New York in late 2007 should boost visitation from the northeast USA.

Opportunities and benefits created by the growth of tourism

Economic

In one of the smallest countries in the world (both in area and population), international tourism offers St Kitts and Nevis one of the few avenues for economic development. The country's main advantages include:

- its all-year-round sunny and warm climate
- its well-educated workforce — 98% of the population are educated to secondary level

- English is spoken as the native language
- political stability — it is perceived as a 'safe' destination by tourists
- its geographical proximity to North America — St Kitts and Nevis are two of the closest tropical islands to the USA and Canada. For most North Americans they are closer than Hawaii.

The further expansion of international tourism should create significant opportunities for St Kitts and Nevis. It will strengthen the country's economy and improve both the standard of living and quality of life of its people.

Despite having a gross national income (GNI) per capita above the world average in 2006 (US$12 680 compared with US$10 180), St Kitts and Nevis lag a long way behind MEDCs such as the UK (GNI per capita US$35 690). One in three inhabitants is poor, with incomes that do not meet minimum requirements for food and other basic needs, and 11% are classed as extremely poor. Moreover, with the ending of the sugar industry, unemployment levels, especially among young men, are high. Although former sugar workers received severance payments and re-training, the country's welfare system does not provide unemployment benefits.

The expansion of international tourism will provide a range of benefits:

- Jobs are created directly by tourism, e.g. hotel receptionists, waiters, porters, maintenance workers, cleaners, guides, security staff etc.
- Spin-off jobs are created indirectly by tourism, e.g. taxi-drivers; workers in gift shops, bars, cafes, restaurants and laundries; opportunities for beach and street hawking; farm workers supplying food to hotels and restaurants; construction.
- Tourism will improve the balance of trade and generate foreign exchange.
- Skill levels will be increased and developed through work in the tourism industry.
- Tourism will attract foreign direct investment to upgrade tourist infrastructure, e.g. international airports, hotels and resorts, harbours, marinas, roads.
- There will be incentives to protect and conserve the natural environment for ecotourism.

Michael Raw

Photograph 8.6 *North Frigate Bay on the Atlantic coast of St Kitts is the largest concentration of tourism development on the island and includes the 648-room Marriott Hotel; the area in the foreground is the site of the Ocean Edge development, due for completion in 2010*

Tourism infrastructure

The development of sustainable tourism relies on a substantial tourism infrastructure that provides accommodation, transport and other services.

St Kitts has a modern international airport. Its recently upgraded runway can now handle the largest wide-bodied jet airliners. Excluding other Caribbean countries, there are scheduled direct flights to St Kitts from the USA (Miami, Philadelphia and Charlotte, South Carolina), Canada (Toronto) and the UK (Gatwick). Connecting flights from neighbouring islands such as Antigua and St Martin bring tourists from elsewhere in the USA, Canada and the UK, as well as from France and Germany.

Cruise ships are an important source of tourism income. Basseterre harbour has two deep-water berths for cruise ships up to 75 000 t. Sixty per cent of roads on St Kitts and Nevis are tarmacked, including the main roads that encircle the islands and run along the coast.

There are a number of hotels. By far the largest is the Royal St Kitts Marriott (see Photograph 8.6). Opened in 2002, it is owned by a major US hotel chain, and has an 18-hole golf course, spa, casino, swimming pools and beach access. There are also large numbers of condominiums, time shares and second homes (Figure 8.21). Development is geared to the upper end of the market. Nevis, for example, has the 200-room Four Seasons resort — the only five-star hotel in St Kitts and Nevis. As a relative late-comer to international tourism, the St Kitts and Nevis government has opted for a largely upmarket rather than mass market tourism industry. Future developments will undoubtedly consolidate this policy.

Environmental protection

International tourism has provided a spur to protect the natural environment of St Kitts and Nevis. New developments are regulated to ensure that they do not damage the islands and are sustainable. Planning

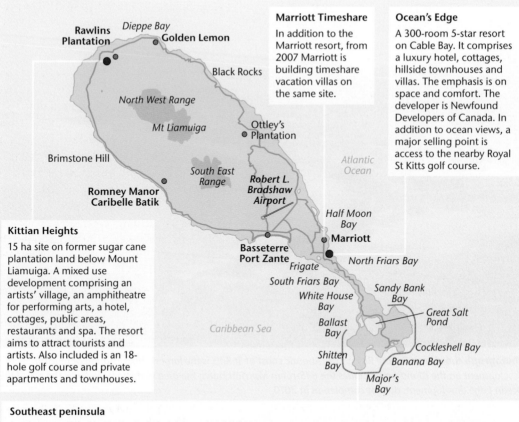

Figure 8.21 New and future tourism investments in St Kitts

regulations in the past have often been ignored. Now developers have to carry out an environmental impact assessment to preserve the islands' natural and cultural heritage. The rainforest is protected by law and there are limits on the height of new buildings.

Problems created by the growth of international tourism

There are a number of general problems associated with the development of international tourism in LEDCs:

- Much of the revenue from tourism goes overseas to MEDCs. For example, most large hotels and resorts belong to international chains in North America and Europe. Profits from these companies will be transferred to shareholders in MEDCs.
- International holidays are arranged or booked through tour operators in MEDCs.
- Air transport is usually by carriers based in MEDCs.
- Resources such as fresh foods may be imported rather than sourced locally.
- International tourism is highly sensitive to any downturn in the global economy (e.g. an increase in oil prices) or to political developments that threaten people's security (e.g. 9/11).

- International tourism is highly competitive and notoriously fickle. Tourism destinations often mature rapidly, go out of fashion and are abandoned for novel destinations.

In the context of St Kitts, the specific problems caused by international tourism derive from the type of tourism, and its environmental impact.

Cruise ships

St Kitts and Nevis, as well as other small island states in the eastern Caribbean, have experienced problems with the growth of international tourism. Cruise ships are an important element in terms of visitor numbers. But as floating hotels they bring only limited benefits. Average spend by tourists on cruise ships is only US$30 per person. On a small island, large numbers of cruise-ship passengers often cause congestion and overcrowding at sensitive beach and other tourist sites. There are also environmental implications: garbage left behind, effluent dumped at sea, oil spilled in coastal waters, and damage to coral reefs caused by ships' anchors.

Over-stay tourists: enclave tourism

Over-stay tourism is often concentrated in resorts and hotels that are exclusive geographical enclaves and owned by foreign companies. Many large resorts such as Marriott at North Frigate Bay are completely self-contained, with bars, restaurants, shops, gyms, golf course, pools and a beach. Others provide 'all-inclusive' holidays with meals, drinks and entertainment included in the package. The result is a kind of 'resort ghetto' segregated from the local population and rest of the island. Many visitors will remain in the resort for the whole of their stay. Thus, spending in local shops, bars, restaurants and tourist sites, which would benefit local people, is often minimal.

With development mainly concentrated in small areas such as North Frigate Bay, large parts of St Kitts appear to be excluded from the direct benefits of international tourism. For example, there is little evidence that tourism has had any impact on the villages northwest of Basseterre on the island's coastal road. **Enclave tourism** often increases levels of inequality within the host population between the relatively small number of local people who find employment in tourism, and the majority who are excluded.

Environmental impact

Large-scale tourism on small islands often puts pressure on limited water resources. Although rainfall on St Kitts averages 1270–1905 mm a year, rapid runoff, high evapotranspiration and little water storage capacity mean that current resources are inadequate to meet the demands of its rapidly growing tourism industry. Already, some parts of the island suffer shortages during the dry season. Moreover, water demand per capita by tourists is three times higher than by domestic consumers. Any additional demands will be unsustainable. The Marriott resort solved its water problems by installing its own desalination plant.

Of even greater concern is the lack of sewage treatment facilities on the island. The island's only sewage treatment plant is located in the tourism hotspot at Frigate Bay. Elsewhere there is reliance on soakaways, septic tanks and pit latrines, which cause some environmental pollution. Without investment in sewerage infrastructure, continued population growth (currently 1.7% a year) and soaring visitor numbers will further degrade the environment, polluting coastal waters and threatening coral reefs. So far the St Kitts and Nevis government has designated no marine parks, which would otherwise afford protection to coral reefs and marine life.

Tourism can further damage the environment through poor planning and the failure to enforce existing planning restrictions. The scale and design of development may be inappropriate. The huge multi-storey Marriott complex dominates the Frigate Bay area and is visible for miles around. Building lines need to be set back from the coastline to ensure adequate protection against storm waves and erosion, and to give free access to the shore. Developers often prefer cliff-top and other prominent positions with sea views (Photograph 8.7). Recent developments in the extreme southeast of St Kitts overlooking the straits to Nevis are visually unattractive. They are made worse by their isolated locations, reached by tracks that scar the coastal slopes.

Photograph 8.7
St Kitts's southeast peninsula is the driest part of the island and is the site for several major resort developments; the island of Nevis is visible in the far distance

Michael Raw

Box 8.3 International tourism and poverty

- International tourism can make a significant contribution to the economies of the poorest countries. Eighty per cent of the world's poor (i.e. those living on less than US$1 per day) live in 12 countries. In 11 of these, tourism is significant and growing.

- The main aim of governments is to maximise income and foreign exchange earnings from international tourism.

- The impact of international tourism varies between different social groups (e.g. literate/illiterate), gender and type of tourism (mass tourism and ecotourism).

- International tourism creates opportunities for the poor and for women in particular.

- International tourism allows the expansion of employment in the informal sector in LEDCs (i.e. the selling of goods and services to tourists). This is because the customer comes to the product.

- Tourism is labour intensive and creates jobs.

- International tourism provides economic potential in micro-states that have few competitive exports.

- Some tourism activities are based on the culture and know-how of local people — assets that many of the poor have.

- Cruises and enclave tourism create the fewest economic linkages and fail to spread effects that benefit the poor.

Case study   **Tourism and economic development in Tenerife**

Physical background

The Canary Islands are situated off the coast of west Africa in the east Atlantic, between latitudes 27°N and 29°N (Figure 8.22). All the islands belong to Spain, an MEDC that ranks 17th on the UN's human development index. The Canaries lie on a hotspot and all have a volcanic origin. Today active volcanism is confined to Tenerife, La Palma and Lanzarote.

Tenerife is the largest island in the Canaries, with an area of just over 2000 km². It is dominated by a huge strato-volcano — Mount Teide — which last erupted in 1909. Teide, at 3718 m, is also Spain's highest mountain (Photograph 8.8).

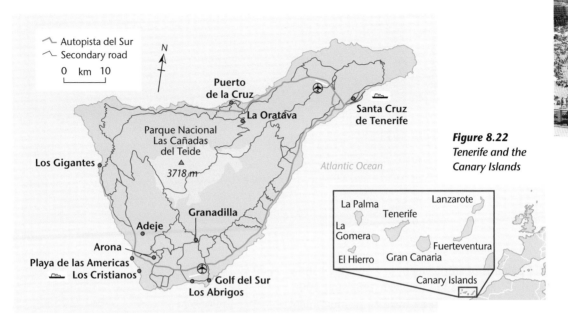

Figure 8.22
Tenerife and the
Canary Islands

Photograph 8.8
Mount Teide, and
Las Cañadas
National Park and
World Heritage Site

Economic background

The resident population of Tenerife at the last census in 2001 was 778 000. This relatively large population on a small island results in a high population density of 380 persons per square kilometre.

Tourism first developed as a major industry in the 1960s and today accounts for approximately 80% of the island's GDP. Most employment also depends either directly or indirectly on tourism (Figure 8.23). In 2005, around 70% of the workforce was in service activities, most of which were linked to tourism. In addition, the construction industry, heavily geared to providing tourism infrastructure, employed a further 16% of workers. Although only 5% of employment was in agriculture, a significant part of farm output supplies hotels and restaurants on the island.

343

Figure 8.23
Tenerife:
employment
change by sector,
1987–2005

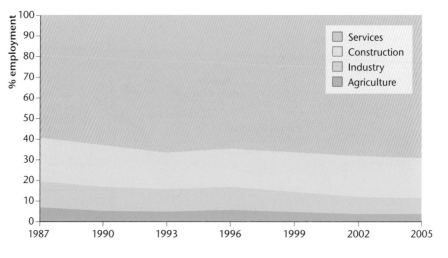

The patterns of employment in Figure 8.23 show relatively little change between 1987 and 2005. There was a slow but steady increase in employment in services, which offset the equally slow decline in agriculture and industry. Overall, we conclude that tourism on Tenerife is in the later 'mature' stages of Butler's model (see Figure 8.6 on page 322). In other words, the industry in the early twenty-first century is at a crossroads. The challenge for the island is to maintain its position as a leading holiday destination for European tourists.

Resources for tourism

Climate

Tenerife has a humid, sub-tropical climate. The moderating influence of the Atlantic Ocean means that seasonal differences in temperature are small. Mean monthly temperatures range from 18°C in December and January to 25°C in July. Temperatures are slightly depressed for the latitude by the cool Canaries ocean current. Sea surface temperatures peak in September at 23°C. However, average monthly minimum temperatures never fall below 15°C. This favourable temperature regime makes Tenerife and the other Canary Islands all-year-round tourist destinations (Figure 8.24).

However, within the island there are striking contrasts in climate. This is mainly due to huge variations in altitude over short distances. The windward north coast and coastal slopes, exposed to onshore

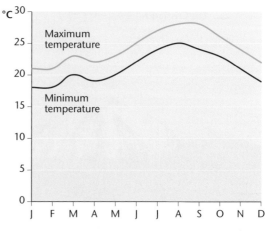

Figure 8.24 *Tenerife: mean monthly maximum and minimum temperatures*

trade winds, get relatively large amounts of rainfall (Figure 8.25 and Photograph 8.9). The south and east — the main centres of mass tourism — lie in the rain shadow of Mount Teide, have semi-arid conditions and the most sunshine.

A distinctive feature of the climate is the orographic effect of the mountains, forcing air to rise, condense and form clouds between 1000m and 2000 m. This cloud layer is a permanent feature of the island's climate. Above 2000 m, cloud development is arrested by subsidence, creating an inversion and clear skies. For this reason, Mount Teide and its caldera is, unusually, one of the driest and sunniest places in Tenerife (Figure 8.26).

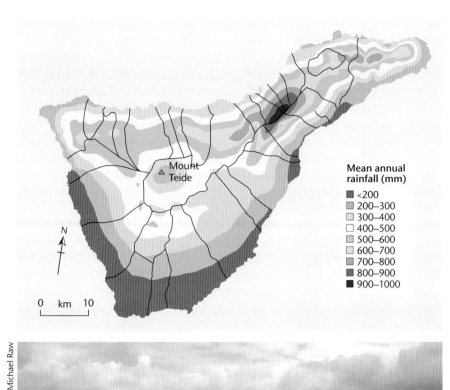

Figure 8.25
Tenerife: mean annual rainfall
Source: Consejo Insular de Aguas de Tenerife

Mount Teide

N

Mean annual rainfall (mm)

■ <200
■ 200–300
□ 300–400
□ 400–500
□ 500–600
□ 600–700
■ 700–800
■ 800–900
■ 900–1000

0   km   10

Michael Raw

Photograph 8.9
Cloudy windward north coast, near Puerto de la Cruz

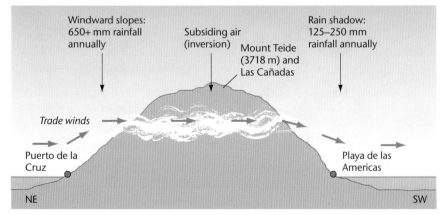

Figure 8.26
Climate and relief in Tenerife

Windward slopes: 650+ mm rainfall annually

Subsiding air (inversion)

Mount Teide (3718 m) and Las Cañadas

Rain shadow: 125–250 mm rainfall annually

Trade winds

Puerto de la Cruz

Playa de las Americas

NE

SW

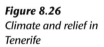

345

Other tourism resources

Tenerife is a rocky, volcanic island with few natural beaches. Beaches in the mass tourism resorts of Playa de las Americas and Los Cristianos are small, and rely on imported sand. Northern Tenerife is less dependent on beach tourism. Its sub-humid climate supports a biodiverse woodland ecosystem known as 'monteverde'. Located in a zone between 600m and 1200 m on the windward coast, it coincides with the belt of cloud caused by orographic uplift. It provides an interesting habitat for eco-tourism and guided tours. Similarly, attractive hiking country is provided at higher altitude in pinewoods dominated by the indigenous Canary Island pine. Like many plants in the mountains, it gets much of its moisture from cloud and fog.

The huge caldera of Mount Teide (see Photograph 8.8 on page 343) at 2300 m attracts thousands of coach parties and day-trippers from the coastal resorts. It is the centre of Las Cañadas del Teide National Park. Its extraordinary volcanic landscapes and unique vegetation adapted to the high-altitude desert climate led to its designation as a World Heritage Site in 2007. Most tour parties stop at the picturesque Roques de Garcia (Photograph 8.10). A cable car gives access to the summit of Mount Teide. Apart from day trippers, Las Cañadas attracts hikers

and eco-tourists. Tourist accommodation is confined to one luxury hotel located in the caldera.

An outstanding cultural attraction on Tenerife is the mysterious step pyramids of Güímar situated on the east coast. Built by the native Guanches in prehistoric times, the pyramids show strong similarities to step pyramids found in Peru and the Middle East. Some archaeologists suggest that the Canary Islands were 'stepping stones' in the diffusion of Middle Eastern culture to South America in prehistory.

The growth of tourism

Before the advent of package holidays and cheap air travel there was little opportunity for the development of mass tourism in an isolated island group like the Canaries. However, in the 1960s and 1970s cheap air travel and longer paid holidays fuelled a tourism boom in the Canary Islands as well as in southern Europe. Tenerife was the main focus for tourism in the Canary Islands. As in mainland Spain, tourism developed rapidly, was subject to limited planning controls and was aimed at the mass market (Figure 8.27).

In Tenerife, tourism originally developed on the north coast around Puerto de la Cruz (Photograph 8.9) and La Oratava. By the late nineteenth century this region had already become a fashionable area for upper-class tourists from Spain and the UK. It offers a

Photograph 8.10
Roques de Garcia, Las Cañadas

Michael Raw

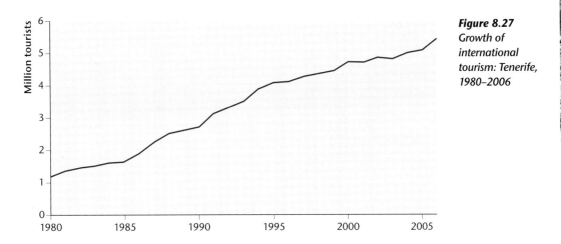

Figure 8.27
Growth of international tourism: Tenerife, 1980–2006

varied environment, with harbours, beaches, spas, gardens and historic buildings. It also remains the most popular tourism region for Spanish visitors to Tenerife.

With the mass tourism boom of the 1960s and 1970s the main concentration of tourist activity shifted to the south-west coast (Figure 8.28). Tourism growth was accompanied by rapid urbanisation and investment in infrastructure. The outcome was a continuously built-up stretch of coast between Los Cristianos and Playa de las Americas, comprising hotels and apartment complexes. Today this area attracts nearly 60% of the island's tourists and is home to large numbers of expatriates (Figures 8.28 and 8.29). It is especially popular with British tourists: over 95% stay in

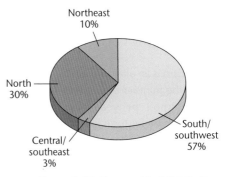

Figure 8.28 *Geographical distribution of tourists on Tenerife, 2006*

Figure 8.29 *Origin of international tourists: Tenerife, 2006*

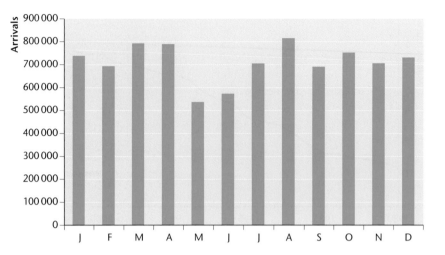

Figure 8.30
Monthly passenger arrivals at Tenerife South airport, 2006

the south of the island. The resorts specialise in low-cost tourism centred on the beaches and the sunny climate.

Tourism is an all-year-round industry on Tenerife. In fact the number of passenger arrivals at Tenerife South airport between November and January exceeds those for June to August (Figure 8.30). For north Europeans seeking winter sun, the Canary Islands are the nearest option.

Opportunities created by tourism

Employment

Overall, tourism has had a positive influence on Tenerife. Before the development of mass tourism in the 1960s, Tenerife was an isolated and backward part of Spain. Most people were poor and agriculture and fishing were the leading economic activities. Lack of employment opportunities forced many young people to leave the island to find work in mainland Spain and in Latin America.

Mass tourism led to huge growth in the Tenerife economy, stimulated inward investment and created thousands of new jobs. Today nearly two in every five jobs are in tourism or related activities, and tourism generates 60% of the island's GDP. Apart from direct employment opportunities in hospitality, tourism is indirectly responsible for the growth in jobs in areas such as catering, car rental, laundry services and water supply. Moreover, thanks to Tenerife's warm climate, tourism is an all-year-round activity.

Infrastructure

With a tourism industry geared to 5 million visitors a year, tourism has been the main driver for improvements in Tenerife's transport infrastructure. Mass tourism, concentrated in the southwest corner of the island, is served by Tenerife South international airport. Completed in 1978, it is Spain's sixth busiest airport. The opening of the airport gave a further boost to tourism on the island. Tenerife has a second airport close to the capital Santa Cruz in the northeast. The two airports are linked by a motorway along the south coast.

Environmental protection

Tenerife has a diverse natural environment with many plant and animal species endemic to the island. The growth of tourism in Tenerife has underlined the importance of the natural environment as a resource. The Teide National Park, itself a major tourism attraction, was designated in 1954 and now is protected as a UNESCO World Heritage Site. On the lower slopes of Mount Teide, the Corona Forest Nature Park protects stands of the endemic Canary Island pine. Meanwhile, many natural and semi-natural habitats are protected as nature reserves.

Although rapid expansion of tourism and economic development on Tenerife has put pressure on the environment, it has, at the same time, helped to protect the environment, which is itself a major attraction for visitors.

Problems created by the growth of tourism

Much of the infrastructure developed to support mass tourism has created low-quality urbanisation in southwest Tenerife. Meanwhile, mass tourism has caused localised degradation of the physical environment, depleted resources and undermined the island's traditional culture and society.

Environmental degradation: the built environment

The rapid growth of mass tourism and its concentration in southwest Tenerife was characterised by a lack of planning and low-quality construction. Meeting the demand for package holidays in the 1960s and 1970s was the priority. This headlong drive for development, which started from scratch, was largely uncontrolled. In places like Playa de las Americas (Photograph 8.11) it created what the tourist guidebooks describe as 'a concrete jungle of tackiness and a jumble of high-rise hotels'. The built environment is visually unattractive, the roads are congested and there are few open spaces. This low-quality development inevitably drove tourism downmarket. Nightlife centred on bars, restaurants and shops on the main streets of Playa de las Americas and Los Cristianos. Drunkenness and rowdiness among young visitors added to the poor image of mass tourism on the island.

Worldwide Picture Library/Alamy

Photograph 8.11 *Playa de las Americas*

Overdevelopment is also a feature of the southwest conurbation. In the south of the island population growth averaged 3.2% a year between 1980 and 2001, compared with an overall average for Tenerife of 1.1%. Population growth in the two municipalities that include Los Cristianos and Playa de las Americas was unprecedented (Figure 8.31). This was caused by massive in-migration from mainland Europe into newly built *urbanizaciones*, and by influxes of islanders from elsewhere in Tenerife (Photograph 8.12).

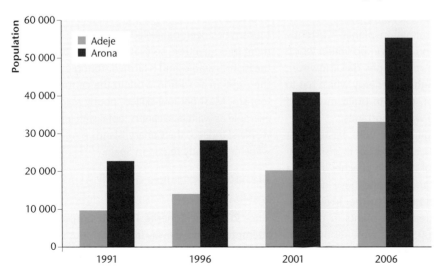

Figure 8.31
Population change in Adeje and Arona, 1991–2006

Michael Raw

Photograph 8.12
Adeje: in-migration has led to rapid population growth and urbanisation in the past 20 years

Environmental degradation: the natural environment

Mass tourism in Tenerife, in its present form, is widely seen as unsustainable. In other words, on current trends the industry will be unable to maintain its viability in future. The major cause for concern is water scarcity. Demand for water, particularly from tourism and irrigation agriculture, continues to rise while water resources remain fixed. Most water is derived from aquifers. Over-exploitation of groundwater has caused water levels to fall and water quality to decline. There is a need for new resources to be provided either by recycling waste water or by installing more desalination plants. Currently there are two desalination plants in operation which produce 60 000 cubic metres per day. However, desalination relies on high-cost energy which has to be imported. Moreover, plans to build more golf courses will only add to water shortages.

An effective sewerage system with waste water treatment plants is an essential part of tourism infrastructure. Although all of the main beaches in Arona and Adeje meet EU standards and have good to excellent quality bathing water, further investment is needed in sewage treatment plants to prevent coastal pollution. In 2005 there were reports that three treatment plants between Playa de las Americas

and Los Gigantes were discharging raw sewage into the sea. Further east, at Los Abrigos, raw sewage entered the sea from private urban developments at Golf del Sur.

Beaches in the southeast are largely artificial and rely on sand that is either imported from Africa or dredged from offshore. Offshore dredging destroys marine habitats and threatens marine biodiversity.

Community structure

Because the island is swamped by foreign tourists, especially British, there are concerns that local culture and society have been undermined. The growth of tourism has been paralleled by a decline in employment in agriculture, so that today only one-third of the island's arable land is farmed. Young people leave the rural areas to find work in the centres of mass tourism. Most get low-skilled, poorly paid work, for example as waiters, cleaners, hotel staff and building workers. Indeed, the Canary Islands have the lowest wage rates of any region in Spain.

Management: new directions for tourism

Since 2001, the Tenerife Tourism Corporation has attempted to move away from mass tourism and the negative images that surround it. This is partly due to strong competition from cheaper destinations such as Morocco, Croatia and Turkey. Reduced competitiveness has been a problem since 1986, when Spain joined the EU and labour costs increased. Also, recent declines in visitor numbers suggest that the island's attraction as a mass tourism destination is stagnating. Today's tourists have high expectations and are no longer content with the quality of experience that satisfied tourists in the 1970s and 1980s.

A number of five-star hotels, boutique hotels, spas and golf courses have been completed with the aim of attracting more affluent tourists. While this policy might result in fewer visitors, per capita spending should rise. At the same time, pressure on the environment would be reduced. However, the move to higher-quality tourism is not easy. First there is the legacy of decades of sub-standard development; and second it is difficult to compete with unspoilt destinations. Eco-tourism and heritage tourism, based on activities such as whale watching, scuba diving, hiking and sightseeing, are also being promoted as sustainable alternatives to beach tourism.

Box 8.4 Economic assistance from the EU

The Canary Islands, the Azores and Madeira face particular economic problems because of their remoteness from mainland Europe and their dependence on tourism.

Unemployment has been well above the EU average for many years, and the Canaries have a GDP per capita that is less than 80% of the EU(15) average. As a result, the islands qualify, as Objective 1 areas, for the highest level of assistance from the European Regional Development Fund (ERDF). The fund is the main instrument for closing the gap between rich and poor regions in the EU.

Between 2000 and 2006, the Canary Islands, the Azores and Madeira received €145 million in economic assistance from the ERDF. Approximately one-third of this money was for upgrading the islands' infrastructure, for example by improving water supply, water quality and management of waste. Money was available for the sustainable development of natural and cultural resources and the upgrading of tourism assets.

Managing tourism to ensure sustainability

Key ideas

➤ Managing tourism to ensure sustainability is about balancing socio-economic and environmental needs.

➤ Sustainable tourism, including ecotourism, often operates in conjunction with communities and the environment.

The management of tourism to ensure sustainable use of resources is nowhere better illustrated than in national parks and other conservation areas. In this section we shall look at how management and planning in the Lake District National Park over the past 50 years has been crucial in protecting landscape and environment. (In addition, the Arches National Park case study, page 182, shows how different issues lead to management responses that aim for sustainability in the long term. And the section on the Annapurna Conservation Area in Nepal, page 155-57, shows how the involvement of indigenous people can help to protect the environment and ensure its future sustainability.)

Box 8.5 Sustainable tourism

- The principle behind sustainable tourism is that development 'meets the needs of the present without compromising the ability of future generations to meet their needs' (Brundtland Report).
- Tourism depends on a range of environmental resources. Whether these resources are physical, historical or cultural, sustainable tourism should, in theory, cause no resource loss or decline in the quality of the environment.
- In practice it is difficult to see how the development of tourism can avoid any damage to the environment. Sustainable tourism must rely on careful management and planning.

- Tourism often has a strong impact on local economies and communities, and these too should be managed sustainably. Local economies must continue to flourish alongside tourism, partly through the involvement of local people in the tourism industry, and partly through government support for other economic activities.
- Sustainable tourism will respect and maintain the traditions, culture and values of local communities.
- Sustainable tourism also extends to ideas of equity — that all groups (local, ethnic, disadvantaged etc.) should benefit.

Case study **The English Lake District**

The Lake District occupies the northwest corner of England and is one of the most distinctive regions in the UK: its character is shaped by its geology and physical geography, as well as human activity

Although its highest point — Scafell Pike — is only 978 m above sea level, the Lake District is the only truly mountainous region in England. This is because the upland, carved in the last 2 million years by a succession of ice sheets and valley glaciers, is rugged, steep and craggy (Photograph 8.13). Deep glacial valleys, many occupied by ribbon lakes, radiate like the spokes of a wheel from the central core of ancient volcanic rocks (Figure 8.32).

Human activity has also left a deep impression on the region's landscapes. Grazing on the fells over many centuries has removed the original woodland cover. Farming and settlement are concentrated in the valleys, which are sheltered and have fertile soils. Picturesque villages surrounded by woodland, and fields enclosed by stone walls, contrast with bare hill-

sides covered in bracken, and rocky cliffs at higher levels (Photograph 8.14). A distinctive element in the human landscape is the vernacular architecture, using local blue-green slate for walling and roofing. In the nineteenth century the Victorians created landscaped gardens, planted exotic trees and built large houses in areas such as Windermere, Grasmere and Ullswater, adding to the attraction of the region's human landscape.

This human landscape is dynamic and has evolved over centuries. What is certain is that it will continue to evolve in future according to the tastes, values and economy of society.

The origins of tourism

Before the nineteenth century the Lake District was regarded as a wild, remote place of no interest to tourists. All this changed in the first half of the nineteenth century. The writings of romantic poets such as Wordsworth and Coleridge, and the paintings of Turner and Constable, transformed the popular view

Michael Raw

Photograph 8.13
Rugged mountain scenery in central lakeland, with glacial troughs, cirques and hanging valleys

of mountain regions in general and the Lake District in particular. Wordsworth published the first guide to the Lake District in 1810 and later in the century Victorian resorts developed around the major lakes, especially at places such as Windermere and Keswick connected to the railway. Pleasure steamers plied the larger lakes such as Windermere, Ullswater and Coniston Water. Most visitors belonged to educated

middle and upper classes. They were drawn by the lakes, the mountain scenery and the Lake District's literary associations. Towards the end of the nineteenth century, other literary figures with strong Lakeland associations, such as John Ruskin and Beatrix Potter, strengthened the region's cultural attraction.

Although the region's popularity as a tourist attraction grew steadily between 1900 and 1950, it never

Michael Raw

***Photograph 8.14** Grasmere from Loughrigg: a typical lakeland scenery of valleys, hills and picturesque villages*

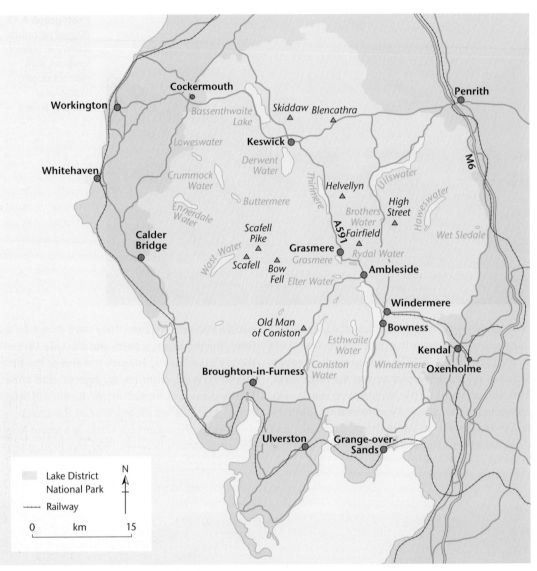

Figure 8.32 *The Lake District National Park*

experienced the boom of mass tourism of the UK's seaside resorts. Even so, by 2004 tourism contributed £534 million to the regional economy, attracted over 8 million visitors and supported 22 000 jobs.

The creation of national parks

The need to protect and manage areas of outstanding scenery in England and Wales was recognised in the 1930s. However, the national park movement began much earlier, in the USA. Due to

the efforts of environmentalists like John Muir, the world's first national park was established at Yellowstone in Wyoming in 1872. This was quickly followed by Yosemite and Sequoia.

Tourism developed in the Lake District because of the region's exceptional landscape quality. However, this fragile resource, increasingly threatened by economic pressures in the inter-war years, needed conservation and management. In 1949 the British government legislated to protect and conserve the highest-quality landscapes in England and Wales for future generations. While the primary aim of the 1949 National Parks and Access to the Countryside Act was conservation, it also stated that national parks should be accessible for the enjoyment of the public through quiet recreation.

The 1949 act led to the designation of ten national parks in England and Wales in the 1950s, and came just in time. In the 1950s, rising standards of living and car ownership meant that visitor numbers to the most popular parks soared. In the past these areas had been protected by their relative remoteness. But increasing levels of car ownership and personal mobility made them more accessible and more vulnerable. Since the 1950s, two other parks have been designated in England and Wales (The Broads and the New Forest), and two in Scotland (Cairngorms, and Loch Lomond and the Trossachs) (Figure 8.33).

***Figure 8.33** National parks in the UK*

Compared with the US national park system, the national parks of England and Wales were more difficult to establish. There are two main reasons for this. First, the US parks were largely uninhabited wilderness areas, with little permanent settlement. In contrast, the parks in England and Wales had been settled for centuries and contained sizeable populations. This meant that economic activities such as farming, mining and quarrying were already long established, providing employment for thousands of people. Second, whereas most of the land in the US parks is owned by the federal government, in England and Wales most of it is in private hands. The National Trust is the biggest single landowner in the Lake District. It owns nearly 25% of the land, much of it in the most picturesque valleys such as Borrowdale, Patterdale and Langdale.

The Lake District National Park

The Lake District National Park, set up in 1951, was one of the first to be designated under the 1949 Act. At 2300 km^2 it is the largest national park in England and Wales.

Its overall success can be gauged if we compare today's landscapes with those of 50 years ago. For the greater part, little has changed. Classic views such as Great Langdale from Chapel Stile, or Great Gable from Wasdale Head, are largely the same today as they were 50 or indeed 100 years ago. Thanks to the creation of the national park, visitors and future generations can enjoy the beauty of the Lake District in the same way that earlier generations did.

Managing national parks

National parks are managed by National Park Authorities (NPAs). These consist of elected local authority councillors, parish councillors and members nominated by the Secretary of State at DEFRA. The NPA is the sole local planning authority in national parks, and is responsible for control, development and the allocation of land use (Figure 8.34). Its general brief is to:

■ conserve and enhance the park's natural beauty, wildlife and cultural heritage

- promote opportunities for the understanding and enjoyment of the special qualities of the park by the public

In pursuing these aims the NPA also has a duty to:
- foster the economic and social well-being of local communities within the national park

Where conflict arises between the aims of national parks that are not easily resolved, conservation has priority. This is known as the 'Sandford Principle'. Thus, above all other considerations, primacy is given to outcomes that 'leave the natural beauty of parks unimpaired for the enjoyment of this and future generations'.

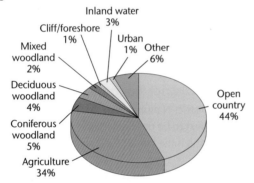

Figure 8.34 *The Lake District National Park: land use*

Planning policies of NPAs follow guidelines issued by central government. The UK's national parks are funded directly through central government and local government. For example, the Lake District gets an annual grant of £6.6 million from DEFRA and Cumbria County Council. On top of this, one-third of the park's income comes from fees for parking and planning applications, and sales to tourists at visitor centres.

Each national park has a National Park Management Plan, which is updated at 5-year intervals. The plan sets out the vision, policies and strategies of the NPA. It is guided by principles such as conservation and enhancement of the environment, sustainability, equal access for all members of society, and the economic viability of local communities. This plan complements the Lake District Local Plan, and the Cumbria and Lake District Joint Structure Plan, which

gives details of policies. National park management is also affected by a range of directives from European to national, and regional to local levels.

In addition to planning control, the NPAs are also responsible for managing footpaths, providing a ranger service and supplying tourist information.

Issues in the Lake District National Park

In the Lake District, a number of tourism-related issues are addressed by the NPA. The main ones are:
- excessive traffic and traffic congestion, particularly on the A591 access from the M6, which links the three largest towns in the park — Windermere, Ambleside and Keswick
- threats to the quality of the landscape caused by changes in farming practices and land-use changes
- conflict among recreational users
- lake management
- pollution of larger lakes such as Windermere and Coniston Water
- footpath erosion on popular walking routes
- the quality of tourism infrastructure, such as hotels, campsites and static caravan sites

Traffic congestion

More than 8 million people visit the Lake District National Park every year, and eight out of ten people travel by car. The larger settlements such as Windermere and Bowness become heavily congested during bank holidays and in the summer, causing air pollution and noise (Photograph 8.15). At these times, long traffic queues build up between the M6 and Ambleside as cars enter and leave the park. Moreover, at busy times parking is inadequate in the main Lakeland towns. Although the number of visitors has hardly increased in recent years, traffic conditions are getting worse, making the current situation unsustainable.

The NPA has made a number of proposals to ease traffic problems in the park. They include the introduction of shuttle buses, levying a congestion charge for entry to the park, raising parking fees, encouraging hotels to provide minibus services to collect and transport visitors, and promoting alternative

Ashley Cooper/Alamy

Photograph 8.15 *Traffic congestion in Ambleside*

forms of transport such as cycling, walking and horse riding. In the USA, some of the most popular national parks like Zion and Grand Canyon operate shuttle bus services. While these schemes have been successful, they operate in very different conditions. For example, in most US parks, visitor attractions are geographically more concentrated, there are fewer access roads and resident populations are small.

Charging visitors in cars to enter the park is feasible, though it would be unpopular with visitors and with the tourism industry in Lakeland. At the moment, the introduction of a congestion charge similar to the one in central London is some way off. Less controversial are decisions to raise parking fees and limit parking spaces in the main tourism centres.

Managing socio-economic and environmental needs

The NPA's primary obligation is to protect and enhance the beauty of the landscape, wildlife and cultural assets of the Lake District. We have seen that

the traditional Lakeland landscape is the main attraction for visitors. Fifty-five per cent of the area of the Lake District is farmland. As a result, farming is the major influence on the human landscape.

Changes in farming practice due to EU policies have implications for the landscape and require careful monitoring. For example, the deintensification of hill sheep farming, and the reductions in stocking levels on the fells in the past 15 years, could threaten the open nature of the landscape, leading to the invasion of scrub and woodland. On the other hand, increases in stocking have in the past caused overgrazing, soil erosion and degradation of the upland environment. If the modern rural landscape that visitors cherish is to survive, farmers must use traditional methods and materials. We saw in Chapter 5 that both the EU and DEFRA have a raft of environmental policies designed to do just this, and to encourage biodiversity and sustainable agriculture.

Forests and woodlands have a huge impact on the landscape and need careful management. Extensive planting of coniferous woodland for commercial timber production occurred in several parts of the Lake District from the 1920s to the 1970s. Some plantations drastically changed the landscape and were highly controversial. However, modern management increasingly views the plantations as a resource for recreation and wildlife. Grizedale Forest, between Windermere and Coniston, has been successfully opened to the public for recreation (Photograph 8.16), and the Whinlatter plantation near Bassenthwaite Lake attracts visitors as the nesting site for the Lake District's only pair of breeding ospreys. Meanwhile, the Wild Ennerdale project is funding the gradual change of woodland in Ennerdale from predominantly coniferous to native woodland.

Through its planning procedures, the NPA protects and conserves the landscape, controlling afforestation, new building and road construction, and blocking inappropriate development. Planning controls are strictly applied. Where approval is granted, building styles and materials have to be consistent with traditional architecture and blend in with the landscape. However, some building and road improvement must be permitted if local people

Photograph 8.16
Grizedale Tarn,
Grizedale Forest

are to maintain their livelihoods, and have access to affordable homes.

Land-use conflicts

Tourist and recreational activities sometimes come into conflict. This is inevitable, given the range of resources within the park and the pressure of visitors. A well-documented example was the conflict between high-speed motorised water sports such as power boating, jet skiing and water skiing, and quieter forms of water-based recreation on Windermere. In 2005, the NPA implemented a 10 mph speed limit on the lake, which ended all high-speed water sports. The following year saw a huge increase in sailing, canoeing, windsurfing and rowing on the lake.

The NPA can also pre-empt conflict by zoning different land uses. Past policies have tended to impose blanket controls on the whole of the park. A zonal approach reserves particular land uses and activities for specific areas (Figure 8.35).

The NPA draws a broad geographical distinction between two types of area in the Lake District National Park: the busier central valleys such as Langdale, Borrowdale and Ullswater, and the 'quieter areas' which form the bulk of the park. Overall,

planning aims to maintain the character of these two areas. The busy central valleys cater for large concentrations of visitors, attracted by waterfront locations and easy access to the fells. Management is more intense in these pressured areas. Planning aims to limit traffic volumes, visual pollution, noise pollution and other forms of disturbance.

In quieter zones, management in less intrusive. These areas correspond to remote uplands in the north, east and central fells set aside for activities such as hill walking, climbing and scrambling. Forest zones, which in addition to commercial timber production provide opportunities for walking, cycling, picnicking and observing wildlife, are located between Windermere and Coniston Water in the south, and between Bassenthwaite and Buttermere in the northwest.

Figure 8.35 shows that intensive recreation based on man-made and managed tourist attractions is concentrated in the park's three main urban centres: Windermere–Bowness, Keswick and Ambleside. These centres provide the bulk of holiday accommodation, and have busy shopping areas and lakeside locations giving access to boats, steamers and other water-based activities. Essentially they cater for a type of mass tourism.

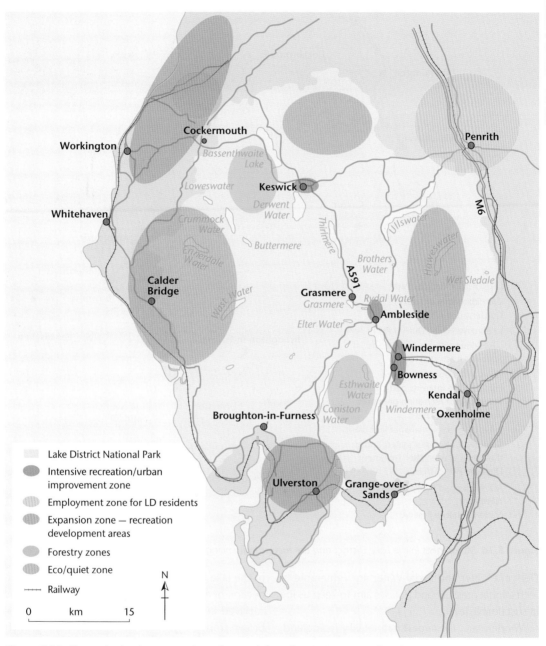

Figure 8.35 *Illustrative land-use zones in and around the Lake District National Park*
Source: *Lake District Economic Futures Study: Stage 2 Report*, Regeneris Consulting, 2004, p.19

Lake management

The NPA manages the 16 major lakes and smaller water bodies in the Lake District (Figure 8.36). Strict development control is applied to all lakes in the quieter areas, such as Wast Water and Ennerdale Water. They are protected from economic and recreational pressures that might alter their character. Some of the most popular lakes such as Windermere,

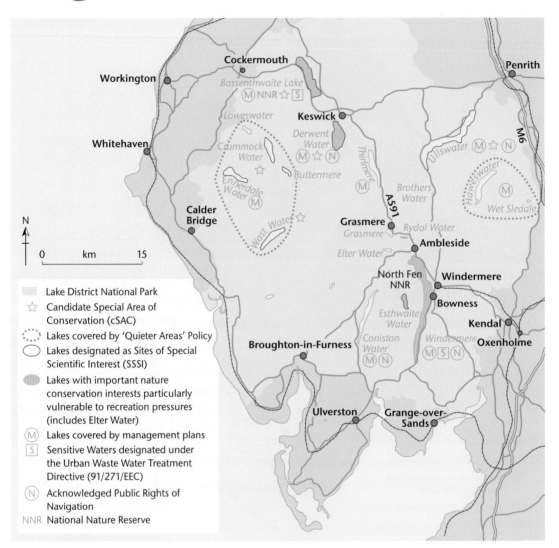

Figure 8.36 *Major lakes in the Lake District and the factors influencing lake management*

Derwent Water and Rydal Water are vulnerable to recreational pressure and policies aim to keep usage at sustainable levels.

Windermere, the largest natural lake in England, is under particular pressure (Photograph 8.17). The settlements around the lake support a resident population of 17 500 — a number that increases significantly in the tourist season.

Pollution from treated sewage discharged into Windermere has increased phosphorus loads since the 1960s. Resulting algal blooms in the late 1980s caused dissolved oxygen levels in the deepest parts

of the lake to fall to zero during the summer. The decline of arctic char — a trout-like fish which has survived in Windermere since the last ice age — brown trout and salmon, is linked to algal growth and oxygen depletion.

By the early 1990s, algae dominated the lakeshores, altering the natural habitat for young brown trout. Water quality has improved since the introduction of tertiary treatment to some wastewater treatment works. There has consequently been a reduction in the number of algal blooms and an upturn in the arctic char populations.

Photograph 8.17
Windermere

Footpath erosion

There are nearly 3000 km of footpaths and bridleways in the Lake District. They are a key resource for outdoor recreation such as hill walking, horse riding and mountain biking. Walking is one of the most popular activities in the Lake District. In 2002 one in three of visitors went for a walk lasting at least 4 hours. Some footpaths in the more accessible hill areas in Great Langdale and the Coniston Fells have suffered severe erosion (Photograph 8.18). One footpath in Wasdale recorded nearly 30000 walkers during the month of June 2005. Excessive use damages vegetation cover, and exposes the underlying soil, peat or clay to runoff and erosion. During periods of heavy rain, paths become temporary stream channels, causing ugly scars visible for miles around.

The management response is footpath restoration. Partnerships between the NPA, the National

Photograph 8.18
Footpath erosion in the fells

Trust and Natural England, together with Lottery funding and volunteer workers, have rehabilitated tens of kilometres of upland paths with stone surfaces and drainage.

Tourism infastructure

Tourism is crucial to the economy of the Lake District and the NPA has a responsibility to maintain and enhance the tourism industry. Although stay-over tourists represent only 28% of visitors, they account for 75% of spending. Only 8% of visitors are from overseas, but they stay longer and spend more. Most visits focus on town-based activities in shops, restaurants and pubs.

Conscious of the need to promote and upgrade tourism, the NPA's policies aim to:

■ improve both the range and quality of retailing in the towns
■ encourage more and longer stay-overs
■ raise the overall quality of accommodation
■ diversify tourism, possibly by developing a cultural attraction of national significance in the park

Examination-style questions

Table 1 *International tourist arrivals by region, 1990-2004*

International tourist arrivals (million)					%share
	1990	1995	2000	2004	
World	442	538	682	763	100
From:					
Europe	253	307	390	431	56.5
Asia and the Pacific	60	89	118	151	19.8
Americas	99	108	131	128	16.7
Middle East	9	10	15	22	2.9
Africa	10	13	17	18	2.4
Unspecified	11	11	11	13	1.7

1 (a) Describe the pattern of international tourist arrivals between 1990 and 2004 shown in Table 1. (4 marks)

(b) Suggest two possible reasons for differences in the regional percentage of tourist arrivals in 2004 shown in Table 1. (6 marks)

(c) Explain why there is a relationship between tourism and development. (6 marks)

(d) With reference to one or more named examples, explain how the growth of tourism can bring economic and environmental opportunities to an area. (9 marks)

2 With reference to named examples, explain the importance of managing tourism sustainably. (25 marks)

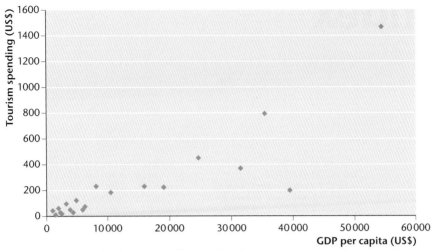

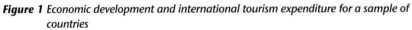

Figure 1 *Economic development and international tourism expenditure for a sample of countries*

3 (a) Describe the relationship between economic development and expenditure on international tourism shown in Figure 1. (4 marks)

(b) Suggest reasons for the relationship you described in 3(a). (6 marks)

(c) Describe how the growth of tourism can have both a positive and a negative impact on local communities. (6 marks)

(d) With reference to one of more named examples, explain how the growth of tourism can lead to environmental degradation. (9 marks)

(e) With reference to named examples, show how management and planning can contribute to tourism's sustainable use of environmental resources. (25 marks)

Index